Double Vision

THE INSIDE STORY OF THE LIBERALS IN POWER

Edward Greenspon and
Anthony Wilson-Smith

Doubleday Canada Limited

Canadian Cataloguing in Publication Data

Greenspon, Edward
    Double vision: the inside story of the liberals in power

ISBN 0-385-25613-2

1. Canada – Politics and government – 1993-   .* 2. Canada –
Economic policy – 1991-   .* 3. Liberal Party of Canada. I. Wilson-
Smith, Anthony. II. Title.

FC635.G74 1996   971.064'8   C96-930585-0
F1034.2.G74 1996

Front jacket photographs by Peter Bregg/*Maclean's*
Jacket design by Avril Orloff
Text design by Heidy Lawrance Associates
Printed and bound in the USA

Published in Canada by
Doubleday Canada Limited
105 Bond Street
Toronto, Ontario
M5B 1Y3

*To my mother, Rosalie Greenspon, for the right hemisphere,
and my late father, Mort Greenspon, for the left.*

E.G.

To my parents, Dick and Audrey Wilson-Smith.

A. W.-S.

Contents

Where there is no vision, the people perish.

Proverbs 29:18

PREFACE

From conception to delivery, this book was a collaborative effort. First, it is the product of two authors. But it is also a work that would never have existed without the cooperation and support of family, journalistic colleagues, editors, sources, and the subjects of these pages themselves.

Writing this book posed the particular challenge of capturing a work in progress: the Chrétien government. Not only did that mean that the target of our inquiries kept moving (who could have anticipated, for instance, the dramatic near-miss of the October 1995 referendum or the hash of GST changes), it also meant that a government scorned could take its retribution. For the most part, therefore, our sources demanded anonymity in exchange for their cooperation. This is an occupational hazard with which we must live.

By necessity, accounts of private meetings have been reconstructed through the recollections of those involved or from their recitations to secondary sources. Where quotations are used, these have been provided by sources who attended the particular meeting being depicted. Sources are a journalist's most important tools. Protecting the identities of those who helped us plumb the depths of this government was integral to being able to tell its story. To the nearly two hundred people who spoke to us, our thanks for your insights and for the considerable time spent with us. A special thanks to those willing and able to speak on the record, including Prime Minister Jean Chrétien and Finance Minister Paul Martin.

Our publisher, Doubleday, has displayed an admirable enthusiasm for this project from the outset. We thank John Pearce for recognizing the book's potential before it was readily apparent, and we commend the entire team, up and down the line, for all their efforts in making sure that somebody would actually read it. Two people stand out, above all, in turning our manuscript into a book. Over the years, we have come to appreciate greatly the contributions of editors, the invisible collaborators in any journalistic endeavour. In this case, we had the pleasure of working with two complete professionals, Rick Archbold, who from our first meeting made it clear that he understood the book in his bones, and Barbara Czarnecki, who shepherded us on the final trek up the mountain. They taught us a great deal about book writing along the way — enough, we hope, to make their task much easier the next time around.

Edward Greenspon writes: I wish to single out my colleagues at *The Globe and Mail* for special thanks. In early 1993, editor-in-chief William Thorsell was gracious enough to release me from a managerial commitment in Toronto so that I could apply to become Ottawa bureau chief. He has displayed confidence in my judgments — sometimes even, I suspect, over his own better judgment.

I was fortunate enough to move into a bureau overflowing with talent and motivation. The collective knowledge of this extraordinary journalistic team — including my predecessor, the estimable Graham Fraser, who provides his counsel over the phone line from Washington — provided me with instant historical context for the political events that have unfolded over the past few years. I owe all my colleagues over that period an exceptional debt of gratitude. I extend particular thanks to Jeffrey Simpson, who was kind enough to read early drafts of many of these chapters with the proviso that he would be brutally frank (unfortunately, he kept his word).

I am indebted as well to Sylvia Stead, our rock of Gibraltar in Toronto, Colin MacKenzie, my former managerial partner who has justifiably risen up the ranks, and John Cruickshank, who helped me finagle my way to Ottawa in the first place. Along the way, many other editors have given me the chance to develop my craft, people like Jack Schreiner, Dalton Robertson, Geoffrey Stevens, Tim Pritchard, Peter Cook, and Peggy Wente.

As a graduate of Carleton University's School of Journalism, I was particularly pleased when director Peter Johansen and Professor Chris Dornan offered me a position during the winter semester of 1996 as the school's journalist-in-residence. With the post came Daniel Leblanc, an exceptionally resourceful graduate student in journalism who provided me with research assistance as well as numerous suggestions for improving the manuscript. He was a wonderful bonus.

Finally, and I leave the most important to the last, my family. Nobody felt this book as keenly as they did. When I started out, my daughter, Bailey, then five, unhappy with my self-imposed exile in the attic, resolved that she would write a book as well: "What It's Like to Grow Up," by Bailey Greenspon. She joined me upstairs, clicking away studiously on an old Mac Plus, her manuscript as confounding to me as this one, no doubt, is to her. My four-year-old son, Joshua, contributed weekly ideas for the title, most of them revolving around some variation on Jean Chrétien and Batman, as unlikely a duo as I can imagine. Our youngest, Jacob, sat on my lap through some of the toughest slogging, inspiring me with the delight he derived from his random slapping of the keyboard, which produced some interesting inserts into my carefully crafted prose.

Lest I create the false impression that I took care of these children during the year this book took over our lives, I must end with an expression of appreciation and awe for the most important collaborator on this project and in my life, my wife, Janice Neil. Her sainthood would be assured if only for the disproportionate share of the household load she carried over the past year. But she also fortified me with the confidence that somebody would read the fruits of my labour and the assurance that even if nobody did, she would still hug me at the end of the day. I am blessed to have in her not just a partner-in-life, but also an editor-in-residence. As a journalist herself, she has always provided a chillingly honest but non-threatening assessment. When I am in doubt, she brings clarity — in life and in journalism. Without that, I would never have started this book, let alone completed it.

Anthony Wilson-Smith writes: I'm grateful to many journalists who have shared with me their time and knowledge. More than anyone else in this regard, I am indebted to my editor at *Maclean's* magazine and friend of more than thirteen years, Bob Lewis. He has given me the opportunity to report from more than twenty-five countries, had the wisdom, humour, and good grace to tell me both when to speak up and when to shut up, and, along with his wife, Sally, has alternately prodded and nursed me through all manner of challenges, both personal and professional.

Former *Maclean's* editor Kevin Doyle is another to whom I owe great thanks, and others in the magazine who have been especially helpful over the years include my partners in crime Bruce Wallace and Warren Caragata, as well as Mary Janigan, Peeter Kopvillem, Andrew Phillips, Brian Bethune, the late Ann MacGregor, and bureau colleagues E. Kaye Fulton and Luke

Fisher. Earlier in my career, I was helped and encouraged by Mark Harrison, Bob Walker, Mel Morris, Michael Cooke, and Jim Peters. Most of any good habits I have acquired as a journalist come from working alongside, and watching, such consummate professionals and friends as L. Ian MacDonald, Bernard St. Laurent, Graham Fraser, Benoit Aubin, and Jeff Sallot. Similarly, I have learned much about Parliament Hill from the encyclopedic knowledge of people like Doug Fisher and Don Newman, and about politics in general from Montreal's best lunchmate, Jim Robb.

On a personal level, I thank Dianne Rinehart for all that was and all that she is. I owe more than I can ever express to my parents, Dick and Audrey Wilson-Smith, to whom this is dedicated with great love, and to Michael, Kerry, Christopher, and Stuart Wilson-Smith.

Most of my contribution to this book was written by laptop computer on a now well-worn and occasionally abused kitchen table. Its owner provided me throughout with comfort, solace, patience, encouragement, and the frequent assertion that my one obligation in return was to make this the best piece of work I am capable of. For better or worse, it is — but I owe Deirdre McMurdy so much more in return than that.

1

CHRÉTIEN
TAKES CHARGE

As he strode purposefully up to Rideau Hall for the swearing-in with his wife, Aline, Jean Chrétien declared to waiting reporters: "It's a working day."

The air was crisp with anticipation, like the first day of school. The governing Tories had cratered into near oblivion, and nearly everyone gathered on the governor general's lawn felt at least a twinge of satisfaction. The reporters, by and large, had come to Ottawa during Brian Mulroney's reign. His crassness and striving, not to mention the litany of scandal and the hints of corruption swirling around his government, had stoked their natural adversarial bias. Now the Liberals were back, ready to exercise the prerogatives of power, as they had for much of the century.

Clean-shaven and conservatively attired, Pierre Trudeau disembarked from a limousine and pronounced on the meaning of it all: "I woke up this morning and I said, 'There will be a Liberal government in Canada today.' So I shaved my beard."

Chrétien wasn't prone to philosophizing. He simply wanted to get to the office and begin ticking off those election promises. He emerged first from Rideau Hall. "Bonjour. Any questions?" He fielded the inquiries effortlessly before a reporter directed a hot one at him about Quebec's demands for labour market training. "I'm the prime minister now since an hour and forty-five minutes," he said. "Give me a break." Asked about his approach to being prime minister, he replied that they all knew his style. "You've seen me in operation a long time. Do you think I will start to change? I'm about to start running. Bye-bye."

That first day had been carefully scripted months earlier, with an eye to setting, in the words of the transition documents, a distinctive tone.

The new government wanted to demonstrate frugality, decisiveness, and integrity.

Frugality came first. The Liberal transition documents spoke at length about the need to take swift symbolic action to demonstrate that the new government could relate to the concerns of ordinary Canadians. Like Chrétien, most of the incoming ministers had either walked up the long driveway of the governor general's residence or arrived in their own cars. Sergio Marchi, slated for Immigration, came in his Subaru. Veteran Herb Gray dropped his wife and daughter near the door and drove off to park his sedan. A red import unloaded the new secretary of state for women, Sheila Finestone, scrunched in the middle of the front seat, her broad-brimmed hat pressed against the ceiling. Nova Scotia kingpin David Dingwall climbed out of the back.

After the swearing-in, the ministers headed off to their new jobs in waiting mini-buses, the inescapable message being that the presidential era of Brian Mulroney was over. Jean Chrétien, a man of modest tastes, would preside over a modest government, precisely as Canadians desired. Just in case the reporters at Rideau Hall missed the point, Liberal spin doctors fluttered about, talking up the significance. Nearly all dispatches dutifully noted the use of the mini-buses.

Nobody thought to follow the buses, which took their passengers to the rear of the Centre Block on Parliament Hill, away from prying eyes. Liberal strategists were petrified someone would watch the scene there, but it passed unnoticed. A cavalcade of highly polished government sedans were idling, waiting for the arrival of the new political aristocracy. The drivers carried photos of their assigned ministers, so they could identify their charges coming off the mini-buses. A man came up to Sergio Marchi, freshly sworn in as minister of citizenship and immigration, and introduced himself as his driver from the Immigration Department. Marchi asked him to wait ten minutes while he slipped upstairs and shared a bottle of champagne with family and friends. As he worked his way over to the rear door, another man stopped him. He was the driver from the Citizenship Department. Marchi, who an hour earlier had arrived at Rideau Hall with his wife in their family car, made his first ministerial decision: he told them to work out which one would take him to the departmental office in Hull. The mini-buses, having evoked their symbolism, disappeared forever.

Cabinet held its first meeting in mid-afternoon. Six ministers — Chrétien, Lloyd Axworthy, Gray, André Ouellet, Roy MacLaren, and

David Collenette — had served, some just briefly, in earlier Liberal cabinets. Many of the rest had wondered for years about the appearance and atmosphere of the cabinet room, situated on a corridor next to the prime minister's office on the third floor of the Centre Block. They had watched covetously as ministers, attended by clutches of assistants, ambled in and out of the suite of rooms behind the wooden door with panes of frosted glass. As they entered for the first time, the rookies couldn't help but notice that in the anteroom where ministers retired to phone their offices and work their side deals, the attentive minions from the Privy Council Office had placed giant containers of headache and stomach pain remedies.

The room itself, built in the 1970s, looked like somebody's nicely finished basement, a large rectangular chamber covered in beige carpet and oak panelling. An inscription on the wall cited the Wisdom of Solomon: "Love justice you that are the rulers of the earth." Chrétien's advisers and the senior Privy Council officials sat around the perimeter, like the spectators at a poker game. The proceedings made up in formality what they lacked in setting. The prime minister kept a speaking list, but names were rarely invoked in cabinet. Those who spoke (or "intervened") referred to the comments of the minister of justice or the solicitor general, not Allan or Herb.

The cabinet table was a huge oval carved from oak, constructed for the larger ministries of the 1970s and 1980s. Microphones were embedded like hunting knives in the table; a glass booth at the near end of the room housed the translators. Right in front of them rested a coffee urn, a pop-up toaster, and plates of digestive cookies. The room looked out over the front lawn of Parliament Hill, which ended at the black cast-iron fence just beyond the Centennial Flame. Directly opposite, the Stars and Stripes fluttered over the entrance to the U.S. Embassy. But the ministers didn't notice the view; the curtains remained forever drawn. Sometime later, when U.S. President Bill Clinton visited Ottawa in February 1995 and met with Chrétien in the cabinet room, he took in the splendid view and wondered why the curtain wasn't left open. "So your guy won't be able to see what we're doing up here," Chrétien quipped, pointing to U.S. Ambassador James Blanchard, who could eye the cabinet room from his embassy desk.

As the ministers filed in, they noticed name tags arrayed around the table. Chrétien seated himself in the centre of the room, with his back to Jim Blanchard's desk, the same spot used by Brian Mulroney. The back of his green armchair was ever so slightly higher than the others. Across the room, a portrait of Canada's first prime minister, Conservative John A. Macdonald, watched over the proceedings. He wouldn't last, replaced in short order by the turn-of-the-century Liberal whom Chrétien so admired, Sir Wilfrid Laurier. Deputy Prime Minister Sheila Copps sat immediately to Chrétien's right. Herb Gray, the most senior minister in terms of parliamentary service, was on the left. The three Davids — Dingwall, Anderson, and Collenette — were grouped together. Rookies like Anne McLellan and Allan Rock sat on the wings.

Lloyd Axworthy, a veteran of the Trudeau ministry, took his place near the middle of the room, next to Gray. Already, his mind was scanning the possibilities for making a mark in Human Resources Development, the colossal new department in charge of more spending than the rest of the government combined. It had been created specifically to effect large-scale reforms to Canada's social policies. At Rideau Hall a couple of hours earlier, he had lined up to take his place in the official group photo of the cabinet, shook his head, and marvelled at the wonders of the world.

Many of the people around the table enjoyed relations of long standing. They had sat in Parliament together or crossed paths at countless party events over the years. But few of them knew the spherical, balding man with the clipped moustache, a Liberal only since June. For Marcel Massé, upon whom Chrétien had bestowed the twin responsibilities for intergovernmental affairs and public service renewal, it was all so familiar yet so foreign. He had been a senior adviser to governments for most of his adult life, and had attended cabinet meetings in that capacity under Pierre Trudeau, Joe Clark, and Brian Mulroney. Now he had crossed over from public servant to elected politician. In his former capacity, he had been relegated to the periphery of the room, where senior officials watched and recorded the proceedings. Now he found himself for the first time in the centre, although precisely how central he would become no one could have imagined.

Chrétien banged his gavel and called the meeting to order. (He would wield the small wooden hammer at the start and end of meetings and, occasionally, to hush his ministers.)

Finance Minister Paul Martin's place was directly opposite Chrétien, under the portrait. But it remained vacant on this day. As the rest of the ministers huddled together for the first time in Ottawa, Martin sat alone puzzling over his briefing books at the Hôtel-Dieu Hospital in Windsor.

Chrétien had arranged for Martin to be the first of his ministers out of Rideau Hall so that he could return to the bedside of his dying mother. After a few brief remarks to the press — he didn't yet know the size of the deficit, low inflation was essential for low interest rates, he looked forward to sitting down soon with Bank of Canada governor John Crow to exchange ideas and opinions, the job was a great challenge and a great opportunity — the second most powerful figure in the new Liberal government dashed for the airport, where a Challenger jet waited to whisk him to Windsor.

Eleanor Martin, a woman who had spent most of her eighty years on the edge of the political limelight, was floating in and out of a coma. Nell, as she was universally known, was working as a pharmacist in her family's drugstore in Windsor in the 1930s when the young MP for Essex East, overhearing her say she would never marry, interjected that yes, she would. And she would marry *him*. From the time of their wedding in 1937 until the death of Paul Martin Sr. in 1992, she managed the domestic side of their life, caring for their two children and keeping her husband on an even keel, through both his considerable achievements and his crushing disappointments. Her political instincts, honed at his side, remained sharp to the end.

At one point, she awoke in the hospital to see her son, Paul, and her daughter, Mary Anne, hovering over her. "Why?" she asked weakly.

Martin, thinking she was asking why both her children had come from out of town, started to answer that they were there because she had been ill and they wanted to see her.

"No," he reported her cutting him off. "Why Finance?"

As Martin sat in the chaplain's office flipping through the three bulky black binders prepared by his new department, he must have wondered why himself. The books were standard fare for a Finance bureaucrat. But to Martin, they were as hard to decipher as the catechism. The four-ring binders ran to hundreds of legal-sized pages, each page stamped "Secret." The first book amounted to the in-basket for the new minister, setting out the dozens of issues that had backed up during the election and outlining the decisions required of him over the next few weeks. The other two exposed the inner workings of the government of Canada, with special emphasis on the dismal state of its finances. The books provided him a glimpse, through the eyes of his officials, of the challenges he would face over a five-year mandate.

"How much fiscal action is required in the February 1994 budget?" one of the books asked. "No one can give the precise answer to this question as it must carefully balance economic and political risk. Certainly the larger the deficit reduction in the near term, the greater the chances of achieving lower interest rates and the less discretionary fiscal tightening that will be needed later in the mandate."

Back in Ottawa, Martin's executive assistant, Terrie O'Leary, was thumbing through her own copies of the binders. They exchanged calls, trying to figure out what this or that meant. Buried deep in the book, they found one item they both could understand all too well: the deficit was running $6 billion higher than had been forecast in the April 1993 budget. And it would be another $6 billion over the forecast in the next fiscal year.

It was a measure of Chrétien's political maturity that he had handed the most important portfolio in any government, but particularly in this deeply indebted one, to his main rival from the 1990 leadership race and, in the minds of many, the pretender to the throne. Chrétien had first-hand experience of coming second and, in his view, of being treated shabbily. He made no secret of his feelings that he had been humiliated by John Turner in the aftermath of his unsuccessful 1984 leadership challenge, and he believed that, as a result, the Liberal Party had suffered unpardonably.

He would not do the same to Paul Martin. He made him co-chair of the party's platform committee, an appointment some Martin supporters thought was designed to marginalize him, but one the runner-up parlayed into the wildly successful Red Book. Now Chrétien didn't hesitate to put him in Finance. "For me, it was essential that you turn the page," Chrétien explained in an interview. "If you don't do that, you don't have a party."

The ministers listened intently as Chrétien launched into an introductory speech prepared for him months in advance. He wanted to impress upon his team that their jobs began right away. For many this was their first cabinet meeting and they should cherish the memory, but the moment had arrived to get down to business. He reminded them that Canadians had elected a large contingent of Liberal MPs and that they would have to be sensitive to that caucus. They could not behave like an elite up here on the third floor, detached from the members downstairs. He insisted that they attend the weekly caucus meetings — a sort of clan gathering of Liberal MPs and senators. Indeed, they were astounded to discover that Chrétien took attendance of ministers at these meetings, conspicuously ticking their names off a list as he spotted them around the room. If they missed too many caucuses, he didn't hesitate to let them know. Only by virtue of the election of those members did they enjoy the privilege of their position; they must never forget that. He also served notice that his government would conduct itself with the highest possible ethical standards, resisting the inevitable temptations available to politicians, as he had for thirty years. He had plenty of talent in the 177-member caucus upon which to draw. "The first person who makes a mistake will be out," he stated, exposing canines far more menacing in appearance, as it turned out, than in actuality.

The prime minister spoke as well about the relationship they should develop with their deputy ministers. He recounted how, in each of his portfolios during seventeen years as a cabinet minister, he would tell his deputies: "You make me look good, I make you look good." The position of chief of staff, a senior political position superimposed on ministerial offices during the Mulroney years as a check against the bureaucracy, no longer existed, he said. (He would keep a chief of staff in his own office, however.) Partly, this was as a demonstration of Liberal frugality. But partly it was to remove a disruptive layer between ministers and their departments. They should meet with their deputies every day, as he would with the clerk of the Privy Council. (Later in the afternoon, he imparted the same message to a standing-room-only audience of about three dozen deputies crowded into the small boardroom on the fourth floor of the Langevin Block.)

The last point he made concerned the Red Book. The Liberals had carefully catalogued their commitments in a polished 112-page election platform, and Chrétien had made a point at almost every campaign stop of reminding voters that, four years on, they could come back to him and tote up the promises kept and the promises broken. He didn't intend to come up short; the first half of the government's mandate would be devoted to the achievement of Red Book promises.

The Red Book had been the sensation of the campaign. The publication of an election manifesto was uncommon in Canada. But the Liberal leadership had felt it was required to help weld together a divided caucus as well as to arm Chrétien against the long-standing charge that, as a leader, he was as devoid of ideas as he was uninterested in them. He waved it around wherever he went, using it more as a shield than as a lance. Until mid-September, polls showed the election virtually tied. Around September 17, the day after release of the Red Book, the Liberals pulled ahead a couple of points, never to look back.

For Michael Marzolini, the Liberal pollster, the Red Book proved to be as important for its existence as for its content. The public's profound sense of alienation had made a deep impression on Marzolini, and on all political pollsters, as he prepared for the 1993 election. In his first focus group after being appointed party pollster the previous January, he had watched from behind the one-way mirror as a panel of ordinary voters vented about broken promises and lying politicians. If a politician made a promise and kept it, the moderator asked, how would you react? Marzolini didn't miss the significance of the response. "Show me a politician who makes a promise and keeps a promise, and I can know it, and I'll vote for them forever," a participant responded, to nods all around.

Accountability, Marzolini concluded, would be the real underlying issue of the campaign, the necessary precondition for discussion of all other issues. "With that mood in mind, verbal promises from politicians were not enough to satisfy the electorate. They wanted accountability — a written contract, signed and costed from each party and leader," he wrote in a forty-eight-page post-election analysis circulated to his firm's clients. "By listing the Liberal initiatives and providing an itemized costing — and through Chrétien's speeches linking the [Red Book] to 'accountability' — Canadians gained a perception of this document being a 'contract" between them and the leader. In the public opinion environment of 1993, this type of accountability was a necessity."

Chrétien now intended to make good on that contract. Asked three weeks earlier at a high school in Welland, Ontario, what his first three orders of business would be, he hadn't hesitated in rhyming off approval of the $6-billion infrastructure program, cancellation of the EH-101 helicopter contract, and a halt to the privatization of Pearson Airport in Toronto. Now his cabinet acted on all three. Chrétien didn't like to dither. "First item, helicopters," he intoned. "Cancelled." His cabinet would be a decision-making body, not a debating society. He had loathed the Trudeau government's time-consuming labyrinth of cabinet committees and subcommittees. Unnecessary discussion tried his patience; he was renowned for cutting people off in mid-sentence if he found them repeating themselves or even echoing a previous speaker. "Chrétien doesn't like discussions for the sake of discussion," said Jean Pelletier, his chief of staff. "At that first cabinet meeting, he said, 'Everyone can speak, but don't speak if it's only to agree with someone.'" Meetings of full cabinet would begin on time and end on time, two hours gavel to gavel. Major discussions would be saved for the streamlined system of two cabinet committees: Social Development and Economic Development, whose meetings the prime minister did not have to attend.

With the helicopter contract out of the way, cabinet authorized the federal contribution to the $6-billion infrastructure program. Finally, it rubber-stamped a quick-and-dirty inquiry into the Pearson Airport privatization. "It was bang, bang, bang — and then we were out of there," recalled one minister.

Their first cabinet meeting over, Chrétien went across Wellington Street to the National Press Building to inform the country about his government's fast start. His ministers, meanwhile, retired to their offices to study the so-called mandate letters through which the prime minister had transmitted his expectations for each portfolio. The day had been exhilarating, but disorienting. Many had been surprised by Chrétien, by his briskness and self-assurance. A few would later confess to feeling even somewhat intimidated. He had been there before and seemed to know everyone's portfolio. "You can't bullshit him," one of the many cabinet rookies commented after Chrétien interrupted at one point to recall that he had heard that same argument twenty years earlier.

Mostly, though, the select group anointed to sit on the third floor were bathing in contentment. They had been entrusted with stewardship of a great but difficult land, a country more indebted to foreigners than any major economy on earth and a country in a never-ending civics debate about whether its continued existence made sense. Nobody shied from the responsibility. In parliamentary politics, two goals supersede all others: to get into the House of Commons, and to progress to the front benches. Jean Chrétien and his ministers savoured their place at the summit. For some, like the prime minister himself, it had been a hard climb.

2

BACK ON THE ICE

Anyone who had watched Chrétien during his first year as Liberal leader would have marvelled at the confident and commanding figure he had become by the autumn of 1993. The election campaign had shown him at his best: sober, sure-handed, supremely well schooled in the political arts. As he returned to government after nine years in the wilderness, he carried himself with a new sense of maturity, even gravitas. He had seen it all and didn't rattle easily. Nor did he possess an overweening need, like Mulroney, for the spotlight. For perhaps the first time in his career, he had outgrown the look, in the immortal words of Dalton Camp, of the guy driving the getaway car.

On his long ascent, Chrétien had always projected the image of a man in a hurry. He strode, never ambled, to his next destination. He galloped up stairs two at a time. From the moment of his first election to the Commons in 1963, a skinny, brushcut lawyer less than three months past his twenty-ninth birthday, he had his eyes fixed on the front benches. Shortly after that election, Doug Fisher, later a journalist but at that time an NDP member of Parliament, showed the freshman MP where he would sit in the back row.

"Yes, but someday I will be sitting there," responded Chrétien, pointing to the front bench. Fisher told him he would have to be prepared to work hard. "Don't worry," Chrétien assured him. "I will work."

Work he did. In 1981, Aline Chrétien told *Saturday Night* magazine that her husband had always plotted a career that went straight upward. "It was to always advance, to keep moving up." He would serve one of the most complete apprenticeships of any leader in Canadian history: nine cabinet portfolios, including finance minister (he was the first French Canadian to hold the post) and Trudeau's constitutional deal-maker, always moving up until his bitter defeat to John Turner in the 1984 leadership race.

As Bill Clinton would later marvel, John Kennedy was still president at the time of Chrétien's first election to Parliament. Seven more U.S. presidents had since followed. In 1967, Lester B. Pearson had made Chrétien the youngest Canadian cabinet minister in the century. He had studied his craft under the best and now stood ready to take his place in the Liberal pantheon, a seasoned professional steeped in politics as the art of the possible.

In February 1979, German Economics Minister Otto Lambsdorff visited Ottawa and met with Chrétien, then minister of finance. Lambsdorff, a serious-minded veteran of European politics, opened his briefing books and proceeded to review in stultifying detail the state of German-Canadian economic relations. After he had finished, Chrétien perfunctorily commented on Canada's economic outlook and then drew the session to a quick conclusion. "Thank you, Herr Minister. Now I know all I need to know," he declared. Lambsdorff, offended, stormed out of the Centre Block. He refused the car provided for him and marched across Parliament Hill in the cold, muttering, "That man is an idiot."

In fact, Jean Chrétien wasn't an idiot. He just didn't like to sweat the details. He had officials for that. Ministers should concentrate on the major political issues and stay out of the hair of their departments on the nitty-gritty. His political mentor, Mitchell Sharp, finance minister in the Pearson era, had a favourite story he liked to tell in the 1960s when people complained about his parliamentary secretary's lack of intellectual rigour. The story was about a government backbencher, early in the life of the country, who wrote to Prime Minister Macdonald asking to be made a minister. Sir John A. told the MP to forget it: he lacked the education, the intelligence, the background. A few days later, Macdonald received a second letter from the ambitious politician saying there must be a misunderstanding: he was only asking to be a minister, not a deputy minister.

But Sharp was struggling uphill as he sought to persuade first Pearson and later Trudeau of Chrétien's worthiness for ever-increasing cabinet responsibility. Without his mentorship, Sharp conjectured in a 1995 interview, Chrétien would never have been given the opportunity to scramble to the top of the heap. He might have ended up one of so many undistinguished backbenchers, possibly fulfilling his initial ambition of a judicial appointment. Michael McCabe, who watched it all from his bird's-eye seat as Sharp's right-hand man, concurred. "Chrétien was there to be made and shaped. He put himself entirely into Mitchell's hands. He understood what the opportunity was."

Whatever Chrétien lacked in rigour, he made up for in shrewdness. McCabe recalled visiting him shortly after he had been made minister of national revenue in 1967 and inquiring how he was making out. "You see that pile over there?" Chrétien replied. "Those are the things the deputy minister wants. When I get one of the things I want, he gets something he wants."

That native intelligence would never abandon him. In 1984, in the anguish of his leadership loss to John Turner, Chrétien was the only one among all the old hands in the new Liberal cabinet who wasn't fooled by the party's illusory uptick in the public opinion polls. Only Chrétien, the sullen and embittered Chrétien, advised against calling the disastrous 1984 summer election that reduced the Liberals to a rump of forty seats. Roy MacLaren, also a minister in that government, recorded in his diary on July 11, 1984: "Everyone except Chrétien urges an early date… He argues vigorously for a late autumn election so as to allow us to put our campaign organization and finances into better shape. By waiting, he believes that we'll gain some new faces, field better candidates. Chrétien also contends that we can only benefit from Turner being seen for a while as PM — accompanying the Queen and the Pope during visits to Canada, at the UN General Assembly etc…. Chrétien's various arguments are not well received. Some muttering about sour grapes."

His sound advice notwithstanding, the charge of sour grapes contained more than a kernel of truth. Chrétien felt that the better man had lost the leadership, a judgment reinforced by the election débâcle. He resented the manner in which the spoils had gone to the victor, mentally cataloguing the perceived snubs both of himself and of his supporters for some future day of reckoning.

On February 27, 1986, after a year and a half of increasing frustration, Chrétien delivered a handwritten note to John Turner, resigning his seat in the Commons. Turner acknowledged the hole left behind by the loss of someone who had been "minister of almost everything," but added, "I suppose there can only be one leader." Chrétien did not depart with enthusiasm. Aline Chrétien, packing her husband's bag for a farewell trip to his constituency, vented her frustration to CBC reporter Jason Moscovitz at the way the party had treated him. "He doesn't have to take that shit," she hissed.

Chrétien moved into an office tower a couple of blocks from his beloved Hill, joining his long-time aide Eddie Goldenberg at the Ottawa outpost of the Liberal Toronto law firm Lang Michener. He established business relationships as well with Gordon Capital Corporation, the secretive wheeler-dealer of Bay Street, and provided his counsel to a trade consulting firm created by another of his former officials, Gordon Ritchie, who had been Canada's deputy chief negotiator for the Canada-U.S. Free Trade Agreement. He joined some big corporate boards: the Toronto-Dominion Bank; his friend Ross Fitzpatrick's Viceroy Resources; and Consolidated Bathurst, the owner of the Shawinigan paper mill where his father, Wellie, had toiled. In short order, Chrétien became a wealthy man, joining at one point with two others in a $1.25-million purchase from Consolidated Bathurst of the company country club outside Shawinigan. He also became a bestselling author, proving his continued popularity with the astounding sales of his ghost-written autobiography, *Straight from the Heart*.

But he didn't appear content. Every few weeks, he would fly to Toronto on business, often dropping in on Donald Macdonald, the former Liberal cabinet minister whose law office was five floors below the Gordon Capital headquarters. Chrétien would pop in unexpectedly, just to say hello or perhaps to see if his old friend had time for lunch. Macdonald recalled the great pleasure Chrétien would experience when strangers recognized him. One day, shortly after Chrétien's resignation, they lunched near Toronto's O'Keefe Centre. Several people approached Chrétien in the restaurant to offer him best wishes. As the two men chatted on the way back to their office tower, a woman walking in front of them suddenly stopped, reeled around, and said, "Mr. Chrétien! I thought it was you." He had been feeling bad, even despondent, according to Macdonald. "That just picked him up." He was a born politician.

He pined for a return. Meanwhile, Chrétien loyalists like David Dingwall, Brian Tobin, Sergio Marchi, and Alfonso Gagliano — the so-called four horsemen — kept up their agitations against Turner's hapless leadership. When the target of their efforts finally called it quits in 1989, after leading the Liberals through their two worst back-to-back election performances ever, Chrétien's team was in fighting trim.

He announced his bid on Tuesday, January 23, 1990, emphasizing that he was the man to beat Mulroney and that the Liberal contest was one between friends, not adversaries. To run the campaign, he turned to John Rae, the diplomat's son who had started out as a twenty-one-year-old aide with Chrétien in the 1960s. They had first met in 1966, when Rae was working at the United Nations in Geneva and Chrétien came through town with a visiting delegation of MPs. Although both were intensely private men, they clicked immediately and went off skiing in the Alps together.

Rae, the older brother of Bob Rae, was a serious-minded, hard-working guy, the kind of person of whom subordinates would say, "Still waters run deep." He could impart messages to underlings just by the way he cocked his head in a meeting. He was unfailingly polite and thorough, but, as his brother once joked, even as a boy Rae didn't give much away. He once astounded a colleague by placing a comforting arm around her shoulder; Rae simply wasn't the sort to make physical contact. Behind the controlled exterior, though, lurked a strongly competitive spirit. A long-time friend thought the key to penetrating his psychology lay in understanding that he had excelled as an athlete in boyhood but had ultimately been frustrated by his small stature.

Chrétien had been so impressed by Rae that in 1971, when Rae took up a career with Power Corporation of Montreal, he tried to recruit his younger brother — Bobby, as he called him — to take his place. Chrétien travelled to Britain to twist the arm of the Rhodes Scholar and later premier of Ontario. I'm a socialist, Bob Rae protested. Chrétien said he didn't care.

But John Rae was only a phone call away in Montreal and — however reluctantly — always returned at vital moments. By 1993, a national campaign without him would seem unthinkable. In fact, the four horsemen told Chrétien that their three top candidates for campaign chief were John Rae, John Rae, and John Rae. Chrétien could not take no for an answer, they said. He was the only one with both the total confidence of the leader and the universal respect of the caucus.

The other dominant figure around Chrétien was Eddie Goldenberg, who came to work for him as a summer student in the early 1970s on the recommendation of Rae. With the exception of only a few brief sojourns, he never left. The son of Senator Carl Goldenberg, a distinguished Montreal labour lawyer, he was a small, socially awkward man with a knack for finding solutions to problems and a cautious streak that put even Chrétien to shame.

From a distance, people thought of them as like father and son, or perhaps friends. Neither description fit. Theirs was an intimate but business-like relationship — Chrétien clearly the boss and the one who could be as brusque with Goldenberg, or perhaps more so, as with others. Whereas

Rae acquired an independent cachet over the years and came to be treated as an equal — in large part because he eventually went out on his own — Goldenberg never graduated from the ranks of valued, even prized employees. Some people likened him to Jean Chrétien's *Reader's Digest*, the guy who actually read everything and reduced it to manageable proportions. Chrétien described Goldenberg to author Lawrence Martin as his "pocket computer." Certainly, he understood Chrétien's mind better than anyone. In 1990, while Rae was running the shop at headquarters, Goldenberg travelled the country with Chrétien, whispering advice in his ear.

Chrétien's closest political advisers, people like Rae and Goldenberg, tended to be anglophone Montrealers, disciples of Pierre Trudeau and with a very distinct vision of federalism. They believed deeply in official bilingualism as a force to bind the country together, supported strong central government, and bitterly criticized Quebec nationalism amongst themselves while defending it just as vehemently any time they discussed it with people from other provinces. A cartoon by the Montreal *Gazette*'s Aislin described their attitude well: in it, a patient-looking anglo Montrealer says to an obvious visitor, "Of course, it's difficult for an outsider to grasp the subtle complexities of the situation" — as the two of them walk past wall graffiti that reads "Speak French, English dogs."

Leadership races, by definition, are civil wars. Thanks to the nature of the delegate selection process, the combat is waged door to door. Still, in 1990 veterans of past Liberal campaigns could remember none quite this nasty. The contest coincided with the prolonged death rattle of the Meech Lake Accord, Brian Mulroney's constitutional deal with Quebec, giving it an even nastier edge. Nor were matters helped any by the stubborn, scorched-earth tactics of Chrétien's main challenger, Paul Martin Jr., whose supporters had managed to have the normal three- or four-month process stretched out for more than a year.

Martin had planned to run on his mind-numbing economic platform; Chrétien on his winnability. But nobody could run away from Meech. Chrétien opposed it; Martin was a fervent supporter. The fate of the leadership candidates and the accord would be decided on the same day, June 23, 1990 — the day of the Liberal vote and the deadline for provincial ratification of the constitutional deal.

Few people cared about Chrétien's views on the subject while he was retired from politics, and the accord at first seemed sure of passing. But by late 1989, with the deal hitting a variety of roadblocks and John

Turner's future behind him, the issue took on new importance. Increasingly, people asked where Chrétien stood. The answer was that several aspects of the accord deeply disturbed him. By far the most troubling was the notion that recognition of Quebec as a distinct society in the preamble might allow the province's legislature to override the Canadian Charter of Rights and Freedoms, which he had been so instrumental in adopting.

Martin, on the other hand, strongly supported Meech. Like Brian Mulroney — who was, in fact, a close friend — he viewed the accord as the minimum package necessary to bring Quebec into the constitutional fold and bury sovereignty as an issue. The natural polarization of a leadership race and the intoxicating passions of constitutional debate served to magnify the differences between the two camps. The resulting tensions between the two candidates and their followers grew to extraordinary proportions during the policy forums and other pre-convention events.

The convention in Calgary, with Chrétien's big first-ballot victory, seemed anticlimactic. The accord died on Friday, June 22, when Newfoundland Premier Clyde Wells refused to allow a vote on ratification in his province's legislature. The announcement of the news elicited a spontaneous cheer from the Liberal audience. Several Quebec supporters of Martin took to wearing black armbands. The next day, Wells showed up in Calgary, where he and Chrétien were shown in a televised embrace that immediately became infamous in Quebec. Chrétien would survive Martin's challenge but would never recover from Meech.

Chrétien couldn't let on, of course, but he understood the extent of his political trouble in Quebec. The Saturday after Calgary, on the morning of June 30, Chrétien and John Rae met up at a country house in Pointe-au-Pic, Quebec, to indulge in their great shared passion: eighteen holes of golf. It was the long weekend leading into Canada Day, and just a week since Chrétien had won the leadership. It was a difficult time for Chrétien: more than 100,000 people had marched in the Fête Nationale parade on Monday, June 25, in support of sovereignty, and Premier Robert Bourassa had given a speech in the National Assembly grimly asserting Quebec's democratic right to choose its own constitutional future. The image of Chrétien at the convention, embracing Wells, was repeated endlessly on the evening news. Some long-time friends wouldn't speak to him, and others did so only to rebuke him.

Now, to add injury to those insults, Chrétien and Rae were stranded on the road to the golf course. Thinking the distance was walkable, they

had set out from the cottage on foot. When they realized they'd under-
estimated, they did the only thing they could think of: they stuck out
their thumbs to hitchhike. Soon they were on their way, courtesy of the
first vehicle that happened along, a newspaper delivery truck making
morning rounds. There they were, one of Canada's most prominent
business executives and the newly minted leader of her Majesty's Loyal
Opposition, huddled uncomfortably alongside stacked bundles of that
day's news. Rae looked over at Chrétien and Chrétien looked back at
Rae and said: "You know, John, it's gonna be very tough right now, but
we'll get through it. We're gonna face a very tough year."

It turned out to be a far tougher year than Chrétien would ever have imagined. He had become stained as a traitor to Quebec, his behaviour in the
1982 patriation of the Constitution now reinterpreted as having stabbed
Quebec in the back. He appeared stumbling and uncertain in public; his
once charmingly fractured syntax was now simply fractured. Chrétien
operated best when he felt comfortable. After Meech, the subject of vilification in his home province, he had been stripped of his confidence. His
previously keen judgment abandoned him as he suggested defusing the
Oka crisis by letting armed militants go and then arresting them later. On
the GST, the biggest issue of the year, he had spent the entire leadership
campaign resisting rash promises to scrap it before delivering precisely
such a commitment in October 1990. He couldn't decide at first how long
to wait before running for a seat in Parliament, and when he did, in late
1990, he chose Beauséjour, a safe Liberal redoubt in New Brunswick,
bringing on the taunts of Quebec nationalists. His advisers, eager to make
him look more prime-ministerial, handed him rambling discourses on
matters of high policy that bored the speaker, and his audiences, to tears.
In a year-end interview, Chrétien had to concede: "It was not a good start
for me."

   It got worse before it got better. In January, he again looked ridiculous in trying to square the circle of anti–Gulf War sentiment in his caucus — led by Lloyd Axworthy and Allan MacEachen — by vacillating
over Canadian participation in the Western mission and then, in a classic
Chrétien compromise, calling for the removal of Canadian troops if shooting broke out. Then he fell ill. A benign tumour was removed from his
lung in late February. His recuperation stretched out to five weeks, three
more than predicted. Speculation mounted that he might have to relinquish

the leadership — a rumour fanned, naturally enough, by those who supported other potential candidates.

But he used the recuperation period well. The doctors had been forced to break his ribs during the operation. He later told intimates that because of the pain he had lain awake at night, thinking about his lengthy career in politics and of his desire, if he had one shot at the top job, not to screw it up. He and Aline took long walks on the shore at Delray Beach, Florida. Aline was the person he relied upon most completely, emotionally and intellectually. She and Chrétien had been teenage sweethearts, both from the same pulp and paper town; she understood his rhythms, his strengths and weaknesses. "I'm telling you that when she tells me something," Chrétien told Hana Gartner in a 1993 interview with the couple, "I listen a lot."

Aline kept a low profile by choice, but she had a big interest in what was good for her husband. She had talked him out of politics after his leadership loss in 1984, saying, "You owe nothing more," and had insisted on a cold calculation of his leadership chances before consenting to his return in 1990. Now she told him that he had gotten this far by trusting his instincts. His advisers, with their TelePrompTers and laborious speeches, may have been well intentioned, but he needed to be Jean Chrétien. When he returned to Ottawa, he did so with a renewed determination to succeed.

First, he fixed up his own office, which had descended into squabbling and recrimination under the leadership of Eddie Goldenberg. Goldenberg had many fine qualities, but people skills did not rank high among them. He tended to be needlessly secretive and hesitated to delegate. Caucus, as well as aides, chafed under his command. In May 1991, unknown to Goldenberg, Chrétien asked a mutual friend to contact Jean Pelletier, a former college classmate who had just stepped down as mayor of Quebec City. They met after a Liberal fundraiser in the Quebec capital. Chrétien explained his problems and asked the courtly Pelletier to take over as his chief of staff.

Goldenberg only learned about the appointment through a newspaper leak in mid-June. Coming across the clipping, he bolted out of a morning tactical session. His assistant Warren Kinsella caught up with him. They went across the street to the Plaza Café. Goldenberg said he was going to quit, Kinsella recalled; he was angry and hurt at Chrétien's handling of the matter.

When Pelletier came on board the day after Canada Day, he concurred with Chrétien's negative analysis. "I decided to meet every employee in camera. After two weeks, I knew what was wrong." Pelletier imposed order on the chaos: meetings at the same time every day, flow charts of who reported to whom; red file folders for matters to go to the leader, blue files for Quebec issues. In order for Chrétien to perform at his best, Pelletier said, "he needs order, control, and stability around him." Pelletier also worked out an accommodation with Goldenberg, the only guy who didn't fit neatly on the flow charts.

With a precise eloquence in French and English, Pelletier seemed like a latter-day version of Charles Boyer. But he could also be terrifying: "the elegant executioner" was how at least one member of Chrétien's staff depicted him. A backbench MP, after his first encounter with Pelletier, described him as being "like a Second World War–era French mayor — Vichy, of course." A serious political party requires discipline; Pelletier was the disciplinarian.

The addition of Pelletier gave Chrétien the orderly base from which to proceed. At the same time, Peter Donolo came on board to address Chrétien's communications problems, recruited by Goldenberg, who affectionately called him "the court jester." But Donolo's value extended far beyond an acknowledged and too often indulged penchant for bad puns. He was thirty-two and working as press secretary for Toronto mayor Art Eggleton when he was hired in August of 1991. No one in Chrétien's office even knew him then; Goldenberg had read about him in a Michael Valpy column in the *Globe and Mail*. Valpy described him as perhaps the best press secretary in the country because of how he had enlivened the otherwise drab Eggleton's image. A little asking around revealed that Donolo was a long-time Liberal despite his youth, a Montreal anglophone from Pierre Trudeau's Mount-Royal riding who began working for the party while still in his early teens.

Donolo would put Chrétien into the denim shirts that became a staple of his campaign appearances (and were shelved once he became prime minister) and began inserting jokes into his speeches. Donolo did not create the Red Book, but he made sure that in Chrétien's hands, it became an effective tool for both the public and the leader himself to believe in. "Think of it as your Bible and yourself as Billy Graham," was how Donolo pitched him time and again. There were inevitable comparisons between Donolo and Bill Clinton's young and hip media maven, George

Stephanopoulos. Except that Donolo, a baby-faced figure fighting a constant battle with his waistline, was determinedly un-hip: he cared little about modern-day trends but could spend hours reciting the dialogue from 1930s or '40s movies, and had a huge collection of compact discs of jazz and big bands from that era. Despite his sociability — among his attributes was his ability to make Chrétien laugh — he liked nothing better than an evening alone in his basement thumbing through his collection of *Maclean's*, *Esquire*, *Life*, and *Look*.

Goldenberg got over his initial hurt and became Chrétien's chief troubleshooter, working especially closely on policy matters with Chaviva Hošek, the opposition leader's director of policy and research. Chrétien now had in place much of the team that would carry him into the Prime Minister's Office in two years. But he still needed to bridge the yawning policy differences in his party.

Chrétien had been around politics long enough to recognize that unless the Liberals could establish their capacity to govern themselves, they would never be trusted to govern the country. Patiently and methodically, he set out to suture his party back together, even if it sometimes took baling wire and airplane glue to do the trick.

John Turner and the Liberals had failed to carry the country in the 1988 free trade election. But many of their MPs nonetheless credited their individual victories to their heartfelt crusade against the Canada-U.S. pact. This created a classic political dilemma for the runner-up party. "The difficulty in opposition," Goldenberg later noted, "is that you get elected on a platform that the people have rejected. By definition."

Among the MPs from the Class of '84 — an overwhelmingly left-wing caucus — feelings ran high to keep the trade issue alive. But the 1988 election had brought a vanguard of articulate business Liberals back into Parliament. Ripping up trade agreements did not conform to their understanding of the behaviour of a natural governing party. Roy MacLaren, Paul Martin, and former Ottawa board of trade president John Manley conspired to pull the party back towards the centre on trade. MacLaren, who had written a book on Canadians operating behind enemy lines in World War II, thought of the three Ms, as he liked to call them, in those same terms. He would later laud them in a speech as a small band of insurgents who viewed free trade as not just a practical necessity but a guiding ideal.

Chrétien intuitively grasped that the Liberals couldn't go on fighting the last war. "None of us in the group around Mr. Chrétien thought that was the way to go," said Chaviva Hošek, his policy chief. "Whatever our feelings about free trade, it was not smart for that to be the issue of the [next] election... Do you want your leader to fight the fight that the previous leader fought and lost?"

Planning had begun in late 1990 for a conference of top Liberal thinkers, who would chart a new direction for a party trying to find its way in a world of deficits and globalization. They gathered in November 1991 in Aylmer, Quebec. The Aylmer conference, modelled on a similar event in Kingston thirty years earlier, provided the 1988 election campaign and 1980s leftward Liberalism with a decent burial. From there began the difficult process of cobbling together a consensus between the wings of Liberalism that had always competed for influence — left versus right; social versus business; nationalist versus free trade.

Out of Aylmer flowed the policy platform, chaired by Paul Martin and Chaviva Hošek. The Liberals had looked inept in 1988 when they couldn't even explain their own daycare policies. This time out, they felt the need to provide a thorough description of their plan and a detailed accounting of its cost and financing. Martin and Hošek met repeatedly with caucus in their attempts to forge a consensus. They toured the country, hearing out Liberals and gauging the public mood, discovering that the party was ahead of the caucus on the subject of fiscal responsibility and, equally, on law and order issues. At the first meeting, in Vancouver, they had booked a large room to discuss the economy and a small one for justice issues. They had to move the latter session.

The document they wrote grew in importance beyond their wildest imaginations in the 1993 election, gaining fame as the Red Book. The first person to call it the Red Book was Kim Campbell — she compared it to Mao's Little Red Book — and the name was picked up in the media. But back in the writing phase it lacked a name — it was known simply as the platform — and a look: the first cover design wasn't even red. And its two authors fought daily over its contents. "I want a divorce from him and we're not even married," Hošek would grouse good-naturedly about the unrelenting Martin.

By the autumn of 1992, the Liberals were starting to detect the sweet fragrance of power wafting in their direction. Mulroney's popularity rating was mired in the teens; with the failure of the Charlottetown Accord, a second attempt by Mulroney at constitutional change that was rejected in a national referendum, his defeat appeared inevitable. Jean Chrétien thought the time had come to begin preparing to become prime minister. He invited David Zussman, one of his least-known yet most important advisers, to drop by his Parliament Hill office.

The pair sat and discussed the state of the nation. The blackness of the public mood weighed heavily on Chrétien. He was convinced that whoever took up residence at 24 Sussex Drive would enjoy only the briefest of honeymoons. "He would," Zussman described in a post-election lecture, "be allowed little time to prove his worth and his worthiness before the electorate wrote him off as one more 'all talk and no walk' politician."

Zussman, a Montreal native, had first encountered Chrétien a dozen years earlier at the University of Victoria, where he was teaching at the time. In 1980 the federal minister of justice inaugurated the university's law school. In the heart of WASP Victoria, Chrétien addressed the students, faculty, and dignitaries for five minutes in French. He then switched official languages, saying that for those who didn't understand him, he would repeat himself in English. But he hoped that the next time he visited the campus, they would be able to follow him in his mother tongue. The audience gave him a standing ovation. Zussman was smitten.

Two years later, Chrétien, just shuffled into the energy portfolio, telephoned Zussman, by then an official in the Privy Council Office, out of the blue and asked him to accept a secondment as his executive assistant. Right after making his pitch, Chrétien heard from Eddie Goldenberg, who had briefly gone off to practise law, that he would like to return to his old job. Mindful that he had just offered the position to someone else, Chrétien phoned Zussman and explained his jam. "So you and Eddie work it out," he instructed, hanging up. They did; they both became special assistants, with Goldenberg handling the oil and gas files and Zussman the rest.

Chrétien came to rely more and more heavily on Zussman's advice. Zussman, who held a Ph.D. in social psychology, seemed to soothe him. In times of crisis — during the trial of his son, Michel, for sexual assault and on the night of the October 1995 referendum — Zussman could be found by his side. His judgment was sound and he was discreet, a quality Chrétien prized.

By the fall of 1992, Chrétien already had a fairly clear idea of the approach a Liberal government would have to take. "The people," Zussman later recalled him saying, "are fed up with lies and scandals and excuses.

They want integrity and good government. Integrity and good government must be the beginning, middle, and end of every policy and plan we develop." No matter who the leader opposite would be, he planned to run against Brian Mulroney. Chrétien, fearing he would be exposed as presumptuous, kept the transition work heavily under wraps.

Zussman knew Chrétien well and understood that his strength lay in his values and political instincts, not his grasp of policy. At the leadership convention in 1990, Chrétien told a CBC interviewer that "leadership is to make the people feel good about themselves, and challenge them." He was more inclined, though, to the former than to the latter. Zussman didn't want Jean Chrétien to become prime minister without a good deal of exposure to the enormous pressures hemming in all Western governments. He felt the decade — with its high deficits, global integration, and aggressive individualism — was too challenging, too mystifying, too different from Chrétien's experiences for him to rely on instincts alone. His challenge in preparing for the transition included preparing the leader for these new realities.

He put together a team of four outside advisers: Judith Maxwell, the former chair of the Economic Council of Canada; Donald Savoie, an Acadian academic and authority on bureaucracies; Sheldon Ehrenworth, executive director of the influential Public Policy Forum; and Daniel Gagnier, a former Intergovernmental Affairs official who had worked with Chrétien in the early 1980s. They pored over public opinion data and read all the latest musings of the think-tanks and political philosophers. Restoring confidence in public institutions would pose the first challenge of any new government, they concluded. The members of the group were persuaded that government could still be a force for good in society. But a new government would need to convince Canadians of its fidelity to the public interest before it could even begin to contemplate soliciting their support for badly needed policy changes.

One issue, above all, haunted the group: the ever-mounting public debt. They found it impossible to fathom a plan of governing without due attention to regaining control over public finances. Maxwell, the member of the group with the most impressive economic credentials, hardly rated as a deficit fanatic. Her reputation came more from the social side of the agenda. But she would sometimes wake up in the morning, listen to the CBC Radio news, and wonder if this was the day that Canada would hit the wall.

On February 8, 1993, Zussman persuaded Chrétien to host a working dinner at Stornoway, the leader of the opposition's residence, with his quartet of policy wonks. Chrétien was reluctant and again feared word would leak and he would be made to look grasping, even ridiculous. But Zussman, still not satisfied that Chrétien possessed the depth of understanding he would need to cope with the constraints on governing in the 1990s, pushed hard. He knew Chrétien learned best through conversation; an evening of purposeful talk would fit the bill.

His misgivings notwithstanding, Chrétien proved a convivial host, directing the guests to the beige patterned couches in the living room and charming them over drinks with war stories from the political trenches. But as they followed him through the French doors into the dining room, members of the Zussman brain trust found his easy smile and quick resort to anecdote troublingly reminiscent of Ronald Reagan. Like Reagan, Chrétien was more deeply rooted in values than in policies. If he were a chief executive officer, one of the diners would remark later, he would be all corporate values and no strategic plan.

As the hired help unobtrusively replaced the plates of chicken and rice with bowls of crème brûlée, the guests persisted in their attempts to glean some overarching insight from Chrétien. Savoie, increasingly exasperated, pushed him to define his vision of the country ten years down the road. Why did he want to be prime minister? Chrétien groped for an answer, dwelling on his qualifications. Finally, Gagnier, who knew him best and understood that his mind didn't work in abstract terms, asked Chrétien his priorities if he won the election.

"I have three priorities," Chrétien replied, finally engaging his audience. Then he listed them: To keep the country independent from the United States. To keep the International Monetary Fund out. And to maintain the unity of Canada. There it was — Jean Chrétien's checklist for the end of the millennium. In many ways, his priorities were the priorities of every prime minister since 1867. Noble goals all. But several of his dinner guests couldn't help grimacing at their unadventurous and defensive nature. He wanted to keep bad things from happening. He seemed to have little sense of the good works he hoped to accomplish.

When it came to politics, Jean Chrétien played defence. He prided himself on being a pragmatist, on eschewing grand plans. The vision thing, as George Bush might say, wasn't his thing. His thing was to go into the office in the morning and deal with the two or three most important files sitting in his in-basket. And to clean out that basket by the end of the day. In his book *The Game*, former Montreal Canadiens goalie Ken Dryden describes the approach teammate Bob Gainey took to hockey. If at the end of every shift he had moved the puck up the ice, to the opponent's end, it was a good shift. "He wants the game under control." Chrétien looked at governing in the same way.

Papers in, papers out, that was his idea of a good day. He was a transactional kind of guy; he dealt with the game in front of him. Like Gainey, he was a defensive specialist. He looked down his nose at politicians, like Brian Mulroney, with visions of filling the net with rubber. Invariably, they were caught up ice when the play turned.

Chrétien thoroughly imbibed the lessons of the wiliest Liberal of them all, the exasperating but politically gifted William Lyon Mackenzie King. "The secret of political success is not what you do right," King instructed his newest cabinet minister, Lester Pearson, in 1948, "but what you avoid doing wrong." It became Jean Chrétien's iron law as well. Two characteristics defined him above all: caution and pragmatism.

Chrétien, not by nature a patient man, was forced to sit and wait as first Mulroney announced his resignation and then the Tories selected Kim Campbell in June as their new leader. Nobody lamented Mulroney's departure as much as the Liberals. He had been their greatest asset, the lightning rod for every discontent ever to fester in a Canadian household. His residual negatives would continue to sustain the Liberals for a long while, but at first Campbell's aura overshadowed her much-dreaded predecessor. Chrétien, whose very longevity rendered him a proxy for disaffection with the political system, suffered by comparison.

On September 8, Campbell visited Governor General Ramon Hnatyshyn, sounding the starting gun on the ultimate test of public opinion. The two main contenders both stumbled coming out of the starting gate. Outside Rideau Hall, Campbell strayed way off message with her glum prediction that the unemployment rate wouldn't dip below 10 per cent until the turn of the century. "I can say how many jobs I'd like to create, but that's old politics," she lectured reporters.

Chrétien, blissfully unaware of Campbell's gaffe, waited under the Peace Tower for the television networks to cut to him. Her typical tardiness — Chrétien, in contrast, was a stickler on the subject, telling aides that punctuality is the politeness of princes — delayed his start just long enough that the clock hitting 11 a.m. drowned out part of his opening statement.

It might have been better if nobody had heard. Chrétien pledged, as scripted, to revive the economy with a $6-billion 1960s-style public works program to build roads, bridges, and sewers in cooperation with the provinces and municipalities. But then, responding to a reporter's barb about his sunny rendition of days past, Chrétien defended a "return to the good old days."

At the campaign headquarters a half-dozen blocks away on Laurier Avenue, Liberal strategists tore their hair out. They had worked long and hard to overcome Chrétien's image as yesterday's man and to couch their message of economic hope within the realities of fiscal constraint. They knew the Tories must already be salivating over the opportunity to portray Chrétien as a throwback to the good old days of tax-and-spend Liberalism.

The Ottawa-based strategists phoned the campaign bus heading down the road from Parliament Hill. At his next stop in Hawkesbury, an hour southwest of Ottawa, Chrétien deftly deflected attention from his own remarks. "The Tory priority is to create jobs for the year 2000," he said, mischievously jumping on Campbell's blunder. "The Liberal priority is to create jobs in 1993, right now, and we'll start in November."

It would be like that for forty-seven days. John Rae, the understated Liberal campaign coordinator, allowed in the final days before balloting that he had sometimes felt like a kid let loose in a candy shop. Some days, he struggled to decide whether to take advantage of the shower of opportunities or stick to the intended message of the day.

The Campbell mistakes were so frequent that Chrétien's team had to work out a system for handling them. Bruce Hartley and Michael McAdoo, two young Liberal aides who had worked together in Herb Gray's office during his stint as interim leader, were on either end of a quick warning system. When Hartley, in Ottawa, learned of a Campbell gaffe, he would immediately alert McAdoo, travelling with Chrétien, by calling his beeper number. McAdoo would phone back at the earliest opportunity for details and then discuss the best possible response with the more senior aides travelling with Chrétien. The calls became so numerous that the pair devised a coding system, adding certain digits to the end of Hartley's telephone number, so McAdoo could ascertain the magnitude of the latest faux pas and decide whether he should tear himself away from the campaign event immediately to find a secure telephone or whether he could wait.

Afterwards, with the Conservatives reduced to two miserable seats, it would seem as if the election had always been in the bag. But the opening polls indicated that it was anybody's to win — or, in the case of Campbell, to lose. A poll published at the start of the second week of the campaign gave the Tories a three-point edge based on positive perceptions of Campbell's leadership.

In his post-election analysis, Liberal pollster Michael Marzolini disclosed that on the day of the writ Canadians believed Campbell would be a better prime minister than Chrétien by a two-to-one margin. They viewed her as stronger, more decisive, more honest, more apt to keep campaign promises, and more likely to restore prosperity and control government spending. Chrétien had experience going for him and an image of being more in tune with the average Canadian. The leadership effect was such, according to Marzolini, that the Liberals led the Conservatives by five points if only party names were mentioned, but trailed by six points if the question identified the party leaders.

Even in mid-campaign, polls showed that nearly half of Canadians could not picture him as their prime minister, with the highest percentage of naysayers situated in Quebec. Results like these encouraged the Tories to attempt their ill-fated face ad late in the campaign. To them, Chrétien represented the greatest Liberal vulnerability. Privately, Liberal strategists acknowledged that the Tories had probably pressed the right button; they had simply made the fatal mistake of doing it in a manner that Canadians found highly offensive.

Ironically, the ads designed to portray him as unfit to be prime minister probably helped create the base for the phenomenal run of popularity he would enjoy after the election. Canadians could identify with the harshness of the treatment and the dignity of his well-prepared response. The Liberals had been waiting for the Tories to get personal. "It's true that I have a physical defect," he told a crowd in New Brunswick. "When I was a kid people were laughing at me. But I accepted that because God gave me other qualities and I'm grateful."

According to the internal Liberal polling, the day before the ad ran, Campbell and Chrétien remained tied in perceptions of who would make the best prime minister of Canada. Three days later, it was the Liberal leader's turn to lead two-to-one, and Conservative support had tumbled another seven points. He knew the election was his. "In the last days of the campaign, when I was in the plane, I was already thinking about how

I will do it, and I was already planning the take-over," he later said.

The crowds grew at every stop as it became apparent that yesterday's man would be tomorrow's prime minister. But the wave failed to carry into his home province. It even threatened to bypass his own riding. In the forty-eight hours leading up to the election, Chrétien's advisers were frantic that he would lose Saint-Maurice, undermining his already wobbly credibility as a voice for Quebec. Two of his senior aides, Peter Donolo and Eddie Goldenberg, arriving with him in the riding on the Saturday before the election, spent the next two days badgering local Liberal organizers about his prospects. The modest turnout at his campaign events and the advanced age of the crowds had them badly spooked.

Chrétien himself would later bitterly blame the media for spreading falsehoods about his imminent defeat. The regional paper, *Le Nouvelliste*, had published a story in Sunday's edition suggesting a sweep by the Bloc Québécois in Mauricie and the demise of Jean Chrétien. But that morning, as he showed the press around his home town, including an unscheduled romp around a boyhood haunt at Shawinigan Falls, he predicted a close fight himself. "It will not be like the good old days, when I had a 25,000-vote majority."

That Sunday, October 24, Jean Chrétien finally stopped running for office so that he could finalize preparations for assuming it. He returned to his cottage early in the afternoon for a long meeting with Jean Pelletier and David Zussman.

Zussman arrived at lunchtime at the A-frame dwelling on Lac des Piles, just on the edge of the giant national park Chrétien had created in the 1970s. As the RCMP waved him through a checkpoint at the top of the gravel road leading to the lake, the gravity of the moment suddenly dawned on Zussman. He had known Jean Chrétien for a dozen years at that point; he understood his strengths and weaknesses. Chrétien embodied the best values of the country, Zussman thought, but required a strong team around him to translate those values into policy. Now he was going to be prime minister, and Zussman would have to help make sure he had the appropriate support systems.

He, Pelletier, and Chrétien reviewed the governing system they would put in place. Zussman had customized it to suit Jean Chrétien — orderly, professional, decentralized, with a minimum of meetings. Ministers would be given their head; bureaucrats would regain influence. Chrétien wanted a small, tightly knit cabinet; he had detested the sprawling ministries of the Trudeau years, so big that real power flowed upward to the Priorities and Planning Committee. In any case, small ministries made for good politics in the frugal 1990s. They had decided months earlier on a twenty-three-person cabinet, including the prime minister. To ensure a sound reading of a disparate country, they would add a small second tier of junior ministers.

As they reviewed the transition material, Pelletier, who had chosen to run for the Liberals in Quebec City, said that he would lose. Chrétien, trying to be upbeat about his own problems, waved off the pessimistic judgment. But the chief of staff, a hard-edged realist, insisted the two situations could not be compared. Quebec City would fall to the Bloc Québécois. Chrétien finally relented — if so, he told Pelletier, meet me at the airport in Trois-Rivières the morning after.

As Zussman prepared to depart that Sunday evening, Chrétien rhymed off a list of close advisers he wanted to help with the final phase of the transition, particularly the making of a cabinet. He gave precise instructions: Zussman should phone and invite them to a meeting Tuesday in the boardroom of the Leader of the Opposition's Office. But he should not begin to place any calls until the Liberals went over the top on Monday evening. Whether because of humility or superstition, Chrétien was self-conscious about jumping the gun.

Chrétien watched the returns on October 25, 1993, at his cottage on Lac des Piles surrounded by his immediate family. Across the country, his victory was termed a sweep. Certainly, it looked big, 177 seats in a 295-member House of Commons. But such numbers can be deceptive. The Liberals attracted just 41 per cent of the popular vote, enough to reward them handsomely thanks to the collapse of the NDP (7 per cent) and the Reform-Tory split west of the Ottawa River (19 and 16 per cent respectively). In Quebec, Chrétien was the first francophone Liberal leader in the country's history to fail to deliver his native province, taking just nineteen seats out of seventy-five. The Bloc confined the Liberals — with two exceptions, including Chrétien's riding — to a Montreal-area enclave and the Ottawa Valley region. The Liberals were the second party in Quebec, as well as in British Columbia and Alberta, the country's fastest-growing provinces, where the upstart Reform Party dominated.

The 1993 general election was actually the result of three distinct campaigns: one in western Canada, where the deficit was the prime issue; one in Atlantic Canada and Ontario, where jobs came first; and one in Quebec, with its own particular rhythms. The Liberals, despite gaining representation in all ten provinces and thus rightfully claiming status as the only surviving national party, won only one of these contests. But their victory in Ontario, Canada's largest province, was sufficiently convincing — ninety-eight seats out of ninety-nine — to put the old hand of Canadian politics in command of a troubled country.

Chrétien knew it would be a challenge. Voting at an elementary school earlier in the day, he had articulated, in his distinctive way, a sense of political fatalism. "Politics is made of this thrill that you skate on thin ice. You never know when there will be a hole that will gobble you up, and it's over forever." Jean Chrétien would seek to minimize those thrills. He lived to play defence.

3

PRIME MINISTER
IN A HURRY

On the morning of October 26, 1993, Aline Chrétien woke her husband in their cottage outside Shawinigan. "Do you want a coffee, Prime Minister?" she inquired playfully. He had toiled long and hard to command that lofty honorific: Prime Minister. He liked the sound. Fittingly, his partner through it all had been the first to say those cherished words. They had been up unusually late the night before, till 3 a.m. Normally, she would have let him sleep in. But the demands of high office were already pressing in upon Jean Chrétien. The president of the United States was scheduled to phone shortly after 8 a.m.

Chrétien's four grandchildren had come over from the cottage next door to eat breakfast. He told them about the important call their grandfather was expecting. Would they like to listen? Chrétien returned to his bedroom to speak for the first time to the U.S. president, his grandchildren gathered on the floor by his feet.

Clinton offered Chrétien the customary congratulations and hailed the strong similarities between the Liberal campaign and the Democratic one of a year earlier. Chrétien offered regards from one of his former officials at the Department of Indian and Northern Affairs, an Oxford classmate of Clinton. Then the president brought up a matter of the utmost importance to relations between the two countries: the fate of the North American Free Trade Agreement, the trade deal Brian Mulroney had initialled with the U.S. and Mexico. Chrétien and the Liberals had called in their campaign platform for NAFTA to be renegotiated, a demand that Clinton feared would kill his chances of winning passage in an upcoming vote in the U.S. Congress. He wanted Chrétien to think through Canada's position very carefully.

"I see no reason to renegotiate the agreement or any grounds or basis for it, and I think we should just go ahead," Clinton told White House reporters after speaking to Chrétien. "I think that all the countries involved have a lot at stake in proceeding, so that's what we plan to do." He apparently read no omens into the fact that the line had gone dead in the middle of their conversation.

For Chrétien, getting right down to business seemed natural. But he valued order, and first he had a transition to which to tend. Decisions taken in the ensuing days could be among the most important of his prime ministership. He already had the plan — the Red Book — now he needed to put the team in place to implement it. His transition papers detailed thirty-eight individual tasks to accomplish before the government could be sworn in, everything from physically moving into 24 Sussex Drive to making a cabinet, from arranging training courses for those new ministers to hiring a prime-ministerial staff.

At fifty-nine, with his craggy features softened by age, the young man on the make had finally arrived on the doorstep of the best political address in the country. He couldn't wait to get over the threshold. His advisers wanted two full weeks in which to prepare an orderly assumption of power. They also pressed him to take a brief holiday after the gruelling forty-seven-day campaign. He wanted to chair his first cabinet meeting already. Exercising his executive prerogative, he overruled them. A ten-day transition would be sufficient, he pronounced. He could holiday some other time.

At mid-morning, Chrétien left Shawinigan after a brief stop at his campaign headquarters to thank local supporters and mingle with his brothers and sisters, who had returned to their home town to witness the final graduation of the eighteenth of nineteen Chrétien children. As always, he moved briskly, leaving his staff gasping after their wild night spent imbibing champagne and smoking cigars in the tacky Kontiki room of a local motel.

The small motorcade drove the half-hour down Highway 55 to the airport at Trois-Rivières. As Pelletier had predicted, he had lost badly in Quebec City, but Chrétien, of course, had prevailed, gaining a comfortable 25,200 votes to 18,896 for Bloc Québécois candidate Claude Rompré. Finding Pelletier on the tarmac, the prime-minister-designate took him aside and asked him to return as chief of staff: "Your loss is my gain," he said.

At 2 p.m., back in Ottawa, his advisers got down to the transition work in the leader of the opposition's boardroom on the fourth floor of the Centre Block building on Parliament Hill. Around the table sat the Chrétien brain trust: Pelletier, David Zussman, Eddie Goldenberg, John Rae, Peter Donolo, Chaviva Hošek. Joining them were Gordon Ashworth, Rae's second-in-command during the campaign; Ross Fitzpatrick, the British Columbia mining magnate who had befriended Chrétien while working on Parliament Hill in the 1960s and headed his B.C. team; and Senator Joyce Fairbairn, the former Trudeau aide who had travelled with Chrétien throughout the campaign. Others came in and out at various points.

While Chrétien retired to his office to phone winning and losing candidates from the previous evening, Zussman handed out a sheet listing the twenty-two vacant cabinet positions with blanks provided to write in four nominees. The advisers then debated their preferences. Zussman and Pelletier listened to the arguments and prepared a final list of recommendations to be taken to Chrétien. Neither knew what he had in mind. Over the previous months, both men had inquired a number of times whether Chrétien had given thought to who should be in his cabinet. Chrétien replied in the affirmative, but refrained from volunteering information.

The formation of a cabinet is probably the most important decision any prime minister can make. These are the men and the women who will run the departments of government and be relied upon to furnish sound advice on the great issues of the day. In a country with the diversity of Canada, a prime minister must strive for balance — regionally, linguistically, ideologically, and, in more recent times, on gender and ethnic lines. But the cabinet also must function effectively, capable of achieving the consensus a government requires to implement an agenda.

In Chrétien's case, cabinet selection was doubly important. He was determined to return to a style of government rooted in the days of Louis St. Laurent and Lester Pearson, a time when strong cabinet ministers managed their portfolios largely as they saw fit. Chrétien would not be a micro-manager, and he would not allow the Privy Council Office, the central bureaucratic agency that worked alongside the Prime Minister's Office, to monopolize power either. He had chafed under the central PMO and PCO controls imposed on ministers in the Trudeau years. He and Zussman had extensively discussed Chrétien's preference to keep out of the hair of his ministers except in the most unusual circumstances. "Your role as Prime Minister," Zussman had written in the transition documents, "is not to implement or 'do'; rather it is to set the agenda and have in place a team carefully chosen for its ability to carry that agenda out. Vis à vis this team, however, you must always be in a position to be the supreme arbiter both in cabinet and in caucus."

Chrétien had been on the wrong end of a cabinet of unequals. No matter how far he rose with Trudeau, he could never hope to compete with Marc Lalonde for influence with the prime minister or clout over the Quebec wing of the party. He wanted to avoid a class system within his cabinet. David Dingwall had served as Chrétien's parliamentary secretary in the Trudeau years and had been one of his most fanatical supporters through two leadership campaigns. When his father died in the first year of the new government, Chrétien decided not to attend the funeral. His aides argued with him, reminding him of Dingwall's loyal service. He was a friend more than a minister. Chrétien asked them what would happen the next time the parent of a cabinet minister died — he couldn't attend all their funerals. "There is only one kind of cabinet minister," he declared. "They must all be equal."

At 5 p.m. on that first transition day, Zussman and Pelletier sat down with Chrétien to listen for the first time to his thoughts on the cabinet. They reviewed the recommendations from the group in the boardroom. Paul Martin was everyone's first choice for Finance, with only two other nominees, Roy MacLaren and John Manley. Lloyd Axworthy's name appeared beside both Foreign Affairs and Human Resources. They had elected 177 members in the 295-member House of Commons. But their success had been uneven, limiting the cabinet possibilities. More than half their members came from Ontario; another 18 per cent from Atlantic Canada. In British Columbia and Alberta, the Liberal contingent was largely composed of political novices, few of them well known to Chrétien or his advisers. In Quebec, the party had doggedly recruited a number of so-called star francophone candidates, people like Jean Pelletier. But the Bloc Québécois had mowed most of them down.

Chrétien went over the pool of victorious candidates province by province, ticking off those he thought qualified to sit in his cabinet. At the end of the working day Tuesday, Zussman provided a list of almost forty names to the RCMP so that they could begin their security checks.

On that first day, Chrétien took time out for one other matter, a special phone call to an eighty-two-year-old man who had been a finance official during the government of Mackenzie King, a deputy minister under Louis St. Laurent, and a Liberal cabinet minister in the Pearson and Trudeau years. Chrétien liked to describe himself as a Mitchell Sharp Liberal, by which he meant a politically cautious, fiscally conservative, personally incorruptible politician wedded, above all, to a single credo: pragmatism. Now Chrétien intended to govern in the Sharp model. But on election night, as calls of congratulations poured into Shawinigan, his éminence grise had been notable by his silence. The star pupil called to find out why his mentor hadn't phoned. A somewhat sheepish Sharp said he thought the prime-minister-designate would be overwhelmed by well-wishers — and that he and Chrétien would have plenty of opportunities to talk anyway. Which they would. Chrétien asked him to become a special dollar-a-year adviser, with an office in the PMO.

The following day, October 27, at 10 a.m., Chrétien held his first news conference as prime-minister-designate. The opening question concerned the fate of the North American Free Trade Agreement. Chrétien chose his words carefully. The Tories had bulldozed the NAFTA implementing legislation through the House of Commons and Senate, but had chosen not to proclaim it into law until the other partners completed their legislative approvals. Chrétien stated that his position remained the same as before, but he steered clear of the controversial language contained in the Red Book, which said a Liberal government would consider abrogation if renegotiation failed.

"My position is very clear," he replied to a question about whether his government intended to proclaim the NAFTA bill into law. "In Canada, no law is effective until it is proclaimed. So we have still this option." His cautious skating notwithstanding, Chrétien's words landed him in the soup in Washington. At this uncertain moment in Canada-U.S. relations, the Americans were easily moved to hysteria. Officials there immediately got on the phone to the U.S. Embassy in Ottawa demanding to know what in God's name Chrétien meant.

A few hours later, Canada's two top trade bureaucrats, Allen Kilpatrick and John Weekes, accompanied by Jim Judd, the chief foreign policy adviser in the Privy Council Office, were ushered into the leader of the opposition's suite to brief Jean Pelletier and Eddie Goldenberg on the situation. The Clinton administration was days away from presenting its NAFTA implementation legislation to Congress. Under the so-called fast-track provisions in force, once a trade bill is tabled, there is no opportunity to amend it. Unfortunately from Canada's perspective, the Clinton draft contained serious, indeed inexplicable, flaws. Canada's hard-won cultural exemption had been mysteriously altered. Some versions making the rounds in Washington even suggested that U.S. domestic courts would be able to overturn the decisions of NAFTA's trinational dispute panels. None of this, the trio maintained, reflected the actual negotiations. Pelletier's initial reaction was to remind them that Chrétien was only prime-minister-designate. "I said go see Campbell." But the bureaucrats explained that the outgoing government had all but vaporized.

The NAFTA crisis didn't catch Chrétien's advisers entirely by surprise. Indeed, the two trade bureaucrats, Kilpatrick and Weekes, had provided the Liberals with an extraordinary heads-up almost two weeks earlier. Talking things over in the suite of offices they shared at the Department of International Trade in the Lester B. Pearson Building, the pair anguished over the ability of any new government to react promptly enough to the events in Washington.

From Kilpatrick's office on the eighth floor, they looked down on 24 Sussex Drive, home of the prime minister of Canada. They had followed the campaign intently and could see clearly enough that Jean Chrétien would be taking up residence there shortly. The Liberals had been unalterably opposed to free trade during most of their years in opposition, but the officials felt heartened by comments Chrétien had made during a mid-campaign appearance at a nursing home in New Westminster, B.C. Challenged on whether he would tear up the agreement, he told an anti-free-trade nursing student that if she wanted to vote against NAFTA, she should support the NDP. "We're in a democracy and for me I have a different view," he disclosed in his clearest statement ever on the subject. "You cannot build a wall around Canada as the NDP are proposing. It's not very realistic and it will be self-defeating."

The trade bureaucrats decided that Weekes should make secret contact with Liberal trade critic Roy MacLaren, whom they both knew. They informed neither the clerk of the Privy Council (their immediate superior) nor their doomed and barely visible minister of the previous three months, Conservative Tom Hockin. They fortified each other with their belief that nothing less than Canada's national interest was at stake. "Technically, we shouldn't be doing this," they told each other in the privacy of Kilpatrick's office. "But the people who are going to need our help tomorrow are the Liberals." Weekes placed the call with ten days left in the campaign.

The Americans were watching the campaign and the polls, too. James Blanchard, the new ambassador in Ottawa, had arrived in August, just as the city's political movers and shakers were preparing to hit the election trail. Blanchard, a former governor of Michigan and, in the shorthand of Washington, Friend of Bill, was enough of a political pro to know that neither August nor an election campaign was a sensible time to spend in a political capital. So he and his wife, Janet, who had served briefly in the White House as Clinton's appointments secretary, headed off on a two-part, twenty-nine-city train journey across Canada. The first trip took them from Toronto to the west coast; the second from Newfoundland to Montreal.

Blanchard had one overriding objective in the election campaign: to keep the United States from becoming an issue. He understood the sensitivities that existed in the wake of the Mulroney years, the feeling that the former prime minister had been too cosy with the Americans. He watched in the pre-writ period as Jean Chrétien cleverly pushed those buttons. If relations with the United States arose as an election issue, he worried, one or more of the party leaders might be backed into a statement that would restrict their options later. So throughout the train trip he kept in close touch with Washington, doing his best to ensure that none of the myriad trade disputes constantly simmering in the Commerce and Agriculture Departments would come to a boil at such an inopportune time.

At fifty-one, with a boyish grin and an unambassadorial yen for a smoked-meat sandwich and Coke, Blanchard brought to the job an understanding of Canada garnered as a governor of a Great Lakes state with extensive north-south industrial links, connections right into the Oval Office, and tons of political savvy. He could spot the political angle in a government initiative the way Mario Lemieux could find the hole in a goalie's pads. On his first meeting as ambassador with Chrétien, the prime-minister-designate paid him the ultimate compliment, remarking, "You're a politician, aren't you?"

Blanchard took satisfaction in the progress of the election campaign. The New Democrats had tried to turn NAFTA into an issue and had crashed on take-off. The Liberals, concentrating their campaign message on jobs and hope, preferred to keep their ambiguous NAFTA policy out of view. Blanchard duly noted that when forced to respond to the anti-NAFTA nurse in New Westminster, Chrétien had suggested she vote NDP. All was going well.

Down in Washington, though, senior administration officials were increasingly antsy. Despite its global reach, Washington is as myopic a capital as any on earth: it pays scant attention to the nuances of political discourse beyond the territorial limits of the United States, and least attention of all to good old reliable Canada. The Clinton advisers and cabinet members knew little about the Liberals other than that they had vowed to tear up the earlier Canada-U.S. Free Trade Agreement in 1988, had voted against NAFTA in Parliament the previous May, and had seized upon some fuzzy election formulation that contemplated abrogation.

Clinton, bracing for a mid-November vote in Congress on NAFTA, would have to shame, strong-arm, or bribe enough reluctant Democrats and shaky Republicans to push the key administration initiative over the top. But these congressmen had already started pestering the White House, asking why they should risk incurring the wrath of voters by supporting NAFTA if the new Liberal government in Canada intended to force new negotiations in any case. "Every Democrat I knew was looking for an excuse not to have to vote on that thing in Congress," Blanchard later said.

The ambassador's first worry was not so much that the Liberals would resist NAFTA, but that they might inadvertently detonate it. If Chrétien forcefully demanded renegotiations on election night — before he even had a chance to speak to Clinton — that alone might lead to its collapse in Congress. Blanchard agreed with Washington that he would have to open a line of communication to the Liberals. But he understood it could compromise Chrétien to meet him in the midst of the campaign, given the rhetoric about how relations with the United States would be different under a Liberal government.

The last leg of the train tour took Blanchard from Moncton to Montreal. The following morning, on October 21, he flew to Quebec City for a top-secret meeting with Jean Pelletier, still in the midst of his fight to win a seat in the provincial capital.

Blanchard told Pelletier he had been reassured by Chrétien's NAFTA remark in British Columbia. But he explained that Washington remained nervous and that he hoped the Liberals would be mindful of the delicacy of the situation in Congress. "I want you to know that you have life-and-death power over it," Blanchard warned. Talk of "reviewing" the deal or discussing "concerns" would be manageable. But "just don't use that word 'renegotiate'" he continued, "because I think you'll kill it. And if you want to kill it, Mr. Pelletier, it will be a very swift way of doing it. You can pretend not to have known what the consequences would be before Congress. You can kill it without leaving a fingerprint."

But Pelletier responded that he didn't want to kill NAFTA. Those around Chrétien had heard such warnings before. In fact, the previous June, Mark Boudreau, the policy analyst in the Opposition Leader's Office responsible for NAFTA, had sent a note up the line with a remarkably similar message to Blanchard's. "Mr. Chrétien must not get 'boxed in' by stating that he will renegotiate the NAFTA which means re-writing the agreement (a promise on which it would be impossible to deliver). That is not to say that there will not be plenty of scope to improve the agreement in future," he continued, borrowing from a formulation proposed by Roy MacLaren's policy adviser, John Hancock. "Mr. Chrétien could say that once the agreement is in place he will work to improve, enhance or change the agreement."

Nobody went out of their way to change the Red Book wording, but Chrétien chose to duck the issue as much as possible during the campaign. With the election days away, Pelletier told Blanchard that the Liberals favoured NAFTA. They had spent several years painstakingly burying their 1988 anti-free-trade position and preparing the party to forge ahead into the new global economy. They had concerns, to be sure. But they wanted to make it work.

Now, precisely one week after that secret meeting, Chrétien had stated in his first press conference — well, typically, it required a cryptologist to decode precisely what Chrétien had stated. He deliberately cloaked himself in ambiguity, believing it irresponsible, according to John Rae, to stake out hard positions on issues until absolutely necessary, a tendency that grew naturally out of his poor language skills. Blanchard fielded a series of frantic calls from Washington. "Don't worry, he didn't use the word 'renegotiate,'" he said. What did they expect, he asked, that Chrétien would repudiate the Red Book the day after the election?

Blanchard's instincts told him Jean Chrétien would be there for Clinton, but that he would need to save face. He knew politicians, and this guy was a veteran. He would know how and when to move, he told the callers. "He knows what he's doing. He's for NAFTA. But there's got to be some adjustments." Blanchard knew he was dealing with some very nervous people in Washington, but he told them, "Trust me, if he'd wanted to kill it, it already would have happened. All he has to do is pull out his Red Book."

The Canadian officials, like Blanchard, quickly concluded that the Liberals had no desire either to blow up NAFTA or to let it expire on its own. The discussion with Pelletier and Goldenberg revolved around how to cope with the situation, not whether they wanted NAFTA. Chrétien's advisers, not yet installed in the Prime Minister's Office, immediately began working the phones to Washington. In the absence of a Canadian trade minister, it fell to Goldenberg to explain Liberal thinking on NAFTA to U.S. Trade Representative Mickey Kantor. Working amid a sea of packing boxes in the Leader of the Opposition's Office, Goldenberg found it all a bit unreal.

In a sense, the crisis atmosphere comforted officials in both International Trade and the Privy Council Office, all of whom favoured NAFTA. It meant that decisions would have to be made quickly and that the matter would not drag out long enough to become the subject of a major cabinet debate. They had more confidence in the group around Chrétien than they did in the still unformed cabinet, especially given their fears that Lloyd Axworthy, the arch-foe of NAFTA, could be named foreign affairs minister.

"At the point at which they actually got elected, we were really at the fifty-ninth minute of the eleventh hour on NAFTA," said Glen Shortliffe, who at the time was the clerk of the Privy Council. "It was take it or leave it in a sense. Had we been at the fifteenth minute of the eleventh hour, as distinct from the fifty-ninth, I think it could have been a very different ball game. But we weren't."

Later that first week, as Chrétien began meeting with his potential ministers, he ran headlong into the stubborn will of Paul Martin Jr., the Montreal MP whose father had sat in cabinets under four Liberal prime ministers. On the first day of the transition, Chrétien had expressed certainty about just two positions, those destined for his two leadership rivals from 1990. Sheila Copps would be deputy prime minister — if, that is, he opted to have a deputy prime minister. And Martin would go to Finance. He and Martin had known each other for many years; they got together once or twice a year to fish or golf, usually with John Rae. The relationship had frayed during the bitter leadership race. But while many of their followers would carry their animosities forward into government, Chrétien and Martin, at least, seemed to have made their peace. In Martin, the prime-minister-designate thought he had a figure with the requisite credibility in the business community and the resolve to take on the key finance portfolio.

But that resolve now worked against Chrétien. Martin didn't want the job. He dreamed of becoming the modern reincarnation of C.D. Howe, the powerful 1950s industry minister. He had listened at his father's knee to the stories of Howe's extraordinary power in the King and St. Laurent years and of how he had retooled the postwar Canadian economy. His father had told him that Howe in Industry had been more powerful than any finance minister. The idea took root in his mind that Industry would be the perfect spot for him to make the transition from the corporate world to the political world.

In the final days of the election campaign, as speculation mounted about a Liberal cabinet, Martin broadcast his distaste for Finance far and wide. He had steeped himself in the works of industrial policy gurus like Robert Reich and Lester Thurow, translating their thoughts, as well as he could, into the Red Book. Now he wanted the opportunity to take command of a souped-up Industry Department and grow the Canadian economy just as, in the private sector, he had grown his shipping company, Canada Steamship Lines. Besides, some of his closest political advisers, people who had been with him during the leadership race, warned him that Finance could prove a political graveyard. They still harboured ambitions for him as a future prime minister and didn't want him saddled with the reputation of Jean Chrétien's minister of debt.

With the campaign still in its final lap, Arthur Kroeger, a retired public servant who, as deputy minister of transport in the early 1980s, had known Martin the shipping executive, returned home one day to find a message on his answering machine from the Liberal politician. The call surprised Kroeger. Although they would occasionally bump into each other around Ottawa, about a decade had passed since they had been luncheon companions. He phoned a number in Vancouver. Martin told him that a lot of people thought he should be minister of finance. But he wanted Industry. "All you can do in Finance is run a slash-and-burn exercise," he protested.

Kroeger, who had served as industry deputy minister after his time at Transport, agreed that Industry was a major portfolio, but advised Martin that Finance differed qualitatively from any other job in government. A finance minister, through the budget, could define the content of the entire government, he said. Only the finance minister and the prime minister enjoyed that power. Martin thanked him and said he would just as soon treat the call as if it never happened.

In the days that followed, Ed Lumley, a former industry minister and boyhood friend from Windsor, delivered the same message, but more bluntly. He and Martin spoke several times that week. Lumley told Martin he was crazy. The depth of the deficit crisis meant that the finance minister, a hugely powerful figure in any government, would be even more central. Did he want to be the person who had to go to the finance minister, cap in hand, looking for money? Or did he want to be the person other people came to? While he, in Finance, would be able to protect someone else as industry minister, there was no guarantee that someone else in Finance would furnish him that same support. Given the fiscal situation, he might find himself without any of the tools required to renovate the Canadian economy.

Chrétien met Martin during the first week of the transition and implored him to take Finance. Martin resisted. Chrétien discussed Martin's reluctance with David Smith, a former cabinet colleague who had graduated to the top ranks of Bay Street lawyers. Smith had chaired the federal campaign in Ontario, and lent an occasional hand with the transition. "I told Chrétien he couldn't take no for an answer. He had to press him into service." The Liberals, with the exception of Martin, who had established his bona fides by taking a troubled company and turning it into a success story, still lacked credibility with the business community, Smith said. The fiscal crisis demanded that Chrétien settle for nothing less than the best possible choice.

Martin phoned Smith and quizzed him on his advice to Chrétien. Smith, who as a young Liberal aide in the 1960s had accompanied Paul Martin Sr. on foreign trips, said that the younger Martin was obviously fixated on the Industry Department of a bygone era. The present-day Industry Department was a shadow of the empire C.D. Howe had ruled. He should be careful about misreading the situation.

Martin was demonstrating a pattern of decision-making that would become familiar. He tended to take a long time to come to decisions, initially resisting advice and then agonizing his way through an internal dialectic process before finally settling, forcefully, on an answer. He couldn't let go of his idealized view of Industry and the role he would play in building a better economy. Despite all he had been told, he still feared that at Finance he would be relegated to the worthy but tedious role of government beancounter.

The matter dragged late into the week of the swearing-in, complicating the task of cabinet-making. Chrétien wanted Roy MacLaren, a former diplomat and magazine publisher with strong ties to the business community, for International Trade. But Chrétien also alerted him that if Martin didn't capitulate soon, MacLaren should be prepared for Finance. The arm-twisting continued. Lumley even received an extraordinary call from David Dodge, the deputy minister of finance, whom he knew from his Ottawa days. Dodge said it was essential that Martin, whom he knew only by reputation, take the job. Finance faced a critical situation and needed a minister credible with caucus and unafraid to challenge the prime minister when necessary.

It took two more meetings with Chrétien before Martin reluctantly acquiesced. The night before the swearing-in, he took his extended political family for dinner at Café Henry Burger in Hull. They didn't know whether to celebrate or mourn. In his mind, Martin still hadn't mapped out a mental picture of a finance minister who was anything other than Michael Wilson, the bloodless Mulroney-era minister of finance who had authored so many of the policies the Liberals had railed against in opposition. His advisers, still mistrustful of Chrétien, worried that he had set out to inscribe Martin's political tombstone.

While the drama with Martin played itself out, Chrétien faced up to some of his other tricky challenges. On the weekend of the transition, he met with Lloyd Axworthy, one of his most senior frontbenchers and a pillar of the party's left wing. The veteran Winnipeg MP longed for External Affairs — Chrétien would rename it Foreign Affairs — a post he had held in the shadow cabinet. But Chrétien felt more comfortable with André Ouellet, a political survivor unlikely to rock the boat, in a position that had evolved into more of an economic ministry.

Axworthy's strong opposition to free trade and his animus towards the business community would have made him a risky choice, especially given the delicacy of the NAFTA file. The Chrétien team was highly conscious of the messages their selections would impart to their trading partners, the financial markets, and the public at large. Axworthy at Foreign Affairs would transmit the wrong signal. In any case, Ouellet, who had served faithfully as campaign chair, stood ahead of him in the line for rewards.

With External and the major economic ministries as non-starters, Human Resources Development was a natural alternative. Clearly, Axworthy had the right stuff, or, in this case, the left stuff. The country's social safety net required a major refashioning, a point Goldenberg and Zussman pressed upon Chrétien at every opportunity. The transition documents dwelt on the implications for government of the rise of a new economy, one built on a foundation of human knowledge rather than physical or financial assets. "Canada is moving out of the mass manufacturing phase and is already in the new technology cycle," Zussman wrote. "It will be crucial that the new government put in place mechanisms which will aid workers making the transition from the old economy to the new."

Axworthy possessed the requisite intellectual capacity to undertake a complex overhaul of a system that involved social, economic, and jurisdictional issues. But more important, he would be a credible reformer: his reputation as a compassionate Liberal would come in handy in challenging the status quo. The transition team often compared the idea of Axworthy reforming social policy to Nixon opening up China. Only a true Cold Warrior like Richard Nixon enjoyed the credibility on the right to pull it off. Axworthy boasted the same attributes on the left. His would be the social face of the government.

The Chrétien team still had to settle the question of whether to bother with a deputy prime minister. The position wasn't constitutionally mandated, and many Chrétien advisers thought it should be discontinued. Trudeau had initiated a tradition when he handed the title to Allan MacEachen in the mid-1970s as a reward for his loyal service. The Tories subsequently invested the role with great authority under Donald Mazankowski, who effectively served as the government's chief operating officer, making sure the wheels moved in the same direction and brokering deals between gridlocked ministers. But Chrétien, despite his aversion to detail, wanted to be his own chief executive officer and chief operating officer. In his mind, he had no need for a deputy in the Mazankowski mould, especially since he intended to relax central control over the government by farming power back to individual ministers.

As a House of Commons man, though, he favoured having a single person to answer questions in his absence. By that criterion, Sheila Copps would be his choice. She had served as deputy leader in opposition and, party polling showed, was one of the few Liberal MPs actually recognizable to a majority of Canadians. Chrétien liked her take-no-prisoners style in the chamber. In the course of their cabinet interview, he told Copps about his dilemma. If there was to be a deputy PM, she would be it. But he remained undecided.

Both the cabinet-making and the NAFTA crisis came to a head at the same time. The Liberals had naturally assumed that they would put their government in place first and then petition the Americans and Mexicans to address the matters flagged in the Red Book: a better deal on energy, and the adoption of common trade rules on subsidies and dumping. But first the Liberals had to deal with the flawed American bill, the one the Canadian officials called NAFTA minus.

Clinton planned to send his bill to Capitol Hill on Wednesday, November 3, a day before Chrétien would name his cabinet and officially take over as prime minister. Despite the diligent efforts of the trade bureaucrats and Goldenberg, the adjustments Canada required to secure its consent were not moving forward. The Canadian officials, free traders all, no longer worried about the Chrétien Liberals destroying NAFTA. But the self-absorbed Americans scared them silly. If they didn't give ground soon, they would leave the Liberals no choice but to walk away.

For once, the Canadians felt they enjoyed some leverage over Washington. But they recognized its ephemeral quality. Once Congress voted, Canada's advantage would vanish. And if Canada overplayed its hand and actually scuttled NAFTA, it could look forward to at least three more years of unhappy relations with a wounded president, not to mention the opprobrium of financial markets already suspicious of the returning Liberals.

Finally, with time running out, exasperated U.S. trade officials told John Weekes the logjam could be broken only at the highest level. Canada's complaints hadn't broken through the Washington policy gridlock. His bureaucrats offered Chrétien a couple of options, including a direct appeal to Clinton. Chrétien chose to call in Blanchard for a one-on-one, figuring that if that didn't yield results, he could still phone the president. And so late on the afternoon of November 2, with less than twenty-four hours to go, Goldenberg telephoned the U.S. Embassy across from Parliament Hill and informed Blanchard that Chrétien would like to meet with him.

"I said, 'Great. When would you like to do it?'" Blanchard recalled.

"Well, actually we're over here right now," Goldenberg replied.

Blanchard had met Chrétien only once before, two years earlier, at the Liberal International convention in Lucerne, Switzerland. Blanchard had represented the Democrats, Chrétien the Canadian Liberals. Chrétien had asked him who he favoured for the Democratic nomination, still a year away. Blanchard mentioned his friendship with Clinton. "Tell him health care is the smartest thing we ever did," Chrétien volunteered. "People love it. Why your country doesn't have it I don't understand. Tell him he needs to stress health care." Democrats in the northern states were already predisposed towards health care reform. Blanchard had lobbied for its inclusion in Clinton's platform. When he got back to the States, he recounted the conversation and reminded Clinton of the enormous political credit still accorded the Liberals for universal health care.

Blanchard dashed across Wellington Avenue to the barren office of the outgoing leader of the opposition. He and Chrétien exchanged pleasantries, reminiscing about the previous meeting in Lucerne. Then the prime-minister-designate laid out his position. Canada was a trading nation and its growth depended on opening up foreign markets. It wanted NAFTA. But there would have to be changes. The package on its way to Congress was unacceptable.

"Tell your president that you have to fix the cultural issue or else we won't sign it," Chrétien stated. "And if you don't believe me, give me the phone and I'll tell him myself."

Blanchard wondered about the extent of Chrétien's authority, noting he hadn't even named a cabinet yet. "I said to him, 'What happens if we work all this out and then your new trade minister doesn't agree?' "

"And he said, 'Then I will have a new trade minister the following morning.' "

Blanchard, impressed by Chrétien's resolve and thinking how nice it would be if Clinton could muster similar fortitude, retraced his steps and placed a conference call to the White House and the Trade Representative's Office. The trade bureaucrats had waited outside Chrétien's office while he met with Blanchard. Then they held their breath. At suppertime, the phone rang in John Weekes's office. It was Rufus Yerxa, his U.S. counterpart. "So what is it you need?" he asked. Blanchard had succeeded in just a couple of hours in kicking Washington into gear.

Weekes and Yerxa and their key officials worked through the night to rewrite the offending passages of the U.S. legislation. NAFTA, for now, had been saved by a Liberal Party that only five years earlier had threatened to tear up the free trade agreement and until weeks earlier was still flirting with the possibility of abrogation.

Just twenty-four hours remained to the November 4 swearing-in, and still Chrétien had not settled on ministers from the two westernmost provinces, Alberta and British Columbia. Not for want of trying either. Chrétien's advisers liked Hedy Fry, the past head of the British Columbia Medical

Association and the victor in Vancouver Centre over Kim Campbell. Fry boasted the added attributes of being a woman and a member of a visible minority group, important political considerations in a party with such a strong following among new Canadians.

But Fry had entangled herself in a mini-scandal during the election campaign when she boasted about writing a prescription for a woman who had insurance coverage, knowing that the medication was meant for her lesbian partner. Most Liberals regarded her transgression as trifling — even humanitarian — but Chrétien's determination that integrity would be the byword of his government ruled her out. A mild reprimand issued by the British Columbia College of Physicians and Surgeons a few days before the swearing-in confirmed her fate.

The Chrétien team settled next on Herb Dhaliwal, a Westernized Sikh businessman with a big smile. They penciled him in for Revenue. But Dhaliwal sat at the centre of a private family enterprise with major dealings with the federal government, including a contract to clean Toronto's Pearson Airport. He couldn't bring himself to distance himself as thoroughly as demanded. At the last minute, Chrétien crossed him off the list.

Meanwhile, Alberta presented its own drama. The Liberals had broken through in the province for the first time since 1968, eking out wins in four Edmonton ridings. The transition team liked Anne McLellan, a constitutional law professor at the University of Alberta who had absorbed Liberal values growing up in Nova Scotia. But McLellan had barely squeaked through on election night, and a judicial recount had been ordered to begin on Monday, November 1. The evening before, she had received a call from the transition team asking her to come to Ottawa for an interview. She met Chrétien on Tuesday and told him about the recount. He said he would need to know a result by Wednesday morning at the latest.

Time was tight. With fifteen hours to go, the fate of four potential ministers still hung in the balance. Glen Shortliffe, the clerk of the Privy Council, called Jean Pelletier. Legal documents needed to be prepared. Press information had to be assembled. What should he do? Pelletier told him to prepare for all possible permutations.

McLellan waited it out at the Westin Hotel. Just in case she didn't make it, the transition team had put Judy Bethel, one of the other Edmonton Liberals, on stand-by in a different hotel. By Wednesday afternoon, the recount remained incomplete. McLellan figured she was out. Then at 11 that night, her phone rang. "You won," Gordon Ashworth, the transition team member responsible for Alberta, told her.

"Really," she replied wearily.

"By eleven votes."

She said she guessed they hadn't been able to wait on naming an Alberta minister. But Ashworth informed her they had. She would be minister of natural resources, which included responsibility for energy, so important to Alberta. She should be at Rideau Hall at 10 the following morning. All the pent-up exhaustion of the previous week washed over her. "I remember sitting on the edge of the bed just being overwhelmingly tired. I didn't feel particularly excited or exuberant or anything, just tired. The next day it all hit me that this actually had happened." At 11:30 p.m., Zussman phoned Chrétien at home to tell him who his minister from Alberta would be. Nobody bothered calling Judy Bethel.

Meanwhile, Chrétien and his advisers reluctantly bumped Victoria MP David Anderson up from the tier of junior ministers, where he had been slotted in as a secretary of state for the Asia-Pacific region. Chrétien knew Anderson from a previous stint as an MP in 1968 to 1972 and felt that he had a tendency to shoot his mouth off. Also, he had badly wanted a minister from Vancouver. But he had run out of best options, so Anderson would be it.

To fill the job first intended for Anderson — the government's travelling salesman in the Pacific region — they tapped Raymond Chan, a west coast human rights activist of Chinese origin. The decision came so late that Chan arrived in Ottawa on the red-eye from Vancouver only on the morning of the swearing-in. Mitchell Sharp and Allan Lutfy, an Ottawa lawyer and former Trudeau aide, were in charge of screening candidates for potential ethical problems; one question, in honour of Ted Kennedy, asked if they had ever been caught cheating on an exam. Sharp and Lutfy picked Chan up at the airport and subjected him to the standard grilling. Except in this case, the interrogation took place in the back of a car as they rushed him to his hotel for a quick shower and change of clothes before heading off to Rideau Hall. Only the sharpest-eyed reporters noticed that in the last-minute rush of the previous night, Chrétien's communications people had forgotten to made the switch in the French-language press kits. They had Anderson listed as both secretary of state for the Asia-Pacific region and revenue minister.

Mitchell Sharp had first come to Ottawa as a Department of Finance official in 1942. In the 1950s, he had served as deputy minister to C.D. Howe. After switching to electoral politics in the 1960s, he served in the Pearson and Trudeau cabinets as industry minister, finance minister, and external affairs minister. In the late 1980s, when he was well into his seventies, the *Globe and Mail* wrote his obituary as a newsmaker in a column called "Didn't You Use to Be?" The judgment turned out to be premature. He was back and, more important, so was his approach to government as passed on to his eager apprentice, Jean Chrétien. "The main thing is he, like me, is not ideological," Sharp reflected in a 1995 interview. "This is essentially why he's a Mitchell Sharp Liberal."

Governing as per Sharp meant, first, always erring on the side of caution. The best way to run a country like Canada, with its unpredictable centrifugal forces, was with great deliberation and care. Second, all good things flowed from a sound economy. Sharp believed nothing could be constructed unless the foundation was secure, which is why he had pushed in 1967 for a delay to the implementation of medicare. Third, Sharp, who had come to Ottawa out of the Winnipeg grain trade, abhorred protectionism, coming down on the side of open trade over attendant issues like human rights. Fourth, Sharp, although on the right of his party, believed in a social safety net. He had come of age in the Depression and, like others of his generation, believed governments had a duty to alleviate genuine suffering. Fifth, Sharp, the former mandarin, believed in ministerial autonomy and in a partnership between politicians and public servants, in the grand tradition of a bygone era when Ottawa had attracted the best and the brightest. Lastly, he stood for the highest ethics in government: he provided Chrétien a model of probity.

Chrétien probably couldn't articulate it, but he actually possessed a philosophy of government of sorts, one rooted in the values learned from Sharp. Unlike most Liberals of his generation, he harboured deep suspicions of big government. He didn't subscribe to legislative fixes for all that ails society. Many problems, he felt, were best left to sort themselves out. Although far more of a scrapper, particularly in matters of national unity, he admired Ontario Premier Bill Davis and his credo that bland works. In many ways, Chrétien was a throwback to Sharp's golden days in Ottawa under Mackenzie King and Louis St. Laurent, an era of pragmatic

Liberalism based on managerial competence. "I think Chrétien skipped the Trudeau generation," Michael McCabe, Sharp's long-time executive assistant, commented.

On November 4, 1993, with the election behind him and his new government sworn in, Jean Chrétien fulfilled his dream of going home to 24 Sussex Drive, despite a last-minute snafu. In the course of the transition, Privy Council officials had alerted his advisers to problems with a leaky roof at the residence. It needed extensive repairs. The officials wanted Chrétien to delay his move; they didn't think the house fit for prime-ministerial habitation. He waved them off: he was moving in, leaky roof or not.

On the first weekend after the Liberal restoration, John Rae, who had first gone to work for Chrétien when Lester Pearson was prime minister, went over to 24 Sussex Drive for dinner with the Chrétiens. Rae again urged the new prime minister to take a few days off after all the pressures of the previous couple of months. Go play golf. Go to a hotel or something, he pressed.

Chrétien looked around the house, raised his hands, broke into an impish grin, and said: "Why would I want to go to a hotel when I have this as my home here now?" Then he and John Rae enjoyed a rare and hearty laugh.

4

MARTIN
AT THE HELM

The evening of November 4, 1993, after the government's first cabinet meeting, David Dodge flew down to Windsor to meet the new minister of finance in his temporary quarters in the chaplain's office of the Hôtel-Dieu Hospital. Dodge, a Princeton Ph.D. and former economics professor at Queen's University, had served as a senior Finance official for nearly ten years, arriving as Marc Lalonde was going out the door and serving throughout the tenures of Michael Wilson and then Don Mazankowski. Martin would be his fourth minister. Dodge was blessed with a supple mind, one inclined to analysis as well as computation. He was tall and balding with a gravelly voice that rose to a surprising squeak when he was agitated. Outfitted in rumpled jackets and with his ubiquitous pipe gripped in his mouth, he still looked more the academic than the Ottawa power-broker.

Dodge harboured no doubt that whoever came to power, the country's high deficit and ever-mounting debt load would quickly establish themselves as the central facts of life. In his previous job as associate deputy minister, the sign on his office door read: "Due to current financial restraints, the light at the end of the tunnel will remain off until further notice." But after his work for the previous government, he couldn't be certain that he would be around to illuminate the incoming Liberals as to the inescapable realities of the situation.

Among the 600 employees of the Department of Finance at the Esplanade Laurier offices on O'Connor Street, the orthodoxy prevailed that Canada was approaching the indeterminate point at which investor confidence would vanish. Dodge hated the analogy of hitting a wall. He didn't think it happened that way. He thought of it more as walking on the edge of a cliff. As the winds grew stronger, the chances of losing one's balance multiplied. The first fall might not be fatal: you might hit a ledge. But by then it would be harder to scramble back and far easier to keep tumbling downhill. As far as Finance was concerned, if action wasn't taken to rein in government spending during the course of the next mandate, Canada would be hurtling towards the abyss.

The deputy had set out his thinking at a seminar on the deficit and debt organized by Auditor General Denis Desautels the previous April. The point wasn't just to eliminate the deficit, he argued, but to create a big enough surplus out of regular spending to cope with steadily growing interest payments. The Mulroney government had succeeded in trimming spending to 17 per cent of gross domestic product from a high of 20 per cent, bringing it back to 1970s levels. The next challenge would be to reduce spending to 14 per cent of GDP, which, he said, "will be the lowest we've been, at the federal level, in the postwar years."

That was radical enough, but the route to Dodge's destination traversed political territory any self-respecting Liberal would most assuredly declare off limits. His first target was OAS, the old-age security system, which cost Ottawa $20 billion a year and gobbled up an ever greater portion of spending every year. Old-age pensions (no relation to the Canada and Quebec Pension Plans) must be tackled before the baby-boomers caused the system to implode, he warned. "If we are looking for one issue, OAS is it." As well, action would have to be taken on social program payments to provinces, regional and industrial supports, and unemployment insurance — pretty well everything that imbued Liberals, Paul Martin among them, with their sense of political identity.

At the end of every term of government, Finance organizes a planning exercise that it calls "The Next Mandate." Martin in Windsor was struggling with the output of the most recent one, begun in the spring. Sometimes the department finds its thinking in close harmony with the incoming minister, which is what happened when the Next Mandate book became the basis of Michael Wilson's November 1984 economic position paper. But the Liberals presented a quandary. They clearly lacked conviction on the deficit. To the department, they didn't even really seem to have a strong understanding that it was the accumulated debt — then approaching $500 billion for the federal government alone — and not the annual deficit that formed the real problem. It was the sheer volume of debt and the need to borrow more and more money every year just to keep up with the compounding interest that was driving the country ever deeper into hock.

The challenge for the next government, Martin's briefing books explained, went beyond just taming the deficit. It would be to reverse the inexorable rise of this stock of debt as a proportion of the overall economy, a situation made all the more precarious by the ever-increasing share owed to foreigners. The upward movement of that debt-to-GDP ratio would have to be turned back during the course of the mandate, Finance warned, or else the government risked losing the confidence of its lenders.

The Liberals had debated the proper emphasis to place on fiscal prudence in their party platform. The party would be engaged in a two-front electoral war, particularly in Ontario, where it needed to lock in NDP defectors on the centre-left at the same time as picking off disenchanted Tories from the centre-right. The Liberals, pragmatists through and through, understood two things about the deficit: one, that a political party seen in the 1990s to be profligate would lack the credibility necessary to win the public trust; two, that the public didn't have a great deal of patience for the intricacies of the subject. Party pollster Michael Marzolini's research underscored the difficulty of running a Tory- or Reform-style deficit-centred campaign. His quarterly public opinion trackings turned up the contradiction — familiar to all pollsters — of a generalized concern about government spending and the deficit coupled with calls for increased spending in a majority of areas. The level of economic illiteracy among the public floored analysts. Liberal research showed that fewer than half of Canadians could say how many millions were in a billion and only one-quarter could identify the correct description of a deficit from a set of five options. A perplexingly large number of Canadians considered agriculture an industry of the future.

For its two-front war, the party came up with a two-track message: jobs, most certainly, but within fiscal reason. There would be an infrastructure program, but it would be financed by the reallocation of existing spending. They would promise daycare, but only in years when economic growth exceeded 3 per cent. The Red Book would set a moderate target of reducing the deficit to 3 per cent of gross domestic product, about $25 billion, in three years to inject the necessary fiscal balance into the jobs message. "The Liberals were addressing the most important issue in the minds of Canadians," Marzolini would write about the infrastructure program in a post-election analysis, "but lacked a credible overlay of fiscal responsibility until the introduction of their *Creating Opportunity* platform document."

The Finance officials snapped up the Red Book as soon as it became available early in the second week of the election campaign. They didn't find much of comfort. To the fundamentalists in Finance, the promise to restrain the deficit to 3 per cent of gross domestic product within three years was a bad joke. The goal, as far as they could tell, came out of some erroneous reading, probably deliberate, of commitments in the European Community's Maastricht treaty, which established 3 per cent of GDP as the maximum acceptable deficit for a country wanting to join the proposed European monetary union, not as an ideal. Moreover — and this was the kind of basic misunderstanding that really disgusted the persnickety Finance officials — the Liberals were comparing apples and oranges. Unlike most European countries, Canada was a federation with constituent parts that ran their own deficits and borrowed on international capital markets. Even if the central government got to 3 per cent, the national deficit, which included the provinces, would be more like 5 per cent. For Canada to get to 3 per cent would require the federal government to come in at 2 per cent or lower. The Next Mandate book counselled the minister to think national, not federal.

The Liberals talked about fiscal prudence, but to Finance they seemed to favour most existing government programs and even wanted to launch major new spending initiatives for infrastructure and child care. They averted their eyes from the runaway costs of unemployment insurance or the demographic time bombs planted in old-age pensions and aboriginal programs. The Liberals identified defence spending, a classic soft target, for the chopping block, and little else of substance.

The officials, finding this all as hard-edged as porridge, concluded that everything would have to be presented in the context of trade-offs. If you want to bring the deficit down to the 3-per-cent target and add child care, where is it you want us to cut, Mr. Minister? Or which taxes should we raise?

The Red Book's ambivalence towards the deficit reflected the party perfectly. In the spring of 1993, just six months before they would take power, Liberal MPs and senators from Atlantic Canada had invited the Acadian academic Donald Savoie to address them. Savoie had once worked in Ottawa for Fisheries Minister Romeo LeBlanc, the codfather of New Brunswick in the Trudeau years. He knew the Liberal Party and he knew the Atlantic region, with its big appetite for federal dollars.

Like many other scholars, he had come to the conclusion that global-ization had eroded the very foundations of public administration and that deficits were forcing governments to try to effect repairs without tools. Savoie warned the Liberals assembled in one of the meeting rooms on Parliament Hill that on the day after the election, should they win, their world would change dramatically. Putting Ottawa's fiscal house in order would become their biggest priority. Officials would arrive with stacks of briefing books outlining in gory detail the impact of the deficit. They would have little choice but to pay attention, to wipe the scales from their eyes. He told them how left-of-centre governments had come to the same conclusion in Australia and New Zealand; that these were realities, not ideologies, he was talking about. And he told them who would pay the price of failure. "I said if they lost the battle over the deficit and debt, the biggest losers wouldn't be on Bay Street, they would be in Atlantic Canada." Programs would be slashed overnight. Government would be taken over by the bankers.

When Savoie had concluded, Cape Breton MP David Dingwall, who chaired the session, threw open the discussion by asking Senator Allan J. MacEachen, the most powerful Atlantic politician in the Trudeau years, to respond. MacEachen excelled at wielding a stiletto. "Now that we've heard from the good professor," he opened up, "let's talk politics." Savoie's woolly theories were quickly shorn and discarded.

MacEachen agreed that officials with briefing books would arrive on the first day of a new Liberal government and would try to break its will. The key, he counselled, was to put out as many commitments as possible before that day so there would be little choice but to follow through. Savoie was as horrified by the 1970s mentality as he was hurt by MacEachen's condescension. "When we finished, I felt like a lonely cow-boy in the meadow," he recalled long afterwards. "I walked away quite shaken."

The politicians weren't yet persuaded of the absolute necessity of deficit reduction. But the senior ranks of the bureaucracy had overwhelm-ingly arrived at that conclusion. The deputy ministers, shuttling around Ottawa in their chauffeur-driven cars, had bought into the deficit message after years of guerrilla warfare. The late 1980s and early 1990s had been trying times for them. The implementation of emergency mid-year cuts, as Finance inevitably fell short of its published deficit targets, had become a regular feature of the political calendar. Bureaucrats like Robert Fowler, the deputy minister of defence, expended inordinate intellectual energy squabbling over the shrinking federal pie. By 1993 Fowler had evolved from a bureaucratic resistance fighter to a resigned supporter of tough fiscal medicine to one of the newly frocked priests of government austerity. He felt the government couldn't simply continue tearing at the carcass; a more profound approach was required. A friend sent him a videotape of a February *W5* segment on New Zealand's deficit experiences by the conservative journalist Eric Malling. It made for powerful television, with its depiction of a social democratic nation reduced to shooting a baby hippo in the zoo for lack of money to house it. Fowler, who felt that official Ottawa remained in a state of denial about the potentially cataclysmic consequences of allowing the deficit problem to drift, dubbed several dozen copies and sent them around town to the other deputies.

A couple of weeks later, on March 16, Arthur Kroeger, the former mandarin who had taken early retirement, witnessed the emerging bureaucratic consensus on matters fiscal during a dinner for about a dozen deputies in a boardroom atop the Department of Industry building. Kroeger, chairman of the nonpartisan Public Policy Forum, was putting together a study on governing in the 1990s to serve as a blueprint for whoever succeeded Mulroney. He had arranged the dinner to provide him with high-level input into the project.

But the deputies had something else on their minds: the deficit. "They were preoccupied with it — totally," Kroeger recalled. "They were debt and deficit obsessed." Their preoccupation hijacked the entire evening, with the discussion failing to rise above the black clouds. They lacked confidence that government could be made to work. It very well could be beyond repair. They mused openly about whether it would be necessary for the International Monetary Fund to come in before a Canadian government actually steeled itself to balance the books.

But the new minister and government seemed more in accord with the muddled thinking of the public at large. Martin's early comments suggested a profound lack of comprehension of the problem, as far as Finance was concerned. Coming out of Rideau Hall after the swearing-in ceremony, he remarked that high unemployment and high deficits both had their roots in the same cause: the ailing economy. "And that is what we want to address." To the zealots at Finance it looked as if their new minister still believed that by adopting the right policies, the Liberals could grow their way out of fiscal trouble. It was the first resort of all new governments. They would have to disabuse him of that simplistic notion.

Martin surprised Dodge, first by his composure in the face of his mother's illness and then by how little he seemed to actually know about government, especially for the son of a long-time cabinet minister. The deputy was a bit taken aback by the forthright simplicity of some of the questions. As Finance would learn, Martin liked things simple, and he didn't mind at all letting you know he hadn't the foggiest idea what you were talking about.

Although he was fifty-five years old at that point, with hangdog eyes giving him the sad look of a butcher caught with his thumb on the scale, Martin's most interesting trait was his childlike curiosity. He disarmed people with his absence of pretension, showing no fear of appearing naive or uninformed. Bob Rabinovitch, a Montreal executive and a senior civil servant in the Trudeau years, recalled first meeting Martin in the early 1980s as a fellow board member of the Canada Development Investment Corporation, a holding company for Crown corporations. Martin would pepper him with endless questions about government. How did it really work? What was it like being in a cabinet meeting? Did they actually raise their hands to vote? (The answer was no.)

Paul E. Martin was born on August 26, 1938, in the same Hôtel-Dieu Hospital where he now kept vigil, induced into the world ahead of schedule to satisfy his father's need to sail for Europe to represent Canada at the League of Nations Assembly in Geneva. Martin Sr., an ambitious Franco-Ontarian raised in the Ottawa Valley town of Pembroke, won election to the House of Commons in 1935 at the age of thirty-two from his adopted home town of Windsor. In the ensuing three decades, he racked up nine more election victories and served as Canada's health minister and external affairs minister in the years after World War II.

Family and friends marvelled at Martin's devotion to his father. Most regarded it as the most unusual and intense father-son relationship they ever witnessed. Martin Jr. put his father, a gifted but difficult man, on the sort of pedestal erected by many boys — but he never took him off. Even as an adult, Martin would speak to his father every day, often more than once. In the 1980s, he bankrolled Martin Sr.'s laboriously researched three volumes of memoirs. After the elder Martin died, his millionaire son inherited his car, speeding to and from his farm in the Eastern Townships in a black Chrysler Imperial suited to a man thirty years his senior.

Martin Jr. got a relatively late start in politics, entering his first contest for public office in 1988 at the age of fifty. His father never disguised his hesitation about his son's political ambitions and repeatedly counselled that he wait until he was at least forty-five and had established himself in some other field. Trained as a lawyer, the young Martin did just that, moving to Montreal in the late 1960s to start a career in business working for Maurice Strong at Power Corporation. He stayed on when Paul Desmarais took over the company, then struck out on his own in 1981 in a management buy-out of Power's Canada Steamship Lines.

In the early 1980s, Martin's name began to circulate in Liberal circles as a future leadership contender. He enjoyed outsider status among party elements fed up with the controlling tendencies of the insiders. A delegation of Young Liberals, seeking to organize a conference to express their revulsion at the tactics of Trudeau advisers like principal secretary James Coutts and Senator Keith Davey, sounded out Martin about being their keynote speaker. Three of them went down to Montreal: Peter Donolo, later Chrétien's communications director; Terrie O'Leary, who became Martin's executive assistant and alter ego; and Alfred Apps, a quasi-cult figure among disaffected Liberal youth, who later moved to Germany.

Their conference had been inspired in large part by Trudeau's appointment to the Senate in the summer of 1981 of an undistinguished, forty-five-year-old MP named Peter Stollery. The sole motive was to clear Stollery's Toronto seat for Coutts, who longed to move into the front rooms. The manipulation represented precisely the sort of cynical, self-interested politics the youth wing had come to despise. Ushered into Martin's office, the three Young Liberals gave voice to their loathing in no uncertain terms. Martin interrupted. "Jimmy is one of my best friends," he cautioned. "Jimmy"! They couldn't believe their ears. Nobody they knew called Coutts "Jimmy."

All told, the scheduled forty-five-minute meeting went well. The visitors stayed three and a half hours and snagged their speaker. The high-profile youth conference in November 1982 elevated Martin's profile in the party — despite his lacklustre presentation — and paid huge dividends down the road by plugging him into a network of smart, young political dynamos.

Martin flirted with a leadership run when Trudeau resigned in 1984. But he had not yet secured the success of Canada Steamship Lines and didn't like the advice that he should run to come second, positioning himself for the next time out. He was an all-or-nothing kind of guy. Finally, after considerable soul-searching, he issued a statement, saying: "I strongly believe in the ideal of public office and it is my hope to serve in some capacity eventually."

When he ran for Parliament in 1988, Martin did so with the intention of challenging for his party's leadership. By the time it came open in 1990, he had a team in place. Martin's youthful crew of organizers, attracted by his energy and embrace of new ideas, considered themselves superior in so many ways to the Chrétien campaign. Inside his campaign headquarters, they referred to Chrétien by the nickname "Potato-head." The candidate wasn't party to such name-calling, but he, too, lashed out at an opponent seemingly more intent on declaring his love for Canada than on engaging in intellectual debate about its direction. "One has the right to ask of somebody who wants to become leader of a party and a country if they have any firm views on the crucial subjects of the hour," Martin, obviously trailing, beseeched.

The most crucial subject of the hour was certainly the Meech Lake Accord. The worst moments of the leadership race came during a policy forum in Montreal on Sunday afternoon, June 3, long after Chrétien had built an insurmountable lead. Canada's first ministers had gathered in Ottawa that day in a last-ditch attempt to save the accord, and everyone's nerves were on edge. When Chrétien rose to speak, some youth delegates bedecked with Paul Martin buttons chanted "Judas" and "Vendu." A newswire story the previous day had incorrectly suggested that Chrétien, a staunch foe of the accord, now wanted it passed without amendment. Although a correction had been issued within hours, the impression had been left of a flip-flop. The Martin youth went for the jugular. "Le flip, le flop, Chrétien is going to drop!" Chrétien never forgot the moment. In an interview six years later, he complained bitterly that the agitators had largely come from Toronto. True enough: one Martin delegate confessed that with little understanding of French, he had confusingly been chanting the word "Fondue."

Sheila Copps and Martin picked up the theme in attacking Chrétien, with Martin's tone particularly harsh. In sharp contrast to Chrétien, he had supported Meech unequivocally. Chrétien and his advisers were livid. This was no way for Liberals to behave, resorting to scorched-earth tactics after the battle had already been decided. Allan Lutfy, the former Trudeau aide now advising Chrétien, was renowned for his precise, Jesuitical sense of logic and unfailing politeness. But his voice trembled with rage as he described being "sick to my stomach. I have never been more ashamed to be a Liberal." John Rae, the epitome of calm under fire, turned crimson at the memory six years later as he recalled being "goddamn furious."

The two of them waited until the next day to contain their rage somewhat, then contacted Martin's campaign manager, Michael Robinson. When they sat down for lunch with Robinson back in Ottawa, Rae — who knew Martin well and considered him a friend — said grimly that his campaign's behaviour had been absolutely, goddamn unacceptable, that Martin was going down to defeat but seemed determined to drag the whole party down with him. But Martin, a candidate possessed, persisted. The following Thursday in Toronto, he again levelled the flip-flop charge at Chrétien. "Now at the last minute he says, 'Oh, I was wrong.' It's obviously going to call his judgment into question." Martin suggested he might not stay on if Chrétien won. "There are a lot of Liberals who are going to say to hell with it." Asked if he would be among them, he shot back: "I'll see you on the 24th," the day after the convention.

By the 24th, Martin had calmed down. The Liberal caucus met early on the Sunday morning after the leadership vote. Martin arrived by taxi at the same time as several of his supporters. They walked in together. Chrétien, already at the front of the meeting room, came down from the podium, kissed MPs Christine Stewart and Mary Clancy at Martin's side, and accompanied the runner-up back to the stage. It was a small gesture of reconciliation, meaningless in itself, but of comfort to Martin's knot of caucus supporters. Clancy, for one, immediately felt better. "What he basically said was, 'You give me your best and I'll give you my best.'" Like his father before him, who had lost Liberal leadership contests in 1957 and 1968, Martin overcame his disappointment and proved himself a valuable team player. But the two camps would never fully trust each other. In power, Martin's people felt systematically snubbed by Chrétien's loyalists when it came to invitations to state banquets or appointments to government positions. The sole Martin supporter to make it into cabinet was Ralph Goodale — the only Liberal MP from Saskatchewan with any legislative experience.

On Friday, November 5, with David Dodge still in town, John Crow, the governor of the Bank of Canada, also made the pilgrimage to Windsor. His journey was perhaps a portent: Crow's plane was diverted to London by bad weather, and he was forced to complete the trip by bus. Unlike

Dodge, Crow was anything but the anonymous public servant whispering words of advice into the ear of his political masters. His position accorded him tremendous latitude over Canadian monetary and economic policy, and the manner in which he performed the job of governor gave him an extraordinarily high public profile.

In his seven years at the helm, Crow had reshaped the culture of the central bank in the image of the German Bundesbank, aping its absolutist drive for price stability. The policy made him the toast of the international financial set. Unfortunately for him, Canada lacked Germany's history of hyperinflation, a searing experience that had spawned a unique hard-money culture. Canada remained, at least psychologically, a frontier economy in perpetual search of cheap capital to sink the next mine shaft or log the neighbouring timber stand. Crow didn't have much of a domestic constituency for his tight money policies.

Crow had evolved into a highly politicized personality: hero to the gnomes of Zurich; villain both to the Canadian left and to the entrepreneurial community, including people like Paul Martin. His anti-inflation crusade was blamed far and wide for exacerbating if not causing the recession in Canada in the early 1990s, a charge he found ludicrous, pointing at the global nature of the economic downturn. But many economists countered that the Canadian economy had stalled earlier — and fallen harder. In opposition, the Liberals had sermonized endlessly against Crow's fixation with price stability and his seeming insensitivity to the human toll.

In the days leading up to the 1993 election campaign, Jean Chrétien suggested that the Liberals would rein in Crow. He would be ordered to relax his inflationary obsession and pay heed to job creation. "We want people to get back to work," the Liberal leader stated in an interview with the *Globe and Mail*. And if Crow refused? "I'm telling you that he's an official of the government," Chrétien responded in an apparent challenge to the governor's cherished independence.

But John Crow wasn't the type to yield to anyone's marching orders. He was a remote figure — brilliant, cocky, and contemptuous of those who challenged the wisdom of his policies, accusing his critics of an absence of "clear thinking." He had clashed with a number of Liberal MPs during his tenure, many of whom had now graduated to the Chrétien cabinet, and he wasn't about to change his tune just because they had switched sides in the House of Commons.

Martin's voice could be counted in the chorus critical of Crow's strict monetary policy. During the 1990 leadership campaign, Martin had remarked that it might be time to think the unthinkable and consider dumping the Bank of Canada governor if he refused government direction to lower interest rates. "I don't believe you just fire the governor of the Bank of Canada. That's very, very drastic," Martin told an interviewer. "But it is incumbent on the minister of finance to lay in front of the governor a deficit reduction plan that is credible. At that point, I think one is entitled to say to the governor, 'We would like over the next twelve to fourteen months for you to get interest rates down to their traditional levels.' And the governor has his choice of accepting or resigning."

Ten years earlier, Martin had bet the farm — literally, in the case of his 400-acre spread in the Eastern Townships — on a leveraged buy-out of Canada Steamship Lines. Martin lined up a partner to help him cover the $195-million price tag and borrowed heavily at a time when the Bank of Canada was driving interest rates to a record high of 22.75 per cent. Martin eventually steered CSL into safe harbour, but not before developing the entrepreneur's disdain for high interest rates. John Crow's policies in the late 1980s and early 1990s deeply offended him, both personally and politically. He thought it irresponsible to stifle economic growth and snuff out so many thousands of companies and jobs — not to mention exacerbating the deficit problem — in the single-minded pursuit of zero inflation. Martin would have wholly endorsed the sentiment of Robert Reich, one of his favourite economic thinkers, who wrote in his 1991 book, *The Work of Nations*: "In the life of a nation, few ideas are more dangerous than good solutions to the wrong problem."

But by the time John Crow came to visit him in Windsor, the Bank of Canada had finally relaxed monetary policy. By 1993, interest rates were down to thirty-year lows. Asked about Crow by the financial reporters as he came out of Rideau Hall, Martin said he saw no reason why the two of them shouldn't get along. "Low inflation is an essential ingredient to keeping interest rates low, there's no question about that," he remarked.

Martin understood that the new Liberal government lacked credibility in domestic and international financial markets, credibility that Crow possessed in spades. Foreigners held 40 per cent of Canada's debt, a dependence that grew with every budget. The country chronically consumed more than it produced, with foreign borrowings bridging the gap. The outflow of interest payments dwarfed Canada's annual trade surplus, leaving the country in a chronic balance-of-payments deficit. Canada had left itself vulnerable to the bond traders of the world, and the Liberals — the party that had opposed free trade, blocked foreign investment, and nationalized oil companies — hardly inspired confidence. Crow represented a huge national asset in a world in which Canada was, by dint of its foreign borrowings, a supplicant.

Paul Martin had until January to announce whether John Crow would be reappointed to a second term. They dined together on that Friday night in Windsor, beginning the process of sizing one another up. Martin felt little sympathy for John Crow. He would just as soon have replaced him, and he understood that the governor's reappointment would be a hot-button issue within the newly formed caucus and cabinet. But over the following days, he relegated such concerns to the dead-letter file, accepting the view of his new officials and nearly every person he knew in the private sector that it would be better to stick with his party's monetary *bête noire* than risk a financial market insurrection. He spread the word to his kitchen cabinet that John Crow was safe.

In the meantime, Martin had more pressing matters demanding his attention. Returning to Ottawa after his mother's funeral on November 13, he immersed himself in the incredible joylessness of being minister of finance. The deficit shocked him: the final tally topped $40 billion for 1992–93 and it looked headed towards even more dizzying heights in the fiscal year then in its eighth month. Making the 3-per-cent target would be tougher than he had figured.

Martin took stock politically. Cabinet and caucus didn't appear prepared for tough medicine. The Liberals were fresh from a big election win in which mentions of the deficit had been nearly as rare as testimonials to Brian Mulroney. Chrétien had repeatedly warned that the scorched-earth deficit policies of the Tories and Reform would put the country into a depression and lead to rioting in the street. The 3-per-cent commitment notwithstanding, Chrétien, a natural optimist out to convey an electoral message of hope, had so seldom mentioned fiscal rectitude that his advisers had considered releasing the Red Book early to provide a degree of balance.

In his first month in Ottawa, Reform leader Preston Manning astutely noted the consequences of the Liberal failure to secure an electoral mandate for containing the deficit. Now that they were in power, now that they were furiously leafing through those briefing books that Donald Savoie had warned about, they would have to seek a retroactive mandate. "People are going to say to them, 'Well, you never talked to us about this during the election,'" Manning commented, rubbing his parson's hands in barely concealed delight. He warned that it would be tough to build such a mandate after the election. Martin could see the same challenge ahead: he would have to educate the cabinet, the caucus, and the country. In the meantime, the federal share of the infrastructure program would put him another $2 billion in the hole.

On November 16, David Dodge gave cabinet its first Department of Finance slide show. He stood in the back of the room while two technicians fed a steady diet of unpleasant charts and graphs through the overhead projectors. A number of ministers found the message of sobriety infuriating. Liberals aren't slashers and hackers, Herb Gray acidly reminded the assembly when the lights came back on. Other ministers questioned why they should trust anything coming from the very same officials who had advised the Tories — and had continually got their numbers wrong in the process. The hostility bounced off the cabinet walls with the intensity of India rubber. It didn't escape Dodge's notice. But for now his more immediate challenge was Martin. It wasn't clear that Martin had even bothered reading the Next Mandate book — Michael Wilson, the best assistant deputy minister the department never had, read everything — let alone digested the true depth of the fiscal challenge.

Over the strong objections of his officials, Martin launched his public education process in a major speech to business students at the Université de Montréal on November 29. He laid out the extent to which the Tories had lost control of the deficit and vowed that his government would not waver in its promise to reduce the deficit to 3 per cent of GDP. "No one should be under any misapprehension about that." But he emphasized yet again that he saw growth as an indispensable tool in deficit reductions.

He had already disclosed that the final accounting of the deficit for 1992–93 had come in at $40.5 billion, $6 billion more than the Tories had projected. Now he revealed even worse numbers for the fiscal year in progress. He had resolved some outstanding accounting disagreements with the auditor general, which inflated the numbers somewhat. Still, he projected that the deficit would be a staggering $44 billion to $46 billion, the largest budgetary shortfall in Canadian history. (It would actually end up at $42 billion.)

The department had argued strenuously against the speech. Officials lobbied for a traditional fiscal and economic statement read in the House of Commons. They also objected to Martin restating the deficit numbers in the middle of the fiscal year and to his use of a range rather than a precise figure. (This penchant for precision, in the full knowledge of its unattainability, was one of the pretensions of economists that most infuriated Martin.) The officials felt he had made them look bush-league.

Which was exactly Martin's intention. The huge discrepancy between the projections in the last Tory budget in April and the actual numbers in November astounded him. At first, he wondered whether the department had been forced by the Tories to publish doctored forecasts. Whatever the case, either the department had known the numbers to be wrong or it had got them wrong. He would never allow it to happen to him, he told his officials in no uncertain terms — never. "You have been goddamn wrong in your forecasts for ten years," he shouted. If they were ever to err again, they would err on the side of prudence. He couldn't believe the number of times that Michael Wilson and Don Mazankowski had been subjected to the humiliation of having to admit the error of their estimates. The officials defended themselves, arguing that economic circumstances change. Revenues continued to collapse with the end of the recession. Nobody could have foreseen the growth in the underground economy.

Martin decided to bring in an outside panel to audit his department's forecasting capacity. The officials swallowed hard. They could give the minister what he wanted, play it safe. They understood his frustration. But the external audit would be a waste. They confided to Terrie O'Leary that a public flogging would undermine the department's credibility both publicly and within the federal bureaucracy.

Martin didn't relent. In his Université de Montréal speech, with his senior officials sitting in the audience, he focussed on all the ways the projections had been wrong and announced the independent study into the department's forecasting methods and performance. "Regardless of the reasons, no government, no organization, can long operate effectively when its projections fall consistently short of the mark." The officials looked ahead stone-faced, doing their best to disguise their embarrassment.

Meanwhile, Martin and Crow were running into problems of both personality and policy. The governor and the minister — they always used formal titles with each other — met often over the government's first six weeks, usually at Martin's office seven blocks from the Bank of Canada tower on the Sparks Street Mall. They spent hours and hours together, probing each other's thinking, trying to establish a comfort level. But it wasn't coming together.

Martin accepted that, having extracted a big toll to rid the economy of inflation, the bank should remain vigilant in not allowing it to return. But with inflation already below its level in the United States, he didn't want to pay a further price to continue driving the rate down. Fresh from the election campaign, Martin felt strongly about the government's growth agenda. Could he count on John Crow to be there for the government in a crunch? Crow, on the other hand, insisted on maintaining the course of inflation reduction, pushing for a reduction of the government's inflation targets to between zero and 2 per cent; Martin preferred to recommit to the existing range of 1 to 3 per cent.

They also were having trouble getting their personalities to click. If there was one thing Paul Martin couldn't stand, it was being lectured at. And if there was one thing John Crow couldn't resist, it was lecturing. Martin could not reconcile himself to Crow's refusal to accept blame for the recession. He found him rigid in his opinions, a hard man to deal with. But as far as Crow was concerned, the Bank of Canada had one job and one job only: to protect the value of the Canadian dollar. In other words, to stamp out inflation, which ate away at currencies as assuredly as termites working the night shift in a lumber yard. He wasn't in the job creation business, no matter what Jean Chrétien thought. Crow railed against the folly of those who counselled just a little inflation. How much was a little? he would ask, like Socrates with his slowest students. A little inflation invariably led to a lot of inflation. He was doing his job; the problem in the economy was that spendthrift politicians had failed to do theirs.

Martin's edginess about Crow was reciprocated. An acquaintance ran into the governor walking to work down Bank Street one day in mid-December. He inquired about relations with the new finance minister and asked if Crow had noticed how Martin never said things were very good or very bad, but always *very, very* good or *very, very* bad? "Yes, he talks just like my teenage daughter," the governor snorted.

Martin's refusal to be pinned down on the Crow appointment drew fire in the financial press. The Business Council on National Issues, the representative of big business, issued a statement calling for the governor's reappointment. Messages poured into Martin's office from business acquaintances overseas and from bank executives in Canada. The uncertainty was jeopardizing the dollar, they all said. Crow should be reappointed right away.

On December 13, as part of his pre-budget consultations, Martin held a televised round-table discussion with a group of thirty-eight economists in the basement of the government conference centre in Ottawa. After a lunch break, Michael Walker, head of the right-wing Fraser Institute, interrupted the proceedings to report that he had informally polled his fellow economists during the break and that twenty-three thought Crow should be reappointed, six did not, and nine had abstained. Martin, publicly ambushed, shot back that he would conduct a poll to see if Walker should remain chief of the Fraser Institute.

The department also lobbied Martin; the officials lived in mortal fear of how the markets would respond to Crow's departure. A run on the dollar, a hike in interest rates — either would damage the new minister's shaky credibility and put yet more pressure on the deficit.

But Martin was a risk-taker. He had gambled in snapping up Canada Steamship Lines in 1981, overriding the concerns of even his worried father. It wasn't in his character to play it safe. Martin had a bad right knee, one that acted up when he sat for a long while. In time, he would need an artificial replacement. The knee had been operated on five times since he first hurt it when, as he liked to say, he was "young and stupid." The initial injury occurred while he was water-skiing in Muskoka, the cottage region north of Toronto. He had swung out towards the side of the boat, picking up speed as he approached the shore after a run. Preening for his friends standing on the dock, he cut in as close as possible so he could splash them. Unfortunately, he failed to notice another boat, with a short anchor rope, waiting to go out. Martin hit the rope, flew up in the air, and crashed into the dock, his right knee smashed to pulp.

That's the way he was: a bit of a showboat, a guy who played close to the edge. He was spontaneous, curious, unafraid of life. One day in the 1970s, he heard on the radio that the Hell's Angels had taken over the streets of Sorel, Quebec. The police had blockaded the town. It sounded interesting. He jumped in his car and drove out to watch the action.

He certainly lacked the inbred caution of a Finance bureaucrat. Nor did he have any intention of deferring to them. "The day the bureaucracy wants to spend its time in church basements getting elected," he liked to say, "is the day that they can run the government."

Martin hadn't set out to get rid of John Crow. But he didn't like being backed into a corner — not by the markets, not by his officials, not by the

Fraser Institute. Privately, he worried that if the markets perceived that he had capitulated, their ransom demands would escalate the next time around. The issue had evolved beyond John Crow to one of who controlled the decision: the minister of finance or the financial markets.

The final determination of Crow's fate occurred at a five-hour meeting in Martin's office on Friday, December 17. The two most powerful economic figures in the country continued to talk around and around their differences. Martin favoured a more balanced approach, one that stressed job creation and economic growth along with low — but not the lowest — inflation. Crow refused to compromise his monetary beliefs. He had invested the bank with tremendous credibility: he didn't want the crusade placed on cruise control. They couldn't bridge their divergent views. Nor could they find a personal comfort level. By late afternoon, it was clear to both of them that they would never come to an understanding and that the relationship would not work. They agreed to disagree. Crow withdrew his name from consideration.

Despite his bluster, Martin shared the nervousness of others about market reaction. "We were petrified, absolutely petrified," Terrie O'Leary, his executive assistant, confessed. He spoke over the weekend with Chrétien, and they met for forty-five minutes on Monday. Chrétien had quietly shared many of Martin's misgivings about Crow. As was often the case with Chrétien, his concept of a central bank governor was rooted in personal experience. In the late 1970s, when he had served in Finance, Gerald Bouey was governor. Bouey came from a small Saskatchewan hamlet called Trossachs and began his career as a teller at the Royal Bank. Bouey was grey and self-effacing; 98 per cent of Canadians had probably never heard of him, which was, according to Chrétien's thinking, precisely the way it should be with a central bank governor.

Crow's high profile and his hectoring manner with elected officials offended Chrétien's sense of the proper order of things. As prime minister, he didn't like the idea of having to watch his Ps and Qs because of the governor. As he had stated in the pre-election interview, the government enjoyed a mandate from the people; the governor was only an appointed official. There was a hierarchy to these things, one that Crow obviously was too independent-minded to respect. But most of all, Chrétien bristled over what he viewed as a high-level lobbying campaign on behalf of the governor, perhaps even orchestrated by him. Chrétien found it unseemly. Determined to let his minister of finance exercise the prerogatives of the position, Chrétien had kept his counsel. Now he gave Martin his full support.

They decided that thirty-year bank veteran Gordon Thiessen, who as Crow's senior deputy was intimately associated with the anti-inflation battle, would make the best possible replacement under the circumstances. His appointment would reassure the markets that the man was being replaced but not the low-inflation policy. Chrétien also liked the fact that Thiessen, like Bouey, hailed from Saskatchewan.

Martin at once felt more comfortable with Thiessen, a far more easygoing individual than Crow. He asked him that Monday to take the job, and they quickly came to an agreement on inflation targets for the next three years — a perpetuation of the 1 to 3 per cent band. A minority of commentators suggested the new governor had accepted a softer formulation, one that would allow the Liberals more wiggle room if inflation began to resurface later in their term. But most said nothing had changed: Thiessen was merely John Crow with a smile. That was precisely the message the government wanted to get out. It would be emblematic of so much they would do: Tory-style policies but with more pleasant packaging.

Three days before Christmas, Chrétien broke the news to a surprised cabinet — he had been surprised himself when Martin had called — while his minister of finance went across the street to introduce the new governor to the media. As the press conference ended, O'Leary phoned back to the department for a status report. The markets, seeing a familiar face at the helm, sailed through calmly. It looked like Martin would escape unscathed.

And so John Crow became the first governor of the Bank of Canada to depart after a single term, going out, in the view of Martin's advisers, quietly and with class. In taking his leave, he illustrated for the first time two critical traits about Canada's new finance minister: Martin was his own man, and he was willing to court risk. Those close to him believed that the episode had emboldened him on both counts.

5

LIBERAL ON HIS KNEES

Patrick Johnston got off the elevator on the fourteenth floor of Phase IV of Place du Portage, the public service monstrosity just across the river from Parliament Hill in Hull. A commissionaire directed him past an empty reception area and down a long corridor. He was struck by the aisle after aisle of empty cubicles — not a soul in sight, not a picture or calendar on the walls. Chairs had been tucked neatly under desks. Even the paper clips had vanished. It looked as if the new tenant had wanted to wipe away all traces of the previous occupant.

The date was November 8, 1993, the first Monday of a new national government. Johnston made his way through a set of wooden doors and past a second reception area, finally arriving at his destination. A middle-aged man with sandy hair and round glasses greeted him, Johnston, a Liberal who had worked for Ontario Premier David Peterson and now headed the Canadian Council for Social Development, sat down for his first meeting with the new minister of human resources, Lloyd Axworthy.

The morning after the swearing-in, Johnston had received a call from Axworthy, a man he had met only casually. Could he drop by that afternoon and kick around some ideas? Johnston was tied up and begged off until Monday. Over the weekend, he read a newspaper interview with the newly installed minister in which Axworthy advertised his intention to launch a comprehensive review of the country's fabled social safety net.

Johnston was surprised to find Axworthy nearly by himself. The only staffer around was a woman named Patricia Neri. She was, she explained, Axworthy's new executive assistant, his most senior aide. She had no experience in government or even in the Liberal Party. Johnston asked her how long she had known the minister. "About two days," she replied.

Many months later, long after their adventure together had gone awry, that initial impression of desolation stuck vividly in Johnston's mind. "You would have thought he would have had his own people," Johnston reflected. Indeed, it seemed curious that a veteran politician like Axworthy, one who had been in the front ranks of his party for nearly fifteen years and had three times flirted with runs at the Liberal leadership, would return to office seemingly so isolated.

Axworthy had been renowned in the early 1980s, when he served as minister of employment and minister of transport, for having the best — and biggest — political staff on Parliament Hill. Now, a decade later, one of his department's outside consultants sized up the crew of relatively inexperienced aides and concluded that Axworthy must have a kitchen cabinet stashed somewhere to provide him with the high-quality political advice such a large and sensitive portfolio demanded. But he didn't.

Johnston came to that first meeting determined to put across two major points. If Ottawa entertained any hope of fundamentally reforming social security — as Axworthy apparently wished — it would need to tear down the Iron Curtain that had descended in the latter years of the Mulroney administration between the federal government and the provinces. Ottawa's unemployment insurance system was too intermeshed with provincial welfare and education systems for the federal government to go it alone. Quebec, as always, would pose particular problems, especially with an election coming up. But Ontario's NDP government, also near an election and wallowing in grievances towards Ottawa, required tender care as well. Second, Johnston said that unless Axworthy worked in concert with the Department of Finance, many of the people he needed to draw into the process would be leery of his capacity to pull off reforms. Suspecting the social security review would be hijacked down the road, they would limit themselves to the role of interested observers.

Axworthy already had some strong ideas of his own and waved off Johnston's suggestions. "I think non-responsive is how I would characterize his reaction," he later said. "He heard me but he didn't really say yes or no or anything." The minister wanted to form a task force of outside experts to furnish him with an action plan that he would then take to cabinet, the provinces, and the country. And he wanted, as far as possible, to move away from the system by which Ottawa provides grants to the provinces to top up their social programs. He hated this role of silent partner. Instead, he argued that the federal government should identify areas of special interest and enter into direct relationships with individual Canadians, as it did in delivering old-age pension cheques to seniors.

He had in mind that the next great federal crusade would be child poverty. He would bypass the provinces, their constitutional competence in that area notwithstanding. He invited his visitor to come work with him. Liberal friends warned Johnston to steer clear — that Axworthy, despite his thoughtful manner, made for a difficult boss — but who could resist the siren call of a major social policy reform.

Curiously for an initiative rapidly promoted as a cornerstone of the new government's mandate, social policy reform had not appeared — at least not explicitly — in the Liberal Red Book. Both the Liberals and the Conservatives had judged social policy too hot to handle in an election campaign. The only difference was that Prime Minister Kim Campbell was injudicious enough to say so. Conservative slippage in the polls turned into an avalanche on the day she told the press that an election campaign wasn't the best time to debate serious issues like social policy reform. Bernard Valcourt, the Conservatives' human resources minister, had argued for making such a reform the centrepiece of the Conservative campaign. In the dying days of the Tory government, his department had prepared a White Paper outlining a break with the "liberal entitlement" psychology in favour of an approach emphasizing self-reliance and individual responsi-bility. But other factions in cabinet judged the subject too incendiary, espe-cially given the party's negative image on social issues. They would be smeared as slashers and hackers rather than reformers. Cabinet passed on the Valcourt paper, which didn't see the light of day until someone leaked it to the *Globe and Mail* in mid-campaign.

On the Thursday before Thanksgiving, Sheila Copps received a brown envelope with Valcourt's White Paper inside. She was preparing to fly out to New Brunswick for an evening rally in the riding of Pierrette Ringuette-Maltais, the Liberal contesting Valcourt's seat. Copps couldn't believe her good fortune. She felt the Liberals had failed to exploit earlier leaks sufficiently. Now she had the goods on Valcourt and the perfect forum in which to make a splash.

Copps spoke to fellow Rat Packer Brian Tobin in Newfoundland, who shared her enthusiasm about launching a social policy salvo against the Tories. Throughout the day, they went back and forth on the phone with Eddie Goldenberg, travelling with Chrétien. Copps could barely contain her excitement. But Goldenberg nixed the idea. The Liberals were edging towards almost certain victory. He was looking beyond the campaign. "We might be doing that ourselves," he told Copps.

The giant Department of Human Resources Development had been created by the Campbell government in June — stapled together might be a better term — for the express purpose of reforming the country's social programs. It grouped programs previously dispersed among four and a half departments — job training, unemployment insurance, labour standards, welfare (social assistance), post-secondary education funding, student loans, old-age pensions, and child tax benefits. Both the Conservatives and the Liberals concluded that by housing all these responsibilities together, the new department could look at the best structure for social programs in the 1990s without regard to bureaucratic turf. For instance, social assistance could now be blended with the child tax benefit or with training funds to help low-income families more efficiently.

HRD was responsible for $69 billion of spending. Axworthy's domain included two of the major vehicles, called transfers, through which Ottawa contributed to and influenced social programs in the provinces: Established Program Financing (Education) and the Canada Assistance Plan. These two sources accounted for about $14 billion in post-secondary education and social assistance funding. (Two other transfers, Ottawa's contributions for health and the equalization payments made to poorer provinces, were outside Axworthy's department.) But transfer payments had been declining for some years, with an accompanying shrinkage in Ottawa's ability to impose its social views.

The HRD officials, like everyone else, gobbled up the Red Book upon its release in the second week of the campaign. Although it steered clear of explicit policies, its analysis of the social challenges dovetailed with the department's view. "It is our goal to help people on social assistance who are able to work, to move from dependence to full participation in the economic and social life of Canada. The current passive support programs, which offer income to people in need but no plan for achieving self-sufficiency, are not enough," the platform stated. Reading it over, Jean-Jacques Noreau, the deputy minister, was pleased. "If they believe that," he thought, "they're not very far from the kind of thinking that has occurred here." He ordered the briefing books for the incoming minister to be prepared with an eye towards reviving the social security review that had stalled under Valcourt.

In selecting Axworthy, the new government made a strong statement that it intended to make social policy changes a priority. The hot blood of a natural-born reformer coursed through Axworthy's veins. In Britain, it had been said of Margaret Thatcher that she couldn't walk by an institution without hitting it with her handbag. Although his politics were situated on the other side of the political spectrum from the Iron Lady, he shared with her an utter contempt for the status quo, a quality that put him at odds with Chrétien and his cabal of cautious advisers. Axworthy was an activist, an interventionist, not one apt to leave things to work themselves out.

Over the years, Axworthy had told acquaintances about one of his first cabinet meetings in 1980, when Chrétien, by then a veteran minister, had taken him off to the side to explain the secrets of success in government. Try not to have too much legislation before the House of Commons, Chrétien advised. And try not to bring too many submissions to cabinet. It was Chrétien's minimalist orientation, perfectly suited to a minister who was, at heart, suspicious of government intervention, and one who lacked the vision, rigour, and command of language to argue in favour of complex pieces of legislation. Around Axworthy's office in those early days, the staff would mock Chrétien and his advisers, Goldenberg in particular, as the Jean "Don't Act Until It's Past Urgent" Chrétien team.

Axworthy took comfort in the emphasis Chrétien had placed on ministers running their own shows. Others, however, worried that an assignment as complex and politically delicate as revamping the country's social programs absolutely required the active support of the entire government, particularly the prime minister. In October, during the election campaign, Harvey Lazar, the top policy expert in the Human Resources Department, had been invited over to the Privy Council Office to discuss a social security review. He told the PCO officials that a strong minister would be a necessary but not sufficient condition for success. The government as a whole would have to limit the policy clutter in order to concentrate all its firepower on such a major undertaking. The prime minister, whoever that may be, would have to be willing to give the effort his or her full backing in the understanding that it could well extract a heavy political toll along the way, especially in Quebec. Later, in the privacy of his department, Lazar would confess that he had been speaking only in general terms. If he had considered Chrétien specifically, he would have expressed reservations about proceeding because of the new prime minister's incrementalist approach.

Atop the dome of the Manitoba legislature in central Winnipeg stands a famous statue called the Golden Boy. The four-metre-high gilded figure carries an illuminated torch aloft with his right arm, rallying youth to his cause. Inside the legislature from 1973 to 1979 sat another golden boy: Lloyd Axworthy, the thirty-something Liberal MLA for Fort Rouge, arguably the most intelligent, articulate, and sparkling figure among a largely grey lot of provincial politicians.

Born on December 21, 1939, in North Battleford, Saskatchewan, and raised within the rich tapestry of north-end Winnipeg, he excelled at school and starred in sports. His father, Norman, was an insurance agent, a petit bourgeois among his working-class neighbours. His mother, Gwen, was a community activist, steeped in the progressive ideals of the United Church.

Decades later, when he was a powerful minister in the Chrétien government, friends would say that the attitudes developed in the north end of Winnipeg still shaped Axworthy. He evinced a natural sympathy for the underdog and harboured a visceral antipathy to business, especially big business. "You can take the boy out of the north end, but you can't take the north end out of the boy," said Peter Smith, who first hooked up with Axworthy as a Young Liberal in the 1960s and later worked for him on Parliament Hill.

In a community dominated by immigrant families from eastern Europe — Jews, Poles, Ukrainians — the Axworthys were of British stock. Lacking in the indignity of being subjected to discrimination himself, Axworthy appropriated the indignities of others. He can still conjure up the anger that welled inside him when a classmate arrived at school one day with a new position on the alphabetical roll call. The boy's father had been informed that an anglicized name wouldn't hurt his chances for promotion at the department store where he worked. "I was so mad at that kind of thing. It was so fundamentally unfair," Axworthy recalled.

Above all, Axworthy attributed his social conscience to one influence: his upbringing in the activist, social gospel United Church system, what he calls "the protesting part of Protestantism." His parents attended church regularly, a habit he never lost. "People used to say it was the Liberal Party on its knees. You showed your belief in God by what you did to help those in your community who were less fortunate. There was a certain liberation theology to it."

At Princeton University in the 1960s, Axworthy became acquainted with a style of politics that fascinated him — politics as waged by the Kennedys. They blended a United Church–style public activism with a worldliness that appealed to him. "They were very pragmatic. There was a wonderful use of language which I've always admired. But at the same time they were very tough, smart politicians." He particularly worshipped Robert Kennedy. John Kennedy's assassination shocked him; Bobby Kennedy's reduced him to tears.

Axworthy's years at Princeton coincided with the emergence of the civil rights movement. The South was on fire as blacks, supported by the federal government, sought to assert their civil rights against the power of state governments and their police forces. For a young man who had been so outraged by the demands on his friend's father to change his name, it marked a deepening of his commitment to social justice coupled with a sense, he said later, that the programs of the New Deal had failed blacks, that they needed to be given their own means of succeeding.

In 1963 Axworthy experienced the first of what would become, over the years, a multitude of crises with big-L Liberalism. Lester Pearson had flip-flopped on whether Canada would accept the placement of U.S. Bomarc missiles, with nuclear warheads, on Canadian soil. Axworthy, distressed, broke with the Liberals and flirted with the New Democrats. But after a couple of meetings, he judged them too doctrinaire for his liking. They lacked the pragmatism and toughness he so admired in the Kennedys. By election day, he had returned to the Liberal fold, reasoning that while he opposed the party's position on the Bomarc, he favoured its progressive tilt on social issues and health care. "I was torn. You know politicians well enough. There's never one ball in the air. There's usually several that you're juggling at the same time. I supposed that's why I still feel happier or better as a Liberal working these things out and going through these different exchanges as opposed to having a kind of purity of things, which means nothing ever gets done."

For Axworthy, it was the start of a recurring pattern: a challenge to his fundamental principles, a physical or psychic withdrawal from fellow Liberals as he struggles with the demon of the moment, and finally a reconciliation in which the course of pragmatism triumphs and he soothes himself with the knowledge that he fought the good fight and, at least, will be around to fight it again. If he can assign himself the role of martyr, so much the better. In 1986, he told Carleton University students how he had come close to resigning from Pierre Trudeau's cabinet three years earlier over the testing of the Cruise missile in Canada. But again he found a reason to stay — this time in Trudeau's subsequent peace mission. It was ever thus with Axworthy.

In government in the Trudeau years, Axworthy earned a reputation as a high-spending, hard-working, nationalistic minister whose social conscience was outweighed only by his penchant for pork-barrel politics. Federal money rained down on Winnipeg. Later in opposition, his attacks on free trade and his slanging matches with the business community reinforced the image of Axworthy as a leftist. Axworthy considered the label a misrepresentation. After all, he had explicitly rejected and then fought the New Democrats. He had also set out in 1980 — without success — to reform unemployment insurance and, shuffled to Transport in 1983, had authored the first wave of deregulation of the Canadian airline industry. As he would demonstrate again in 1994 with his attack on middle-class students, he hated privilege of any kind.

"I suppose if there is one area that has been difficult," he said in an interview in late 1995, "it has been a lot of the expectations that were created as much for me as by me: the darling of the left and the advocate for the downtrodden.

"A lot of people said to me, How can you be doing the things you are doing? And I keep saying to them, You don't know my history very well. I came out of a sixties mentality that was fighting city hall, fighting bureaucracy, fighting big programs, turning power back to the people — that was my growing-up frame of reference in the sixties. I never believed that big welfare programs or benefit programs were all that effective."

Some of his closest associates suggested that to understand Axworthy, it was necessary to think of him as an American Democrat, like the Kennedys. He worked off a base of idealism but would not hesitate to employ raw power in pursing his goals. At the end of the day, the ability to continue exercising power — some might call it ambition — outweighed any particular use of that power, or the social good. In other words, as it did for Democrats, and nearly all Liberals, pragmatism would prevail.

Perhaps the greater paradox in the Axworthy character, however, was the juxtaposition of his compassion for humankind with his poor interpersonal abilities. Axworthy had little or no curiosity about those around him and would discard inconvenient staffers like yesterday's sandwich wrap. His relations with bureaucrats were crisp. He was quick to blame others for his shortcomings and slow to reach out.

Unfortunately for Axworthy, the participatory brand of politics practised in the 1990s demanded people skills. Building a consensus by throwing money at a problem wasn't feasible any more. Time and again, Liberals insiders watching his failings in the social security review would return to the story of his encounter in 1981 with feminist Doris Anderson, the head of the Advisory Council on the Status of Women. As a progressive Liberal, he had been given responsibility for women's issues in Trudeau's cabinet. When the government decided that a planned women's conference on the Constitution would prove embarrassing, it fell to Axworthy to persuade Anderson to call it off.

His attempts to strong-arm the independent-minded government appointee failed miserably. In January 1981, with a small knot of male Liberal advisers gathered in his office, Axworthy berated Anderson on the telephone in no uncertain terms. There would be no conference, he decreed. Finally, he hung up and looked around. "That's the last we'll hear from her," he stated with finality.

He was wrong. The following day, Anderson went public with complaints about ministerial interference, sparking a bitter public feud that persisted for months and caused irreparable harm to the rookie minister's progressive image and leadership ambitions. For close observers of Axworthy, the incident exposed a number of problematic character traits. Put in charge of calming a manageable situation, he allowed it to escalate into a full-blown confrontation. He personalized the differences, and he misjudged the capacity of his opponent to make an impact. The same behavioural pattern would re-emerge in the social security review.

In 1919, at the convention at which they selected Mackenzie King as their leader, the Liberals pledged to institute "so far as may be practicable, having regard to Canada's financial position, an adequate system of insurance against unemployment, sickness, dependence in old age, and other disability, which would include old age pensions, widows' pensions, and maternity benefits."

Once in power, King treated the 1919 resolution merely as a "chart on which is plotted the course desired by the people of the country." Even through the human devastation of the 1930s Depression, he demonstrated no rush to reach that destination, expressing deep skepticism of Roosevelt's

New Deal. He continually rebuffed the progressive wing of his party, including an ambitious young lawyer from Windsor named Paul Martin.

The war, however, broke the mould of Canadian politics in a way the Depression had failed to do. It demonstrated to Canadians that government could manage the economy, King's misgivings about state planning notwithstanding. The bureaucrats — seared by the Depression and tempered by the war — had gained new confidence in their abilities, and conveniently possessed an alluring blueprint for their putative interventions in John Maynard Keynes's *General Theory of Employment, Interest and Money*. Mitchell Sharp's generation couldn't bear the thought, after all the wartime sacrifice, of Canadians again being thrown to the vagaries of the market, especially now that the state boasted the scientific tools to prevent Depression-like ravages again.

King prepared to satisfy the public's craving for greater social security in the postwar world, an urge being reflected in alarming support for the left-wing Co-operative Commonwealth Federation. He promised in the 1943 Speech from the Throne "a charter of social security for the whole of Canada," and followed that with a series of progressive reports and measures, including family allowances.

By the time King went to the people in June 1945, he had largely completed his redefinition of Liberalism. Still, it was, as he himself would note, a "very near-run thing." The Liberals lost fifty-eight seats but held on to power, with the Conservatives winning official opposition status and the beset CCF relegated to third place.

The wartime blueprint took a generation to put into practice, the King and St. Laurent Liberals ever mindful of the 1919 caveat "so far as may be practicable, having regard to Canada's financial position." The final pieces wouldn't be implemented until the 1960s, with Lester Pearson residing at 24 Sussex Drive and an ambitious young MP named Jean Chrétien seated on the back benches.

By November 1993, with Lloyd Axworthy ensconced in Place du Portage, the postwar social security system looked badly tattered. The previous year, 3.7 million Canadians had cycled through the unemployment insurance program at one point or another; joblessness touched the lives of more than 6 million family members. Another 3 million Canadians collected social assistance, twice as many as a dozen years earlier, a figure that expanded in good times and failed to contract in bad. More than 1 million children lived under the poverty line. Between 1975 and 1992,

federal and provincial spending on Canada's social programs, not counting health and education, rose from $12 billion to $75 billion, an increase
of more than 50 per cent even after discounting inflation. But it didn't
seem to be helping.

Axworthy surveyed the scene in the fall of 1993, laying the groundwork for his social policy reforms. As always, he looked outside his department for ideas, recruiting social policy experts to work with Patrick
Johnston to design a new social security system for Canada. Among those
he tapped was Judith Maxwell, former head of the Economic Council of
Canada.

In Axworthy, Maxwell was eager to believe that the man had finally
met the moment. Maxwell, the Mother Teresa of the policy wonks, despaired
of the state of Canada's social programs. For years, finance ministers had
nickel-and-dimed the system without bothering to shore it up. She accepted
the primacy of the deficit fight. But still she felt sorrow over the misdirec-
tion of scarce funds in these tight times into outmoded social policies.

The October election revived her spirits. Earlier that month, she had
participated in a panel discussion at the Château Laurier Hotel with
Michael Walker, head of the conservative Fraser Institute. He prattled on
about the deficit, and about the need for the new government, whichever
party won, to eliminate it. Frustrated over his domination of the session,
she blurted out that while the importance of deficit reduction could not be
denied, not only the fiscal deficit but also a social deficit demanded attention. The phrase "social deficit" resonated. A wave of applause rippled
through the room.

Shortly before Christmas, Axworthy read an article Maxwell had just
published titled "Globalization and Family Security," in which she enu-
merated the pressures for change and offered a number of strong recommendations, including a policy that would deny anyone under twenty-five
the right to collect unemployment insurance. Instead, jobless young people would be given a choice of enrolling in formal education or training or
a Job Corps. That sort of tough-love approach appealed to Axworthy. He
invited her for lunch in his office on the last working day before the holidays, outlining his plans and asking her to join his task force. "He wanted
to think big," she recalled.

Social policy, conveniently, was one of the few areas of policy-making
in which nation-states clearly retained their ability to make a difference in
an age of free trade and global competition. Unlike capital and technology,

human beings — labour — were unlikely to bolt across the globe in a nanosecond. Lester Thurow had told Liberals at the 1991 Aylmer conference that a state could make no better investment in the global economy than supporting its own citizens. They represented the only competitive advantage you could hang on to.

If Canadian workers were to be subject to the sudden upheavals of a global economy — and where could they hide in this age of debt and globalization — then government needed to help workers adjust. So social policy would have to be adjustment policy: labour market training, continuous education, literacy, numeracy. These were the tools workers required to survive. Income redistribution by itself, Maxwell had written, "provides palliative care but offers no remedies."

For Axworthy, the social security review would mark his second pass at these problems. Although the pace of change had accelerated, many of the underlying challenges remained the same as those that had existed in his previous stint at Employment in the early 1980s. Back then, Axworthy wanted to reorient UI programs from passive income assistance to active measures, like training. Even then, Axworthy used a term that would become central to his vocabulary in his later incarnation: that unemployment insurance must increasingly become "employment insurance." But after the onset of the 1981–82 recession, the most severe downturn since the Depression, long-term planning gave way to stopgap measures. He devoted his energy to make-work job creation, running up the deficit in the process.

Now, a decade later, he would not get sidetracked again. The size of his department delighted him. He would not have to waste valuable effort hammering out compromises with the welfare minister or the labour minister or the employment minister — what he called "boundary management." He wore all the hats. In fact, as he surveyed the cabinet, he could see only one minister who would require special attention: the guy who controlled the purse strings, the minister of finance. Paul Martin also recognized that his relations with Axworthy would be integral to the success of the entire government.

Their life experiences were markedly different: Axworthy came out of the contemplative world of the academy, Martin from the fast-paced world of commerce. One was an urban planner, the other an entrepreneur. Martin was in charge of containing government spending; Axworthy was a spender in the government's biggest spending department.

But they enjoyed much in common as well. They were of the same generation, each with deep roots in the party; they both loved ideas, the fresher the better; and they both believed in the power of government to do good deeds. Martin had a romantic attachment to the 1950s cabinets of Louis St. Laurent, which had been anchored by Industry Minister C.D. Howe on the right and, in Martin's telling, his father, Paul Martin Sr., on the left. He thought of himself and Axworthy as the modern equivalents.

In many ways, Martin admired Axworthy, clearly one of the smartest people in government and blessed with a commendable ability to process complex information. He told an associate in the early weeks of the government how lucky Lloyd had been to have had the best staff on the Hill when he was a minister in the 1980s. He envied Axworthy's assignment to modernize the country's social programs — far better than hacking and slashing at Finance — and his ready credibility with the party's progressive wing.

Axworthy, in turn, appreciated that Martin regarded himself as a progressive. But he never got over his natural skepticism of businessmen cavorting as social reformers. He had deeply resented the manner in which Martin supporters on the Liberal Party executive had set the spending limits in the 1990 leadership race well beyond the means of ordinary mortals like himself. If not for lack of money, he might have run. Axworthy sometimes found himself wondering about the sincerity of Martin's commitment to the social Liberalism espoused by his father. He would hear Martin talk the talk, and then go off with his buddies at the Business Council on National Issues, a group for whom poverty was a problem of time management. He was a hard guy to figure.

Ed Lumley, the former industry minister, was a friend of both. He had known Martin since the two were teenagers in Windsor in the 1950s. He and Axworthy had been seatmates in the Commons in the early 1980s and had forged a friendship despite residing on different sides of the ideological tracks. Lumley travelled to Ottawa in the early days of the government to participate in an orientation exercise for new ministers. He tried to impress on both these friends the importance of working with each other.

Lumley assured Axworthy that Martin was a guy with a heart. Beneath the corporate exterior lurked his father's son. He wasn't, by nature, a slash-and-burn kind of guy. He told Martin, in turn, that Axworthy should never be dismissed as a simple left-winger. He was a thoughtful guy with a passion for changing things. The key to getting along lay in treating him with respect. Patiently and persistently explain your position. He was, despite appearances, flexible. He would eventually respond to the logic of any given situation.

Martin took to thinking of cabinet not in terms of left and right but rather as traditionalists and activists. The former group, whether left or right, tended to go along to get along. The latter group, of which Axworthy was a charter member along with Transport Minister Doug Young on the right, made things happen no matter the constraints. Martin lauded Axworthy's refusal to live with the status quo. It was an instinct he shared. "I would rather have left-wing activists than right-wing traditionalists," he would say, "because right-wing traditionalists won't do a goddamn thing except take the situation as it is." Martin thought he could do business with a reformer like Axworthy.

Axworthy, too, could identify common ground. The two sides of Liberalism came together, he figured, on the need to push back the country's growing entitlement mentality in favour of one of more individual responsibility. "We lost that over a period of time," he said. "Maybe during the Trudeau years, this notion built up that somehow government owed everybody something. I think there has been a swing back, and Liberals are reflecting that."

Indeed, to those who knew them best, their differences weren't so much about values as about personality and temperament. Mary Clancy, the gregarious Halifax MP, liked to count both among her friends. In the early weeks of the government, she spotted them at one of official Ottawa's favourite hangouts, Mamma Teresa's.

"I look up from the table and coming downstairs are Paul and Lloyd," she recounted. "I jumped up to go talk to my two favourite cabinet ministers and caught my foot in the handle of my briefcase and fell forward to the floor." Somehow, Axworthy and Martin missed the display. Embarrassed, Clancy caught up with them and described how she had just made a complete fool of herself.

"Lloyd says, 'Oh my God, are you hurt?' And Paul says, 'I missed it. Can you do it again?'

"To a large degree that explains the equal appeal of them. There is an empathy in Lloyd. There is a true empathy that comes out and sometimes because he cares to such an extent, it is harder for him. Paul cares too, absolutely. But Paul has an easier personality. So he can say and do things and not have to work so hard to get people to go along with him. The good fairy gave him the charm. I love them both. But they are very different men."

Early in the life of the government, the pair were teamed up with Industry Minister John Manley at a special G-7 jobs summit in Detroit organized by President Clinton. It was an enjoyable meeting — they hob-nobbed with U.S. Labour Secretary Robert Reich, the industrial policy guru whose works both had read avidly — and they were in good spirits at the wrap-up press conference. They divvied up their comments by language. Axworthy spoke first in English. Martin followed him to the rostrum, jokingly introducing himself as Axworthy's translator. He then repeated the spiel in French.

A reporter from the *Detroit News* walked away impressed by their evident warmth. In the next day's paper, he referred to "a cheerful, red-faced sort ... with a Québécois accent" who "gleefully translated" Axworthy's closing remarks. "If the bilingual bonhomie going back and forth between the translator and Axworthy is any indication, our favorite northern neighbor isn't likely to rip itself apart any time soon," he wrote. They had a good chuckle over that one. But it wasn't always so smooth.

6

TRADING PLACES

On the evening of November 18, Jean Chrétien, prime minister for two weeks, sat down in Seattle, Washington, with U.S. President Bill Clinton to put NAFTA to bed. The meeting had been arranged almost a month earlier, during U.S. Ambassador James Blanchard's secret mid-campaign visit to Quebec City to discuss the tottering trade deal with Chrétien's chief of staff, Jean Pelletier. The advisers decided their respective bosses should get together soon after the election — but not in Washington, in light of Chrétien's determination to project an image of greater independence from the United States, nor in Ottawa, given the long lead time required for security arrangements. They settled on Seattle, where both leaders would be attending the Asia-Pacific Economic Council summit.

Right up to the last minute, neither could be sure there would be a NAFTA. Clinton's crucial congressional vote on the agreement had taken place only the day before and looked like a near thing right to the end. Chrétien learned the results over a radio-phone on his Challenger jet as he flew out west for the summit. The White House, pulling out all the stops, had gone over the top in the final thirty-six hours, winning by a healthy 234-to-200 margin in the House of Representatives. Chrétien and his advisers sat aboard the plane ruminating over the administration's evident political skills in turning the vote around. Back in Washington, the president was ecstatic. He had put his credibility on the line for NAFTA and won big. He stayed up all night sucking on a cigar and phoning around the country to thank supporters.

By the time Clinton arrived in Seattle, his eyes were puffy and red from lack of sleep. He begged his advisers to postpone the session with Chrétien for twenty-four hours, but they persuaded him that the increasingly anxious

Canadians shouldn't be left dangling. At this point, only Jean Chrétien stood in the way of finally nailing down the largest free trade zone in the world. Clinton's advisers wanted it signed and sealed before anything could go wrong.

By and large, the details had been hammered out over the previous two weeks. On the day of the Chrétien government's swearing-in, the Prime Minister's Office passed the NAFTA file to the responsible minister, International Trade Minister Roy MacLaren, the party's strongest free trader. Three Red Book items remained to be addressed: realization of Canada's long-held desire for common codes on subsidies and dumping, which the Liberals felt would reduce trade harassment from the protectionist Congress; and an exemption, similar to one granted Mexico, from NAFTA trade and investment rules for the energy industry.

Rhetoric aside, Chrétien didn't really have much of a quarrel with the state of Canada-U.S. relations under the Tories. He shared with the vast majority of Canadians a desire for positive relations with the Americans. As his former business associate Gordon Ritchie, Canada's second-in-command in the free trade negotiations, said, Chrétien knew that the only thing worse than getting along with the Americans was not getting along with them. The economy of his district, Chrétien noted in an interview, depended on exports of pulp and paper and aluminium.

But he felt Mulroney had erred in allowing himself to look like a supplicant. Chrétien vowed he would refrain from fishing with the president of the United States. The symbolism changed. The first time Chrétien wrote to Clinton, the Privy Council Office, employing the style favoured in the Mulroney years, drafted a letter with the salutation "Dear Bill" and sent it over for Chrétien's signature. It came zipping back within hours with a terse message attached. All correspondence with Clinton would open "Dear Mr. President."

On NAFTA, though, Chrétien had talked himself into substantive differences. The deal's supposed "energy give-away" troubled him greatly. Former advisers described Chrétien as an unusual politician to brief. He refused to engage in hours of discussion weighing the pros and cons of a given issue. "The art of briefing him is to get it out fast and give him just what he needs to know," said one bureaucratic veteran. At these briefings, Chrétien would appear totally disengaged, as if not listening. But in reality he was scanning the information, trying to situate it on a grid composed of his instincts and his experiences. Suddenly, he would lock in his coordinates and want to hear no more. At that point, it became almost impossible to change his view.

On the NAFTA promises, MacLaren and a variety of advisers explained that the Calgary oil patch actually favoured NAFTA and that the provisions in the agreement merely reflected Canada's obligations, in any case, as a member of the International Energy Agency. But Chrétien, who had served in Liberal cabinets in an era of energy shortages, not surpluses, refused to adjust his coordinates. He worried about Canada's energy security in the face of a future OPEC crisis. The others found the concern out of date and out of touch. But he was the boss, so MacLaren cast about for a means to address his concerns without jeopardizing NAFTA overall.

As he suspected, the Americans refused to budge on energy. Canada, like Mexico, already enjoyed a NAFTA exemption, but had chosen to apply it to cultural industries. Working with his officials and Goldenberg, MacLaren persuaded the Americans to accept a unilateral Canadian declaration setting out that "in the event of shortages or in order to conserve Canada's exhaustible energy resources, the government will interpret and apply the NAFTA in a way which maximizes energy security for Canadians." The declaration would not be part of the agreement and would not bind the other trading partners. It was designed to satisfy the prime minister of Canada as much as anyone else that the "energy give-away" had been addressed.

The Americans also told MacLaren they would agree to establish two side panels to work on the subsidies and dumping issues over the following two years — the other main Liberal demands. But there would be no renegotiation of the overall agreement. Approval of NAFTA would proceed regardless of the output of these working groups.

Blanchard also came up with a symbolic gift for the Canadians. On his cross-country rail journey, he had stopped in Winnipeg and met with Lloyd Axworthy. The Manitoban expressed strong concerns that Canadian water could be diverted under NAFTA. Neither Blanchard nor the Canadian officials shared this analysis. But with nothing to lose, Blanchard secured a letter for Canada assuring that the United States had no designs on its neighbour's water resources. In the opinion of the Canadian trade negotiators, the letter merely restated the terms of the agreement. But it gave Chrétien another piece of paper to wave around.

By the time they arrived in Seattle, the outline of the deal was well in place. After a quick round of introductions, Chrétien and Clinton retired to a pair of wing chairs in the middle of the room while their retinues of advisers scrambled to their places. Their seats fanned out from the leaders in a horseshoe shape, making it difficult to hear their conversation. The room lacked any semblance of intimacy, the ambience was further spoiled by Clinton's fatigue — it was already 11 p.m. Washington time.

Clinton's advisers, mindful of his exhaustion, had suggested that the president take the pressure off himself by seeking out Chrétien's views on a variety of foreign issues. He asked what Chrétien thought they should do about the slaughter in Bosnia. Chrétien hadn't been briefed on the subject. His row of aides had prepared him to talk trade. "That's a very tough one. I don't know," he replied. Clinton tried him on Haiti, but again the conversation failed to take flight. The meeting had a stiff, awkward feel. Everyone could tell Clinton desperately wanted to be somewhere else.

Finally, they turned to NAFTA. On this, Chrétien came prepared. He explained the significance to Canada of the subsidy and dumping issues. He also argued for the energy exemption, although it seemed futile to his advisers by that point. Clinton, slouching in his chair, said he would abide by the terms that their officials had worked out. With that out of the way, Clinton relaxed a bit, telling Chrétien that he had read his autobiography and couldn't believe the number of cabinet posts the prime minister had held at one time or another. He said he had been left wondering why this guy couldn't hold down a job. Chrétien replied in an equally light-hearted manner, to Clinton's obvious delight. By the time he took his leave to go upstairs to bed, a bonding process had begun.

The Americans wanted to announce the deal then and there. But Chrétien felt he should discuss the decision further with some of his cabinet ministers, at the very least so they didn't learn about it first in the media. In any case, his advisers worried about the optics of him flying to Seattle, being squeezed into Clinton's schedule at night, and then acceding to U.S. demands to sign NAFTA. The scene lent itself to a potential media interpretation of Chrétien as a supplicant, a prime minister who said he would be businesslike with the Americans and then caved in at his first opportunity. The Chrétien advisers insisted on putting some distance between Seattle and its outcome.

Canadian media coverage of the trip focussed almost entirely on Chrétien's brief meeting with Clinton. But the Canadian delegation had an agenda extending far beyond NAFTA. The APEC meeting presented an ideal opportunity, they thought, to cultivate Asian relationships, most notably with China.

Chrétien devoted special attention to Chinese President Jiang Zemin, who, under APEC's protocol of arranging leaders in the alphabetical order of their countries, conveniently sat next to him at all events. Jiang arrived determined to mount a charm offensive that would make his hosts — and everyone else — think more about China's future than of the bloody images of the massacre of students in 1989 at Beijing's Tiananmen Square. They had their man in Jean Chrétien.

Privately, Foreign Affairs officials thought Jiang, a sixty-seven-year-old lifelong Communist, almost spectacularly unimpressive. A confidential briefing note described his manner as "rambling" and "buffoonish" and observed tartly that he "thinks he is sophisticated." He was, the note concluded, most likely "a transitional figure" among Chinese leaders. But nothing in Chrétien's manner suggested anything other than the greatest reverence for his Chinese counterpart. Jiang, Chrétien announced at a news conference, "is a really extroverted guy. I spent a lot of time talking with him." Enough time, anyway, that he elicited an invitation from Jiang to come to China the following year.

The Seattle summit provided important early clues about the character of the Chrétien Liberals. They made their peace with the Americans and aggressively courted the perpetrators of Tiananmen Square. They would be a party for trade, even at a cost to concerns like human rights or the environment.

Jean Chrétien, the guy who had skipped the Trudeau generation, was determined to return the Liberals to their trade roots as the party of reciprocity, of lower tariffs, of the Auto Pact. The Conservatives, the authors of the National Deal, had historically protected the interests of the entrenched central Canadian business oligarchy by erecting tariff walls. In 1891, as Liberal leader, and again in 1911, as prime minister, Sir Wilfrid Laurier challenged this compact by proposing trade deals with the Americans, going down to defeat both times. In 1947, Mackenzie King negotiated a secret free trade deal with the Americans, but got cold feet before making the fact public.

Postwar Canada, under the economic leadership of C.D. Howe, minister of everything, and his able deputy, Mitchell Sharp, welcomed American capital to develop the country's resources and expand its industry. Over time, a backlash developed against Howe, finding its most eloquent expression in the voice of a patrician Toronto accountant and Liberal

activist named Walter Gordon, the scion of the Clarkson Gordon accounting firm. In the 1957 report of his royal commission on the country's
economy, Gordon lamented the infiltration of Canada by more and more
American branch plants. He was disturbed by the stultifying effects on
Canadian technological development, and he worried that Toronto, rather
than serving as the business capital of a sovereign nation, would be relegated to some northern version of Philadelphia, a once-proud financial
centre condemned to the minor leagues. The issue wasn't really trade but
investment, and its main champion was more conservative than radical.
Gordon's Liberalism — with its emphasis on nationalism, intervention, and
social justice — fit perfectly in an era under the influence of expatriate
Canadian economist John Kenneth Galbraith. Gordon's ideas dominated
the Liberal Party policy conference at Kingston in 1960.

But for all the noise it would make and the following it attracted, most
Liberals remained wary of Gordon's nationalism. At the party's 1966
national policy convention at Ottawa's Château Laurier Hotel, the free
trade wing, led by Mitchell Sharp, routed Gordon and his disciples. Sharp,
who preferred to judge corporations on the basis of their performance
rather than their citizenship, lined up the support of every delegate from the
free trade stronghold of western Canada, save the two Axworthys, Lloyd
and Tom, and one long-forgotten other. The Liberal Party was not yet
prepared to say no to the Americans and to the prosperity Canada had
imported along with their capital. "Liberals are a patriotic lot," Jean
Chrétien's mentor wrote in his 1993 autobiography. "Not all of them, however, equate patriotism with economic nationalism of the kind espoused
by Gordon and his followers."

The two poles of Liberal trade policy continued their competition over
the next quarter-century. Gordon inspired a generation of brilliant political operatives, people like Keith Davey, Jim Coutts, and Tom Axworthy.
These children of Gordon would exercise tremendous influence during the
Trudeau years, pushing the party, despite Trudeau's intellectual hostility
to the concept, in new nationalistic directions. But the Sharp wing continually blunted their advances. Even at the 1984 leadership convention —
after one of the most nationalistic terms in Liberal history and with the
party's western flank badly diminished — a survey of delegates found that
46 per cent supported free trade while 47 per cent opposed it.

Intellectually exhausted in his last term, Trudeau had turned to a former finance minister, Donald Macdonald, to head a royal commission into

Canada's economic prospects, just as St. Laurent had turned to Walter Gordon a generation earlier. Macdonald made for an interesting choice. He hailed from the geographic centre of Gordonism, downtown Toronto, recruited at the age of thirty by the Liberal patriarch of economic nationalism himself to run in Rosedale. At the 1966 convention at which Gordon and Sharp had crossed swords, Macdonald had organized the floor for Gordon. In caucus, he championed such nationalistic causes as pulling Canada out of NATO and breaking with the American isolation of China. As minister of energy, he personally oversaw the creation of Petro-Canada.

But after quitting politics, Macdonald went to Bay Street to practise law and, in short order, came to view the world through a different lens. He did not set out to support free trade. But his travels across the country with the royal commission convinced him that for Canadian business to break out of its torpor, governments would have to remove the last vestiges of John A. Macdonald's protective barrier. He reflected with regret on many of the initiatives he had sponsored or supported as a politician: the Foreign Investment Review Agency, the creation of Petro-Canada, a made-in-Canada oil policy, and ultimately, after he had quit politics, the National Energy Program. "In due course, I looked back after fifteen years of effort and realized that very little of what we had done had actually served our purpose. The U.S. companies were still powerful and Canadian competition had been badly stifled," he said in an interview. With the election of the right-of-centre John Turner as leader in 1984, the Liberals appeared to be tacking back towards a less ambiguous pursuit of liberalized trade and investment. The Ottawa bureaucracy, wanting to shield Canada from the protectionists on the warpath south of the border, prepared for the inevitability of free trade negotiations with the Americans, whichever party won the 1984 election.

But the election débâcle — with the Liberals reduced to forty seats — left Turner powerless. The business wing of the party was, by and large, routed. The shrunken caucus consisted overwhelmingly of a generation of Liberals, like Lloyd Axworthy and the Rat Pack, who had been inspired by Walter Gordon's economic nationalism and had come of age under Trudeau. When Macdonald's report was released in 1985, his call for Canadians to take a "leap of faith" in favour of free trade stuck in the craw of this new, decidedly more left-wing Liberal caucus. In the 1988 election, where the Canada-U.S. Free Trade Agreement was the defining issue, the Liberals and Conservatives soaked in each other's historic bathwater.

Parliament was called back in December 1988 for a special session to pass the free trade bill. It received final reading in the Commons after an all-night sitting that lasted into the early hours of December 24. After the vote, David Walker, the rookie Liberal MP from Winnipeg, walked out the west exit of the Centre Block with Lloyd Axworthy, the most articulate and passionate of the anti-free-trade crusaders. Parliament Hill, bathed in 23,650 Christmas lights, projected a wondrous lustre. As they strolled down the hill into the deserted downtown core, Axworthy reflected on the lost battle. "It's not the end of Canada," he remarked wistfully. "The country will survive. But it will be a much different place. We lost a certain dream with that vote. We will have to do things from now on in a very different way."

Jean Chrétien, upon taking over in 1990, knew the party had to move forward. He named MacLaren, the party's purest free trader, his critic for international trade. Typically for Chrétien, he didn't articulate his reasoning. He phoned MacLaren in Toronto and simply said he knew where he stood on the issue and wanted him for the post. But Chrétien, ever the gradualist who felt safest in the middle, at the same time named Lloyd Axworthy external affairs critic. He gave them adjoining offices, although the passageway saw little traffic.

MacLaren's appointment represented a reprieve for him. Despairing of his party's positions on the deficit and trade, he had decided earlier in the year that he had no political future. As Liberal finance critic following the 1988 election, he hadn't been able to bring himself to join the chorus criticizing the Tories over the deficit, trade, or the GST. Out of sync with caucus sentiment, he gave up his critic's post in the summer of 1989, seven months after assuming the role. When he hired John Hancock, a Cambridge University Ph.D., as his policy adviser and speechwriter in early 1990, he warned that it could be a short-term position. He was close to packing it in and returning to Toronto.

Chrétien's call revitalized him. In June 1991, MacLaren laid out a radical free trade agenda in an internal discussion paper called "Wide Open," one approved for dissemination by Chrétien. "The fundamental flaw of the current government's trade policy is not that it has opened our economy to the United States, but that it has done so to the exclusion of the rest of the world," the paper declared. He called on Canada to become "aggressively global" in launching free trade talks with Asia, Europe, and Latin America — placing the 20 per cent of its trade with the rest of the world on an equal footing with the 80 per cent with the United States. He was the crazy Canuck hurtling down the hill in pursuit of this liberalized world order. "The task for the Liberal party," he wrote, "is not only to convince Canadians of these realities but to demonstrate why it is best qualified to confront them." He believed this possible in Jean Chrétien's Liberal Party.

Typically, Chrétien had never taken a strong stand on this issue that divided Liberals. He campaigned against "the Mulroney deal" in the 1988 election, but those closest to him knew his instincts were not those of an economic nationalist. They also knew that whatever he thought, he would act pragmatically.

To Maude Barlow, the energetic anti-free-trade crusader and former Liberal, there was nothing ambiguous about Chrétien's trade stance. Before the 1990 Liberal leadership race, she and other anti-free-trade activists had met with Chrétien. He told them of his experience on the board of Consolidated Bathurst — he always called it Connie B. — and recounted how his father had worked at the company's mill in Shawinigan. Connie B's take-over by U.S. forestry giant Stone Consolidated saddened him. But the pragmatist in Chrétien told him the time had arrived to move on. By the time of the next election "the monster will have had too many babies," Barlow recalled him saying.

The Aylmer conference in November 1991 marked the turning point, a three-day event meant to drag a Walter Gordon caucus into a Mitchell Sharp era, just as the Kingston conference of a generation earlier had set the tone for a C.D. Howe party refashioning itself in Walter Gordon's image. But how hard to push and how fast? The organizers debated whether to use the word "globalization," which sounded like a Tory plot, in the titles of the sessions. Eddie Goldenberg and Chaviva Hošek decided in the affirmative. They chose American economist Lester Thurow to deliver the keynote address. Before he took to the stage, Kenneth Courtis, a Canadian economist living in Japan, and Peter Nicholson, a Liberal banker with a formidable intellect who would re-emerge later as Finance Minister Paul Martin's personal economics guru, softened up the audience. Courtis described the challenge posed by Asia, and asserted that those Canadians who reject the high social costs of adapting to new global realities had it wrong. "The social cost of not moving to adjust is going to be even greater." Nicholson warned that societies that boycott the competition for global investment "can, at best, look forward to a life of genteel decline and at worst, a descent into social chaos."

Chrétien sat through the entire proceedings, sharing a table with Roy MacLaren. The message was twofold: to let the party know he took the subject seriously, and to disabuse the public of the stubborn notion that he took no interest in issues. At the conference's end, he embraced globalization with uncharacteristic clarity. "Protectionism is not left-wing or right-wing. It is simply passé," he declared in wrapping up the event. "Globalization is not right-wing or left-wing. It is simply a fact of life."

Walter Gordon's intellectual offspring found Aylmer and its carefully crafted message galling. The 1960 Kingston conference had penetrated deeply into their psyches. Kingston had laid the groundwork for the social reforms of the Pearson years and opened up a world of possibilities. What were they to make of this? That the global economy precluded much. Neo-liberalism, as articulated in Aylmer, looked to many just like neo-conservatism, except brought to you by a nicer group of people. In the corridors, disconsolate left-wing Liberals moaned about the party's surrender to the corporate agenda.

In one of those Kodak moments that perfectly captured the debate between the two wings of Liberalism, Peter Dalglish, a social Liberal out of the Axworthy camp who had founded an organization called Street Kids International, challenged keynote speaker Thurow from the floor abut the so-called virtues of the Asian model. Thurow had extolled the Japanese education system, praising the fact that 96 per cent of kids graduated from high school, which meant that "Japan's team" in the new global economic competition came to the game better prepared than the American team. Dalglish stood at a mike in the rear of the room and demanded to know about the other 4 per cent. "A lot of the other 4 per cent commit suicide," he asserted. "Japan has one of the highest adolescent suicide rates in the world." The global system created winners and losers, he said. The responsibility of government was to care for the losers.

Thurow refused to bend. "It is certainly true that a very small number of Japanese high school students commit suicide. A much larger number of American students commit suicide because of drugs, pregnancy, whatever. And if you tell me a child is going to commit suicide, which is horrible, but my only choice is if they commit suicide over teenage pregnancy or school exams, I think I know which way I want them to go."

Dalglish went after him again, about Japan's environment record. "The Japanese never will care about the environment. Why? Because it doesn't reflect in their bottom line. They only care about winning."

Thurow shot back that he wasn't telling Dalglish to become Japanese; he couldn't even if he wanted to. "But I'm telling you you're going to have to play in this economic ball game if you want a world-class standard of living."

The exchange exposed the true schism between social and business Liberals. Except for the extreme wing of nationalistic protectionists like Maude Barlow, Edmonton publisher Mel Hurtig, and Winnipeg business-man William Loewen (all of whom would leave the party), most progressive Liberals, when they bothered to think about the issue, realized, as Nicholson had said, that there was no place to hide from globalization. But whereas the business Liberals like Nicholson, MacLaren, and Martin emphasized creating Canadian winners in the global economy, the social Liberals like Dalglish and Axworthy focussed on the protection of the losers. Neither approach precluded the other, but suspicions between the two camps ran high.

To MacLaren, "Aylmer was the watershed." The weekend couldn't have gone better. He had often said fibre optics is neither right nor left; now Chrétien mouthed his language. He would look back on Aylmer as a pay-off for the missionary work he and Martin and Manley had undertaken in the post-1988 caucus. "Once Aylmer happened and the leader of the opposition endorsed its discussion, as he so clearly did in the summing-up speech, to a real degree the debate was over."

Rather than sit through it, Axworthy fled Ottawa for a prearranged date to attend the Grey Cup game in Winnipeg with his brothers (the weekend marked the first anniversary of their father's death). Before departing, though, he made plain his take on Aylmer, telling a reporter: "All this talk about globalization is just a cover for right-wing ideology."

Even in Winnipeg, he couldn't escape news of the rightward drift. A boom mike caught MacLaren sounding triumphal at the conference's end. Asked by a colleague how he thought Axworthy would react, MacLaren broke into his impish smile and, unaware of the eavesdropping press, declared: "Eat your heart out, Lloyd Axworthy!"

Axworthy tried to stake out a new position a few weeks later in a speech at the McGill University Faculty of Law, stating that "globalism did not come as a revelation in a burning bush at Aylmer for most, if not all, Liberals," but warning against what he called a new "globalism Realpolitik" gaining currency in parts of the party. He beseeched Liberals not to follow the siren call of a world order guided by transnational corporations and unfettered markets; that was the way of the Tories. MacLaren regarded it as a final bleat of defiance.

Indeed, the pragmatic streak in all Liberals, Axworthy included, drew the Liberals back together as the prospect of power grew stronger. "All of us felt an overwhelming sense that the factionalism could not be allowed to continue," Axworthy acknowledged several years later. "With the Tories collapsing the way they were, clearly it became really important to find an accommodation between the different views."

In the run-up to the party's policy convention that winter, Liberal MPs cobbled together their compromise. Delegates rejected a resolution committing a Liberal government to immediately abrogate any free trade agreements, with Axworthy publicly speaking against it. Instead, they endorsed the motion that stated essentially the position that would go into the Red Book: "abrogating trade agreements should be only a last resort if satisfactory changes cannot be negotiated." It was vintage Chrétien, resorting to just the kind of ambiguity he so preferred over clear, polarizing choices. Abrogation if necessary, but not necessarily abrogation.

The resolution didn't end the differences, but it succeeded in bridging them. Axworthy read the Liberal position as a course leading to probable abrogation. "We should put down our list of areas for renegotiation and go down to Washington and see if they're interested," he said in March 1992. "If they are, you sit down and do it again. If they're not, I guess you exercise your right to abrogate."

MacLaren, meanwhile, continued to press against calls for renegotiation. In the aftermath of the policy convention, he wrote to Chrétien accurately forecasting that the Americans might refuse to renegotiate, leaving the Liberals with the stark choice of continuing with the existing agreement or following through on abrogation. "I urge we use the word abrogation sparingly," he counselled.

Chrétien worked diligently to hold his fragile consensus together. In May of 1993, the Conservatives tried to smoke out the Liberals by introducing the NAFTA bill into the House of Commons. Most of his advisers, including Eddie Goldenberg, pleaded with Chrétien to support the bill and purge the Liberals' anti-free-trade record, once and for all, as a potential election issue. But Chrétien countered that the party could not promote a policy calling for improvements to the deal and then vote in favour of its original form. The Liberals settled on a position that allowed them to oppose the bill for peripheral reasons.

Still, Chrétien didn't seem comfortable about the vote, at least not to MacLaren. The two of them flew back together from Toronto that day. Chrétien's driver got them to the House of Commons just as the division bells stopped ringing. They slipped into their seats with seconds to spare. Along the way, they had joked about how much easier it would be to miss the roll call altogether. But they did their duty: both stood to vote against NAFTA, knowing full well that, once seated on the other side of the House, they would take a decidedly different position.

Six months later, they were on the other side. On Thursday, December 2, Chrétien informed his cabinet of Canada's intention of proclaiming NAFTA into law, creating a continental trade bloc of 360 million people, larger than the European Union. After the Seattle summit, he had canvassed key ministers privately. On this morning, he chose to present the decision to cabinet as a fait accompli, raising the matter at the end of the agenda and then adjourning the meeting without inviting debate. In the early days of the government, with the prime minister firmly in charge, nobody presumed to challenge his quick draw on the gavel. In any case, it would have been hard to resist given the support of the three major economic ministers, namely the three Ms — Martin in Finance, MacLaren in International Trade, and Manley in Industry.

As it turned out, the Liberal demands on NAFTA did not result in the change of a single word in the 2,000-page text. Instead, Chrétien secured three pages of side agreements, including a unilateral and altogether meaningless five-paragraph declaration on energy security and a non-binding joint statement calling for the three countries to spend the next two years talking about subsidies and dumping. These talks did not commit the parties, in the words of U.S. Trade Representative Mickey Kantor, to "any particular outcome." NAFTA would go ahead as it was.

Like Clinton, who had emerged as the belated champion of George Bush's deal, it had fallen to Jean Chrétien to pilot into port the trade deal negotiated by Brian Mulroney and Michael Wilson. The gap between Republican and Democrat, between Conservative and Liberal disappeared. Liberalized trade enjoyed a bipartisan consensus.

Chrétien came to office with a limited feel for foreign policy. He lacked the same experience in External Affairs — he had served in the portfolio for just a matter of weeks before the 1984 election — that he enjoyed in economic ministries. Issues like Canada's presence in Bosnia perplexed him. The long sweep of alliance-making did not lend itself to his instinctive judgments. His meetings with foreign leaders tended to be more about comparative domestic politics than any exploration of the intricacies of international diplomacy.

But trade was a different story. As industry and trade minister in the 1970s, he had loved the part of the job that took him around the world as Canada's chief salesman. He would subsequently resurrect the role in his high-profile Team Canada missions, investing these missions with an importance beyond that ever accorded to the promotion of Canadian goods and services abroad.

For Chrétien, such an emphasis fit perfectly with his election promise to concentrate on jobs and economic growth. It had become obvious that a historic shift had occurred in the Canadian economy. In the late 1980s, exports had accounted for just 25 per cent of economic activity. Now they represented nearly 40 per cent, a staggering increase in such a short period. All the growth in the new global economy was on the trade side.

Naturally enough, Chrétien, elected on a jobs and growth agenda, set great stock by expanding Canada's trade links, especially as other avenues of job creation proved themselves dead ends. The government lacked the money to create jobs directly, and quickly learned that the prescriptions of the Red Book worked better in theory than in practice. Over time, trade policy would pretty well subsume industrial policy. A few years earlier, environmental considerations had been hot, even if they meant restricting trade. Now the opposite would be true. The same situation prevailed with human rights. The denizens of Jurassic Park, as the trade bureaucracy was known to its rivals, became one of the most powerful influences in Ottawa. The new prime minister equated foreign policy with exports and exports with jobs. That was what he had promised. This was how he would deliver it.

After cabinet, Chrétien and MacLaren walked across the street to the National Press Building to report on the outcome of the NAFTA negotiations with the Americans. MacLaren, who had left his coat behind, would remember feeling cold on the exterior but warmed inside. Two years past Aylmer, his "Wide Open" vision had triumphed. Chrétien, on the other hand, looked ill at ease. He worried that he would be branded as having caved in to the Americans and broken a promise. It could be the end of a short-lived honeymoon. "It's not a perfect situation, but that's not possible in life," he shrugged when challenged by the reporters. "We have done, in my judgment, more than people said we would."

With that, the Liberal government buried the legacy of the 1988 free trade election. Liberals once again, in the spirit of Laurier and C.D. Howe, stood for free trade and would, over the coming months, pursue its attainment with abandon. But for now — just a month past the election — Chrétien didn't want Canadians to dwell too much on a breathtaking reversal. The following day, he announced the cancellation of the controversial Pearson Airport privatization, knocking NAFTA off the front pages.

Chrétien need not have worried. He seemed coated in Teflon; nothing stuck. Canadians didn't seem to care about anything other than the fact he wasn't named Brian Mulroney. As his first Christmas as prime minister approached, he could look back on the opening months with satisfaction. His government had gotten off to a fast start and he had slipped into the role of prime minister of Canada like a pair of old slippers. Despite deep-seated public cynicism about politicians, Canadians seemed perfectly at ease with a lifelong politician who, only a few months earlier, had been dismissed as yesterday's man. His government had already slid by two potential crises unscathed — the adoption of NAFTA and the replacement of John Crow — a sure sign Canadians wanted to believe in their government again after all the upheavals of the Mulroney years. He had set a tone and a direction.

On New Year's Eve, less than two months into office, Chrétien invited his relatives to 24 Sussex Drive to help him ring in the new Liberal era. A little after midnight, some of them decided to go for a swim and sauna in the poolhouse built for Pierre Trudeau. Giddy at their new station in life, they frolicked on the way back to the house. Jean Chrétien gazed up at the sky. Next door, looking down on the ruckus from a window in his residence, he could see the ambassador of France taking in the scene of the prime minister of Canada making angels in the snow.

7

A MAN WITH
A PLAN

As the new Liberal government settled in during the early weeks of 1994, Paul Martin and Marcel Massé began to talk. Like most Liberals, Martin was a bit mystified by the well-spoken, bald-headed man seated among them at the cabinet table. Massé had come to politics late in life. At fifty-three, he was a political novice, with less than six months as a member of the party. But as a lifelong public servant, he probably knew more about government than anybody else in the room, including Chrétien.

Although he enjoyed little public profile, his impact was immense. It would be hard to consider the inner workings of the Chrétien government without reference to Marcel Massé, O.C., Q.C., B.A., LL.B., Dip. Int'l Law, B. Phil., Rhodes Scholar, Nuffield Scholar, graduate of the Quiet Revolution. At the tender age of thirty-eight, he served as clerk of the Privy Council in Joe Clark's short-lived 1979–80 government. While other Liberals sulked in opposition, he served the Mulroney government, lastly as secretary to the cabinet for intergovernmental affairs, a position he had also held under Trudeau. In the interim, his experience included two stretches as president of the Canadian International Development Agency, a period as deputy minister for external affairs, and four years at the International Monetary Fund in Washington.

This well-seasoned rookie had been handed a special assignment by the prime minister, one not well understood by Martin or the other ministers. His job title read minister of intergovernmental affairs (simple enough) *and* minister responsible for public service renewal (whatever that meant). Under the rubric of "getting government right," he explained to Martin, he was charged with both restructuring the operations of the government of Canada and reordering relations with the provinces.

Paul Martin had a strong but unformed sense of the failures of government. But he didn't have the foggiest notion of how to fix them. Marcel Massé shared with Martin a view of government in the 1990s. It did too many things, and not enough of them well. The difference was that he had a plan, a comprehensive mental map that connected the dots between the deficit, federal-provincial relations, and increasing public dissatisfaction with public services. He knew the government inside out, and he possessed the sort of analytical mind that could turn Paul Martin's unformed urges into a coherent strategy.

But Massé lacked one thing Paul Martin possessed in spades: clout. If that hadn't been apparent to him from day one, it certainly became clear on November 16, the day that David Dodge made his initial presentation to cabinet on the government's woeful financial condition.

Nobody in the room — not Martin, not MacLaren, not Chrétien — had a better appreciation of the deficit's corrosive impact on Ottawa's ability to govern, indeed on the nature of the federation itself. Massé had devoted his final months of public service to the subject, chairing a committee of deputy ministers considering the way ahead. Now he made one of his first interventions in a cabinet meeting, underlining the seriousness of the challenge laid out by Dodge. His sure grasp of the matter was indisputable, which wasn't of much consequence since none of his colleagues chose to dispute him. Instead, they ignored him. The discussion went on for another forty-five minutes, with another dozen or so ministers speaking. Only one of them made even the most oblique reference to Massé's remarks.

Massé analyzed the situation as it unfolded. He was more confused than crestfallen. He sought out a familiar face, catching Glen Shortliffe, his former colleague and still the clerk of the Privy Council, before he left the room. "Glen, I'm curious. Was there something wrong with my intervention? Was I unclear?" he asked.

Shortliffe laughed. "No, Marcel," he replied. "But you have just learned your first lesson about cabinet. It's not what is said, but who says it." Massé rolled the reply around in his mind. He decided his first order of business would have to be raising his own standing with the other ministers.

As he and Martin felt each other out, he confessed he probably lacked both the leverage and the information required to accomplish his assigned task. His ministry had been situated within the Privy Council Office. He had no real department of his own, no analytical capacity, no institutional or, apparently, even personal credibility. The bureaucrats and other ministers would stonewall him as assuredly as they had stonewalled Conservative Deputy Prime Minister Erik Nielsen's outside advisers a decade earlier when they had taken a run at reinventing the government. Massé suggested a partnership with Martin and his department.

If others among his new Liberal compatriots had bothered to check out Marcel Massé, they might have hung on his words more closely. Certainly, Jean Chrétien saw something he liked. Massé had been one of the party's star candidates, hand-picked by Chrétien to run in Hull-Aylmer riding over the objections of the riding association. The Liberals, in the person of Jean Pelletier, had been after him since the previous October. Unknown to them, he was also being courted by the Tories. Defence Minister Marcel Masse, his namesake other than for the difference of an acute accent over the last letter of the family name, thought he would make a clever successor in his riding of Frontenac.

Scanning his résumé, one could understand the attention. Massé possessed a sparkling record of achievement. But he came to his new occupation bathed in almost total innocence about the real world of politics, as he would demonstrate in his first weeks on the job.

He agonized over his decision to run, even though the Liberals were handing him one of their safest seats and, better yet, the riding where he actually resided. He pulled down nearly $15,000 a month as one of Ottawa's top public servants. As an MP, even a cabinet minister, he would have to take a cut in pay. And he wouldn't draw any salary whatsoever in the period between his departure from the public service and his swearing-in as a member of Parliament.

Certainly Massé felt impelled to run by the political circumstances around him. The constitutional misadventures of the Conservatives under Brian Mulroney deeply troubled him and, even as an apostle of change, he thought the approach being hatched for reform of the public service wrong-headed. A wholly unrelated matter, however, finally pushed him over the edge. Ironically, the man who ultimately persuaded him to take up the Liberal banner — totally inadvertently — was a Conservative, Joe Clark, under whom Massé had worked first in the Prime Minister's Office and then at External Affairs.

From 1989 to February 1993 — during the final operatic scenes of the Meech Lake Accord and the highly improvised Charlottetown exercise — Massé presided over the Canadian International Development Agency. It was his second stint in the post, a job he loved. He had written his thesis at Oxford on the development of the manufacturing industry in Senegal. On field trips to the West African state in the 1960s, he courted his future wife, Josée M'Baye. When it came to CIDA, Massé could actually get lathered up. Which is exactly how he felt in the winter of 1993 when his minister, Barbara McDougall, informed him of her plans to alter the agency's operating practices.

Massé advised her that the charter governing the agency required her to take the matter to cabinet. Then he went off to warn his good friend, the former prime minister and external affairs minister, Joe Clark, now in charge of the constitutional file.

Massé intended to give Clark a heads-up so that he would be prepared when McDougall came to cabinet. But he hadn't counted on Clark's reaction. The veteran politician coolly said that he understood Massé's special attachment to CIDA, but he had to remember that he was just a civil servant, and civil servants obeyed orders. If he wanted to make the decisions himself, then he should run for office. Other men might have blanched, the crispness of the admonition wounding their pride. Massé judged it sensible advice.

But he put off making a final decision. In the midst of these deliberations, in March, he accepted a new post in the Privy Council Office as secretary to the cabinet for intergovernmental affairs. He was in charge of cleaning up after the Charlottetown fiasco. Later, eyebrows would be raised over his decision to participate in some of the innermost deliberations of the Mulroney government while entertaining the Liberal offer. Those who knew him well figured that his Cartesian mind would simply have compartmentalized the two matters, without even considering the appearance of conflict.

Finally in June, Massé made the jump. He took out a small mortgage on his house to provide the bridge financing to his new life. Chrétien was to make the announcement himself at a rally in Montreal on Sunday, June 20. He had frantically sought out star candidates to enhance his battered credibility in Quebec and was eager to trumpet his big catch. The story was leaked to the *Globe and Mail*'s Jeffrey Simpson, who published a column about the impending announcement in Friday's paper. Rumours swirled around Ottawa that Massé had been summarily escorted out of the Langevin Block by Glen Shortliffe. Both denied it. Shortliffe corroborated that Massé had informed him of his imminent departure several days earlier and that he then passed the information to Mulroney. With the news now public, Massé didn't wait out his final working day as a bureaucrat. "I left the office by 10:30 in the morning," he said. "Glen didn't have to ask me to go."

With his round head on a rounded body — a dead ringer for the fictional spymaster George Smiley, figured one John Le Carré fan — Massé was a familiar enough figure in Ottawa. But he was also an enigma, even to many of those who had worked alongside him over more than twenty years in the public service. Unlike so many people who congregate in a national capital, he could not be easily pigeonholed by region or ideology. He seemed to have been born in one of those labyrinthine office towers across the river in Hull, the product of some long-forgotten interdepartmental liaison. Even those close to him knew little of his roots.

André Gourd, who had been Quebec's delegate general in Ottawa under the provincial Liberals, briefly worked for Massé after the PQ victory in September 1994 relieved him of his appointment. Gourd arranged a dinner at Club St-Denis on the eastern fringe of downtown Montreal for the minister. They arrived early and Massé suggested a stroll through the neighbourhood. He pointed out the church where he had been baptized and the school where his father had taught. Gourd had assumed that Massé was from New Brunswick, where he had worked for several years in the 1970s. Certainly, he had never imagined him coming from a working-class Montreal neighbourhood.

Born on June 23, 1940, Massé was the third of twelve children. His father was a schoolteacher, his mother a francophone from Saskatchewan. His father, to whom he bore a remarkable physical resemblance, was a strongly nationalist figure, he recalled years later, who would be called upon at election time to deliver speeches about the protection of the French language and culture. In the classification of the day, he was a *bleu* — conservative, authoritarian, true to a line in Quebec politics that ran from the Ultramontanists through to Duplessis. The senior Massé was the first generation off the farm and the only member of his family with a classical education. Indeed, one of the attributes that distinguished him in the 1940s and 1950s was his passion for schooling. "He didn't have money, but he was going to give us an education as our heritage," his son recalled. Nearly all of his twelve children made it to university.

Marcel's academic brilliance surfaced early. With a little after-hours tutoring, he finished grade one in three months and skipped fourth grade entirely. He completed his seven years of primary education in four years and was accepted into classical college at age ten. It was to be that way through-out his life. He was awarded his B.A. just as he turned eighteen and com-pleted law school a month before being legally permitted to sign a contract.

Massé came of age as the Quiet Revolution flowered. But he lacked the nationalist passions of some of his classmates and relatives. His mother had fostered in him an appreciation of the French fact outside Quebec. "Once you learn that, you cannot consider that Quebec can build borders around itself and forget the other francophones who have fought for the French language and culture as much as Quebeckers," he would reflect. Her son's rebellions would take other forms.

The first of these rebellions took place at seventeen, as he neared com-pletion of his undergraduate studies at Université de Montréal. He decided to apply for law at McGill University. "I wanted to learn English. I couldn't get out in the wide world without speaking English. I wanted to look at other societies." Some of his relatives thought him a *vendu*, a trai-tor to his people. His father, wanting to be supportive of his gifted son, was torn. There was not only the language question, but a religious one as well. The elder Massé wrote to the legendary bishop of Montreal, Cardinal Léger, who ruled that the precocious teenager could go to McGill as long as he joined the Newman Club, the Catholic society on campus.

While at McGill, he struck up a friendship with an exchange student from Poland. Upon graduation, he applied to take a diploma in international law at the University of Warsaw. That was to be his second rebellion. "To go to McGill was to rebel against the ambient society, that is to say, 'You guys want to stick to a kind of francophone mould. I want to try the other side.' Once I had done that, then the next thing was the *rideau de fer*, the Iron Curtain. At McGill, I had begun to learn much more of the wide world, about the left and the right. In French Canadian society, there wasn't much of a left. We were a religious, autocratic society until 1960. And to me, when it started to change, it meant you had to know the left as well as the right. The Iron Curtain meant things that were forbidden. It was like the forbidden fruit. I wanted to live behind the Iron Curtain and see what things tasted like."

Unfortunately, they tasted bad. In its absence, he developed a new appreciation for political and economic freedom, the sort of freedom that Canadians, not knowing such deprivation, took for granted. He made a point of attending mass with his Polish student friends every Sunday, as an expression more of dissent than of faith.

Massé's final rebellion occurred right after Warsaw. He signed up with an organization called Crossroads Africa, one of the many groups of that idealistic era that transported white students from the industrialized world to help with the development of post-colonial Africa. Massé quickly fell in love with a Senegalese woman who ran the country's Cubs program. He went on, as planned, to Oxford, but chose a thesis subject that allowed him to return to Senegal for research purposes. Then, at twenty-four, he married Josée. "That was a no-no in French Canadian society." An English Canadian would have been bad enough, but an African woman was a real challenge to his father's authority, and the traditions of old Quebec.

Thirty years later, Massé would look back on his three rebellions as almost a cleansing experience. "First you get out of your race, then you get out of your ideology, then you get out of your prejudices."

Typically, there had been order and reason to his rebellions. But a lifetime later, they also provided cause for concern given his responsibility, in his intergovernmental affairs capacity, for relations with Quebec. Chrétien had a paucity of talent to draw upon in Quebec. He made Foreign Affairs Minister André Ouellet political minister in the province, in charge of doling out patronage and watching over the party. But Ouellet, like Chrétien himself, lacked the requisite credibility with a new generation of Québécois to provide leadership in a public way. Heritage Minister Michel Dupuy had different shortcomings. Paul Martin was an Ontarian who had moved to Quebec as an adult. In any case, he had his hands full in Finance. That left Quebec to Massé, at least until Lucienne Robillard came along in 1995 and Stéphane Dion and Pierre Pettigrew in 1996.

Certainly, he knew the file inside out from an intellectual perspective. But when you "get out" of your race, your ideology, and your prejudices, it can leave you isolated from political currents. Where other gifted Quebeckers of his generation had worked to modernize the province over the previous three decades, he had graduated beyond it. He didn't know politics and, it could be argued, he didn't understand the people of Quebec, certainly not like a Lucien Bouchard.

In a cabinet of highly evolved political animals — people like André Ouellet and Sheila Copps and Brian Tobin and David Dingwall — Massé must have felt like the first cave dweller to walk upright. Asked to describe him, cabinet colleagues invariably would sneer, "He's a bureaucrat," putting as much pejorative spin on the word as they could muster. They could glean little evidence of his Liberalism.

Indeed, in one of his first interviews as a Liberal candidate, he told Montreal's *La Presse* that he had been increasingly at odds with the Mulroney government. But he also provided strong hints that his views lacked harmony with some of his new brethren. He favoured free trade agreements, without equivocation, and he backed far deeper reductions in the deficit than the Liberals proposed; nor was he a centralist on social policy. In fact, although he didn't say so, he had snubbed an earlier approach to run for the Liberals in 1988 because of these views.

By dint of his different work experience, it shouldn't have been surprising that Massé would have a different take on the deficit. He had arrived in Ottawa in 1971 after spending most of the previous ten years out of the country, the final four at the World Bank in Washington. Then, in the wake of the FLQ crisis, he received a call from a fellow former Rhodes Scholar, Francis Fox, then an aide to Pierre Trudeau and subsequently one of his ministers. He told Massé that the prime minister wanted to recruit more French Canadians into the senior ranks of the public service and wondered if his former classmate was ready to return home. Massé contemplated the financial implications — he paid no taxes as a World Bank employee — but finally accepted a position in the Privy Council Office as an economic adviser.

Two years later, his career took an unusual detour, one that deepened his emerging fiscal conservatism and imbued him with a provincial perspective. Richard Hatfield, the unconventional premier of New Brunswick, wanted a Jackie Robinson–type character to break the linguistic barrier in Fredericton. Hatfield specifically wanted a francophone deputy minister of finance, someone so flawlessly bilingual and with such impeccable academic credentials that the anti-French loyalists in his party would feel incapable of attacking him. Massé — Rhodes Scholar, World Bank graduate — fit the bill.

Hatfield arranged to meet the young technocrat for breakfast in Ottawa. In the course of the meal, he made comments about French Canadians that Massé found offensive. "I thought to myself, This guy is crazy." But he didn't rise to the bait.

Six weeks later, Hatfield called and asked Massé when he could start work. That was when Massé learned the actual position in question, and that the winning candidate had to be someone with the sang-froid to withstand a lot of nastiness. Hatfield was impressed by the manner in which Massé had kept himself in check at breakfast. So Massé and his family moved to New Brunswick, where he served the Tory government for four and a half years, first in Finance and then as cabinet secretary, the top civil service position. The sojourn left him a fiscal conservative. "Once you've been a deputy minister of finance, you never forget that," he liked to say.

There was no disputing the depth of his experience in government. But politics posed a whole host of new challenges. Just days after the Chrétien government's first Speech from the Throne in January, the *Ottawa Citizen* got hold of Department of National Defence flight records from November that showed Massé had taken government jets on trips to Boston and New Orleans. And he had brought his wife along. Within government, there was considerable controversy over how to account for the cost of such trips, given that DND crews were already on salary and the costs of the Challenger jets had been expended whether they flew to Boston or remained on the ground. According to DND, the cost was $42,000. A new formula recommended by Auditor General Denis Desautels put the bill at $172,000.

Either way, it was a long way from the $2,500 that first-class return tickets to the two destinations would have cost. When Reform Party MP Myron Thompson rose in the Commons on January 25 to demand an explanation, Massé was unapologetic. The speeches had been arranged on short notice and his schedule was tight. On the afternoon he spoke at Harvard, Massé explained, he had appointments in the constituency that morning and then needed to rush back for a cabinet meeting the following morning. Commercial connections were impossible.

Privately, Massé fumed that if the people of his riding thought they had elected a dépanneur owner to represent them, they were mistaken. "In the future, I will use taxpayers' money in order to be as efficient as possible, in exactly the way that it was demonstrated by that trip," he told Thompson.

Politically, it was the wrong response. The government had been working assiduously on its integrity offensive. The entire strategy rested on portraying the Liberals as frugal in contrast with their spendthrift predecessors. Jean Chrétien rode around in a Chevy, shunning the presidential-style armoured limousine used by Brian Mulroney. The Liberals put a For Sale sign on the Airbus that had been customized for Mulroney's use. Aline Chrétien gave up the expensively decorated suite of offices in the Langevin Block that had been reserved for Mila Mulroney's use. Reporters knew this because Peter Donolo, the prime minister's communications chief, made sure they knew it.

Now here was Massé, way, way off message. Anyone who knew any-thing about the deficit, like Massé, knew this was all symbolic claptrap. Government operations made up just a small portion of the budget, and the cost of the flights was an accounting fiction. If the deficit was to be truly tackled, the focus needed to be on untouchable items like old-age security and regional development grants, not ministerial flights. But any-one who knew anything about politics, unlike Massé, knew that you could never win public approval for the big-ticket items so long as it looked like the politicians lived high on the hog.

For several of his cabinet colleagues, Massé's fumble was confirma-tion that he lacked the right stuff. But Chrétien had seen something there he liked. He thought of Massé as a modern-day Mitchell Sharp, an expe-rienced hand coming out of the bureaucracy and imbuing the political realm with a sense of serene reasonableness.

The Massé plan — the one he revealed to Paul Martin — had been ges-tating for a long time. It began with a simple conviction: that the political process, especially in an era in which governments were constrained by deficits, was about making choices. For a number of years, he had been the most outspoken critic within the public service of the increasingly com-mon practice of across-the-board cuts, the resort to avoiding hard choices by docking each department equally.

He was one of a select group of high-level officials invited to sit on a special committee that advised the Treasury Board about its policies, a perch from which he pontificated openly and regularly to his fellow bureaucrats that across-the-board cuts represented an abdication of polit-ical responsibility. They allowed governments to wriggle off the hook of tough but rational choices, of setting priorities, of reflecting the values of their constituents, of doing their jobs. "Marcel, as you know, is not given to emotion, but he would lash out on this issue," recalls one of the other participants. "It was a very personal matter for him. It was irra-tional, and it was bad for officials, and it was bad for governments."

Massé pushed his plan for a systematic and comprehensive rethink-ing of government from the moment he first signed on with Chrétien. The previous February, he had set out his analysis in a talk at the Canadian Centre for Management Development, the government's in-house business school. Sounding like a bureaucrat in midlife crisis, he described the lecture as his testament after twenty-five years of public service at the provincial, federal, and international levels.

Massé described three revolutions conspiring to strip sovereignty from national governments throughout the world: a technological revolution, a democratic revolution, and a global revolution. And then there was debt. "Although these three revolutions underlie the need for changing roles for governments in all countries, the initial fact that caused governments to look for new ways of providing public services has been the scarcity of public money and the size of public sector deficits." Government desperately needed to rethink its role in the 1990s, he said.

Early in the election campaign, Massé persuaded Chrétien to let him develop his thinking further in a speech to the Quebec wing of the Public Service Alliance of Canada. The Longueuil speech, as it came to be known, was carefully vetted: Chrétien reviewed it personally with Massé over the phone. It was interesting both for its sharper political edge — he derided the Mulroney-era ministerial chiefs of staff, who had shoved aside public servants, as the "new Clark Kents of government" — and for its more prescriptive nature than the February speech.

At Longueuil he laid out his three-pronged agenda for getting government right: reining in government expenditures, that is, doing only the things you could do well; overhauling the delivery of public services and political institutions to make them more responsive; and reordering federal-provincial relations. On this latter score, Massé felt that the lack of clear lines of demarcation between federal and provincial roles engendered the kind of bickering and tension that so frustrated the public. He wanted the respective roles of different levels of government clarified. But, as he made clear, "We can do this without recourse to constitutional amendment. The last thing this country needs is another round of constitutional conferences."

Massé's three prongs were all part of the same plug. Identifying what Ottawa did and did not do well in the context of where it should concentrate its tax dollars would naturally lead to discussion about whether the provinces could do these things better. Such might be the case, for instance, with job training.

After the election, when Chrétien met with each of his prospective ministers to discuss their cabinet jobs, Massé said he would like to pursue the theme of his Longueuil speech, pulling together a new approach to fiscal responsibility, intergovernmental affairs, and governance. Chrétien wondered what such a portfolio would be called. Massé suggested minister for government renewal. Chrétien wrote it down himself, since there was no such title on his list. Later, a Privy Council official, not knowing what it was about, would change the name to minister for public service renewal.

Massé clearly wasn't the only senior government thinker who had come to the conclusion that Ottawa had to comb through its inventory of programs, one by one, and toss out those that no longer made sense. In fact, it had become the conventional wisdom by 1993. Glen Shortliffe, in managing Kim Campbell's government reorganization in June 1993, stated that the new structure of ministries would be followed by a thorough review of programs, a sequence Massé found irrational. David Zussman and his transition group had been thinking along the same lines. Each could claim some paternity — and did — of the process that would come to be known in the autumn of 1994 as program review. Massé, though, alone among all the putative fathers, was in a position to turn the theory into practice, if he could bring Paul Martin on board.

After his opening discussions with Massé, Martin went away and considered the partnership offer. Some of his advisers were leery. Massé was asking to borrow some of the power and prerogatives of the minister of finance. He would have to know as much as Martin about government spending numbers and trends. At the nitty-gritty level, he would know more. "Martin had to decide if he trusted me," Massé explained in the wake of the 1995 budget. "He needed to think about it. Once he thought about it, he has never come back on it."

Martin realized that Massé brought something to the table, too, something he lacked. Massé understood government and bureaucracy; he breathed process. He had time to dedicate himself to the task at hand. Moreover, he was about as unthreatening a partner as one could imagine. Massé was without great political prospects. It wouldn't be like sharing power with, say, Sheila Copps.

The alternative to Massé's detailed review and rank-ordering of every government program was for Finance to apply its blunt axe. It was, as far as Martin was concerned, a tried-and-failed method. He didn't want to be remembered as another in a litany of finance ministers dedicated to making government leaner. He wanted to make it more responsive as well. He told Massé they would be partners.

In the months to follow, Martin came to think of Massé as his Cartesian other half. They would form the most powerful tandem in Ottawa: the hard-driving salesman lacking in patience for process, and the calm conceptualizer who worked best in the higher reaches of abstraction. Although few would notice it, they would place an intriguing advertisement of their new partnership in Martin's first budget, one that would subsequently change the face of the government of Canada.

8

THREE FACES
OF PAUL

Jean Chrétien and Paul Martin were also talking. Once they had put the matter of the Bank of Canada governor behind them, they turned in earnest to the government's first budget. Chrétien communicated one overriding objective: that the Liberals had to move swiftly to fund the promises in the Red Book. Just before Christmas, Chrétien had signed a national infrastructure deal with the provinces. The premiers had rushed to Ottawa for a special first ministers' conference to grab the $2 billion in federal money before the newly elected Liberals came to their senses.

Martin had already been jolted awake. With the 1993–94 deficit exploding into the $45-billion range, he would have to hack away at existing programs just to cover the added costs from the Red Book, never mind the Liberal commitment to begin lowering the deficit. He began trooping around to a series of one-on-one meetings with his cabinet colleagues. Martin didn't have a lot of time to fashion a fancy budget. He would take two quick swipes — the defence cuts that had already been spelled out in the Red Book and a pre-emptive strike against UI — and then go after the other ministers in his second budget. David Collenette and Lloyd Axworthy would be awarded a bye in round two.

On January 18, Parliament convened for the first time since the previous spring, back when Brian Mulroney had presided over the nation's business. Chrétien was riding high in the polls, his honeymoon with the Canadian people enduring deep into the winter. His frugality and his party's message of economic hope resonated with a long-repressed public. Canadians revelled in his upbeat energy: if he was Reagan, remarked one of his officials, he was Reagan on steroids. Like Reagan, he exuded optimism, and like him, he preferred to ignore a problem rather than confront it. Even when he acted, he sought not to disturb anyone's sleep. His "What, me worry?" demeanour reminded some of his hero Sir Wilfrid Laurier's famous "sunny ways" — a metaphor drawn from the Aesop fable showing the superiority of the sun to the north wind in separating a traveller from his coat. Chrétien's sunny ways were going down wonderfully with a public fed up with the chilly blasts of Mulroney's final years.

He seemed to possess some mystical understanding of the Canadian psyche. Chrétien had ventured during the election campaign that the mere sight of tractors and trucks moving as a result of the infrastructure program would lift spirits and prompt Canadians to get out shopping again. Miraculously, it appeared to be happening. The consumer confidence figures compiled by the Conference Board of Canada spurted upward in the last quarter of 1993 and the first quarter of 1994, breaking out of their postrecession doldrums. Board economists attributed some of the upswing to the changing political mood.

On the morning of the opening of Parliament, Chrétien met his caucus and talked about the importance of restoring the bonds of trust with Canadians. Soon, he would face off for the first time in the House of Commons against Bloc Québécois leader Lucien Bouchard. He clearly had Quebec on his mind. The Liberal way, he declared, would not be to dwell on the Constitution. Canadians — all Canadians — wanted jobs. His national unity strategy would be the provision of good, honest government and economic growth. The proper functioning of the federation would be the ticket for keeping Quebeckers in the fold. Chrétien ended with one of his favourite quotations from Laurier, one he would use the next day as well in his maiden prime-ministerial speech in the House of Commons. It spoke to his very different appreciation of the French fact in Canada from that of Lucien Bouchard. "We are French Canadians, but our country is not limited to the territory around the Citadel in Quebec: our country is Canada. Our fellow citizens are not only those who have French blood in their veins. They are those, regardless of race or language who have come here among us as a result of the vagaries of war or the whims of fortune or by their own choice."

Typically for the image these Chrétien Liberals wanted to portray, the Speech from the Throne — the traditional recitation of the government's legislative agenda — was short and to the point, taking just twelve minutes to read in the Senate chamber. It contained no surprises. The blueprint for this first session of the Thirty-fifth Parliament had been well set out in the

Red Book, with all the familiar promises about youth, small business, home renovation, the GST, and, of course, the infrastructure program. Already, these promises looked like quaint relics of a bygone era. On the day of the Throne Speech, the debt clock outside the Vancouver Board of Trade office — galloping ahead at $1,400 a second — clicked past the $500-billion mark.

Both Paul Martin and Jean Chrétien were fiscal conservatives of a type. They were like members of a religious denomination who rarely attended church, and skipped grace except when the in-laws came for dinner. They knew what the Good Book said, they even believed it, but their commitment was far from absolute. The world provided so much temptation. They weren't beyond backsliding.

Like scores of politicians before them, they had concluded that the deficit demanded action and that the best course lay in growing their way out of hock. It wasn't that they lacked the stomach for cutting programs, even though the Tories had already used up all the easy cuts. It was simply that restoring the economy to health, creating the conditions for strong job growth — this marked the more Liberal approach to deficit reduction. "The number one instrument for reducing the deficit is jobs, the second is cutting spending. And that has been our position all along," Martin told the nation as it awaited his first budget in the unusually cold winter of 1993–94.

As his co-author on the Red Book, Chaviva Hošek, head of Chrétien's in-house policy unit, had become as well acquainted as almost anyone with the internal mechanics of Martin's mind. "What Paul really cares about is innovation and growth. But he knows that unless the fiscal house is in order, it's useless," she would patiently explain. "So I think it is wrong to characterize Paul as caring about the deficit. I think it's right to characterize him as saying that getting ourselves on track so we can grow and have a decent economy is important, and getting control of the deficit will allow us to do that."

Within the small group deliberating over the final contents of the Red Book — Martin, Hošek, Eddie Goldenberg, Terrie O'Leary, and Chrétien — Martin was the deficit hawk. He pressed for the Liberals to commit themselves to a zero deficit. But Hošek judged him far more interested in the symbolism of a zero target than in its substance. Chrétien, on the other hand, was a more experienced politician, one who had seen some of his own symbols come back to haunt him over the years. Circumstances changed, often very quickly, in politics. He reflexively sought that extra inch of wiggle room.

It wasn't so much that a zero deficit target was too radical for Chrétien as that it was too incautious. Early on, in his capacity as a former finance minister, he warned Martin of the folly of long-term commitments. The Tories had promised a zero deficit in five years, the Reform Party had boasted it could reach zero in four. Chrétien knew there would be a lot of water under the bridge by then, and who could say when the river might swell. There might be a war, he said at one point with a shrug. You never knew in politics.

Chrétien loved the middle of the road, the dry ground away from the puddles. He approached the 1993 election determined not to be stigmatized as either a tax-and-spend Liberal or a would-be Tory. Martin and Hošek debated long and hard over the role of daycare in the Red Book. Martin felt the Liberals couldn't afford it; Hošek that they couldn't afford not to have it. Chrétien, in one of his classic fudges, called for daycare if necessary but not necessarily daycare: they would promise up to $720 million over three years for new daycare spaces, but only with equal funding from the provinces and only "in each year that follows a year of 3 percent economic growth."

Chrétien liked the European idea of 3 per cent of gross domestic product as a target for the deficit. That would mean bringing the deficit down to $25 billion in 1996–97 from the $32.6 billion projected in the last Tory budget. It didn't sound onerous, but Mulroney had never done better than 4.5 per cent. So it was decided. The Red Book goal would be 3 per cent of GDP in three years. It resounded with gravitas. Martin wrung out the concession of having it stated as an "interim target."

Outside the Liberal group, real deficit hawks found Martin's conviction a little suspect. In the months leading up to the election, he and Hošek got together with the top-secret policy quartet feeding ideas to David Zussman, Chrétien's transition chief. Each of the four, Judith Maxwell, Donald Savoie, Daniel Gagnier, and Sheldon Ehrenworth, believed the deficit towered over all other concerns. Martin and Hošek briefed them on the economic aspects of the Liberal platform. The fiscal situation hardly rated a mention. Martin preferred to talk about innovation and growth. The group pressed him on the deficit. He seemed perplexed by the fixation. The transition advisers left the meeting very troubled.

A short while afterwards, Martin ran into Maxwell at a parliamentary hearing and accompanied her down Parliament Hill. Martin inquired what she thought the right amount of fiscal stimulus would be in a first Liberal budget. The idea that anybody would be thinking in terms of stimulus in the deficit-ridden 1990s stunned her. He suggested an amount. "Oh, I think that's too high," she demurred.

As she returned to her office, Martin's mind-set and her less than forthright reply gnawed at Maxwell. She decided to break one of her cardinal rules of never initiating a call to a politician. She told Martin that he was looking at the matter through the wrong end of the telescope. The question wouldn't be how much extra spending a Liberal government could introduce, but how much existing spending it could retain. He thanked her warmly for her viewpoint, without passing comment on it.

Martin was under the sway at that point of growth-oriented economists like American Nobel prizewinner James Tobin, people who didn't subscribe to the view of deficits as inherently evil. Martin had read an article from that spring's issue of *Challenge Magazine*, in which Tobin wrote that deficit reduction must not become an end in itself. "Its rationale is to improve productivity, real wages, and living standards of our children and their children. If the measures to cut deficits actually diminish GDP, raise unemployment, and reduce future oriented activities of government, business, and households, they do not achieve the goals that are their raison d'être: rather they retard them." Martin thought enough of the sentiment to highlight the quote in the opening chapter of the Red Book.

Despite their well-deserved reputation for two decades as tax-and-spend politicians, the Liberals weren't historically a party of big deficits. A look at the national accounts for the postwar era makes the point. From 1947, when the wartime demobilization was complete, until 1974–75, when the country caught its first deficit chill, Liberal governments balanced the books, or better, almost every year. The Diefenbaker interlude from 1958 to 1963, during which the country struggled with recession, was the only period of sustained budgetary deficits. The Liberals of the King and St. Laurent eras prided themselves on managerial competence and pragmatism above all.

As health and welfare minister in the 1950s, Paul Martin's father would smoulder year in and year out about the postponement, yet again, of public health insurance and pensions while the finance ministers, Douglas

Abbott and Walter Harris, used their surpluses to cool inflation and pay off war bonds. "Too frequently, an all-knowing finance bureaucracy overruled the judgements of my officials and myself," the Young Turk with the social conscience griped in his memoirs.

The Liberals of his son's generation, including Jean Chrétien and Lloyd Axworthy, basked in their party's central role in creating social programs. But the truth of the matter was they had swallowed their party's propaganda line: while the Liberals wore their double-breasted hearts on their sleeves, once inside the cabinet room they changed into banker's blue. By the time the Liberals actually completed the postwar social safety net, Martin Sr. was close to collecting a pension himself. The party always clung to the wording of its 1919 resolution, that these social programs would be made the law of the land "so far as may be practicable, having regard to Canada's financial position."

In the Pearson years, federal spending crept up, but the Liberals still kept the books in balance while barrelling ahead with their social policies. The national accounts for 1965, the year the parsimonious Mitchell Sharp became finance minister, show that Ottawa brought in $9.1 billion in revenue and spent $7.5 billion on programs. It also paid out $1.1 billion on interest on the national debt, most of it still left over from the war effort. The bottom line: a surplus of $517 million. A typical year.

In 1972, Pierre Elliott Trudeau warned: "If a government wants to do the popular things, it will ruin the economy — real quick." The Trudeau governments, with their easy confidence in the ability of the state to eradicate poverty or even create prosperity in economically barren regions, soon became wedded to doing the popular things. Throughout the Western world, the era of big government was in full swing. According to the philosophy of the times, social programs would be universal, regardless of need. Governments backstopped all citizens in this age of entitlement. Ottawa under Trudeau plunged into housing and urban affairs — areas of provincial jurisdiction — enriched unemployment insurance, left stockpiled eggs and milk to rot, topped up pensions, purchased oil companies, and threw billions at the noble but futile task of eliminating regional disparities.

When the postwar bubble finally burst in the early 1970s, Ottawa responded with a variety of spending measures aimed at recapturing the big growth of years past. But to no avail. In retrospect, an unfortunate confluence of events contributed to the rapid run-up in deficits that began in 1974, many of them beyond Trudeau's, or Canada's, control. Domestically,

Finance Minister John Turner built inflation protection — through index-ation — into social programs in his February 1973 budget while remov-ing the benefits to the treasury of taxpayers being pushed by inflation into higher tax brackets. This decoupling of revenues and expenditures led to an ever-widening gap as inflation galloped ahead over the next decade.

Meanwhile, international factors impinged on Canada. In the wake of the sharp oil price increases engineered by the Arab oil producers the pre-vious fall, productivity gains, the real engine of the postwar boom, slowed to a crawl. With them, so did economic growth. In the two decades up to 1973, productivity growth — the ability of the economy to get more from less — averaged 2.3 per cent a year. In the two decades afterwards, it fell to 1.1 per cent. Unemployment soared and economic growth stalled. Indeed, in the twenty-two years from 1953 to 1974, the Canadian economy grew by 5 per cent or more thirteen times. But in the two following decades, it bettered the 5-per-cent benchmark just three times. Growth in the 1980s declined by half, to just 2 per cent, then vanished entirely in the first half of the 1990s.

The deficit fever the Liberals caught under John Turner came to afflict his successors at Finance, Donald Macdonald, Jean Chrétien, Allan MacEachen, and Marc Lalonde. Each one of this lineup of ministers judged the situation a temporary aberration, one that would be remedied in the next budget, by which time the problem would fall to a new minister. In fairness, few finance ministers ever confronted an array of forces such as stagflation, oil shocks, and the slowdown of productivity growth. The entire Keynesian model — which posited that high inflation and high unemploy-ment could not occur at the same time — had cratered. It took quite some time to understand that the rules of the game had changed irrevocably, that it wasn't an aberration at all.

In short order, the achievement of the postwar Liberals in paying down the huge debts from World War II while rebuilding the economy had been wiped out. The Liberals drove the deficit to an astronomical $38.6 billion in 1984–85, in relative terms the largest budgetary shortfall since 1945. The national debt had stood at 107 per cent of gross domestic product at war's end. From 1947 to 1975, Liberals brought it down to under 18 per cent. The national debt totalled just $27.1 billion in March 1975. At the end of the Trudeau era the figure had bounced up to $199 billion. During his prime ministership, government spending climbed from $12.2 billion to more than $100 billion. The unemployment rate tripled, and repeated

attempts to wrestle inflation to the ground failed. The Liberals, the party
of managerial competence, left office with their reputation for sound
economic stewardship in ruins.

By 1984, the year David Dodge moved over to Finance from Employment, a state of high anxiety had enveloped its bureaucrats. As the election approached, they laboured away in secret on their Next Mandate
planning exercise. Whether the victors would be Liberal or Conservative
didn't really concern them. Either way, deficit containment would be the
defining characteristic of the next government.

When Bay Street graduate Michael Wilson arrived at Esplanade Laurier
in September, he concurred completely with the analysis laid out in the
briefing books. With very little adaptation, the Next Mandate review
became his November 1984 *Agenda for Economic Renewal*. "The fiscal
situation is disturbing," the document said. "The mountain of debt is feeding on itself and the deficit shows no prospect of declining on its own in
this decade even with moderate growth." The paper provided the road
map for the next nine years: the destinations were income tax reform,
deregulation, privatization, free trade, expenditure control, the GST.

But Wilson went down swinging his first time at bat. He never fully
recovered from the débâcle of his government losing its nerve on the partial deindexation of old-age pensions in the face of a sixty-three-year-old
woman named Solange Denis. "You lied to us," she shouted at Mulroney.
"You made us vote for you, then, Goodbye Charlie Brown" — the image
became deeply etched in the Tory psyche. The government was forced into
a humiliating retreat. Canadians weren't primed for tough fiscal action, and
Michael Wilson and his bureaucratic fellow travellers in Finance utterly
lacked the political skills to win them over.

Wilson did succeed in chipping away at the rate of increase in government spending (although spending actually continued to rise) during the
sustained boom of the 1980s, building up annual operating surpluses. But
the Tories could not resist big energy projects and other temptations. In
place of spending cuts, they dumped their problems onto the provinces and
introduced a dizzying array of tax increases. They endorsed John Crow's
war on inflation despite the damage that high interest rates inflicted on
their fiscal efforts.

The national debt doubled on Michael Wilson's watch alone and then
accelerated its upward pace under his successor, Don Mazankowski. Done
in by compound interest and an uncertain political will, in late 1993 the

Tories handed a far more profound fiscal mess back to the Liberals. The national debt — Ottawa and provinces combined — now stood at nearly $700 billion and the country was taxed to the max.

Preparations for his first budget caused Martin to reflect on the nature of the fiscal challenge, but he was still far from the "come hell or high water" deficit warrior he would become. And he was a handful. The senior staff spent nearly as much time managing upward, in the vernacular of organizational behavioural experts, as they did on their regular duties. Terrie O'Leary, his no-nonsense executive assistant, admitted to an interviewer that Martin was a "very high maintenance" boss. "He believes in tension; he sees it in a positive light."

Martin began his stewardship at Finance with a well-intentioned fib, telling the senior officials in their first meeting that reports of his having not wanted the job were untrue. Finance had been his first choice all along. That marked his last attempt at stroking sensibilities.

The corporate CEO turned politician had no patience for the orderly procession of the bureaucratic mind. He just wanted to shoot the rapids. In the early meetings, he made it clear that he had little use for the department, which looked to him to be bare of ideas and congenitally incapable of expressing itself in comprehensible language. He would send back briefing notes, complaining they were too technical. What does this all mean? he demanded, making the authors feel totally inadequate. He wanted it in English, simple, straightforward, no-mumbo-jumbo English. And he wanted solutions to problems, not endless analysis. He had, indeed, drawn lessons from the Next Mandate exercise — just not the ones intended.

The time-honoured departmental approach of snowing the minister under with ten possible scenarios, eight and a half of them impractical, didn't play with Martin. He couldn't care less why a problem was a problem or why particular solutions wouldn't work. He dismissed these offerings as "a lot of crap."

The department had a tradition of conducting long, thoughtful meetings akin to university seminars, aimed at probing the problem *du jour* from every conceivable angle. The sessions, initiated during Mickey Cohen's tenure as deputy minister, were a response to the disaster of MacEachen's 1981 budget. Internally, they still bore the moniker "CMOs" — for Cohen, Minister, and Others. Under Wilson, the others included a supporting cast of a couple of dozen officials, right down to the juniors, who would sit in the back of the room absorbing Finance Think. Wilson loved the cut and thrust of the debates, which could go from morning to night, often stuck on such niggling matters as the tax treatment of muffins under the GST. Mazankowski tolerated the discussions, although he wasn't as open as Wilson in allowing the officials to watch him struggle with decisions. Martin had trouble understanding why he was stuck in a room with a bunch of officials who didn't even know what *they* wanted.

In Ottawa, process was seen to be as important as substance. In fact, one of the major classifications in the bureaucratic nomenclature was the process person. But Martin couldn't care less about the internal dynamics of Ottawa. "What is PCO?" he liked to provoke, referring to the Privy Council Office, the ultimate process people who advised the prime minister and lorded it over the rest of the bureaucracy. To him, they just muddied the waters, and got in his way. They accomplished nothing.

In an interview at his farm in the summer of 1995, he spoke at length of his impatience with the Ottawa system. "The bureaucracy is very process oriented and I'm not. Nobody who has been in business is. I basically want to get a job done. I don't give a goddamn about the process. For the bureaucracy, what's interesting is that as long as the process is working, everybody is happy. The thing can go on for years. We don't *have* years."

Bureaucrats think it's a good meeting, he complained, if "everybody agreed that they knew where they disagreed. Well, screw that," Martin continued. "You know, as long as the meeting breaks up with nobody throwing a punch, everybody in the system is happy. And my view is you're a lot better off to have the meeting end with somebody throwing a punch because at least something gets decided."

The Finance officials were having trouble adjusting to their new corporate chieftain. At times they felt he treated them, in the words of one, "like a CEO speaking to a junior salesman in Saskatoon." Fuelled by more than a dozen cups of coffee a day, Martin always seemed to be on the go. He didn't necessarily distinguish between day and night, weekday and weekend. If an idea popped into his head, he would call the relevant official at home at 10 at night or 8 in the morning. If the phone rang during a family dinner on Saturday evening, Finance officials knew better than to answer. His adrenaline levels were off the chart. At his first meeting with provincial finance ministers in Halifax, reporters on their way down for breakfast stumbled into the new federal minister pacing the corridors — showered, dressed, fed, and anxious to get the damn thing started.

He drove the tax branch particularly hard. Martin was under pressure to find a way to revamp the GST, as the Liberals had promised in the election campaign. And left-wing Liberals in caucus wanted him to lower the maximum contribution limit for RRSPs and get rid of supposed breaks for family trusts. Despite his CEO demeanour, Martin actually sifted information slowly. Achieving a comfort level with new issues often entailed a long, agonizing process.

The tax officials had been through these files a million times before. They were on record as stating that family trusts did not represent the black holes that some claimed they were, and that RRSPs had finally been brought in line with company pension plans, achieving equity for self-employed individuals with salaried employees. But Martin needed to hear it all again. And when he heard it, he raged that he wasn't being given adequate answers, just "a lot of crap."

He didn't hesitate to vent his displeasure with their resistance. "You stupid bastards," the tax officials remembered him screaming after one unsatisfactory discussion of family trusts. "You just don't get it. We are changing it. Now do it." Then he would amiably thank them as they left the room, seemingly unaware of the effect he had on people.

Dodge found that tax matters gave Martin the most trouble. He would push the officials towards unworkable solutions. After hunkering down through yet another barrage about the need to design a method for raising more taxes from seniors rather than reducing benefits, Dodge finally got so fed up that he marched into the minister's office with an income tax form in hand and threw it down on the desk: "I don't think you've ever seen one of these," he conjectured. He then spent two hours guiding Martin through its labyrinthine complexity.

Senior acquaintances in the bureaucracy figured that Dodge would make a quick exit, perhaps back to academe or one of those lucrative private-sector jobs that had provided refuge for a number of his predecessors. Nobody knew of his secret role in plumping for Martin as finance minister in the first place, an intervention he doubtless regretted at that point.

In the early meetings, the officials encountered the volcanic temper that went along with Martin's quicksilver mood swings. He could be genial and charming, but periodically he lost it. His former executive assistant, Richard Mahoney, a Martin loyalist to the core, remembered his first exposure to a Martin tirade. It was May 4, 1989, the day after John Turner quit as Liberal leader. Mahoney had joined Martin's staff just a few weeks earlier, giving up his position at a Toronto law firm with the understanding that he would have to finish off several cases. Martin had been revving up his campaign team for months, but nobody knew when the starting gun would officially go off. On the day Turner finally pulled the trigger, Mahoney was locked in a hearing room in Toronto.

Naturally, nobody cared about John Turner any more. The media wanted the horse race to begin. Martin did interview after interview during the day, sticking with the well-worn but safe line that it was John Turner's day. But Barbara Frum, host of CBC-TV's flagship current affairs show *The Journal*, was having none of it when she finally had her shot at a fidgety Martin that evening, demanding straight answers to tough questions.

Frustrated by his poor performance and stewing over Mahoney's absence, Martin blew. Mahoney recalled, "I'd known this guy for seven years now, reasonably well for four or five years. I had had a very civil relationship with him since 1984 and had lots of chats about the idea of going to work for him and what our expectations were. This was a charming guy. And all of a sudden, we have this blow-out. I'm thinking, 'Yikes, we've probably got a year and a half to go [until the leadership vote]. I'm his number one person here. We've just had this killing discussion. He's never going to have confidence in me again.'"

Nobody had ever spoken to Mahoney like that. "It's just not my style. In my family, we don't do that." He figured their relationship had suffered irreparable damage. It was early days, early enough for Martin to find someone else with whom he was more comfortable. He wrote up a letter of resignation and left it on Martin's desk.

When he saw the note the following morning, Martin, thunderstruck, walked into Mahoney's office and asked, "What's this?" Mahoney reminded him of the previous day's fireworks. "He says, 'I don't know what you're talking about.' It became quite clear to me that we had had two separate experiences. For him, he blew off some steam and he was fine. And for me, I was probably traumatized." Martin apologized and asked Mahoney to please rip up the letter and stay.

Among Martin's political staff, the outbursts were known as the Beatings. Aides learned to roll with them; they were just one of the ebbs and flows of working for any boss, and this one had plenty of compensating flow. When Bob Woodward's book *The Agenda* came out in 1994, detailing the verbal abuse Bill Clinton regularly rained down on aide George Stephanopoulos, David Herle, a Martin loyalist and former employee, called Mahoney and read him the passages over the phone. The Beatings had become a bit of an internal joke by then, a rite of passage that bonded Martin and his team. He could be a bully, but he could also be funny, earthy, and genial. He was jocular with men and charming with women, the kind of guy who would still bow to kiss a lady's hand — and then wink at her companion. A woman never lit her own cigarette in Martin's presence. Nobody picked up a tab, and if they did, he would go back to the restaurant later and have the credit card slip torn up. He was just as fast with a quip, often aimed at himself. He had friends on all sides of the House of Commons.

Martin also took an intense interest in the lives of the young people in his circle, peppering them with questions about their relationships — not always appreciated — and dispensing advice on career choices. They felt as if he was there for them as much as they were for him. In June 1990, a judicial ruling forced Maurizio Bevilacqua, a thirty-year-old MP who had supported Martin for the leadership, to give up his seat until a by-election could be held in December. "The person who called me the most to see how I was doing and how my family was doing was Paul Martin."

The best way to get along with Martin, his friends, family, and close associates learned, was to argue back. Michael Robinson, the high-powered Ottawa lobbyist who managed Martin's 1990 leadership campaign, said, "Paul really loves getting into conversations on substantive matters and to debate them in the most gruesome detail." Nobody could really count themselves an intimate, Martin's friends said, until they had been through at least one screaming match with him. The Martin team was like one huge, brawling family. They worked hard. They argued hard. They partied hard. Chrétien's sober loyalists — who didn't party at all — would marvel at the cohesion of their former leadership rivals. They seemed to move around town in a rugby scrum.

The key individual in Martin's political network was Terrie O'Leary, whom some veteran bureaucrats judged the best executive assistant they had ever seen. Blonde, intense, chain-smoking, and barely five feet tall, O'Leary possessed the finely tuned political antennae that her boss readily acknowledged he lacked. When she joined Martin's staff in 1990 from a job with a Toronto brokerage firm, she was in her early thirties, with a background in the party going back a decade. Her mind worked quickly and words flew out of her in excited bursts of rapid fire. She seemed to exhale more than she inhaled, giving her voice the breathless quality of an asthmatic.

To listen to the way the two of them spoke to each other was to wonder how they survived more than five minutes in the same room without
plates flying. "Jeezus Christ, O'Leary," Martin would invariably begin a
sentence, perhaps merely giving her the gears, perhaps revving up to an
impassioned denunciation or sermon. "Oh calm down now, Paul," she
would snap back dismissively. Or if she really found his argument uncon-
vincing, she would jump right in. "You're wrong, Paul," she would inter-
rupt, gasping for air. "You're wrong." It didn't faze him for a second, but
it left the officials dumbstruck.

On the sidetable to O'Leary's desk, in an office adjoining Martin's,
sat a brightly coloured abacus. Martin presented it after blowing up at her
during a meeting with the officials. "Terrie, you don't understand the numbers," he snapped impatiently. The next day, meeting with the same group,
he walked in with the abacus, a public peace offering. For a tyrant, he
engendered phenomenal loyalty from those hardy enough to survive.

The Finance men, and they were still mostly men and, perhaps surprisingly in Ottawa in the 1990s, still mostly anglophone men, were a less
robust breed. The department attracted a type: smart, earnest, hard-
working, frugal. It was as if they had all sat in the front row in high school,
scoring marks in the nineties, but never landing a date. In August 1994,
after their rapprochement with Martin was well under way, he invited the
senior departmental officials down to his farm in the Eastern Townships as
a reward for the long hours they were putting in. He suggested they bring
their bathing suits and tennis rackets. When they arrived, the weather was
poor. So they and the minister sat around and worked on departmental
business.

Early on, Martin confessed to a certain psychosis when it came to
speeches. It was an accurate description: they could unhinge him. The
preparations to make everything look natural often stretched over weeks
and months. He refused to leave anything to chance. In opposition, he would
memorize his questions on days he was scheduled to speak in Question
Period and then practise them in front of a mirror.

Getting Martin speech-ready was a dreaded ordeal. He demanded the
initial draft of his remarks weeks in advance. It had to be in giant twenty-
eight-point type, the size of a newspaper headline, and even the first draft
had to be written in French and English. Martin then would agonize over
the words, shuffling around paragraphs and toying with sentences, trying
to find a structure that made sense to him. If he made a change to the French

version, the officials would have to scramble to make sure the English copy conformed. They weren't accustomed to this. Almost everyone else in government worked in one language or the other, with translation provided near the end of the process. He rehearsed everything, including cabinet presentations, especially cabinet presentations.

The speeches could bring out the worst of his moods. In the early going, meetings would sometimes degenerate into ranting sessions, with the communications officials made to feel as inadequate as toy tugboats in the ocean. At one meeting, he hurled a bulky draft of a speech across the room in disgust. Within a couple of months, he had gone through two speechwriters. He also wore out the department's communications director, Peter Leibel, who, following the culture of the bureaucracy, preferred to outlast problems rather than confront them. Martin found him timid and ingratiating.

Martin simply couldn't tolerate people who told him what they thought he wanted to hear. He liked to be challenged. He respected people who yelled back. He hated the "Yes, Minister" crap. Soon he got the response he wanted. A deputy minister in another department nearly fell off his chair at a meeting when Dodge interrupted Martin with a succinct "Horseshit!" He had never heard a public servant speak to a cabinet minister like that. Martin didn't seem the least bit put out.

The officials, naturally enough, took the Liberal Red Book seriously. It was to be the guiding light of the government, and their minister was its co-author. But time and time again in meetings in those early months, Martin would savage them for their deference to his handiwork. "Don't tell me what's in the Red Book," he yelled more than once. "I wrote the goddamn thing. And I know that a lot of it is crap. Don't be a slave to it."

On another occasion, he cut off a reference to a Red Book commitment by exploding that the goddamn thing had been thrown together quickly in the last three weeks of July. Things hadn't been properly thought through. "So screw the Red Book." (Martin's people had their own spin on the "Screw the Red Book" comment: first, that he had never said it, and later, that the department had misinterpreted him. It wasn't that he didn't believe in the Red Book, O'Leary explained. He was extremely proud of it. He just wanted the department to understand the need to move beyond it.)

The department had things to teach Paul Martin about economics. But he also had something to teach them: the power of communications. The flip side of his psychosis over speeches was that he had grown into a great showman, much to the delight of those advisers who remembered his awkwardness in the 1990 leadership campaign. All the agonizing and practice reaped dividends. The department had never known a communicator like him. Michael Wilson had been the consummate finance minister. But, like the officials, he was more technocrat than politician. Under Wilson, Finance had the feel of a monastic order, one of its departed officials recalled. The fervour about the deficit was so absolute, the truth so blindingly obvious, that nobody saw much need to explain themselves. Now the department was led, in the words of David Dodge, "by a marketer par excellence. It was like changing the chief executive officer of a company from an engineer to a salesman."

On February 22, 1994, Martin unveiled his first budget. He walked down the west stairway to the Commons with Chrétien, who said something mystifying about his glass of gin being in place. At 4:30, he stood to provide Canadians their first real measure of their new finance minister. "Canadians are fed up with government inertia," he said. "They seek determined, fundamental change. They want their government to have a game plan and pursue it — a strategy for jobs, for growth." Then he took a swig of the water on his desk. His mouth was on fire. The glass contained straight gin. Chrétien had arranged the switch in compliance with a long-held parliamentary custom for rookie finance ministers, the origin of which nobody knew.

The budget, thrown together from a standing start in a hundred days, testified to the conflicts raging within Paul Martin. In the week leading up to his maiden budget speech, John Godfrey, an insightful Liberal MP from Toronto, suggested that the key to understanding this finance minister was to accept that there were three Paul Martins. There was Paul Martin the shipping executive and fiscal conservative; Paul Martin the devoted son of one of the country's social policy pioneers; and Paul Martin the disciple of New Age economic thinkers, like Robert Reich, who took it as an article of faith that governments could still contribute to economic growth.

The fiscal conservative closed military bases and carved $2.4 billion out of unemployment insurance, more than the Tories had ever dared. Both were gutsy moves, considering how they would hit disproportionately in Atlantic Canada, a region that had returned Liberals in thirty-one of its thirty-two seats four months earlier. Lloyd Axworthy accepted that UI presented one of the few areas Martin could hit hard and fast. In exchange, he secured a promise — as did Defence Minister David Collenette — that, having contributed in the first budget, he would be spared further cuts the second time around.

The social activist coughed up $800 million for Axworthy to dabble in social policy experimentation, running pilot projects to determine what worked and what didn't while toiling away on his comprehensive reworking of the social safety net. He gave Axworthy two years of clear sailing on transfers, announcing, however, that their level in 1996–97 would have to be no higher than in 1993–94. Considering inflation and the growing demand for services, the effect was equivalent to a cut of $1.5 billion.

Finally, the industrial strategist funded all those nifty ideas, even the half-baked ones, in the Red Book, programs like technology partnerships and innovation funds. The government's integrity agenda demanded it. Chrétien had made the point at the first cabinet meeting, and many times since. They had been Martin's ideas in the first place.

Martin advertised his document as a two-stage budget, with more to come in the second year. But he wasn't waiting, he insisted, to deliver on the Red Book's critical deficit commitment. "The decisions taken today by themselves set us on a clear path to achieving the government's deficit target of 3 per cent of GDP in 1996–97," he asserted. In fact, all his many actions combined would only trim the deficit to $39.7 billion in 1994–95, just $1.5 billion less than if there had been no policy changes. The bulk of the action in reaching the $25-billion target would occur in the second and third years and would depend largely on revenue growth.

Buried unnoticed in the budget speech would turn out to be its most important line, a lonely sentence — hidden in the thicket — that would take on tremendous significance over the coming months. "The Minister Responsible for Public Service Renewal will review all departmental spending to identify where greater savings are possible through the elimination or reduction of low priority programs," Martin pronounced, imbuing the project of his partner, Marcel Massé, with the added heft he required. Few ministers made note of the sentence. It would be several months before they recognized its — and Massé's — significance.

In a nod to his father, Martin summed up his budget speech by saying: "And so it falls to us, this generation, in our time, to do what those who came before us did in theirs — that is to assume our responsibilities, to create opportunity today. And that is the standard by which we will be judged by those who come after us." With that, he sat down, satisfied that the Liberals had taken the necessary steps to restore their reputation for managerial competence, and without breaking faith with their past.

Afterwards, he returned to the Finance offices at Esplanade Laurier for a post-budget party. He was generous in his remarks, heaping praise on the department for its tremendous contribution to their first budget together. As was his way, he laid it on thick. In the corner of the room, a knot of bruised officials snorted contemptuously: "Wait till tomorrow," one quipped.

9

THE NEW
KID'S SANDBOX

On January 31, less than three months in office, Lloyd Axworthy publicly launched his massive review of Canada's social security system. He disclosed plans for a complicated consultative process that would lead to legislation "later in the fall or early in the next year." Axworthy acknowledged the tightness of the timetable. "This is an ambitious plan," he conceded. "It engages us in a complex task. And it will result in major change. But it is worth doing. It needs doing. Canadians want us to do it. It is the reason for government — to give leadership, to mobilize energy, to foster a common will to improve our common lot." The House of Commons Standing Committee on Human Resources Development would conduct public hearings while a task force of experts helped him write an action plan. Axworthy would bring forth his plan in April, consulting the provinces thoroughly. He intended to strike fast, before circumstances could again, as in the early 1980s, conspire against him. That day marked the high point for his social security review.

Two major obstacles stood between Axworthy and the finishing line. His officials saw them as two filters through which the review would have to pass. He would have to win the cooperation of the provinces, particularly the two biggest, Quebec and Ontario; and he would have to keep his reform process in alignment with Paul Martin's fiscal plans. From beginning to end, nobody could ever discern a strategy for getting through either one, neither on the part of Axworthy nor from the central authorities in the Prime Minister's Office and Privy Council Office.

On Valentine's Day 1994, Axworthy talked for the first time with the provincial ministers. The meeting, closed to the public, went beyond a mere courtesy call. Except in unemployment insurance, Ottawa served as the non-custodial parent in the social policy field, providing financial support but, even at that, rather sparingly in the opinion of the custodial provinces. The delivery of welfare and education — as well as constitutional authority over them — resided in the provincial domain. And they also claimed job training as their own.

Despite his six years in the Manitoba legislature, Axworthy had little natural sympathy for the legitimate role of provinces. As a federal minister in the early 1980s, he had been a larger and more compelling figure than the fumbling Manitoba government of the day. Now his officials concluded that he regarded all provinces in the same manner as Manitoba — as irritants to manage, but not as equal partners with the federal government. He possessed the temperament of a soloist rather than that of the concertmaster. As the provincial ministers gathered at the government conference centre in Ottawa on February 14, federal officials covered their ears in anticipation of a cacophony of protest at the vague and secondary role to which Axworthy had relegated them.

In keeping with the spirit of the day, however, sweetness and light prevailed. Axworthy offered little of substance, but pledged to consult the provinces every step of the way. "We may see each other more often than we see our spouses," he joked. He warned that time was of the essence. Finance officials, with a very different agenda, were breathing down their necks. If ministers responsible for social and employment programs didn't define what they wanted, it would be defined for them, he prophesied. "It is going to happen one way or the other, so we might as well make sure that it happens in a way that introduces some of the priorities and principles that we share." Axworthy told the other ministers that Martin had promised him two years of stable social funding in which to complete the task. If they failed, "ministers of finance will make changes."

The provinces expressed concerns about his task force. They couldn't understand how he could closet himself with a group of experts writing an action plan while supposedly working in partnership with them. Axworthy, who only two weeks earlier had disclosed he would "chair a small task force," now denigrated that particular label as too grandiose to describe their function. The group consisted merely of advisers, he said, nothing so integral as a task force. He promised at least two more full-scale federal-provincial confabulations prior to any decisions: one in April before putting forward the draft action plan, and one in the fall to precede the introduction of legislation.

Axworthy's officials could scarcely believe their ears. They had expected a Valentine's Day Massacre and instead felt like voyeurs at a love-in. The provinces basically took the minister at his word.

The only discordant note was sounded by Joy MacPhail, the rookie British Columbia social services minister. She welcomed the talk of partnership but warned against what she called the sandbox dilemma. "I have a five-year-old son," she told Axworthy, "and we know that five-year-old kids travel in packs. One of his pack this past summer got a new sandbox and invited the rest of the guys over to play. When they arrived, it was awful because the one five-year-old, the owner, had filled the entire sandbox with a castle, and the other little guys had to sit around the edge and observe the castle and admire it. I will tell you what eventually their solution was to that kind of deal: it was that they kicked the shit out of the sand castle." MacPhail said she hoped that Axworthy would not leave everyone sitting around the edge of the sandbox admiring his castle.

Others thought her remarks impudent. But in short order they would find resonance in the sand castle metaphor. Just eight days later, in the budget, the federal government announced the biggest cuts ever to unemployment insurance, cuts bound to throw thousands of UI recipients onto provincial welfare rolls. Axworthy had promised that nothing would happen without consultation — then this. He would never regain the trust of the provinces. Indeed, despite the promises of partnership, the Valentine's Day meeting was the first and last time that he and his provincial counterparts would ever meet as a group.

Axworthy's genius in politics lay in his constant ability to generate new ideas and situate himself on the cutting edge of policy thinking. Politics, especially in developed democracies, is a conservative avocation; its longest-lasting practitioners understand, as Jean Chrétien had stated on election day, that they skate on thin ice. But Axworthy felt most comfortable probing the outer edges. The challenge of a new idea seemed to physically refresh him.

He and Martin were very much alike in their embrace of ideas. But there the similarity ended. Unlike Axworthy, Martin was slow to absorb new information, but once he adopted an idea he would pursue it with ruthless abandon. Axworthy tended to always broaden the discussion. He rarely settled, meandering down path after path, each time demanding his officials work up a new set of options or numbers. He would send his staff scurrying off in twenty different directions. By the time they returned, he had twenty new directions in mind.

Now back in power, the familiar pattern re-emerged. To the delight of the task force that wasn't a task force, Axworthy chose to participate personally in its meetings, at least initially. He came across as articulate and compassionate, impressing everyone around the table with the acuity and flexibility of his mind. But ever so gradually, it began to dawn on them that they weren't getting anywhere, never registering closure on anything. The group would prepare for a particular agenda item, and then Axworthy, responding to an offhand comment, would suddenly veer off in an entirely different direction, indulging his weekly enthusiasm. "It was completely disorganized. The activities were almost random," recounted Arthur Kroeger, a task force member. "It was week after week of just talk. We couldn't get a sense of what he really felt about anything."

Without obvious boundaries — either bureaucratically or within Axworthy's mind — the whole gigantic enterprise became unmanageably fluid. One day he would want to include x; the next day x was out and y was in. The only thing in the department's ambit clearly excluded was labour standards — and Axworthy had commissioned a separate group to examine them. Many of the participants couldn't understand why old-age security, one of Ottawa's biggest social programs, was out (they briefly thought otherwise), but post-secondary education transfers were in. Child care apparently was in, but the child care tax deduction, a largely middle-class benefit, seemed to be out.

Task force members pressed Axworthy to provide them with guidance on the amount of money at their disposal. They could talk all they liked about a new approach to child care or training, but without reference to the government's budget realities, they would never graduate beyond talk. They — and he — needed to consider the real-life trade-offs that made governing in the 1990s so challenging. "Unless you know what your constraints are and what resources you're working with, you never recognize priorities," Kroeger argued. "You just sit there and you talk. You say, Gee, child care is awfully important, and of course child poverty, we really have to do something about child poverty. Then there is the problem with the working poor and an endless list of the good things you'd want to do if you had all the money in the world."

But Axworthy steadfastly resisted. The more politically experienced task force members began to suspect that he had not even considered his end game. They would get nowhere when quizzing him on his strategy for dealing with budget cuts or even his plans for guiding his social security review through the upcoming Quebec election. He now came to their meetings only occasionally.

The intellectual curiosity the members had initially found so attractive in Axworthy came to be regarded as a critical absence of focus and discipline. The group's members, many of whom knew each other from previous pursuits, privately began to despair of his intellectual dilettantism. Ken Battle, director of the Caledon Institute for Social Policy, thought of him as a "classic Shakespearean character" — blessed in so many ways but marred by this one fatal flaw. Kroeger conjured an image of the Stephen Leacock story, with the horse riding off in all directions.

Battle discovered that one moment you were central to Axworthy's efforts and the next you didn't exist. He left the home opener of the Ottawa Lynx baseball season in April 1994 early because Axworthy's driver was coming by to pick up a copy of a task force paper before the minister headed off to England the next day. Battle never again heard a word about the paper.

Close to insurrection, a group of task force members got together in April and decided they should confront Axworthy in what amounted to the sort of intervention that friends might arrange to shock someone with a drinking problem into seeking help. They wanted Axworthy to understand that his efforts were leading nowhere. The delegation cornered him at his Parliament Hill office on a Friday evening, before a task force retreat that Axworthy would be attending. But they toned down their comments as they delivered them. At the rate they were progressing, the advisers told him, the department's staff would never complete an action plan. Axworthy seemed receptive to having the task force members pick up the pen. The minister himself prepared some handwritten directions over the weekend and furnished them to Battle, Maxwell, and Johnston on the Monday. But he hated the version they eventually submitted, they learned long afterwards.

At least the task force members could escape (in fact, they would petition for their own disbandment in May). But his officials, run ragged, could count on no such relief. They had welcomed Axworthy's appointment in November, figuring they had won the cabinet lottery with a minister possessing the intellect and energy and, better still, the stature within the government to push a reformist agenda. But the honeymoon didn't last. The creation of the task force, by its very nature, riled the department, challenging its natural monopoly over advice to the minister. And his seemingly capricious demands further eroded the initial goodwill. Now the officials just wanted a good night's sleep. Several of them had taken to waking at 3 a.m. to keep on top of the minister's demands. One of the policy analysts earned a measure of celebrity for being asleep at his desk most mornings, following yet another all-nighter.

Conflict with his officials had been a leitmotif through Axworthy's ministerial career. He seemed to take a reflexive dislike to his departmental bureaucracies. In his view, they were the protectors of the status quo, employing their energies and considerable resources to fend off true agents of change, like himself.

In the early 1980s, his modus operandi had been both to circumvent the departmental hierarchy and to infiltrate its ranks with his own people. In his book *Regional Ministers*, political scientist Herman Bakvis devoted two chapters to Axworthy's aggressive governing style in the Trudeau years. "Overall Axworthy was deeply leery of the bureaucracy and ... tended to be crisp if not downright rude, a quality that was unlikely to engender a great deal of loyalty and enthusiasm among many civil servants. Largely because of his deep-rooted suspicions, Axworthy, much more so than any minister up to that point, came to depend on his own personal staff, and in so doing broke new ground in the annals of minister-civil servant relations in Ottawa."

Now Axworthy set out to train the slow-moving Human Resources beast. But he had surrounded himself with a relatively weak political staff. And he was hobbled by Chrétien's decree that ministerial offices would be compact, a measure implemented, in part, to stymie ministers like Axworthy who were disinclined towards the sort of relationship between ministers and departments that the prime minister considered appropriate. Axworthy complained bitterly about the hiring limits and sought an exemption. The Prime Minister's Office generally rebuffed him.

The critical relationship between minister and department also suffered from the decidedly different temperaments and predilections of Axworthy and his deputy minister, Jean-Jacques Noreau. Axworthy was an ideas guy, one lacking skill at the often slow process of consensus building. Noreau, on the other hand, was, in the parlance of the business, a process guy. His manner was bureaucratic, through and through; even his moustache seemed standard-issue. The consensus mattered to him as much as, or perhaps more than, the subject of the consensus.

Ministers do not choose their own deputies; they are appointed at the pleasure of the prime minister on the recommendation of the clerk of the Privy Council, the person who can most influence their careers. Noreau, like Chrétien's new clerk, Jocelyne Bourgon, had been among a group of deputies who had strongly supported the devolutionist thrust of the 1992 Charlottetown Accord. In Kim Campbell's brief tenure, he negotiated a hasty August 1993 offer to cede control of labour market training to Quebec. He felt that the federal government had missed too many opportunities to work things out with the provinces and worried about the growing sense of Ottawa being out there with "its big federal feet in other people's territory." Along with Bourgon, he viewed the social security review at least in part as a new opportunity to make peace with Quebec — and other provinces.

Axworthy also thought of himself as a decentralist, but one with a decidedly different bent. He preferred to bypass the provinces altogether and devolve power directly to individuals. Why transfer funding for post-secondary education to the provinces, he wondered, when you could give it directly to students in the form of vouchers? Why cover half the costs of welfare, with no say over how the provinces ran their various programs, when you could transfer money directly to poor children through the child tax benefit? He didn't want a partnership with the provinces in social policy; he wanted a divorce. And he didn't want to pay support.

The presence of two competing visions atop the department further strained the lives of the Human Resources officials. Middle-level functionaries, handed marching orders by Axworthy or his staff, would produce a report and send it up the line, only to see it blocked in Noreau's office one floor below the minister's. He would order it redone in a more "province-friendly" manner. Then the minister would vent his displeasure. The department's apparent resistance frustrated Axworthy's staff. "Every time we sent something downstairs," complained one aide, "it would disappear. And then when it finally materialized, it came back wearing a moustache. You couldn't recognize it."

The officials, feeling trapped, retreated into the safe haven of ambiguity. Noreau wanted to work closely with the provinces; Axworthy did not. "So the kind of solution we would come up with was a meeting with some of the provinces where nothing would happen," explained a weary veteran of the social security review. That would keep them both off your back.

The Chrétien government's post–Red Book agenda had been organized around a Holy Trinity of issues — the deficit, managed by Paul Martin; social security review, in Axworthy's hands; and national unity, run out of the Prime Minister's Office. All enjoyed top priority. But little discussion had taken place as to the interaction among them. In Chrétien's governing model, everyone was on their own. The centre refrained from strategy, restricting itself to problem-solving.

HRD's outside communications consultants — Elly Alboim, the former Ottawa bureau chief for CBC-TV, and David Herle, a politically gifted former president of the Young Liberals — regularly issued warnings to the department about its lack of a plan for dealing with the deficit and national unity. HRD needed to position itself in the slipstream of those two issues, which ultimately would matter more to the government, rather than in contradiction to them, they counselled. But Axworthy seemed indifferent, and Noreau's horizon tended to be limited to the crisis of the day rather than the potential crisis of the next six months.

Outwardly, Chrétien talked up a business-as-usual approach and the equal treatment of provinces, both of which boded well for Axworthy. But the prime minister's musings to caucus, cabinet, and staff made plain that Quebec came first in his priorities. Every Wednesday morning, the national Liberal caucus, MPs and senators, would gather in the old Reading Room just to the east of the Commons chamber. The chairs of the regional caucuses, which had already met individually, presented their reports, and then the floor was opened for questions or observations. Finally, Chrétien would speak, often in a stream of consciousness, one that invariably flowed into the most fertile delta of his thinking, Quebec and its continuing role in Canada.

In January, Daniel Johnson had taken over from Robert Bourassa as premier of Quebec, knowing full well that a provincial election could not be put off much longer and that the governing provincial Liberals were trailing the separatists in all the polls. Johnson, as unequivocal a federalist as had led Quebec for many years, demanded assistance from the Chrétien government. He and his advisers drew up a shopping list of issues, progress on which they felt could demonstrate, in tangible fashion, the flexible nature of federalism and Ottawa's sensitivity to the needs and aspirations of Quebec. The first item on the list was action on cigarette smuggling, much of which originated on Indian reserves. They also sought the complete devolution of labour market training to the province; a Quebec-friendly federal budget; completion of an internal trade agreement with the other provinces; and renewal of a ten-year-old regional development agreement.

The reconciliation of the Liberal instinct for a strong federal role in social policy with the party's historic commitment to national unity had confounded social ministers for generations. As Queen's University academic Keith Banting later wrote in a post-mortem on Axworthy's social security review: "Nationalist forces within Quebec politics have challenged federal leadership in social policy since the days of the Tremblay Commission in the mid-1950s, and since then the politics of social policy in Canada have been fueled as much by inter-governmental struggles over jurisdiction as by substantive differences over program content."

In early February Chrétien took uncharacteristically swift action on tobacco smuggling, cutting cigarette taxes and increasing enforcement measures against smugglers. Johnson was gratified but quickly resumed pressuring Ottawa to get to the next item on his list: labour market training. Johnson's demand put Lloyd Axworthy, like many of his predecessors, in conflict with the Quebec agenda. The province wanted the Chrétien government — following through on the promise of the failed constitutional agreements and the pre-election offer from Campbell — to vacate the training field and hand over the $900 million Ottawa spent on such programs in Quebec.

Axworthy felt tremendous pressure to offer up something. But he had strong reasons not to give away the shop. After all, how could he prejudge the outcome of his social security review by surrendering such an important lever as training, especially given Ottawa's interest in upgrading the job prospects of unemployment insurance recipients, who were its constitutional responsibility?

All through the late winter and spring, top-secret negotiations went back and forth and back again. At one point in March, all the key federal representatives — Axworthy, Martin, Massé, Noreau, and Jean Pelletier — flew to Quebec City for a meeting at the Bunker with three provincial ministers and Johnson's chief of staff, Pierre Anctil.

Back in Ottawa, the Liberals cobbled together an interim offer. Quebec would gain immediate control over delivering the $140 million worth of federal training that Ottawa purchased annually from the province's community colleges and participate in planning of other federal training programs. Massé urged Johnson to accept half a loaf, which was all that could be expected from the cabinet at that point. The documents contemplated further devolution once the social security review was complete. Axworthy asked his Quebec counterpart not to prejudge the review, to treat the offer as a down-payment. But the deal failed to make the grade for Johnson, who feared that if he came home with anything less than had been on the table previously, he would be laughed out of the court of public opinion.

In early April, news of the federal offer to Quebec leaked in the press. Johnson immediately distanced himself, vowing that he would not sign "a bargain basement offer." He also called off the province's participation at Axworthy's second federal-provincial meeting, scheduled for April 18. The PMO advisers, increasingly sour on Johnson, felt he had been looking for an excuse in any case.

Other provincial social ministers, upset over the unilateral UI cuts and the parsimonious doling out of information from Ottawa, also rumbled about a boycott. A week before the meeting, they still lacked any background papers on the shape of the action plan (which, in fact, had not taken shape). How could they prepare? The Valentine's Day spell was broken. "Officially and even unofficially, I know nothing, and I find that disturbing," Joy MacPhail stated, suggesting she and B.C.'s labour minister might not attend.

Ontario also bristled. Axworthy had identified the Rae government as a natural ally in his social security review, and, as an important gesture of goodwill, had promised to end the financial discrimination against the province built into federal social assistance transfers under the Canada Assistance Plan since 1990. But with the Ontario government approaching an election, a rupture existed within its own ranks over the political advisability of cooperating with Ottawa. Ultimately, the hawks gained the upper hand and persuaded Rae to take a hard line.

All sides now pressed in on the beleaguered Axworthy. Even the social policy groups, his natural political constituency, turned against him. His reputed credibility with trade unions and anti-poverty activists had been part of the rationale for naming him to the portfolio. But the groups now dismissed him as a stalking-horse for yet another Finance Department attack on social spending.

As the pressures mounted, Axworthy, who had always exhibited a tendency to blame others, lashed out at those former allies on the left now busy throwing darts at him. These "naysayers" failed to appreciate that he stood between them and a Reform Party solution. He had attempted to buy some trade union support by agreeing to a proposal from Bob White, president of the Canadian Labour Congress, to establish a group to examine the distribution of work in Canada. But the UI changes that had upset the provinces had also poisoned the well with the labour movement. In April, Axworthy delivered an address on the state of the social security review at a jobs conference. In the question-and-answer session, unionists upbraided him for the reduction in UI benefits at a time of double-digit unemployment. A defensive Axworthy beseeched the unions not to take "to the barricades."

The dressing-down, while unpleasant, became regular fare. He treated these attacks — which reeked of the bitterness of brothers betrayed — not so much as differences of opinion, but as challenges to his very integrity. His angry responses to left-wing challenges astounded Dan Miller, the British Columbia labour minister. Such agitations came with the territory in politics, Miller remarked, a fact he figured a politician of Axworthy's experience would have accepted long ago.

Social activists, feeling the sharp edge of his tongue in various public forums, inevitably banded together in a loose-knit victims' group. Jean Swanson, the chairwoman of the National Anti-Poverty Organization, distributed a limited edition of eight buttons to the survivors of various Axworthy public pilloryings. The buttons read: "Axworthy Screeched at Me."

Cracks also began to emerge in Axworthy's relationships with cabinet colleagues. Like the provinces, they resented the primacy of the task force, which seemed to know more than they did about the minister's intentions. The more-political ministers fretted over the crazy concoctions a group of ivory tower thinkers might put forth. They already felt that Axworthy tended to be too academic for his own good, that he relied too heavily on the force of reason rather than a good reading of the public mood. "The task force of super-academics scares the bejesus out of me," Nova Scotia minister David Dingwall confided to some of his colleagues.

On Thursday, April 14, Axworthy acknowledged the deterioration in relations with the provinces and cancelled the federal-provincial meeting scheduled for the following Monday. Task force members, many of them gathered in Toronto for the annual dinner of the Public Policy Forum, refused at first to believe the news. They found it painful to contemplate how far off the rails the social security review had slid in such a short time.

Back in Ottawa the next day, Deputy Prime Minister Sheila Copps responded to the cancellation with the first public glimpse into the cabinet's misgivings. "Everybody wanted to feel very comfortable with the proposals in the action plan before the meeting, and that includes the federal government," she said. Axworthy was furious with Copps, who as chair of cabinet's Social Development Committee would play a key role in upcoming deliberations over his action plan. Both he and the PCO officials had already contemplated going around Copps. Ultimately, they deprived her committee of the right to oversee the Axworthy proposals, creating instead a special committee that included economic as well as social ministers. But Copps, making use of her special access to the prime minister, managed to chair that one too.

Ministers, Axworthy among them, dreaded the Copps treatment. She spewed negativity and held strong views on everything, regardless of her knowledge base. At forty-one, her political approach had been formed by a dozen years spent on the opposition benches in Ottawa and Queen's Park. Sheila Copps knew how to criticize, mock, needle, deconstruct. She had excelled in Question Period in opposition, flustering ministers opposite with her considerable volumes of energy and passion. But could she work effectively with a team of other ministers to construct and govern? When she was a committee chair, others felt she should serve as a neutral force, forewarning ministers of brewing objections and smoothing out conflicts. To many, she seemed more comfortable working against her colleagues than with them.

In May, the special cabinet committee took its first full look at Axworthy's draft action plan. The sweep of the document caught some of the ministers by surprise. A decade earlier, commenting on the National Energy Program, Roy MacLaren had questioned the ability of any government to tackle three goals simultaneously in a single policy. "One is possible. Two is difficult. But to do three things at the same time is virtually impossible. Even the ringmaster of that superb circus in Moscow had, I recall, difficulty in keeping his eye on all three rings concurrently."

Axworthy had settled on reforming three general spheres comprising $38 billion in spending: the unemployment insurance system, including training; social assistance, including the vexing problem of child poverty; and post-secondary education funding. UI alone would be tough enough. Successive governments had chipped away at the liberalization of the program introduced in 1971 by Bryce Mackasey, but all had shrunk from the sort of frontal assault that Axworthy proposed. Although the program had already taken a big hit in Martin's budget, Axworthy intended to shoot again at frequent users of UI, threatening particularly seasonal workers in Atlantic Canada.

His plans for social assistance and especially for post-secondary education also gave cause for concern. To small-l Liberals like Herb Gray, Sheila Copps, and Sergio Marchi, his approach smacked of an abandonment of the welfare state. To the devolutionists, led by Marcel Massé, his desire for a massive federally led overhaul of programs constitutionally outside Ottawa's jurisdiction trod provocatively on provincial territory. Massé, mindful of the looming Quebec election, argued that the paper must be "more green" — by which he meant less categorical — and "more province sensitive," particularly in regard to post-secondary education.

To Axworthy's thinking, he had been given a mandate by a prime minister prepared to let his ministers be ministers. Moreover, the Holy Trinity of issues were all to proceed in lockstep. Nobody had ever stated that one had greater priority over the others. And, he continued to believe, he had two years to get the job done.

The close attentions of his colleagues left Axworthy smouldering. When challenged, he tended to get defensive and withdraw rather than fight back, reinforcing his loner status. Like his task force, his cabinet colleagues were having trouble understanding how all the pieces were going to fit together. One of the other ministers on the committee, watching him during a particularly gruelling session, remarked that he looked "as if he was almost folded upon himself." A couple of others wondered why he tolerated the incursions into his territory — why, like Transport Minister Doug Young, he didn't just stare down his tormentors.

Axworthy, who had come to politics from the academic world, seemed to lack the toughness of a millionaire businessman like Young. And unlike Martin, he had not been blessed with a gift for influencing people through the use of humour or charm. (One minister, commenting on Martin's effectiveness in cabinet, volunteered, "He's nice to the wives.") David Zussman, who had sat on Axworthy's task force and then watched the process spin out of control from his new vantage point working on program review in the Privy Council Office, couldn't help thinking how much better it might all have been if only Axworthy would bother having lunch from time to time with a fellow minister or two.

Axworthy's officials continually badgered him to arrange one-on-one meetings — so-called bilaterals — with key cabinet members to try to assuage their various concerns. In some cases, he could have pacified them by simply providing more information or making a minor adjustment, or even just reaching out.

But Axworthy had never been the most collegial of ministers. In the 1980s his staff tended to win support for his measures through judicious use of the grab-bag of spending envelopes they controlled and the goodies, such as ministerial immigration permits, they could dole out. Axworthy, as the only elected minister from western Canada, sat on most cabinet committees and controlled all kinds of spending. "You didn't say no to Lloyd," recounted a veteran of the era. But the heavily indebted Chrétien government did not afford as many opportunities for such horse-trading.

Now he degenerated from uncollegial to anti-collegial. The requests for bilaterals went unanswered. All ministers have shortcomings — some more acute than others. It is for their advisers to bridge these gaps. Unfortunately, nobody in his immediate entourage seemed prepared to challenge him. As a result, his proposals became mired in committee, the same issues resurfacing week after week. Normally, the chairperson might have moved to break the logjam. But Copps had assumed the role of antagonist, not mediator.

Word of his growing isolation seeped back to former Axworthy staffers and cronies from the early 1980s. These so-called Old Friends of Lloyd had struggled in the early 1980s against his ineptitude at political networking and his insensitivity in human relations. He would regularly bow out of Liberal Party functions at the last minute, especially in those scores of ridings stretching north and west of Winnipeg, embittering the very local grandees whose support he would require in a leadership bid. Assessing his leadership prospects in 1990, he found himself needing to line up several big-name endorsements. His organizers identified Allan MacEachen, the left-leaning Liberal senator who had ruled the Maritimes during the Trudeau years, as a promising target. Rather than take MacEachen to lunch himself, Axworthy assigned the task to David Walker, a long-time friend but a rookie MP.

But even the Friends found the stories of his most recent behaviour disturbing. "It was not like Lloyd to be collegial," one of them remarked. "But it also wasn't like Lloyd to be anti-collegial." Beginning in the summer and continuing through the fall, a group of them tried to arrange a dinner with him to offer some ideas for dealing with his cabinet travails. Three times the Old Friends of Lloyd scheduled the dinner. Three times Axworthy cancelled. Finally, they gave up.

By now, Daniel Johnson had let a June election date slip by. September provided the next window. Axworthy still seemed to be without a rejoinder to the concerns of Quebec ministers that his foray into provincial jurisdictions would undermine the already slim chances of the Quebec Liberals. On the afternoon of July 4, the pressures blew the Axworthy reforms right out of cabinet. Ministers rejected the latest draft of his action plan. They pushed its release, already postponed several times, back to the fall, after the Quebec election. Everything would have to be rethought: the communications strategy, the process for working with the provinces, and especially the federal role in social policy. The department was told that the sections of the paper dealing with post-secondary education contemplated too robust a federal role, failing to pay due deference to provincial jurisdiction. "It was delayed to avoid giving the separatists an easy target," Jean-Jacques Noreau later conceded. The new release would be in September. Tellingly, the document would no longer be referred to as an action plan; henceforth it would be called a discussion paper.

The department arranged a series of post-mortems, dubbed the "Where Do We Go From Here" meetings. On July 6, it concluded that it would have to improve on four counts: the timetable would have to be more realistic; more sensitivity would have to be shown to the provincial role; a better working relationship would have to be established with the PMO, PCO, and Finance; and the department would have to figure out a way to control Axworthy's intellectual meanderings so they could be translated into concrete policy — what they called "getting to the bottom line with the minister." His officials expressed concern about the minister's credibility, both within the government and with the public. He had been badly damaged by his repeated missed deadlines.

Axworthy had been right in thinking that his window of opportunity had come — and gone — in April. Any later, and he would be trying to bring out a controversial social policy reform in the midst of the Quebec election campaign. His review, with its attentions to post-secondary education policies — a certain red flag to Quebec, which guarded its jurisdiction zealously — was comprehensive, all right. It may even have been good policy. But in a federal state like Canada, where power was shared and where Quebec always posed special challenges, its ambition was out of proportion to the possibilities. Rather than expedite the process, at every juncture Axworthy had insisted on broadening the review, on examining one more idea, including one more bell or whistle. And so he missed his window of opportunity and perhaps his chance to make some history.

At the start of the government, Axworthy had been seen as the standard-bearer for the social Liberals in cabinet. But their vision — indeed the Trudeau vision — had trouble getting airborne in this Liberal government. A competing vision, more fiscally grounded and provincially oriented, appeared to be gaining ascendancy, a vision most forcefully propounded by the intergovernmental affairs minister, Marcel Massé, and supported by his partner, the most powerful minister in the Chrétien government, Finance Minister Paul Martin.

10

HANG TOGETHER OR
HANG SEPARATELY

The initial reviews of the February 1994 budget had gratified Martin. A poll by the Angus Reid organization found 55 per cent of respondents judged the Liberals on the right track versus 27 per cent who felt otherwise. The economic commentators were impressed by the prudence of his economic assumptions in contrast to the jiggery-pokery to which they had become accustomed. They hadn't been privy to the battles within Esplanade Laurier over bad forecasts, but they could judge the outcome: his budget was built on rock-solid foundations. He would make his targets, feeble though they may have been.

The team at the Bank of Nova Scotia, in the spirit of the Winter Olympics then under way, gave him a gold for the realism of his economic assumptions, a silver for spending control, and a bronze for leaving taxes largely untouched. The brokerage firm Merrill Lynch judged his projections so conservative that the deficit could actually come in as much as $5 billion lower than stated. Amy Smith, a currency analyst in New York, questioned only one Martin assumption: that short-term interest rates would fall to 4.5 per cent. She maintained they would be far lower than that. By and large, the newspaper reviews were pretty favourable, too, grousing about this or that but accepting the budget overall as a reasonable opening effort.

Except, that is, for the *Globe and Mail*. The national daily, the breakfast companion of the business and political elite, hammered Martin in its editorial pages from the word go. Its editorial the morning after the budget was headlined "Martin cowers before Debt Mountain." "The Liberal government's approach to deficit reduction may be summarized as follows: do not seem to try, and you will not be seen to fail," it thundered about the modesty of his 3-per-cent target.

Two days later, the *Globe* weighed in again with an attack on Martin's personal credibility in an editorial entitled "Cheap tricks for tawdry ends." The piece said it had been a mystery since Martin's Université de Montréal speech in November how the Tories could have been so far off in their deficit projections of the previous April. "Only now, with the release of Martin's own budget, is the answer clear… Mr. Martin fibbed." The editorial described how certain revenues and expenditures had been juggled back and forth between the last Tory budget and Martin's recent offering to inflate Mazankowski's deficit figure and bring down Martin's number. It characterized Liberal efforts as "a pack of lies" and judged that "what is truly appalling about this performance is its duplicity."

You could say a lot of things to Paul Martin — he loved a good argument. He would debate anyone on any topic till 4 in the morning. But the attacks on his personal integrity penetrated like a dagger into his well-developed pride. The editorial left him deeply wounded.

On March 1, he arrived at the *Globe* offices at 444 Front Street West, on the fringe of Toronto's old garment district, for a session with the paper's editorial board. David Dodge and Terrie O'Leary accompanied him, underlining the importance he placed on his media relations. Dodge, knowing the extent of Martin's anger about the editorial, begged him to remain calm. Inflamed passions would not help matters.

Meetings of an editorial board — the group within a newspaper that is in charge of its opinion sections — can be intellectually challenging but are almost always civil. Not this time. Despite Dodge's urgings of diplomacy, both sides sat down loaded for bear.

William Thorsell, the paper's editor-in-chief and a tireless campaigner for rolling back government, opened the session by accusing the Liberals of wanting to grow their way out of the deficit. That set Martin off. He told Thorsell that he had a lot of faith and confidence in the *Globe* and was impressed with the quality of its reporters. But he failed to understand why its columnists and editorialists continually misinterpreted the positions he had taken. He quoted from his budget speech, saying that growth alone would be inadequate to slay the deficit. "I find it hard to believe that anybody would think that I said that … we can grow our way out of this thing." But he also reiterated his view that spending cuts alone represented a "simplistic approach" since the deficit was the product of more fundamental economic problems. "You can cut all you want. You're not going to solve this problem. It is much deeper than any cutting."

Andrew Coyne, the paper's insouciant neoconservative commentator, then heaped scorn on the Liberal deficit targets. Coyne's youthful looks and smart-alecky manner infuriated his legions of critics as much as his sharp-edged views. Martin, who rightly suspected Coyne of authoring the offending editorials, accused him of engaging in a lot of empty rhetoric. He agreed that the level of the deficit "of course, is unacceptable." But the Tories had never reached 3 per cent. The point was to begin moving the deficit downward and proving that this government was capable of achieving its targets.

Coyne went back on the attack, asking incredulously how the Liberals could possibly count among their cuts measures previously announced by Conservative Finance Minister Don Mazankowski. This really galled Martin. The Tories had never enacted the legislation to secure the Mazankowski cuts. As far as he was concerned, they were merely paper cuts, at least until he had made them real. He had taken a pretty heavy beating at cabinet for deciding to implement the Tory cuts. Coyne was acting as if he had caught Martin out, whereas Martin contended that he had been scrupulous in making note of the origin of the cuts in the budget documents.

"I find it very hard to believe that it is a, quote, cheap and tawdry trick that we have followed conventional accounting practices of government that have been established for a coon's age," Martin said, referring to the accusatory editorial. Thorsell defended the piece and criticized the government's accounting practices. Martin countered that while he didn't necessarily agree with Thorsell's view, it represented a reasonable difference of opinion. "It is not a fib. It is not a cheap and tawdry trick."

It was turning into a verbal version of a Saturday-afternoon tag-team wrestling match. Coyne jumped back into the ring, accusing Martin again of playing with the numbers for political gain. Martin repeated that he had been completely up front with how he had arrived at his numbers. "We told the world," he wailed. "So for somebody to turn around then and say they have discovered them — now I know what the Indians felt like when Columbus arrived." Coyne challenged him on his authority to know what was good for business. Martin, flabbergasted, recited his résumé.

Now Dodge, forgetting his own proscriptions, jumped over the ropes. He had been boiling away on the sidelines, disturbed by Coyne's disrespect. His voice rising in anger, his hand stabbing the air, he tried to show Coyne the document laying out what Martin had done. Coyne told him to keep his fingers to himself. "You keep them to *your*self," Dodge shot back angrily. Coyne lashed out again at the timidity of the Liberal targets. He, too, was getting more and more agitated.

Martin and O'Leary looked at each other in astonishment. "Calm down, you're going to have a heart attack," Martin said to Coyne.

"I'm not the one pounding the table," Coyne retorted.

Martin was a man who liked to be liked and hated to be disrespected. The *Globe*'s attacks, which continued apace after the extraordinary session, weighed heavily on him. Some of his advisers believed the paper's unrelenting campaign played a significant role in his transformation to deficit hawk over the coming months. He simply couldn't abide being the whipping boy of the newspaper his friends and associates read. Indeed, a number of his friends, disappointed with his first budget, let him know that if he didn't toughen up the second time around, when it came time to return to the business world after politics he could be perceived as someone who had fallen well short of expectations, like John Turner.

As time wore on, other economic opinion-makers adopted the *Globe* line on the inadequacy of the cuts. Martin wouldn't realize it for some time later — and he would never accept it as just — but the audience that counted, the economic chattering classes and those Masters of the Universe who swapped bonds around the globe in such huge amounts that they said "ten" when they meant $10 million, was turning thumbs down on his first budget.

Indeed, Martin never got beyond his defensiveness over that first budget. He would vacillate between extolling its virtues and making excuses for its shortcomings, often in the same sentence. His tough approach to UI and defence demonstrated the gutsiness that would be confirmed a year later, but it was offset by mounds of mush elsewhere. Martin would beg for understanding, noting that he had had only a hundred days or so to bring the budget down. There was only so much that could be accomplished in the first round. His reaction drove Terrie O'Leary around the bend. She thought there was plenty to recommend in the first budget and persuaded Martin to take to the road during the summer with an elaborate display meant to show the decision-makers that eradicating the deficit wasn't as simple as it looked from Bay Street.

In fairness, the budget featured several innovations that would become the hallmarks of Martin's stewardship at Finance: the use of prudent economic assumptions; the large, $2.4-billion contingency fund; the refusal to finance new initiatives unless the ministers in question could come up with the money by reallocating from other spending. Before Martin, ministers would regularly agree to initiatives without giving any thought to financing them. Such had been the case with the Tories' famous Green Plan, administered by the Department of Environment, and the grants and loans made available for oil upgraders in Regina and Lloydminster. Since these programs were the brainchildren of cabinet committees, no department would take responsibility for them in its budget. Instead, they were financed from reserves. In the weeks following his first budget, Martin learned that certain ministers had taken to charging programs against this contingency fund. He hit the roof, insisting that it was in place to protect against incorrect economic assumptions and for no other purpose. Nothing could go to cabinet without its own financing plan.

Martin had stated from the outset that his opening effort was merely the first part of a two-year budget plan. But his go-softly approach was also a testament to Liberal ambivalence on the deficit. Few ministers had truly bought into deficit reduction. MacLaren was probably over there with the *Globe*. So was Massé. Martin gravitated in that direction. Transport Minister Doug Young, Industry Minister John Manley, and several others were inclined to emphasize fiscal concerns, but by and large, the Liberal spending impulse had not subsided.

On a swing through Edmonton in March, Chrétien caused a flap when discussing the budget on a radio talk show. Host Ron Collister, accustomed to the permanent budgetary revolution carried out by the Klein government, asked Chrétien what areas he would cut next.

"To go to our goal of 3 per cent of GNP, all the cuts have been announced in the budget. There will not be a new round," Chrétien said.

"No surprises a year from now?" Collister persisted.

"No, there may be some changes, but there is nothing. The budget of Mr. Martin last week is all based on the prediction of 3-per-cent growth." It was a typical Chrétien verbal puzzle; it seemed to say something, but revealed nothing — except perhaps confusion, but even that was hard to know for sure. *There may be some changes, but there is nothing.* It was unclear if his 3-per-cent reference was to economic growth or the deficit target or both. Only a professional code-breaker could know for sure.

Two things appeared crystal clear: the Liberals did not think radical solutions were necessary to cut the deficit, and they believed that the 3-per-cent deficit target was in the bag. Within a matter of weeks, they would be proven wrong on both points.

Meanwhile, the biggest fallout from the budget had landed on the national unity front. The budget had contained two major spending measures: deep cuts to unemployment insurance, which came as a complete surprise, and the shutting down of some defence bases. The Liberals had held their breath over UI, privately fretting that this move would surely mark the end of their honeymoon. They had raked the previous Tory government over the coals for similar, indeed smaller, cuts. But with the exception of a rowdy demonstration in Shawinigan, in which the prime minister had been jostled by the crowd and a plate glass window had shattered, the Teflon Man slid through. The closing of the defence bases, while attracting great attention locally, had failed to coalesce as an issue, with one notable exception.

Martin had given Defence Minister David Collenette a savings target and instructed him to keep the specifics of his planned closings to himself. Martin didn't want to know; he would be busy, far too busy to have to fend off the lobbying efforts of individual MPs and regional ministers. Ignorance would be best.

Defence was one of the few areas of government activity not generally popular, which is why the Liberals had been unusually explicit in targeting it in the Red Book. When Collenette arrived in the department, the officials already had options ready for him. Their equation was simple: they wanted to preserve their equipment purchase budgets and were more than willing to sacrifice what they called infrastructure, by which they meant military bases. They bemoaned the loss of the EH-101 helicopters on the first day of the new government as short-sighted and wrong-headed. The unfortunate fact of life, though, was that it was always easier for a government to defer, or even cancel, a capital spending project than it was to devastate a community with a base closing.

At his first briefing, the department gave Collenette its options for the Red Book's promised $350 million in defence cuts in 1994–95 (above and beyond the helicopters). Closing Quebec's Collège Militaire Royale in Saint-Jean-sur-Richelieu, one of the country's three military colleges, was on that first list. "I remember my initial instinct was that this was going to be rough," Collenette later recalled. "I did my French-language training there as an MP. It's a beautiful place. It means a lot and it's quite successful. But we just couldn't keep three military colleges." The military wanted to consolidate the three colleges in Kingston, which entailed clos-ing both CMR and the Royal Roads facility in Victoria. "You had to close both of them," or invite charges of favouritism, Collenette said. "It's either three or one."

The government had decided against the torturous process of public consultations on which bases should go and which should stay. Chrétien, Martin, and Collenette agreed that it should be a budget decision: fast, clean, and hard to go back on. So by virtue of budget secrecy, the informa-tion on which bases would go was held within a tight circle. Even Martin did not learn of Collenette's precise choices until about forty-eight hours before the budget. Other members of cabinet found out only when Collenette furnished affected ministers with letters before they went downstairs to hear Martin's budget. The Quebec ministers would subse-quently complain that such a critical measure had not been subjected to adequate political scrutiny. Jean Pelletier suspected that the military had taken advantage of a young and relatively disorganized government.

It didn't take the Bloc Québécois long to latch on to the closure as a sign of Ottawa's perfidy. Within forty-eight hours, Lucien Bouchard had taken up the cudgel, accusing the government of "taking us back forty years and wiping out a symbol of success for the French fact in Canada." It was indeed a powerful symbol, an institution created to overcome anglo antipathies to French Canadians in senior military positions. Worse yet, officer training would now be consolidated at Kingston, a city widely viewed by Quebeckers as a haven for anti-French sentiments.

Daniel Johnson's new government in Quebec had asked Ottawa to be vigilant against budget measures that might harm his re-election prospects. Chrétien obliged as much as possible, arranging advance briefings, includ-ing a one-on-one between Martin and Johnson. The provincial Liberals had no hint, however, about the CMR closure — not surprising given that Martin himself had chosen to remain uninformed. At first, Johnson mis-read the dangers, shrugging in the budget aftermath that Quebec had to pay the same price as everyone for deficit reduction. But as the outcry spread, he dispatched delegations to Ottawa to try to repair the damage.

Chrétien handed the file to Marcel Massé — who held responsibility for intergovernmental affairs as well as program review — with succinct instructions: the closing is final, now fix the political problem. Ottawa was willing to lease the facility to the province for a dollar a year as an edu-cational institution and maintain its language school at the base. But the provincial Liberals, much to Massé's consternation, didn't want to rush into negotiations, preferring to establish a commission to examine the options. To complicate the matter further, political consideration dictated that any offer to Quebec on CMR needed to be matched by equivalent concessions to British Columbia on Royal Roads. And the Defence Department didn't want to bear any indirect costs.

It would take many months of work for Massé to reach an accommodation with the government in Quebec. Even then, the provincial Liberals chose not to ratify their agreement, leaving the matter open for the Parti Québécois to further exploit when it came to power in September. The lesson of the CMR fiasco was twofold. First, the third prong of the Massé approach — clarifying federal-provincial relations — was easier said than done. Federal interests often diverged and provinces had minds of their own, even when it came to the terms under which Ottawa would give something away. Second, working in tandem even with federalist allies in Quebec — and there had rarely been a Quebec Liberal leader as unequivocally federalist as Daniel Johnson — could never be taken for granted. The provincial party had an agenda of its own, one often very different from that of Jean Chrétien's government.

By spring, it was evident that Martin's budget had crashed against the rocks. With cruel irony, it was undone by a faulty economic assumption, in this case on interest rates. Martin had tried to be prudent, but he hadn't reckoned that the U.S. Federal Reserve Board would aggressively move to snuff out inflationary pressure in the United States with a series of interest rate rises in March and April. Concerns that an imminent election in Quebec would return a separatist government to power and growing disappointment over the budget added to the upward pressure on Canadian rates. To add salt to Martin's wounds, the spread between American and Canadian interest rates had widened. The fact that Canadians — with their lower inflation rate — had to pay more for money than Americans drove Martin wild. In February, with a rookie's naiveté, he had ventured publicly that Canadian rates were soon destined to dip below American ones, causing conniptions in the marketplace, which immediately bid down the Canadian dollar and forced up Canadian rates. Now, in the wake of his budget, the premium an indebted Canada paid for its money was moving in the wrong direction.

By early May, with the budget barely two months old, interest rates stood two percentage points above the supposedly prudent budget assumptions. If the rates didn't fall back fairly quickly, Martin would never reach his 3-per-cent deficit target. Each additional point of interest added $1.7 billion a year to the government's costs — that was the consequence of being $500 billion in hock. Thanks to his contingency fund and the conservatism of his economic growth projections, he looked safe to make his modest $39.7-billion deficit target in the first year. But Finance could see the targets for years two and three slipping out of reach. There would be no way to make the 3 per cent without additional spending cuts — deep, un-Liberal ones.

Suddenly, people paid close attention to Chrétien's offhand comments to Ron Collister in Edmonton. Would a politician so wedded to the safe middle ground countenance radical spending cuts? Right from his Université de Montréal speech the previous fall, Martin had insisted that he would do whatever it took to make the 3 per cent. But did the prime minister share the same commitment? That was the question making the rounds at the smart luncheon spots in Ottawa.

Chrétien and Martin had spoken early in the life of the government of the need for there never to be "any light between them." Chrétien was a big believer in giving ministers their head. He liked to tell the story of how Trudeau had once taken him aside and asked, "Jean, are you mad at me? You haven't spoken to me for a long time." Chrétien replied that everything was fine, he was just doing his job. "My job is not to be a bother." That was Chrétien's model of a good minister: one who didn't bother the prime minister.

But the minister of finance must be a bother. His role is central to the functioning of a cabinet, and any differences or appearance of differences with the prime minister of the day can quickly cripple the entire government. The resignation of Chancellor of the Exchequer Nigel Lawson in Britain in 1990 over policy disputes with Margaret Thatcher's personal economic adviser was part of a chain of events that eventually led to Thatcher's downfall as well. In Britain, the aphorism about prime ministers and chancellors held that they hang together or they hang separately.

Among the many subtle assignments of a prime minister is to watch his finance minister's backside. If he sees a cabinet discussion going badly, a PM can move quickly to defer a decision until a future meeting. He doesn't want his finance minister's authority diminished. Prime ministers and finance ministers must be seen as one. Their disagreements must never spill out, even in front of cabinet. When Chrétien made his remark on spending in Edmonton, his entourage didn't think twice about it. Martin was in New York City at the time, schmoozing the financial community. Terrie O'Leary, who had accompanied him, and Peter Donolo, who was travelling with the prime minister, spoke nightly by phone to compare notes, making sure their bosses were, as they liked to say, on message. The night of the Collister interview, Donolo didn't even think to make note of the matter. It was only over the next couple of days, when he and O'Leary saw that the *Globe and Mail* was treating the story as a split in the top ranks of government, that they rushed to control the damage. They wanted to draw the curtains quickly on any impression that even a sliver of light separated Martin and Chrétien.

As a former finance minister himself, Chrétien had a greater than normal interest for prime ministers in fiscal matters. He had demonstrated through a series of economic portfolios that he had learned the value of fiscal prudence at Mitchell Sharp's knee. As finance minister in 1979, he had been under great pressure to open the vault in the run-up to an election the Conservatives seemed poised to win. But Chrétien opted for a conservative, stay-the-course budget, one he always defended even while conceding that it had been received poorly by the Liberal caucus.

Chrétien's time in Finance had not been easy. The year before, he had suffered through the most humiliating experience of his political career, the famous Guns of August incident. Chrétien, as finance minister, accompanied Trudeau that year to the Bonn economic summit and then returned home while the prime minister went on a sailing holiday with German Chancellor Helmut Schmidt. When Trudeau returned, he announced an immediate $2 billion in budget cuts in a televised address to the nation. Chrétien, who had been involved only in the preliminary discussions, was at the lake near Shawinigan and knew nothing of the speech. "I was made to look like a fool," he wrote in his autobiography. "Normally a minister of finance would resign in such an embarrassing situation. I decided not to mainly because I was worried about the effect of a French-Canadian senior minister resigning when a separatist government was in power in Quebec."

In his memoirs, Trudeau confessed that Chrétien was justified in being upset. "But Jean Chrétien is a good soldier and a happy warrior, and we quickly moved on to fight more battles side by side."

As far as Martin was concerned, the silver lining of the August 1978 fiasco was that he now had a prime minister personally and emotionally resolved to stand behind his minister of finance. "He understood how important it was because of what happened to him." Martin had known Chrétien for many years before entering politics in 1988. His father had sat in cabinet with the young man from Shawinigan in the late 1960s and early 1970s while Martin Jr. worked at Power Corporation alongside Chrétien's trusted adviser John Rae. Martin knew that Chrétien had resented the manner in which the Prime Minister's Office and the Privy Council Office had dominated ministers in the Trudeau years and, so much the product of his personal experiences, would refrain from doing the same. "This is the way he is," Martin said. "I mean, you don't decide your management style in discussion with a bunch of people. You are what you are."

Martin thought of Chrétien in terms of Louis St. Laurent, the 1950s Liberal prime minister who had operated more as a chairman of a board, surrounded by strong personalities doing their own thing. Martin's father had enjoyed working for St. Laurent, despite his frustrations over the snail's pace of social reform, more than for the other three prime ministers he had served. It was an important factor for Martin. He might have returned to his business in Montreal after losing the leadership if he had thought otherwise. He wasn't equipped to be a yes-man.

Chrétien's determination to give his minister of finance running room was so great that he was willing, at least in the early going, to tolerate actions with which he disagreed. In the preparations for the 1994 budget, Glen Shortliffe, still clerk of the Privy Council, went to see Chrétien on a matter under discussion at Finance that he thought would have negative implications for the government. He laid out his concerns to Chrétien, who concurred with the analysis.

"So can I convey that to Dodge and Martin?" Shortliffe asked.

"No," Chrétien replied. "I am not going to tell my finance minister what to do."

As the fiscal picture deteriorated in the spring, Martin tested that resolve. The finance minister decided he would have to impose a freeze on any new spending. He arranged to see Chrétien prior to a cabinet meeting. The prime minister knew how unhappy the freeze would make his ministers, many of them still wet behind the ears and not yet disabused of the notion that the job of government is to find new ways to separate taxpayers from their dollars. Chrétien grumbled and wondered whether it was absolutely necessary. People won't like it, he warned. But if Martin insisted it was the only course, then that was that. The prime minister gave his reluctant endorsement.

Martin announced his spending freeze at the start of the meeting. Across the table, ministers could see Chrétien looking down, seemingly oblivious. It wasn't clear to anyone but Martin that he had even discussed the matter with the prime minister. About ten minutes into the meeting, one of the ministers spoke on a pet project that required some new money. Martin began to interject. But Chrétien cut him off. "Didn't you hear the minister of finance?" he asked. "Just ten minutes ago, he said there wouldn't be any more money." Another ten or fifteen minutes went by and another minister made mention of a new spending initiative. This time Martin turned beet red. But again the prime minister beat him to the punch. His patience was wearing thin, too, as could always be discerned by the way he fidgeted in his chair and tapped his pencil. "Didn't you hear *me* ten minutes ago?" he demanded sharply. "I said there is no money. Can't you guys understand that? The next one who asks for new spending, I'm going to cut his budget by 20 per cent."

It was at that moment, Martin would later tell associates, that he knew Jean Chrétien would be there for him. Certain ministers continued to attempt end runs around him during the preparations for the second budget. Incredibly, some of them were even thoughtful enough to copy to Martin the letters they sent the prime minister complaining about the unreasonableness of Finance's demands. Chrétien never raised these complaints with Martin. He wanted to be kept informed, closely informed, of budget preparations. He had his own thoughts on some of the matters under consideration, often strong thoughts. But he granted his finance minister the autonomy that he himself had expected from Trudeau.

As the budget numbers deteriorated under the stress of the bad interest rate projections, the wallflower of a sentence about reviewing all the government's programs grew in significance. Martin was a big believer in focus. He thought companies should stick to their knitting and he felt the same way about governments. The sentence referred to a plan he had hatched with Marcel Massé to review all the discretionary programs of the government of Canada (except those covered by Axworthy's parallel review) and toss out the ones that made no sense any more in the 1990s. In general, the review would cover "program spending," about $60 billion out of Ottawa's nearly $160 billion in total annual expenditures. Details would be worked out later. Such a strategic review was commonplace in the corporate world, where companies constantly assessed and reassessed their business lines. But governments tended to operate by inertia.

Now with the fiscal noose tightening around him, the so-called program review took on added urgency. The point was no longer just to cut programs that no longer made sense, with savings a probable result. The review now would be driven first and foremost by those desperately needed savings — and reinventing the government of Canada would be the side benefit. Martin had been thinking of a five-year process. He telescoped the timetable down to three years, with as much of the action as possible to occur in years one and two.

Suddenly, the view in Finance of the 3-per-cent target shifted dramatically. No longer was it seen as a commitment so light it could float in air. Now it was discussed as an anchor. The Liberals had fully committed themselves to 3 per cent when they thought it would be easy. It would destroy their credibility if they abandoned their target now that the going had gotten tough. As Martin would later tell an international gathering of central bankers and Finance officials: "Without a target to which we were all irrevocably committed, the natural reluctance of ministers — myself included — to accept cuts in their own domain would likely have caused things to unravel." For eight months, Chrétien had been unyielding in his push to keep Red Book commitments. Ministers were periodically asked to produce report cards on how their departments were faring. There was no way he would back down from the 3 per cent. It wasn't so much that it was a good — or bad — idea. His credibility was nailed to it.

June 1994 was exceptionally hot in Ottawa. The denizens of the capital looked forward to their summer escape to the Gatineaus, which beckoned from the other side of the Ottawa River. The short stroll up Parliament Hill left tourists and regulars drenched in perspiration. Martin's fifth-floor Centre Block office was particularly unbearable. It faced the front of the building just to the west of the Peace Tower, the façade made famous in thousands of postcards and the nightly stand-ups of parliamentary TV correspondents. Occupants of the front offices were forbidden from ruining the aesthetics by putting air conditioners in their windows. Martin had a small floor unit operating at full blast, grinding out more noise than comfort. But that was hardly the most inhospitable aspect of a visit to his office that month.

Invitations — some would say summonses — had been issued to each cabinet minister to drop by with their deputies and hear about something called program review. Martin, with Massé, his Cartesian other half, by his side, and a senior official, usually Dodge, sat down with each successive minister armed with little more than a small table of numbers, two lines over three years. The table laid out the current budgetary allocation for the department in question and the amount by which it was to be reduced in the 1995, 1996, and 1997 budgets under program review. The size of the required cuts left the ministers gasping: in many cases, they were well above 50 per cent.

Anne McLellan remembered reacting quite strongly to the numbers. "Right there, in that simple, deceptively simple, little piece of paper, they were going to destroy the Department of Natural Resources and remove any meaningful federal role in the resource sectors of this country."

Sheila Copps would retain vivid memories of her own meeting with Martin. There was no great love lost between them. They had competed against each other in the 1990 leadership race and, at one level, saw each other as potential rivals the next time out. She found the numbers he now proposed unbelievable. His office window was open and drifting up from the lawn in front of the Parliament Buildings was the music of an oompah band. The entire scene was surreal.

Sergio Marchi wondered who had conjured up these magic targets. Martin was selling program review as a collective exercise in setting priorities, one meant to replace the false justice of across-the-board cuts. Some programs merited more lenient treatment than others. Political judgments had to be made and would be made — by ministers. But who had decided on these opening bids, Marchi asked himself, if not the Department of Finance? Weren't these the same officials who had served Wilson and Mulroney so faithfully? Were they the ones issuing these political judgments?

Dodge had asked the same question when Martin first assigned him to set the departmental targets. The deputy tried to fend him off, saying it was a political decision. Martin didn't have time to waste. He told his deputy that the politicians could work it out later. But he needed something to concentrate their minds right off the bat.

The news of the ministerial meetings soon rippled back to the departments. The town was torn between shock and disbelief. The upper echelons of the public service got on the phones to swap intelligence. The ministerial aides congregated at Clair de Lune and Café Henry Burger, wondering what the Finance officials had slipped into Martin's water. How much did the prime minister know? Would he step in?

The Industry Department took the news particularly badly. On the one hand, Martin had been urging it for months — he had never lost his ardour for its mission and had played a role in making sure it would go to a minister of his liking — to find ways to support growth-oriented companies in adopting new technologies or identifying export markets. Now he was ordering Manley to decimate his department. Harry Swain, the department's acerbic deputy minister, had no intention of playing along. Although he disputed the assertion, he was widely pegged as being opposed to the Red Book's activist orientation. Now he went around town mocking the sessions in Martin's office as the "Come-to-Jesus meetings." He and Manley were not about to throw themselves to the ground in exaltation just because the Industry dart had landed on the 60-per-cent mark.

The June blitz had been timed to coincide with one of the government's thrice-yearly cabinet planning sessions at the Lester B. Pearson Building, just up the street from the prime minister's residence on Sussex Drive. Martin was to make his presentation on the fiscal situation on Saturday morning, June 18. Martin had reviewed his plans in May with the prime minister. They had not discussed the specific targets for each department, but once again Chrétien expressed his willingness to do whatever it took to make the 3-per-cent deficit target. Martin knew that as minister of finance, he could simply impose spending cuts on the departments. But in the preparations for his first budget, he had found that nobody but him and perhaps Chrétien and Massé appreciated the bigger picture. This time around, he would introduce a radical budget, perhaps even a historic one. It would take everyone to sell it. Come budget day in 1995, he didn't want to be standing alone in the House of Commons. He wanted ministers to fan out across the country — indeed the world — taking ownership of the government's agenda.

Martin had thought for a long time about using the 1995 budget to set out a course beyond 3 per cent. In the first budget, he had projected his deficit target three years into the future. Doing another such projection would require a long and difficult cabinet discussion since it would raise the issue of what lay beyond 3 per cent in 1996-97. Martin's advisers told him it would be foolish to fight a two-front war. The imperative now was to secure that first 3 per cent. O'Leary argued that the 3 per cent had become their biggest ally. To push against it on one end would be to invite someone else to push against it on the other. Martin held on for a long time before finally concurring. They would limit themselves to a two-year target in the next budget — the two years already out there.

On Friday afternoon, June 17, word of the Come-to-Jesus meetings seeped out. Reporters in the *Globe and Mail*'s Ottawa bureau had sensed something in the wind all week. On Friday, they figured it out. Under the headline "Martin eyes spending cuts, Cabinet split as interest rates threaten deficit, sources say," the Saturday *Globe* broke the news about the ministerial sessions in Martin's office and played up divisions in the Chrétien cabinet. Prime Minister Chrétien's view of the matter "is the question of the day," one government source was quoted as saying. "I think it's going to be a defining weekend."

The cabinet meeting, which had begun Friday afternoon, reconvened that Saturday morning. Chrétien took little time in making his feelings known. He was furious, as irate as anyone in the room had ever seen him. Chrétien's is a cold anger. He doesn't rant and rave – just the opposite. He becomes quiet. His words come out more slowly, with greater deliberation. He opened the meeting with a long, heartfelt lecture about cabinet confidentiality and government solidarity. Some of the ministers had to strain to hear him. "I want to have a full and frank discussion," he said. But how could they, if it would end up in the media. Somebody had revealed secrets that were not intended for public consumption. Someone had turned a private discussion among ministers into a public conflict. Ministers were being painted into corners. The government was being made to look divided.

If ministers couldn't trust each other, Chrétien said, then a cabinet government couldn't function. The room was dead silent. People could hear themselves breathing. Chrétien went on and on about trust and integrity. He told them that he would not tolerate any further leaks in his government. He would weed out culprits in future and punish them, no matter who was responsible. And then Jean Chrétien uttered words that no minister ever forgot.

"If I can't find out who's doing this," he said, looking around the table, "then I will arbitrarily pick the names of two ministers out of a hat and fire them. And it will be too bad for them. But I want everyone to understand I am serious. I will not tolerate this."

Chastened and incredulous, the ministers sat quietly like schoolchildren caught spitting at one another. "I think everybody was just taken aback by that," one of them later confided. "To just think that quite innocently one could end up out of cabinet."

As a veteran politician, Chrétien knew leakers are rarely discovered. But he wanted to throw a scare into his still-green cabinet, and he succeeded. Leaks nonetheless continued to plague his government, like all others; he never found the leakers or followed through on his threat.

After the sermon, Paul Martin was up. His presentation had been carefully scripted and practised in countless dry runs. He had to remember he was speaking to politicians, not economists. These ministers would be his first and toughest audience, and he needed to convince them that he had a story to tell and that he knew how to tell it. That would be as important as the facts themselves.

After eight months in government, Martin had come to appreciate that cabinet ministers are busy people. Just as he had little idea what was going on in the Department of Fisheries, he figured the fisheries minister or the health minister had little idea what had transpired since the last budget on the fiscal front. They probably hadn't followed every facial twitch of U.S. Federal Reserve Board chairman Alan Greenspan with quite the same intensity as he and his officials had.

He told his fellow ministers that as a consequence of the run-up in interest rates, drastic action needed to be taken or their government, like the Tories, would fall well short of its deficit target. The 3 per cent "was shot to hell." He would be fine in the current fiscal year, thanks to his large contingency fund. Fine, that is, assuming interest rates didn't continue heading north. But he didn't have time to dither. The government's entire economic credibility was tied to the 3-per-cent commitment. It was right there in the Red Book and had been reaffirmed dozens of times since the election. His reputation was on the line. The prime minister's reputation was on the line. The Liberal Party's reputation was on the line. If he was to make the 3-per-cent mark, he had to begin planning for a budget that would be historic in its implications.

Everyone sitting around the table knew their own number. They understood that they had a personal stake in the matter, just as Martin had intended. This was not the usual abstract lecture. The upcoming program review would cut massively into government programs. It would change the relationship between Canadians and their central government. The government would have to go after sacred cows like old-age pensions and transportation subsidies.

Chrétien's intervention had changed the entire dynamic of the meeting. There was still discussion, certainly, even some dissent, particularly when Martin floated an idea to redesign the old-age pension program, which would end universality and target benefits more closely to those worse off, as David Dodge had long counselled. André Ouellet, Sheila Copps, and Fernand Robichaud, the junior minister from New Brunswick, strongly warned Martin that he was playing with political dynamite. A number of other ministers questioned whether Martin was overreacting to a fluid economic situation. The geniuses in Finance had clearly got interest rates wrong in February; what was to say they weren't getting them wrong again in June? Once the Quebec election was over, perhaps rates would come down again. Maybe yes, maybe no. But in the end Martin secured the go-ahead to begin planning his budget. Most important, nobody had dissented from the 3-per-cent target — his anchor was firm.

Martin and Dodge walked away from the showdown meeting pleasantly surprised. They had been braced for a much harsher assault. But the outrage that ministers had been expressing individually failed to coalesce at the critical moment, an outcome no doubt influenced by Chrétien's opening intervention and Martin's strong presentation. "Out of that cabinet retreat," Martin later said, "basically came the mandate: we're going for it. Everybody understood what the hell was involved in losing the game."

The meeting ended just before lunch. Chrétien rushed away to make a tee-off time at the Royal Ottawa. Martin and Dodge headed off to meet Terrie O'Leary for brunch at an eatery on Elgin Street. The task ahead would be daunting, but the meeting had left them in good spirits. Dodge would look back on the June cabinet retreat as the first of two defining moments on the fiscal front. (The second would occur six months later and would lock in their June gains.) The Liberals had granted Finance the mandate it had sought the previous November. But now, seven months after his first audience in a Windsor hospital, he understood that he had a minister blessed with the skills to sell a radical deficit reduction package.

11

GHOSTS OF
MEECH LAKE

By the summer of 1994, the early spirit of cooperation that had existed between Jean Chrétien and Quebec Liberal leader Daniel Johnson was dissipating. Johnson continued to agitate over the decision to close the Collège Militaire Royale in Saint-Jean. He kept pressing Chrétien and Axworthy to do something about handing over control of labour market training to the province. The provincial Liberals were frustrated again when another item on their shopping list, renewal of an economic development agreement, crumbled under fiscal pressure. The Quebec election was now expected in the fall, and the discord was not promising for federalists.

The relationship between Chrétien and Johnson had begun on an upbeat note. After Johnson became premier of Quebec, he and Chrétien spoke every week by telephone. In the wake of the coolness that had existed between Chrétien and Bourassa, almost anyone was an improvement as far as the federal Liberals were concerned. Chrétien had never liked or trusted Bourassa, whose enthusiasm for federalism, he felt, depended on the size of the most recent equalization cheque from Ottawa.

Johnson was different. He described himself as a "Canadian first and foremost" at one point – an almost unprecedented declaration in modern times from a Quebec premier (and one he later backed away from). When he took over as premier, he knew he needed Ottawa's help to be re-elected. For once, the overtures came from Quebec City to Ottawa, instead of the reverse, as Johnson requested the feds' help. Chrétien's anti-smuggling initiatives infuriated Ontario and anti-smoking activists, but reaction in Quebec was favourable. Johnson and Chrétien were ecstatic with the public response. The two leaders still did not know each other well, but Chrétien felt he could do business with Johnson even though he was certain that Johnson had voted Tory in the 1993 election.

Helping the provincial Liberals get re-elected would not be easy. For one thing, the federal Liberals lacked the financial and organizational resources they had enjoyed in the early 1980s, when they held seventy-four of Quebec's seventy-five seats. For another, the federal treasury was at rock bottom, and so was the patience of Canadians for political pork-barrelling. The rest of Canada was in no mood to see any coddling of Quebec: if the government was cutting services elsewhere, it could not be seen to be giving preferred treatment to one province. In early April, Sheila Copps, in her capacity as environment minister, announced that Montreal would be the site of a NAFTA environmental review agency. Fewer than a dozen Canadian jobs were involved, but the Reform Party protested loudly about favouritism to Quebec, and premiers across the country issued ringing denunciations. That response provoked hurt and indignation in Quebec, wiping out any political gain for the original decision.

Chrétien, on the other hand, was feeling increasingly confident about winning a referendum if the Parti Québécois came into power, and was less concerned about the election. Traditional Quebec electoral wisdom had it that 40 per cent of voters were Liberals, 40 per cent Péquistes, and the rest sat squarely in the middle. Anglophone and ethnic voters were unlikely to desert the party in a straight choice between the Liberals and the PQ, so the real key to electoral success lay in winning over the undecided 20 per cent. You could not win elections without some of that moderate nationalist support, Bourassa always said, and he had four majority election wins in five tries to support his theory. And partly as a result of that theory, the provincial Liberals accorded inordinate importance to the youth vote; fully one-third of delegates at party conventions were under twenty-five, and they tended by nature to be more nationalist than their elders. This was also the section of the party that spawned the apparatchiks who ran the party executive, and made most of the important decisions. For example, Pierre Anctil, Johnson's chief of staff, was only thirty-four when he took the job in 1994. Federal Liberals, watching from the outside, felt that Quebec's most important federalist provincial party placed too much emphasis on those who criticized the federal system.

The provincials, in turn, regarded most of the key Quebec advisers around Chrétien as out of touch with the mood of the province. Chrétien and his people liked to go on about the number of Quebeckers in key positions in Ottawa and the policy of official bilingualism as proof that francophones played a key role in the federation, but increasingly, Quebeckers didn't care about those issues and looked to Quebec City for their leadership. The provincial Liberals considered Jean Pelletier a straight-shooter, but aloof and disdainful of any manifestation of Quebec nationalism. They thought Eddie Goldenberg was smart but rigid in his belief in Trudeau-style federalism. Similarly, they respected John Rae but pigeonholed him as the voice of Montreal's anglophone business community. Among cabinet members, the only two who had any real credibility in provincial political circles were Paul Martin and Marcel Massé. It was de rigueur to denounce André Ouellet, despite his legendary reputation as an organizer: he was seen as a dinosaur.

But there was no question what — or who — constituted the biggest obstacle to a federal return to the party's former glory in Quebec. Chrétien, despite being a native of the province, was the problem, not the solution. Through the late 1980s, he had been subjected to a concerted campaign of vilification in Quebec over his role as justice minister in the 1982 patriation of Canada's Constitution and adoption of the Charter of Rights and Freedoms. That was where the problem had begun. That hurt, but his biggest headache went back four years to his handling — or mishandling — of the Meech Lake Accord.

Chrétien's role in Meech, John Rae often said, was never fully understood, by either supporters or opponents of the accord. But by the mid-1990s, and perhaps forever after, Chrétien was stuck in Quebec with the image of a man who, when asked to choose between his home province and the rest of the country, went with the outsiders.

So far as Chrétien was concerned, Brian Mulroney should never have reopened the constitutional file in the first place. After patriation there was relatively little talk of the issue for the next four years. Although Quebec secessionists later characterized the 1981 negotiating session that led to patriation as "the night of the long knives," consigning Chrétien a key villain's role, it was not an issue in the 1985 provincial campaign in which the Liberals swept the Parti Québécois from power. In fact, the PQ, in the final months of René Lévesque's leadership in 1985, relegated sovereignty to secondary status in the party program. After 1982, Chrétien said in a 1990 interview, "nobody talked constitution for several years, we had a lot of other things [in Quebec]."

By Chrétien's telling of it, Mulroney had reopened the issue by encouraging Quebeckers to feel aggrieved that they were not formal signatories to the new Constitution. If you tell people often enough that they have been screwed, Chrétien said to an acquaintance, sooner or later they will believe you, and there is a problem. He expressed the same view when he ran into Mulroney's chief of staff, Stanley Hartt, at an airport shortly after declaring his candidacy for the leadership. "You guys made one big goddamn mistake in reopening the Constitution," said a confident Chrétien. "When I become prime minister, I will fire the first person in my government who even mentions the C-word."

Chrétien laid out his thoughts on the accord in a speech at the University of Ottawa on January 16, 1990. The speech was deliberately given a week before his formal leadership declaration in a futile attempt to compartmentalize the issues. The principal "pen," as speechwriters are called in Ottawa, was Eddie Goldenberg, though Rae and several others had a hand in its contents, and Chrétien made a series of small edits. The accord, he said, in its existing form, "does not promote the fundamental values which I believe all Canadians share." Chrétien called for several changes, including a constitutional assertion that recognition of Quebec as a distinct society would not override the Canadian Charter of Rights and Freedoms. That was always his principal objection to the distinct society clause. He complained that "for all practical purposes... it confines French to Quebec and English to the rest of Canada" because it "does not adequately promote the value we share of a united, tolerant Canada nurturing our two official languages." The problems with the accord, he said, "need not be insurmountable." But he called for a "new negotiation over whatever time it takes" to lead to a "revised, improved and amended accord."

In the months leading up to the June 1990 deadline for passage of the accord, Chrétien's advisers became concerned by the antipathy in Quebec towards the rest of the country that seemed likely to grow if the accord was not ratified. By the end of May, surveys showed that 65 per cent of Quebeckers believed that English Canada was hostile to Quebec, and support for sovereignty over federalism led by 48 per cent to 37 per cent.

Paul Desmarais thought that perhaps it was better to have a slightly imperfect accord for a united Canada than no accord, and a fractured country. The head of Power Corporation wanted to do something about it. He called Mulroney and Chrétien separately. Would they be amenable,

Desmarais asked, to appointing representatives to stage private talks between Chrétien's people and the Conservatives to see if this Meech impasse could be broken?

The choice for the Tories was Hartt, Mulroney's chief of staff, a cagey, bilingual Montreal lawyer. Someone on the Liberal side suggested Eric Maldoff. Another bilingual Montreal lawyer, he and Hartt used to get together in the early 1980s at Hartt's house to informally debate the future of the federation, and of the anglophone community in Quebec. Maldoff did not have much of a history with the federal Liberals, but he and Goldenberg knew each other well. At the time Maldoff and Hartt first met, Maldoff was the first head of the Alliance Quebec English-rights lobbying group. He was eager to do something to resolve the growing mess, and he knew players on all sides, including the provincial Liberals. There had been virtually no contact to that point between Chrétien's people and the provincials. John Rae later confessed that he didn't even know the names of Bourassa's inner circle in 1990.

But the Tories regarded cooperation from Chrétien as essential. They hoped he could bring Newfoundland's Clyde Wells on side as well as Sharon Carstairs, the leader of the Manitoba Liberals. Manitoba Premier Gary Filmon led a minority government, and could not make a move without Carstairs's support. With it, the Tories were confident Filmon would support the deal.

Throughout May and into early June, Maldoff and Hartt met regularly in Montreal. Each brought lawyers with more constitutional expertise: for the Liberals, John Laskin, the son of former Supreme Court chief justice Bora Laskin, and veteran constitutional hand Roger Tassé for the Conservatives. Tassé was a former law partner of Chrétien's: Mulroney chose him in part because of that connection. Often, the meetings went right through the night as they debated the wording of various clauses, searching for more precise definitions of concepts such as distinct society. When the meetings were over, Hartt talked with Mulroney and constitutional adviser Norman Spector (another native Montrealer), and Maldoff called Eddie Goldenberg, who oversaw the file for Chrétien.

At the same time, an all-party parliamentary committee headed by the Tories' Jean Charest was going through the same exercise in public. Each morning, Charest met with Mary Dawson, a high-ranking official in the federal Justice Department. She would hand him a thick wad of carefully worded legal text for discussion that day with committee members: most of those documents were the result of the Montreal negotiations. If Charest knew the source of Dawson's files, he never let on.

Chrétien didn't like any of this: not the public sniping from other Liberals, nor the backroom dealing. It ran against his instincts to be beholden in any way to a political opponent, particularly when that opponent was Mulroney. He didn't trust him, as he later told friends. In his haste to make a deal, Chrétien thought, Mulroney would say almost anything. But Chrétien's advisers wanted him to give cooperation a try. No one, not even MPs within the two parties, was supposed to know that the Liberals and Conservatives were negotiating. It wouldn't help the accord's popularity in Quebec any if nationalists knew that Chrétien had a hand in the contents of the Charest report. Similarly, it wouldn't help Chrétien in some anti-Meech Liberal circles if they knew he was doing backroom deals with representatives of their Great Satan, Brian Mulroney. But somehow, Lucien Bouchard found out. Until the start of May, he dominated Tory cabinet meetings with eloquent but extended monologues on the merits of the agreement. Now, he looked increasingly morose.

Only Bouchard knows exactly when he decided to abandon the Meech talks, and renounce federalism. Some Tories who knew him well later concluded that Bouchard deliberately waited until his resignation would have the most devastating impact on the accord's chances of passage. By making his announcement May 21, with only a month until the deadline for ratification, he succeeded. Hartt bitterly described Bouchard as "a living car bomb, calculated to explode at the most damaging moment."

At that point, Mulroney was negotiating by telephone directly with Robert Bourassa to see if he would accept the Charest report's recommendations. The key recommendation, addressing Chrétien's primary concern that the distinct society clause could override the Charter and largely following his suggested remedy, was the insertion of another clause into the accord asserting that the Charter would be paramount. Mulroney thought he had talked Bourassa into agreeing. Bouchard's resignation letter killed any chance of that: after its contents were made public, Bourassa's acceptance would have looked weak and vacillating. Bourassa put out a statement saying that any modification of Quebec's demands was "out of the question." Bouchard's letter noted pointedly that Charest's report seemed to have been written by "the opponents of the Meech Lake Accord — starting with Jean Chrétien."

As the first ministers met in Ottawa June 2 to 9, Maldoff was there, formally accredited to the Manitoba delegation. Hartt briefed him every day on the outcome of meetings, and Maldoff then went back from the Wellington Street conference centre through a tunnel to the Château Laurier Hotel, where Goldenberg was waiting. No one wanted to take a chance on Hartt and Goldenberg meeting openly: both men were too well known, and a sighting would start immediate, well-founded speculation.

Most of Chrétien's senior people now very much wanted a deal, to get both their man and the country off the hook. Late in the week, as the premiers moved closer to a tentative agreement on Meech, Maldoff brought in a one-and-a-half-page document for Chrétien's consideration. It would amount to an endorsement by Chrétien of the meeting's conclusions. That would be crucial, given that Manitoba's Filmon and Newfoundland's Wells were signing it only conditionally, and wanted to take their document back to their respective legislatures.

Chrétien promised to consider the statement. But the next day's *Globe and Mail* carried a soon-to-be-infamous interview with Brian Mulroney. In it, he appeared to suggest that he had planned the timing of this first ministers' meeting as cynically as possible, intending to turn up the heat on the premiers by waiting until the last second. Mulroney had, he said, "rolled the dice" with the biggest gamble of his political life.

Chrétien and his senior people exploded. Publicly, they remained quiet, so as not to draw attention to their role in almost pushing the accord through. Rae felt betrayed by Mulroney's comments. Goldenberg was more sanguine: like his boss, he was always suspicious of Mulroney, and this just confirmed that his instincts had not betrayed him. There was no more talk of Chrétien publicly endorsing the accord. He spent more than an hour on Tuesday, June 12, in private consultation with fifty Liberal MP supporters, and then refused to discuss his opinion of the accord publicly. Instead, he and Aline retreated to their waterfront Shawinigan cottage to rest and prepare for the convention.

The accord died on Friday, June 22, and Chrétien won the party leadership the next day, but it seemed a poisoned chalice. If the accord failed to pass through the Manitoba and Newfoundland legislatures, Chrétien had said in the final week, that would be a reflection of democracy in action, and no one should fret, the country would still be there tomorrow. Later, Chrétien asserted, with some justification, that he had never spoken out directly against the accord: rather, he criticized the notion of it as a "seamless web" of contents that could not be changed or even questioned without torpedoing the entire agreement. He had wanted the accord's content "clarified," he said, not killed.

But no matter. At a time when every federal political leader and most provincial premiers were on side in supporting Meech, Chrétien's doubts marked him as an opponent. That made him just as much of a hero in some circles in English Canada as it demonized him in Quebec.

That summer, he was publicly characterized by Gilles Rocheleau, one of two Quebec MPs who left the party after Chrétien's victory, as "Quebec's Judas Iscariot," and he was called a lot worse in private. It hurt him deeply. Chrétien did not acknowledge the emotional pain publicly, confiding only in a few friends. "If you know Chrétien at all," Rae said to one mutual acquaintance, "you know how deeply all that tears at his soul."

If Chrétien wasn't loved in Quebec, he could settle for being respected. The federal Liberals had risen in the polls in Quebec since the 1993 election, and by the summer of 1994 Chrétien was only a few points behind Lucien Bouchard when respondents were asked whether they were satisfied with the performance of each leader.

Quebec was a topic Chrétien could never keep from discussing, the itch he just had to scratch. He glossed over events in other provinces but found portents of hope, items to mock, or lessons to deliver in every little sliver of political news from Quebec. So the decline in his enthusiasm for Daniel Johnson was palpable.

At the March 16 caucus meeting, shortly after their collaboration on contraband tobacco, Chrétien had effusively praised Johnson. "It is a long time," said Chrétien, "since we have had a premier like Johnson who we can work with. We have to help him win in June, or all of Canada will suffer." But when Johnson started fed-bashing over labour market training and Collège Militaire Royale, Chrétien did a turnabout. Johnson, he told caucus on May 4, would win or lose on his own. The federal Liberals could not be dragged into Quebec. If the people in Quebec were not satisfied with the Bourassa administration, he said, he could not blame them. None of the feds were happy with Bourassa, either. He was no more kind towards his old nemesis, Brian Mulroney. In rural Quebec, Chrétien said, people were being told stories about the rest of Canada that were unbelievable yet accepted, because it has been so long since anyone vigorously defended federalism. He was disturbed by the lack of generosity throughout the country, pointing again to the fuss over the placement of the NAFTA environmental agency in Montreal. Even the premiers, he noted, had criticized the move. Mulroney ruined the country, Chrétien said, and now the Liberals had to navigate through rocky straits.

Chrétien's favourite subject for castigation was Lucien Bouchard. As the year unfolded, and it became more likely that the PQ would win the election and call a referendum, Chrétien increasingly mocked Bouchard within caucus. It was a constant theme, and reflected his absolute certainty that Quebeckers would never vote for separation. After Bouchard visited Washington in early 1994 and described himself bluntly as a "separatist," Chrétien gleefully told MPs that the federalists had cornered Bouchard in the U.S. We managed that well, he said. He asked caucus for patience for the next six months on issues that could play badly in Quebec, because at the end of the day, Quebec would stay in Canada, and the Liberals would multiply by three their number of seats in the province.

In the spring Bouchard visited Alberta, where he received a polite but cold reception when he talked about sovereignty. It was good for him, Chrétien felt, to see that it would not be a smooth divorce. After Bouchard mused about building a high-speed train line between Montreal and Toronto with federal and provincial money, Chrétien called the Bloc leader "ridiculous." He mocked Bouchard's insistence that a sovereign Quebec could continue to use the Canadian dollar, and joked that he could not imagine another sovereign country, such as the United States, wanting to put a beaver on its money. Bouchard, he insisted on several occasions, helped the federalist side because his appearances in Question Period were drawing new attention in Quebec to the House of Commons. In Pierre Trudeau's day, Chrétien said, only René Lévesque was seen regularly on television. Now, the prime minister and sovereignty's most charismatic spokesperson shared equal time on television newscasts.

Six months into his mandate, Chrétien was philosophical about his government's achievements. The Liberals had done a lot, he said, but the Quebec issue was still there. The saving grace, he concluded, was that "when it will be over, it will be over for a long time." By June, with the Quebec election postponed till fall, an overconfident Chrétien couldn't wait for battle. His disdain for the separatists was bred in the bone. His father, Wellie, had been an ardent federalist, a youthful worshipper of Laurier who, upon being introduced by his son to Pierre Trudeau, said he could now die safe in the knowledge that Quebec would remain in Canada. When other French Canadians of his generation opposed conscription in

World War II, Wellie Chrétien had expressed himself in favour. A son had gone off to fight.

Chrétien created a strategic planning unit to advise him on the referendum, with a bright but strutting foreign service officer named Howard Balloch heading it up. He had first encountered Balloch as an advocate of closer relations with China in preparing for the November 1993 Seattle summit. To some, it was a measure of Chrétien's cockiness that he would put a bureaucrat with little domestic experience, a Newfoundlander at that, in charge of his national unity squad. Veterans of the 1980 referendum, when the best and brightest had been recruited to a similar but more high-powered committee, thought Chrétien was sleepwalking towards the precipice. The Balloch group also suffered from an uncertain chain of command in relation to both the Prime Minister's Office and Intergovernmental Affairs Minister Marcel Massé. Balloch would never become a big player; in Montreal, where the real referendum planning would take place, he was unknown and therefore untrusted.

Just before the summer break, in June, Chrétien was interviewed by *Maclean's*, which gave him an advance look at a poll the magazine had commissioned for its annual Canada Day issue. Ninety per cent of Quebec respondents described Canada as the best country in the world to live; 83 per cent of them, asked whether they meant all of Canada or the specific area in which they lived, cited the entire country. That, as far as Chrétien was concerned, seemed all the confirmation he needed that things in Quebec were going his way. The Prime Minister's Office let it be known that he would not involve himself in Quebec's election campaign, and neither would MPs from outside the province. The government's agenda, said one Liberal adviser, "would not change one iota" because of the election. In response to any provocations from Péquistes during the election campaign, the preferred response from the rest of the country would be silence.

The race began July 24, and Johnson fought a spirited campaign. Throughout it, Chrétien broke his silence only once. Two weeks before the September 12 vote, Placide Poulin, a bathtub manufacturer in Sainte-Marie-de-Beauce, an hour south of Quebec City, picked up his ringing phone at home one day and was startled to hear a voice say it was "Jean Chrétien, the prime minister of Canada." Chrétien was calling, he told Poulin, to give "thanks for your defence of federalism." The reason was that Poulin had expressed his strong opposition to separatism when PQ leader Jacques

Parizeau visited his factory. Chrétien read about the incident in a newspaper, and was moved.

The outcome was far closer than anyone had expected. The PQ won 77 out of 125 seats, but its 44.7 per cent of the vote was only marginally better than the Liberals' result; they won 47 seats with 44.3 per cent of support. Although the PQ would form the government, the outlook for sovereigntists — who had virtually ignored the topic during the campaign in favour of criticizing the Liberals' performance — seemed bleak.

On September 18, Chrétien gave a speech in Quebec City to the Canadian Chamber of Commerce. The second half was devoted to Quebec and gave his first in-depth response to the PQ victory. The prime minister urged the international financial community to stay calm about the prospect of a referendum. He praised Canada as a tolerant country, and said that the best way for him to contribute to the coming debate on the country's future would be to lead a government that would concentrate on "providing good government, jobs and economic growth, on getting our fiscal house in order, on modernizing the roles and responsibilities of the federal government." In other words, there would be no special treatment for Quebec on the eve of a referendum: it didn't need it, and the rest of the country wouldn't tolerate it. In the meantime he would govern as planned, proceeding with Axworthy's social security review, Massé's program review, and Martin's deficit reduction.

On September 21, he gave the same message to his caucus. He couldn't say when the referendum would be, he said, but the sovereigntists were not confident. They knew they could not win.

Chrétien liked to describe Canada as "a solution in search of a problem." And once the referendum was out of the way, he felt in his bones, the solution would remain, and the country's biggest problem would be gone.

12

ON THE
BARRICADES

Lloyd Axworthy awoke with anticipation on the morning of October 5. For nine months, he had pushed against the apparatus of government to be able to bring out his proposals for reforming the social security system. His original timetable had called for an April release, but that had been pushed back to June, then July, then September; and now, with the Quebec election over, he would finally take his blueprint public that afternoon.

Along the way, his action plan had been downgraded to a discussion paper. It offered a series of options for further consultation, a Green Paper in the parlance of Ottawa. But it still contained enough substance, particularly on unemployment insurance and post-secondary education, to really move the yardsticks forward. At last, he would exit the stultifying chambers of the bureaucracy and cabinet and engage the Canadian public in a debate on the need to modernize a social security system designed while he was still a toddler.

He started the day as usual, with a breakfast of orange juice and Mini-Wheats on the second floor of his Ottawa townhouse. Usually Axworthy walked to work, but with the early start to this day his driver, Ron Carrière, was waiting to ferry him the two miles to Parliament Hill.

A sheaf of newspaper clippings sat on the back seat. The minister stopped dead at an article from that morning's *Toronto Star*. Under a heavy boldface headline, the *Star* quoted from what it described as a confidential cabinet document outlining "a secret plan" for an unannounced $7.5 billion in social spending cuts over the next five years. The article charged that Martin and Axworthy had deliberately hidden these cuts, which would not be disclosed until the budget the following February. Axworthy got on the car phone, ordering his personal secretary, Lea Attrux, to call his point man on the social security review, Giles Gherson, and his press adviser, Alec Jasen. Get them into the office, he barked. It was just 7:30 in the morning and already, as he would say later, he had been struck by a boulder.

Gherson and Jasen had been working till 3 in the morning preparing Axworthy's speech to the House of Commons and the opening statement for his press conference. Their wake-up call had been curt. "The minister wants to see you, right away." Jasen was in the shower when the phone rang, Gherson still in bed. They both arrived at the office with wet hair.

The bombshell stunned them. "My first reaction," Gherson would recall later, "is, This is wrong, where does this come from? It's bizarre. Where the hell does this come from?" Then their minds drifted to thoughts of sabotage. Could someone be out to get the minister? They started working the phones, trying to identify the document the *Star* had in its possession.

Terrie O'Leary saw the clips about the same time as Axworthy and was equally dumbfounded. She, too, tried to figure out what the *Star* had. Martin and Axworthy had discussed the savings from the social security review but only in a preliminary way. Indeed, Axworthy had resisted detailed discussions, insisting that he had to address the policy failings before dealing with budgetary matters. He had fought hard to have his discussion paper released before Martin's budget update later that month so as to avoid the impression that Finance was somehow driving his agenda.

Gherson phoned Martin to enlist his support. He feared that reporters might corner the finance minister and get him to say that the $7.5-billion figure could be in the right ballpark. Gherson wanted the number disavowed, but Martin was reluctant to tie himself down. He felt awful for Axworthy, but wherever that figure had come from, who knows, it might prove fairly accurate at the end of the day. They started yelling at each other, angrily hanging up without an agreement.

Axworthy had the wind completely knocked out of him. As the day wore on, his funk deepened. He learned that the document in question was not a cabinet paper but rather the best guess of a Treasury Board bureaucrat. It was little comfort. "We're finished," he moaned. "We're killed. Why bother going ahead." The television set was tuned to Newsworld, with the volume turned down. At one point, Axworthy could see the right-wing economist John Crispo, a foe from the free trade debates, on the screen, apparently talking about the social reform plans. "I know what he's saying. He's dumping all over us," Axworthy muttered gloomily. Gherson turned up the volume. Just to add to Axworthy's foul mood, John Crispo had rallied to his side.

After having his paper rejected by cabinet in July, Axworthy had set about improving both the content of the paper and the management of the review. The two filters — fiscal restraints and relations with the provinces — continued to perplex everyone. With the paper pushed back to the fall, the department increasingly fretted about being ground up in the wheels of the next Martin budget, which promised to be hard as nails.

Neither of these impediments should have surprised Axworthy. Over the course of the months, many advisers had sounded warnings. In the spring of 1994, he had attempted to recruit Francis McGuire, an aide from the early 1980s who had gone on to become New Brunswick's deputy minister of economic development, to return and help him push the review through. McGuire knew both government and the Liberal Party. He came and sized up the operation, quickly concluding that Axworthy hadn't changed much as a boss in the intervening decade. The staff were still running around in a dozen different directions in futile efforts to satisfy Axworthy's whims. The lack of coherence in the department also distressed McGuire, now accustomed to the small and responsive bureaucracies in New Brunswick. He concluded that Axworthy lacked adequate support to pull off such a big task.

But these problems of style and staff could be overcome: the bigger issue was Axworthy's game plan. McGuire had no doubt that Paul Martin would have to take a meat cleaver to government spending in the coming budget. If the social security review had any hope of succeeding, Axworthy needed to lock it in before the knife fell. He had four, five, maybe six months to act, which meant limiting his horizons. Axworthy, though, according to McGuire, maintained that he had twenty-four months as promised by the prime minister and Martin.

McGuire's advice was simple: forget all the public consultations and the fancy program designs. Unilaterally slay the Canada Assistance Plan and lump its monies together with the unemployment insurance fund to create a new national benefits program for the jobless and poor families. But leave billions aside for job training and other active intervention measures, the details of which would be negotiated one-on-one with individual provinces. He figured Axworthy could begin signing deals in a matter of a couple of months, probably starting with New Brunswick, and the political path would be smoothed by the control regional politicians would gain over the delivery of programs. To McGuire, this made for both good politics and good policy: the country was so diverse that the same prescription in northern New Brunswick probably didn't fit the circumstances of Cape Breton Island, let alone southern Ontario or east-end Montreal. He wanted to signal federal flexibility in unmistakable terms by handing Quebec control over labour market training.

Axworthy, concerned that the approach would result in a chequerboard Canada, rejected the advice. "I said, 'Okay, but then you can't win,'" recalled McGuire, who made clear that he liked to win. He took the next plane back to Fredericton. "I made up my mind this wasn't a doable deal." Axworthy later remarked that McGuire, after so many years in New Brunswick, had become "too provincialist."

In the aftermath of the July débâcle, Noreau and Axworthy once again discussed the widespread sense that the minister had not been adequately served by his advisers. He badly needed one person who could run interference among all the disparate groups: his office, the bureaucracy, cabinet, caucus, and the external interests.

At about the same time, David Zussman, the Chrétien confidant who had served on Axworthy's task force, got together with *Globe and Mail* columnist Giles Gherson for lunch. A policy wonk's policy wonk, the veteran Ottawa journalist was nearing completion of a one-year term filling in for the *Globe*'s national affairs columnist, Jeffrey Simpson. Zussman caught him at a vulnerable moment. Uncertain what would follow the Simpson column, he was immediately attracted by the suggestion of helping Axworthy with the social security review. The prospect of observing government from the inside intrigued him.

Gherson went off to see both Axworthy and Goldenberg, and accepted their offer. His appointment as principal secretary to the social security review raised eyebrows. Despite his stature as a journalist, he had no experience in government and even less in politics. He certainly lacked McGuire's hard political edge. Gherson's advantage lay in his analytical mind, profuse energy, and professional writing ability, which, judging from the efforts coming out of the bureaucracy, constituted a precious commodity. He would hold the pen on the discussion paper.

From the moment he arrived in August, he became a powerful force in the social security review. Many in the department thought he complemented Axworthy too closely in their shared enthusiasm for new ideas. Officials joked that they had done a Vulcan-style mind meld. But Gherson succeeded in keeping Axworthy focussed on the finish line.

By mid-August, Axworthy finally felt satisfied with the shape of the discussion paper. He had scheduled a trip to Australia, where he intended to take a first-hand look at some innovative social policy approaches. When he returned, he would bring the paper back to cabinet. A couple of days before his departure, he decided to bring the disbanded task force back for one final meeting to generate feedback on the latest draft.

The Last Supper, as it came to be known, took place at the Westin Hotel on the evening of August 16. The appetizers had hardly been served when the task force's long-simmering disillusionment over the direction of the review boiled over. The task force members could hardly believe the extent to which the bold thinking of a few months earlier had been watered down. The paper failed to tell a coherent story, its content speaking more to the compromises with the Quebec ministers and to the obvious fact that it had been written by a committee than to the social challenges confronting the government. Worse, it still failed after all these months to address the realities of fiscal constraints. Even Tom Axworthy, the former Trudeau aide invited by his brother for the dinner, couldn't think of much positive to say.

Axworthy was shaken. He cancelled his Australia trip and ordered his office to track down Gherson, who had left for holiday in California. Gherson rushed home for a twenty-four-hour whirlwind of emergency meetings with Axworthy and Eddie Goldenberg before returning to California weighed down with the heavily criticized manuscript. The rewriting of the paper began at his sister's home in La Jolla. Gherson shared the task force's judgment of the piece of work in his hands. It lacked coherence, much like the entire process up to then. He thought it needed to tell a thematic story. He settled on employability: the centrepiece of the reform would be "helping people to prepare themselves for work in a changing world." In other words, governments wouldn't create jobs, but with a better labour force, the jobs would come. "The best form of social security," the paper said, "comes from having a job." With Gherson's focus on employability, child poverty became less of a priority.

The ever-cautious Goldenberg, who bore a passing resemblance to Mr. Worry, had been unhappy with the quality of Axworthy's offerings for months. Now he appointed himself an outside invigilator. Once a week,

Gherson would troop over to Goldenberg's office to listen to the familiar exhortation to keep the paper province friendly. The powers that be wanted more diagnosis and less prescription. They insisted on options in place of proposals.

Axworthy bristled under the fine-tooth scrutiny. But Goldenberg could not be ignored. One of his great strengths was his ability to forecast the prime minister's reactions and to interpret them for others. He often spoke on behalf of Chrétien, which, if he was not challenged, made him more powerful than most cabinet ministers. Indeed, when he contemplated running for Parliament himself in the Montreal-area riding of Dollard in 1993, Brian Tobin, a fellow Chrétien loyalist who often competed with Goldenberg for the boss's attention, expressed delight. "I'd like to get him in cabinet with me on an equal footing," he told others. Despite Chrétien's decentralization of power back to ministers, issues that either touched on national unity or sparked internal divisions inevitably ended up on Goldenberg's desk. He was the government's chief fire prevention officer.

Unlike Axworthy, Goldenberg took no pleasure in the quixotic. When a Canadian human rights activist followed Chrétien to Indonesia to hound him on abuses in East Timor, Goldenberg shook his head in amazement at the idealism of those who still believed they could change the world single-handed. Like many in the Prime Minister's Office, he viewed himself as a small-l liberal. But he thought Bill Clinton had been naive at the outset of his presidency in allowing himself to be sidetracked from his economic agenda to champion the cause of gay rights in the military.

The pressure on Axworthy to say less and less grew with each passing day. The referendum was still ahead, and despite Chrétien's comments, nobody wanted to needlessly antagonize Quebec, with its sensitivity to provincial jurisdiction. Axworthy's plans for post-secondary education continued to cause concern. Massé, even while acknowledging the continuing efforts to make the paper more province friendly, warned fellow ministers that it tempted an adverse reaction, that the whole process of social security review would be seen as inherently centralizing.

These had been gruelling, soul-defeating months for Axworthy. Now here he was on October 5 — finally ready to publish his paper on the future direction of social policy — and the whole effort had been hijacked by the *Toronto Star* story about the hidden fiscal agenda. Judith Maxwell, the task force member who had once brimmed over with optimism at Axworthy's efforts, felt her legendary compassion failing her. The task force had pushed and pushed him to face up to the fiscal situation. He had stead-fastly refused, leaving himself vulnerable to precisely the kind of charge now devastating his launch plans. "I'll tell you what I thought that day," she said with uncharacteristic anger. "I thought, I told you so."

The media assault in the wake of the *Star* story was brutal. Axworthy, accompanied by a poker-faced Massé, there to speak in French, met the press after presenting the paper to the House of Commons. Despite the obvious mushiness that had flowed from the pressures of being all things to all people and of ducking the fiscal implications, his eighty-nine-page paper still contained a number of far-reaching, even radical, options. Axworthy floated the idea of increasing the child tax benefit by as much as $1,500 per child and integrating the federal efforts on children with provincial welfare plans. (He gave no hint of where the money would come from or who would be in charge.) He suggested a major restructuring of unemployment insurance, an approach that would treat frequent claimants, including seasonal workers, differently than others by slashing their benefits and forcing them into training programs.

On post-secondary education, Axworthy really displayed his reformist bent. For years, federal post-secondary transfers had gone to the provinces with no strings attached, not even an insistence that the money actually end up in the hands of colleges and universities. Now Axworthy sought to reassert the federal government's control over its funds. He would cut the provinces out entirely and deal directly with students. Under the existing formula, Ottawa's cash transfers would run out in ten years or so. Axworthy proposed the creation of a permanent endowment of $2 billion a year for student loans that would be repaid, with payment schedules based on the future income of the graduate. Assuming — as the auditor general did — that Ottawa would have to write off 25 per cent of these loans every year, the actual cost to the federal treasury would come to only $500 million a year. Axworthy therefore could provide Paul Martin with the $1.5 billion in savings he had demanded for 1996–97 without further impoverishing the educational system or hitting social assistance transfers.

This was all heavy stuff, but not nearly as interesting as whether he was hiding cuts from the public. Reporters challenged him unrelentingly on the credibility of his initiative, prompting Axworthy to plead: "Let's get down to what's in our document."

But it wouldn't be so. "I hate to keep harping on the money thing," Southam News reporter Joan Bryden said. "But I will anyway."

The minister leaned back in his chair, rolled his eyes, and sighed: "Why not?"

Axworthy subjected himself to nine interviews over the next five hours, his day from hell culminating in a brutal exchange on *Prime Time News* with Pamela Wallin. Almost every question homed in on the leak. She didn't seem at all interested in the substance of his proposals. "If you want us all to participate," she stated, "why not treat us like grownups and tell us what the price is?"

Over the coming weeks, the social security review would attract a diversified clientele of detractors among the ranks of professional activists and beneficiaries of the status quo. The great unwashed Canadian public, however, appeared to accept the need for the sort of massive changes Axworthy had proposed, and didn't seem perturbed that deficit reduction formed part of the rationale. A poll taken after the launch by the COMPAS organization found that 91 per cent of respondents strongly or somewhat supported a requirement that some people on social assistance take training courses or do community work; 84 per cent similarly supported integrating federal and provincial benefits into a guaranteed minimum income; 74 per cent supported targetting child tax benefits more closely to the needy; 66 per cent supported his two-tier unemployment insurance system. Only on post-secondary education funding did public approval elude Axworthy.

Aside from the jurisdictional issue, the special cabinet committee vetting the social security review had warned him that taking on students would be politically foolhardy. Even centralists like Sheila Copps, relying on her political intuition rather than a deep appreciation of fiscal federalism, wondered where the benefit lay in challenging students and their middle-class parents. Who were the winners who would rally to his side? She could see only the losers.

But Axworthy hung tight. He argued the centrality of education to his reforms. Improving the employment prospects of Canadians could not be divorced from the education of the workforce. The universities flooded the market with too many political science graduates and too few with technical skills. Axworthy was a former university professor himself. He was damned if he was going to pass up a chance to punt these institutions, and their pampered middle-class beneficiaries, however reluctantly, into the twenty-first century.

Both he and the department felt confident they could sell their proposal on the merits. The Tory approach, he told cabinet, would be to simply chop the $2 billion or more in federal education transfers. His way — the Liberal way — would be to restructure the system so as to perpetuate the benefits and spread them more equitably.

Perhaps it was too ingenious, for he never succeeded in explaining it. Instead, he got ensnarled in a debate about tuition fees. The provinces, with lower revenues from Ottawa, could be expected to hike tuition fees, perhaps even doubling them. Sure, students would have the loans to offset these increases (the new scheme would build on the Canada Student Loans Program), but they would have to go more deeply in debt to get through school. Axworthy's proposal, they complained, amounted to transferring Ottawa's deficit onto their backs.

The students, unlike single welfare mothers, possessed the means to mobilize. They went after Axworthy with a vengeance, loudly making their views known in every community across the country with an institution for higher education.

By this point, it had become clear to Axworthy and his department that he stood practically alone. Chrétien made a single intervention; other ministers, with the exception of Martin, steered clear of championing his paper. Axworthy had particular problems in Quebec because of his weak French. Just prior to the launch, his staff asked the fluently bilingual Sheila Copps if she would go to Rimouski and Sherbrooke after the release. She resented being summoned to a meeting with Giles Gherson: she was a minister and he was an aide. She sent one of her assistants to the meeting; he found the planning haphazard. No audiences had been lined up, no radio talk shows. And why was she relegated to the media backwaters? Copps decided to stay home.

The Atlantic ministers had also gone to ground upon the paper's release. They remained deeply upset about the cuts to UI contained in the previous budget and the suggestion now of further action against seasonal workers. As for the others, they had more pressing concerns. Axworthy now paid a price for not having brought cabinet along with him. If he wanted to play solo, the orchestra would gladly sit out this number.

The provinces had also jumped all over him. Quebec, as expected, went to town on Ottawa's lack of respect for its jurisdictional integrity. Ontario Premier Bob Rae delivered the most cutting line, dismissing the paper as the "Coles notes of Canada social policy." He also ridiculed the dearth of fiscal information. "Talking about social reform without talking about the numbers is a bit like talking about Moby Dick without talking about the whale."

On November 16, students staged a nasty demonstration on Parliament Hill. When Axworthy appeared, they pelted him with Kraft Dinner noodles. He started out by saying: "There is no government policy. There [have] been no decisions taken." They interrupted him with chants of "Bullshit." One of the signs bobbing in the angry mob read: "Suck my dick, Lloyd, it's all I have left."

Shouting over the taunts, he made the case that his proposals would provide more money for higher education, not less. "That is a fact," he asserted, his face flushed red. A raw egg splattered across the left shoulder of his suit jacket. "If you don't want to hear the truth, that's your problem," he shouted, stabbing his right index finger at the crowd. Growing hoarse, he implored the students to get off the barricades and join him around the table in an honest dialogue. "That is what we do in a democracy," the former campus radical said.

Walking back towards the Centre Block, Axworthy couldn't hide his frustration from the reporters taking in the incredible scene. "We're trying to build a future for them. They don't seem to understand that," he remarked, his voice flat. Then, dishing out a customary late hit, he declared that nobody was entitled to special privileges in this country.

Inside the building, other Liberals watched the events on the lawn with mounting dismay. They had been under attack as well in the Commons. Lucien Bouchard, sensing Liberal discomfort, switched to English during Question Period, asking Axworthy about the apparent contradiction in coupling his Green Paper call for the greater acquisition of knowledge with a policy that would restrict access to universities.

The spin doctors were already out, maintaining that the students had lost the day with their rude behaviour. They certainly looked loutish on television. But Axworthy chalked up the biggest loss. A government with a low pain threshold saw little gain in battling students. To one cabinet colleague, Axworthy had looked like an angry man yelling at a bunch of kids, their provocation notwithstanding.

The department worried that the minister had become obsessed with the students. Other aspects of the social security review suffered as a result. The officials noted ruefully how the problem kids always seemed to get the most attention. The child care lobby behaved itself and the minister paid it little heed; the students pelted him with macaroni and dominated his time.

Axworthy had lost control of the critical terms of the debate. He no longer "framed" the question; the students did. For Axworthy, his reforms would perpetuate a federal role in higher education. But to the public at large, it simply seemed a bald-faced attempt by government to double tuition fees. Axworthy's department had been told by pollster Frank Graves in November that Canadians rated education as the number one priority over the next five years for the federal government, even though it was a provincial jurisdiction. At a time when training and education were touted as necessary preconditions to compete for jobs, Graves warned that Canadians regarded education as their passport to a reasonable future. Axworthy's own department acknowledged in its internal papers that cheap, accessible education was seen as a cornerstone of what makes Canada unique. Axworthy, to his own great annoyance, looked to be the enemy of universality, not its saviour.

Axworthy put his office and department on war footing. He ordered the establishment of a Quick Response Unit to speedily counter the students with letters to campus newspapers, leaflets, and the like. He also sought to identify sympathetic academics and student leaders as spokespeople for his reforms. He tapped into the networks of young staffers in his office, former summer interns, and Young Liberal organizations to provide intelligence on campus activities across the country. Axworthy came to loathe the Canadian Federation of Students, which he judged shortsighted and selfish, and unrepresentative. The left-wing federation was under pressure as well on many campuses. Each time Axworthy's office learned of the existence of a rival student union, it would establish contact and encourage the group to make its views known to the local media.

Meanwhile, the Commons Human Resources Committee hit the road to test reaction and got more than it bargained for. Leftist organizers hijacked its meetings in Vancouver, Toronto, and Montreal. The violent pictures from these meetings did little to enhance the public image of the protesters, who appeared to be suppressing legitimate democratic debate. But to Axworthy's colleagues, he seemed to have lost control of the whole exercise. Their confidence level sank to new lows. Atlantic Canada was the next stop for the Commons committee. The Atlantic caucus, leery of the Axworthy exercise from the word go, now discussed asking the prime minister to scrap it altogether.

Politically, the battle with the students proved a disaster. Personally, it also took a heavy toll. Axworthy was enraged when a radical group calling itself the International Socialist Students organized a December 17th protest at his house called "Lunch with Lloyd." They plastered maps all over Ottawa showing where he lived and inviting students to partake of Kraft Dinner outside his home.

Nothing in the entire sorry affair brought Axworthy so low. He fumed at the invasion of his privacy and, worse, that of his wife and son. The family was placed under police protection for several days. Axworthy wanted to confront the protesters at his house, to defend his property. "He was like a cat that has put his paws in the electrical outlet," Noreau, his deputy, recalled. "We had to convince him to go away that day. Go anywhere else, just don't stay home."

Axworthy and his wife, Denise, went to watch their son, Stephen, play hockey while his press secretary, Alec Jasen, and a phalanx of RCMP and city police guarded the house from a handful of macaroni-toting protesters. On the way back home, the family stopped at a convenience store to pick up a couple of items. A young man outside the store began screaming and swearing at Axworthy. There was no escape.

13

THE RED BOOK IN
BLUE TIMES

Sporting a fresh haircut and an altered state of mind, Paul Martin went public with his new deficit warrior persona in a pair of extraordinary appearances before the House of Commons Standing Committee on Finance on October 17 and 18. In the well-rehearsed and carefully choreographed style that had become his hallmark, he would lay out an emerging philosophy for governing in the 1990s and disclose for the first time how much damage had been done to his deficit reduction targets of eight months earlier.

By 9:30 a.m. on Monday morning, Room 253-D of the Centre Block, better known as the Railway Committee Room, was overflowing with journalists, business and social group representatives, bureaucrats, and political staff. The hall — at seventy feet by forty feet, the largest on Parliament Hill — crackled with the expectant air of a courtroom awaiting opening arguments in a sensational murder case.

At 9:32, Finance Committee chairman Jim Peterson, one of Paul Martin's oldest friends in the government, banged his gavel and brought the committee to order. "With Canada's mounting national debt, Canadians are aware that the status quo is not an option," Peterson said as Martin sat down to update his previous budget and launch extensive and unprecedented public consultations on the next budget.

The Honourable Paul Martin had prepared hard for this day. Like a courtroom lawyer — and he was a lawyer by training, not an economist — he didn't leave anything to chance. He was accustomed to high-pressure situations and tended to rise to the occasion. On this first morning, he intended to unveil his Purple Book, which he billed as a "diagnostique" of the country's economic problems, with particular emphasis on the relationship between economic growth and deficits. He hoped that the Purple

Book, officially called *A New Framework for Economic Policy*, would stand as a successor to the outmoded Red Book as the government's bible. Media cynics, rushing for copies of the eighty-seven-page guide, delighted in their quick realization that its hue was the product of blending red (as in Liberal red) with blue (as in Tory blue).

The charge of being a Blue Grit, increasingly expressed in newspaper articles and within corners of his own caucus, disturbed Martin no end. He remained in his own self-image the son of Paul Martin Sr. and not the bastard child of Conservative Michael Wilson. "Martin didn't want to be seen as just a deficit minister," one of his officials said. "He wanted to be a guy with a broader view."

Martin dressed on this Monday morning in a dark blue pinstriped suit and conservatively dotted tie. He had taken the advice of those around him and eschewed his broad-striped shirts in favour of solid white, which was more television-friendly. Propping his text on a Plexiglas stand on the morning of October 17, he propounded on the details of his thinking. "Let me state from the outset that this is not a list of new programs. It is a statement of objectives and a statement of our economic philosophy. The budgetary decisions we make will be consistent with the criteria set out in this framework." He sat alone — unusual for a minister appearing before committee — at the far end of a rectangular box of tables. Over both shoulders, he was flanked by large television monitors. With each new point in his text, graphic images appeared on the screens, visually reinforcing his oral arguments. The sense of his cabinet colleagues the previous June that he had a coherent message to sell and the skill to peddle it was about to be validated.

In sharp contrast to Chrétien, Martin was a table d'hôte kind of politician. He didn't feel comfortable with the à la carte approach to governing of a Jean Chrétien. He liked, even needed, to be able to situate his actions within a framework of beliefs. All summer long, he had searched for some meaning to being finance minister in the 1990s, for a storyline beyond the necessary but soulless task of reducing the deficit.

Martin had been groping his way towards a redefinition of Liberalism even before he ran for Parliament in 1988. He was the sort of guy easily attracted to new ideas. Even some of his most ardent supporters worried about his policy trendiness. They found him too quick to embrace the latest cover of *Atlantic Monthly*, and transpose it to fit his circumstances.

Still, there was something refreshing about a politician intent on broadening his world-view. He reminded many of U.S. Senator Bill Bradley, a so-called Atari or neo-liberal Democrat, a politician open to new solutions for different times. Martin's 1990 leadership campaign had tried to articulate a new Liberal vision — reading his campaign booklet "Nationalism Without Walls," one would have thought he was running against Pierre Trudeau — but the message was lost in the powerful undertow of Meech. The Red Book again marked an effort to bring the party into the 1990s, but, as he had acknowledged to his officials, it was a hastily assembled document, more illustrative than comprehensive, and rendered inconsistent by the exigencies of numerous political compromises. Clearly, it had shut the door on the Liberalism of the Trudeau era, but it had fallen far short of answering tough questions about NAFTA, the deficit, the GST, and social policy.

To outfit him with a new Liberal philosophy, one that truly reconciled the legacy of his father with the Michael Wilson times, Martin now turned to Peter Nicholson, the economics guru whom he had seconded from the Bank of Nova Scotia to bulk up the department's brainpower. Nicholson was an important figure in the Paul Martin story. At fifty-two, he was a few years younger than Martin, but of his generation. He also shared a family grounding in the Liberal Party. His father had once been Nova Scotia's finance minister, and Nicholson himself briefly followed him into politics, sitting as an opposition Liberal MLA from 1978 to 1981.

His education was in physics and mathematics, rounded out by a Ph.D. from Stanford in operations research, a field of mathematics related to military logistics. Along the way, while teaching at the University of Minnesota, Nicholson had read an article pointing out that in every generation there are only a handful of great mathematicians: as for the rest, they probably did little harm. Nicholson wasn't cut out to be a second-rater, so he decided to aim for the top of some other field. Trading on his expertise in operations research — a discipline well suited to the prevalent "limits to growth" mentality of the 1970s — he headed to Ottawa. There, he sunk his teeth into some of the high-protein policy issues of the era, both in government and later as the in-house guru to Bank of Nova Scotia chairman Cedric Ritchie. Nicholson would pop up in the most eclectic places: on the wharves of St. John's trying to make sense of fish allocations, or in a New York bank tower navigating his way through the Third World debt maze, or back in Ottawa, in the midst of the Charlottetown constitutional negotiations, co-authoring a short-lived but highly regarded formulation aimed at breaking the deadlock on Senate reform.

Nicholson and Martin went back. For years, they attended summer think-in weekends organized by former Liberal cabinet minister Hugh Faulkner. Martin had suggested Nicholson as a speaker at the 1991 Aylmer conference, when he warned, with prescience, that "a heavily indebted nation is hostage to its external financiers and thus increasingly constrained to satisfy their objectives rather than its own."

In early 1994, at wits' end over his perception of a lack of original thinking emanating from his officials, Martin enticed Nicholson to come to Ottawa for two years and help him out as the department's Clifford Clark Visiting Economist, a selection customarily made by the deputy, not the minister. Nicholson wasn't an economist by training, but he didn't intimidate easily. "Someone once told me that Wellington's motto was that he always marched towards the sound of gunfire," he liked to say in explaining his career path. He arrived in March, just in time to catch a barrage: interest rates were putting the boots to Martin's first budget.

Quite consciously, Nicholson had chosen over the previous decade to play the role of secretary to a single prince. Now his prince was one of the most influential of all, Canada's minister of finance, investing his secretary with great influence as well. Nicholson's thoughts on economic matters were well documented among his prodigious writings. He favoured free trade and open investment, believed governments must invest in science and technology but generally did more harm than good when dabbling in the economy, and argued that the deficit and debt were a matter of arithmetic, not ideology, and demanded radical action.

Much of Nicholson's writing centred on the nettlesome issue of productivity, that is, the achievement of more economic output with less effort. Invited to speak to the intake of new Liberal MPs in February 1994, he told them: "Rising productivity is the ultimate source of a rising material standard of living. It follows that national policies to enhance competitiveness should, for the most part, be policies to enhance productivity. That, in a nutshell, is my central message." Within four months of Nicholson's arrival in Ottawa, after a great deal of resistance and argumentation, it would become Paul Martin's central message as well.

When Nicholson parked himself on the twentieth floor of Esplanade Laurier, he felt that his prince wasn't yet convinced in his bones of the full horrors of the deficit, or of the central importance to the equation of productivity. The interloper and the department saw eye-to-eye on this and most other matters, and Nicholson quickly picked up on the tensions between the officials and the minister. He hadn't worked for Martin before — had not even seen much of him in the previous several years — and was himself a bit intimidated at his contrarian style. "You say white and he says black," he would later marvel.

At his first meeting with the departmental officials, within days of arriving, Nicholson established his bona fides. They liked his mind and found his manner agreeable. Instead of being stuck with a competing pole of influence, the top officials concluded that they had lucked into somebody who could talk sense, and possibly cut through the minister's stubborn streak without having anything hurled at him. He had credentials they could not match: a private-sector background, a Liberal membership card, and, mostly, a history with Martin that pre-dated his tenure as minister.

Martin's pattern was clear by this point. It took him a long time to assimilate information, to sift through it, evaluate it, integrate it, and translate it into his own words. Along the way, he could be aggressive, a manifestation more of uncertainty than of confidence. The Purple Book, known internally over its summertime gestation as the productivity paper, was no exception. From the outset, Martin was skeptical, even hostile, to its central thesis: that the key to a better economy lay in greater productivity. His intuition told him otherwise, that productivity gains destroyed jobs. How in hell's name, he demanded to know, did the promotion of policies that would see fewer people producing more output serve the interests of a government committed to jobs and growth?

Nicholson and Dodge both understood the difficulties of making the case for productivity. A productivity juggernaut did churn out victims in its wake. Displaced workers would not always find new employment — they might be too old or live in the wrong place or possess the wrong skills. Ultimately, though, labour was redeployed in more enriching pursuits and so societies were enriched. In time, the winners outnumbered the losers.

Knowing Martin's interest in history, Nicholson drew on examples from the past. He reminded him of the way in which the increase of farm productivity had thrown thousands off the land, but allowed for an industrial revolution that drove up standards of living. He established a connection between countries with high productivity, particularly in Asia, and their relatively low levels of unemployment. He tried to relate the productivity thesis to Martin's own business experience at CSL. As was often the case, the people around Martin — in this instance, David Herle, Elly Alboim, and his parliamentary secretary, David Walker — embraced the argument sooner than the minister. They contributed to the efforts to bring him around.

Nicholson would later reflect that there hadn't been a single eureka moment along the way in that long summer of persuasion. But among the many charts he put together, one stood out for the impression it made on Martin: one in which he divided postwar economic performance in Canada into pre-1974 and post-1974 periods. That year marked the end of the robust productivity growth that Canada, and most of the Western world, enjoyed following the war. Nicholson demonstrated that when productivity growth was high, joblessness was low. And vice versa after 1974. It didn't prove cause and effect: productivity improvements didn't necessarily lead to job creation. But it punctured Martin's argument that productivity growth was, by definition, antithetical to a government committed to growth and jobs.

As Martin's comfort level grew with the productivity paper, so did his embrace of radical deficit reduction, which was part of Nicholson's thesis. His intellectual movement on the deficit was visible to the sensitive observer. In early October, he spoke on the subject at an International Monetary Fund meeting in Washington. "Deficit reduction is not an optional course of action," he told finance ministers and central bankers from around the globe. "It is a precondition for sustained economic growth and job creation. Reduced deficits will in turn lead to lower interest rates, to higher consumer and business confidence and to the creation of new and lasting jobs."

It was a long way from Rideau Hall eleven months earlier, when he had declared that "the root cause of the deficit and the root cause of unemployment are one and the same, and that is the ailing economy." Back then, Martin believed that low growth and high interest rates caused deficits. Now he believed that deficits caused low growth and high interest rates. In the eyes of the department, he had come a long way.

Martin's increasingly tough talk on the deficit was also motivated by his growing appreciation of the arithmetic of compound interest. Again, it hadn't come naturally. First the officials and then Nicholson worked on him. The scourge of the 1930s Alberta Social Credit Party became Paul Martin's scourge in the summer and fall of 1994. The debt was growing by $85,000 a minute, all of it interest. "Compounding was the fact beyond all others that convinced him of how essential it was to come to grips with the deficit problem," Nicholson said. "He became completely seized of the arithmetic of compound interest."

Even over the course of one year, Martin could see the corrosive effect that interest costs had on his own ability to do good works. The 2-per-cent run-up in interest rates of the spring had added $3.4 billion to his annual interest bill, and the creation of another $42 billion in debt over the previous twelve months was good for yet another $3 billion in interest charges. A further $6 billion in annual interest costs was a huge whack of cash — more than the annual cost to Ottawa of the CBC, Via Rail, veterans' allowances, and post-secondary education combined. Nicholson ran some numbers that indicated that even with a balanced operating budget — that is, revenues equal to spending on programs, excluding interest — those interest payments would mushroom from $40 billion to $60 billion within five years. These were frightening numbers to a government struggling to identify savings of $100 million here and $100 million there.

To Martin, another $20 billion in interest was an affront. Bad spending chased out good spending, all because interest costs had taken on a life of their own. Money that might otherwise go to combat child poverty or promote industrial growth was being shipped abroad every time bondholders in New York, Tokyo, and Zurich clipped their coupons. Martin now saw clearly that the debt, most of it compound interest with no socially redeeming value, stood between him and his activist impulses. Moreover, the hope he had expressed early in the term of government that Canada, with a lower inflation rate than the United States, should enjoy the benefit of lower interest rates would remain unattainable so long as investors demanded a higher premium to compensate for the risks posed by the debt.

By August, after their summer locked away together in a running tutorial on economics, Nicholson finally felt satisfied that Paul Martin accepted the dangers of the deficit in every pore of his body — intellectually, emotionally, psychically. But Martin also had something more now: in the Purple Book, he found the central thesis that would elevate his mission beyond just the deficit. The answer lay in Nicholson's message on productivity.

There were still three Paul Martins. But they no longer competed for control of his mind: there was a precedence to them now. The fiscal conservative stood first in line. If a stake wasn't driven through the heart of the deficit, then the other two — the social progressive and the industrial activist — would never have their moment in the sun, he reasoned. Fighting the deficit was not an end in itself, as it had been for the Tories, but merely the means to an end.

The Parti Québécois victory on September 12 threw a scare into some of the deficit hawks around Ottawa. They feared that the prime minister would be loath to cut spending too deeply as his government headed into a promised 1995 referendum on separation. Even in better political times, the prime minister had not seemed all that firm in his convictions, they noted, thinking back to his March remarks in Edmonton.

But Chrétien seemed to be on board as well. His first post-referendum speech in Quebec City on September 18 heartened Finance. It was an unusually detailed address for the prime minister, setting out an ambitious agenda for action in the fall, including Axworthy's social security review paper, Martin's budget update, the program review exercise, and a statement on innovation and growth by Industry Minister John Manley. The Finance officials were especially pleased by two lines in the Quebec City speech. The first was a reiteration, again, of the 3-per-cent goal. The second was a quote from John Maynard Keynes himself. It stated that periods of economic expansion were the ideal times to tame deficits. "So now is the time," Chrétien stated.

As he prepared to come clean about the consequences of his incorrect assumptions on interest rates, Martin had to play to three different audiences: the public at large, the Ottawa political system, and the financial markets. His first task was to begin conditioning Canadians for the major spending cuts to come in the February 1995 budget. To some extent, the Liberals were catching up with public opinion, which the previous Tory government had begun to sensitize about the dangers of the deficit. More recently, Reform had lent a hand, as had provincial governments, particularly Bob Rae's in Ontario. Rae certainly wasn't Ralph Klein, but in terms of public opinion the sudden attentions of the NDP to the deficit spoke volumes more about the seriousness of the situation than anything happening in Conservative Alberta.

Second, he wanted to give Marcel Massé's program review a boost within Ottawa as the major vehicle for this collective government assault on spending. The bureaucrats around town, and their ministers, needed a reminder of the government's seriousness.

Finally, Martin hoped that a powerful statement of intent in October would buy time with the financial markets until the February budget. Finance feared that further significant movements in the dollar and interest rates would force them to shoot at a moving target. Therefore, it was important to convince the markets early on that the challenge would be met, and met by cuts on the spending side.

The key to making sure Martin successfully put across his message, particularly to the public, lay in getting it out on television, his communications advisers had concluded. It was well known that the majority of Canadians acquired their news from TV. The problem was that financial stories, with their columns of numbers and accountant's jargon, lent themselves far better to print journalism.

Communications strategy was the domain of Peter Daniel, the department's cagey assistant deputy minister for communications and a former network television correspondent, and the ubiquitous pair from Earnscliffe Strategy Group, David Herle and Elly Alboim. Alboim was instrumental in introducing Martin to a new visual system called Powerpoint, which would help him immeasurably in communicating his message. Its graphics were more sophisticated and dynamic than the customary overhead projections. With high-tech pictures to illustrate the story, it would appeal more naturally to Newsworld, the network news shows, and the other important information programs.

The preparations had been intensive. Martin essentially was to host a pair of live television programs — the committee providing the backdrops — in which he would have to read his prepared remarks, in two languages, making sure he didn't run ahead of or behind his pictures. They worked on it for hours on end, writing and rewriting the speech, then matching it up to the visuals. Sometimes Martin would stand on the sidelines, observing how it looked, as Peter Daniel played his part — Martin loved the sound of Daniel's broadcast voice. In the end, Martin went through three dry runs for each of the two presentations, not including the countless occasions on which he practised the text alone.

His freelance speechwriter, Larry Hagen, who had made his name penning Joe Clark's Charlottetown speeches, was brought in from the beginning so that he could understand the substance and immerse himself in Martin's thinking. If the medium was television, it would require sound-bites. Some of the lines became instant standards. *We are in hock up to our eyeballs* and *It is a target we will meet come hell or high water.*

On the night before the first presentation, Martin and his advisers stole into the Railway Committee Room and staged a final rehearsal with full lights and cameras. Nothing was to be left to chance.

As expected, Martin rose to the occasion. He treated his audience to a condensed version of his summer seminar series with Nicholson, knitting the story of growing public debt and deficits together with the reality of two decades of slow economic growth, stagnant household income, and rising unemployment. The common thread, he told Canadians, was the perplexing 1970s bursting of the productivity bubble. It was the decline in productivity growth that served as the Rosetta Stone for all the themes Martin dwelled upon: skills shortages, slow economic growth, counter-productive social programs, misbegotten business subsidies, and deficits. "In Canada, the productivity slowdown was not sufficiently offset by reducing public and private consumption," the paper commented, "resulting in an extraordinary build-up of debt, both foreign and domestic."

The linkage between productivity and economic growth — the linkage he had resisted so stoutly — could not be denied, he argued. The strong productivity growth of the postwar years had been accompanied by low unemployment and rising per-capita income. "Better productivity is not the enemy of employment," Martin told the committee, "it is our workers' best friend. How do we improve productivity? To my mind and to all of our minds, the answer is clear. We must improve our skills. We must do better at innovation. We must provide a welcoming climate for investment. We must remove the disincentives we have created for both business and individuals — disincentives that encourage dependence and stand in the way of opportunity. Finally we must get our fiscal house in order."

With that, Paul Martin had his new economic philosophy. It sounded simple enough, but it represented a marked departure from Liberal economics of a decade earlier. Social policy was no longer about providing income support to the victims of economic change. Victimology was out. Safety nets were secondary. Policies would be aimed at helping those willing to help themselves back into the labour market. Economically, the nature of state intervention would change. The government still had a role to play in harnessing scientific research and technological advances to private-sector engines, thereby contributing to productivity growth. But megaprojects and regional business subsidies no longer fit the bill. Economic nationalism was bad, overregulation was bad, deficits were awful.

While it wasn't Trudeau Liberalism, neither was it neoconservatism. Reform Party finance critic Herb Grubel generously said he agreed with 90 per cent of the analysis. But the other 10 per cent was inconsistent. On the one hand, Martin had catalogued the high cost of government inefficiency, but on the other he set out new goals for the state. "Do you mean the same people who brought us the post office are now going to bring us more job training?" Grubel wondered.

The Purple Book out of the way, Martin reappeared before the committee at 3:34 the following afternoon to finally admit that, like Michael Wilson, he had been blown off course by economic factors he had not anticipated. Submitting the update document, titled *Creating a Healthy Fiscal Climate* but soon dubbed the Grey Book, he decried "the curse of compound interest" and "the tyranny of interest payments" and vowed to do what it took to meet the 3-per-cent target, "come hell or high water." The country had failed to take advantage of periods of growth in the 1970s and 1980s and could not afford to squander the current economic expansion. "Mr. Chairman, most of us did not choose to enter public life because of a burning desire to dismantle government programs. We came into government to help build a better Canada in terms of jobs and of growth. That is our only goal. It is because of that goal — not in spite of it — that we must act decisively on the debt challenge today. We must not waste this recovery."

Wrapping up his successful television production, Paul Martin took his new economic philosophy and returned to the twenty-first floor of the Department of Finance to work on the budget that would remake Canada. Even Nicholson would subsequently concede that the Purple Book proved, in the final analysis, more of a triumph for its impact on Martin than for its influence on overall government policy. Increasingly, as the fiscal noose continued to tighten between October and budget day, his handiwork would be relegated to the back burner. Nicholson understood. He often used the analogy of the hospital emergency ward: the doctors have to stop the bleeding before they begin to think about physiotherapy. He felt Martin now appreciated the need to stabilize the patient. And so decisions would be made in the short term that ran contrary to the productivity argument. Economic philosophy is fine, Martin would tell fellow ministers in the months ahead, but the country was on the critical list.

14

THE STAR CHAMBER

As Paul Martin went public with the truth about the government's finances, Marcel Massé was already hard at work on their joint project of slashing spending and reinventing the government of Canada. With the deteriorating budget situation, the program review process had taken on added urgency.

Departments had been given their targets in June and ordered to survey their operations and submit business plans over the summer. Axworthy largely had a bye thanks to his parallel social security review, but the others busied themselves figuring out what to keep and what to jettison. It would require more than a search of the books. Before the process was over, most ministers would have to search their souls. Unhappily, Paul Martin's deficit arithmetic did not fit easily with their values as Liberals.

The business plans would be screened by a special cabinet committee. In agreeing to program review and appointing the committee's members, Chrétien had added his own special twist. The financial ministers, Martin, Massé, and Art Eggleton at Treasury Board, would be joined in the exercise by some of his more politically alert ministers, Brian Tobin, Sheila Copps, André Ouellet, Sergio Marchi, and the old warhorse from the left, Herb Gray. For leavening, Anne McLellan, the promising rookie from Alberta, was thrown in. It would be a show-me committee. If you can't get a consensus in the cabinet, Chrétien seemed to be telling Martin and Massé, how can you hope for one in the country?

In billiards, there is a highly skilled stroke called a massé shot. It involves hitting straight down on the ball with the cue held perpendicular to the table. It is a means, when a player is snookered, of getting around a blockage. Now Massé, snookered for so many years by hesitant politicians and timid courtiers, was ready to strike from above, to use his position as

chairman of this critical committee to put into action the ideas for government reform he had long advocated. But he would have to build a
consensus among these less fiscally conservative ministers.

Massé designed a precisely formulated system of inquiry for program
review. Departments would have to subject their activities to six tests. Did
the program in question continue to serve the public interest? Was there
a necessary role for the government? Could that role be better carried out
by the provinces? Could the private or voluntary sector do the job better?
If the program continues, how can it be made more efficient? And, finally,
even if it cleared these other hurdles, the real question: Was the activity
affordable?

A feeling of disbelief had descended over Ottawa after the June cabinet retreat. Senior officials had been through exercises like these before.
At the end of the day, the government either lost its nerve or displayed an
appalling ineptitude at doing its sums. Nonetheless, one had to go through
the motions, so as ministers fled the unpleasant summertime humidity of the
capital for the barbecue circuit in their ridings, their senior departmental
officials were left behind to dutifully prepare the business plans.

The syllabus for the Program Review Committee called for several
overview lectures late in the summer. Martin decided to share with the
committee the "Big Picture," a deeply detailed, long-term analysis of
the government's finances that rarely — if ever — had been seen outside
the Finance Department. It was byzantine material, showing the spending
trends of individual programs, the impact of demographic changes, the
dynamic impacts one program had on another, the options on the revenue
side, and the likely effects on the underground economy. The Big Picture
made for a dark and foreboding portrait. After three such sessions, the committee members were sufficiently spooked to believe that perhaps they were,
indeed, on a path towards the precipice.

Massé also rolled out a ten-year budget forecast he had ordered the
previous spring. (Mid-level Finance officials had tried to stonewall him,
but Martin let them know in no uncertain terms that Massé was his partner.) The long-term forecast showed very clearly that traditional spending restraint would never bring the deficit to zero. Demographic factors
pushed expenditures on seniors and aboriginal people perpetually upward.
The next recession, whenever it came, would eat into tax revenues and
swell social spending, undoing whatever progress had been achieved till
then on deficit reduction. The only way to regain control over the deficit,

Massé told the committee, was to restructure the government's spending patterns. Simple cuts would not suffice.

Brian Tobin, a show-me kind of guy, aggressively challenged the Finance officials in these early meetings. He would sit there during the presentations, his open mouth exuding skepticism. But the fisheries minister, for all his flash, also possessed great dollops of native intelligence. A trip to Japan on behalf of the Liberals in his last year of opposition had impressed upon him Canada's vulnerability to the whims of foreign lenders. With each passing session on program review, he became more and more convinced that the debt was draining the lifeblood out of the country. With his typical irony, he marvelled aloud after one intervention: "I've become the right-wing fiscal conservative of this government."

In the fall, Tobin put his considerable oratorical talents to use in sermons about the perils of debt and deficits. He began to tell audiences that on his first day on the job as an MP in 1980, at the tender age of twenty-five, the country was 113 years old and its total debt stood at $146 billion. With that, Canada had fought two world wars, built the infrastructure to sustain the economy — the two transcontinental bands of steel, highways, seaways, and harbours — developed a health care system the envy of the world, and opened up new provinces and territories. "For $146 billion, I came to the conclusion when I was twenty-five years old and had been an MP for one day that maybe it wasn't a bad deal."

Then he spoke about the second big day of his political life, the day he was sworn into cabinet in November 1993. More than thirteen years had passed, now he was thirty-nine; the debt stood at $500 billion, and the country had nothing to show for it. Worse still, the annual deficit was $40 billion. "That means if we assume the wheel and if we drive the ship neither left nor right, we neither accelerate nor decelerate, if we merely follow the course that she's already on, the one that Mulroney left behind, we'd track up more debt in five years, $200 billion, than Canada racked up in its first 113 years of existence." Even in Atlantic Canada, he felt the audiences coming along. Martin was grateful for the help and promised Tobin, in return, that he would make Newfoundland the first stop on his post-budget tour.

Only after the committee understood the Big Picture did Massé reveal the overall goal. All told, it added up to a massive 20-per-cent cut in program spending over three years. They would have to hack $10 billion over three years from the $50 billion in programs under examination. Later, defence spending was added, bringing the total to $60 billion (and ending Collenette's bye). Pretty well everything under the government's control would be scrutinized, other than the programs already within Axworthy's social security review, old-age pensions, and interest on the debt.

In the usual Ottawa way, the bureaucrats ran a parallel process, one in which David Dodge shared information never before shown to other departments. With that knowledge in hand, the business plans prepared over the summer went to a committee of deputies, chaired by Jocelyne Bourgon, clerk of the Privy Council. It was a peer review and it led, in the euphemism of officials worldwide, to some full and frank discussions, fuller and franker than would be possible between ministers and deputies. Most of the business plans were sent back for major revisions.

Only a handful of departments cooperated fully on the first pass. The prize pupil was Transport, which had zoomed well ahead of the pack in redefining its mission and shedding costs. The department's no-nonsense minister, Doug Young, had already unveiled a policy to place all the airports in the country under the control of local authorities, a truly staggering departure for a Liberal government. Jean-Luc Pepin, the eloquent transport minister in the last Trudeau government, once described airports as "the cathedrals of the twentieth century." They were one of the most visible symbols of the federal presence in communities across the country. Now Ottawa was getting out of the business, a policy started under the Tories but now vastly expanded. Young also intended to sell the country's air navigation system to a consortium made up of its users, and to privatize CN Rail. Much to the consternation of Agriculture Minister Ralph Goodale, Young also had publicly declared his intention to kill the Crow freight rate subsidy for grain, seen as a birthright of Confederation in Goodale's native Saskatchewan.

Early in its life, the Program Review Committee gained an informal appellation, one that packed a pejorative punch. Around town, it was called the Star Chamber, in tribute to the dreaded English institution of the Stuart period that met in Westminster Palace under a roof "decked with the likeness of Stars gilt." Like the ancient Star Chamber, program review was an offshoot of the Privy Council, delegated to issue judgments on matters large and small. Its deliberations were secret and its justice arbitrary, making it a powerful instrument in the hands of the sovereign.

Liberal ministers resented the power and remit of its modern manifestation. The collision of its irresistible force with their immovable departmental functions set off a series of increasingly acrimonious exchanges. Committee members long after would remember the day that Goodale, Paul Martin's best friend in cabinet, delivered a withering challenge to their moral authority. "What gives you the right to act as judges on what generations of other people have created? The future of thousands of people is going to be decided by you nine here. From what divine right do you derive the power to decide that fifty of my scientists will be without work tomorrow? How come you think you know what is right and what is wrong? What is in the national interest or not? You guys get to be here and apply your outlook of the world, your values. And after you decide, then you are going to come to us and tell us what to do. What gives you that right?" More than one of the members of the committee could be seen nodding in agreement.

Sergio Marchi, himself a member of the committee, became one of its first supplicants in his capacity as minister of citizenship and immigration. Marchi, a Canadian of Italian descent born in Argentina, found the process of meeting his departmental targets personally excruciating. The nobility of Canada's open immigration policies animated almost all Liberals. Under Laurier, the party had settled the west, recruiting the legendary men in sheepskin coats from eastern Europe to come and break the unforgiving prairie soil. Generation after generation of newcomers had arrived in Canada brimming over with gratitude for Liberal governments. Immigration was as central to the party's ethos as social programs. That was doubly so for Marchi, at thirty-eight the youngest member of Chrétien's cabinet and the closest of all the ministers to the immigration experience. As a youngster playing hockey, he had gone by the name Jim because the other boys at the rink couldn't pronounce Sergio. "When I was a kid," he once said, "I knew that every time there was a reference to the Mafia or crime or whatever, people would lump my parents in as greasy Italians." To the sensitive and sentimental Marchi, Immigration amounted to more than a portfolio.

Marchi had two heroes in life. The first was his father, Ottavio, a tool-and-die maker who had left his Italian district of Friuli in the 1950s in the classic search for a better life. The other was Mario Cuomo, the son of working-class Italian-American immigrants, who rose to become governor of the state of New York. Marchi admired both his liberal ideals and his awesome oratorical skills. If you want to understand Marchi, read this, one of his officials remarked in the fall of 1995. He threw the transcript of a speech across the table, a speech Cuomo had delivered that September to a Liberal fundraiser in Marchi's riding of York West. It must have made Marchi's heart skip a beat when Cuomo said he had come to the northern reaches of Toronto "especially for Sergio Marchi," who had hounded him for years.

Marchi served as Liberal immigration critic in opposition, forging fast friendships with the legions of philanthropic and self-interested advocacy groups working the beat. He was their parliamentary mouthpiece; they were his instant friends. Despite strong anti-immigration sentiments abroad in the land, Marchi wanted to liberalize immigration, raising the annual intake to the Red Book target of one per cent of the population, roughly 280,000 newcomers. But in short order he was forced into a mental adjustment. At a public consultation session in a Toronto church basement, the mother of a three-year-old girl who had been raped by a Caribbean immigrant confronted Marchi. The father of a three-year-old girl himself, he was shaken by the story. He told his officials, whom he had been hectoring for months over their supposed lack of compassion, that they had to be careful about who they let into the country.

Soon Marchi found himself in a firestorm over two brutal murders in Toronto in which immigrants were suspects. After initial hesitation, Marchi responded by beefing up his department's enforcement capacity, incurring the wrath of his erstwhile friends in the immigration community.

By the time program review rolled around, Marchi's heart-on-his-sleeve Liberalism had been tempered somewhat by the discipline of power. That suited his officials fine. They tended to be far more conservative than the minister. They argued from the moment he entered the department that the beneficiaries of the program, new Canadians, should cover more of the costs of their benefits. His deputy, Peter Harder, had come into the bureaucracy after serving as an aide to Tories Erik Nielsen and Joe Clark, generating an initial wariness on Marchi's part. But he had also quickly established himself as one of the town's younger and more able deputies. (Marchi once confided, "Peter is all right, but he knows that in any showdown, I can get to the prime minister a lot faster than he can.")

The department recognized from the outset that Marchi posed a challenge: he was a sentimental politician carrying a lot of personal baggage whose instincts were out of sync with the political and economic realities. The times demanded a curtailment of immigration, not a bold expansion of its frontiers. Eventually the department, aided by the Toronto incidents, brought Marchi around to its point of view, but it was a constant struggle to keep him from backsliding.

Martin had given Immigration a relatively modest target: to cut 15 per cent over three years. But the department had already been heavily rationalized under the Tories and felt it should be treated as a prototype for program review, not as a victim of it. Massé displayed some sympathy, but said that while the plea might be reasonable in times of a 3-per-cent across-the-board cut, the need to take 20 per cent out of program spending meant nobody could escape.

Immigration officials canvassed the possibilities. They certainly couldn't forsake enforcement, given the political mood in the country. Nor would Liberals want to shut down settlement services, the language, health, and housing programs aimed at helping immigrants integrate into their new communities. The remaining alternative would be to slash immigration levels radically, but again such a move flew in the face of Liberal values, and ultimately it would prove economically counter-productive.

Finance began pushing the idea of charging a user fee to new arrivals to Canada, a so-called landing fee. The officials over at Esplanade Laurier regarded the concept of user-pay as the way of the future and wanted some prominent examples in the budget. Marchi was pretty dubious. Again, the idea was antithetical to everything Liberals stood for. And the fee that Finance was seeking — around $1,700 or $1,800 — would be so prohibitive, he figured, as to effectively bar the door to most immigrants. But his officials found merit in the user fee model. Indeed, the department, under the Tories, had already introduced a $500 processing fee for landed-immigrant applications. They pushed Marchi towards the landing fee (which, in Orwellian fashion, they called the right-of-landing fee). It was two steps forward, one step back, with Marchi trapped and sulking all the way.

From the point of view of the bureaucrats, user fees had the great advantage of bolstering the revenue side of the equation, while leaving the spending side untouched. The Immigration officials recommended a fee of at least $1,500. Anything less, they figured, would provide only temporary relief. After much prodding, Marchi agreed to the concept, but he wanted a token fee of $250. "I am a Liberal and these are not Liberal ideas," he said, speaking from the heart. In his head, though, he knew that it didn't add up.

Marchi felt he had one hope: to subject his fellow program review ministers to the same torment he was undergoing. He would take the user fee idea to the committee and cross his fingers that the others would recoil. Then Marchi could wriggle off Martin and Massé's hook.

His assessment was right — to an extent. The initial reaction of the other small-l liberals on the committee — Copps, Tobin, and Gray — was that Marchi must be kidding. They could never do that. They were *Liberals*. Marchi had good fortune on his side. He was one of the first ministers up, in early fall, and the committee's olfactory senses weren't as acute as they would become. More fundamentally, they did not yet appreciate the irreconcilability of Liberal values and the 3-per-cent target.

Martin seemed as disturbed as the others by the landing fee. But he was focussed on a bigger issue: his deficit. It was immutable. He told Marchi that maybe $1,500 was too high. But the idea itself was sound. He didn't relish the thought of gouging immigrants, but if he let Marchi off the hook, the other fish would break upstream, too. The whole process depended on everyone sacrificing — not necessarily equally, that would be the Tory way — but still one for all and all for one.

Martin reeled Marchi back in. He was sent away to do more work. Back at the department, he reviewed the options again. This time, the dreaded landing fee — which would become almost universally known as the head tax, in memory of the discriminatory fees imposed on Chinese immigrants between 1885 and 1923 — started to make sense.

The arithmetic came down to a stark choice: either impose the fee or kill off settlement services. Neither Marchi nor the committee could stomach the latter course. They looked at the United States and worried that the loss of language training for new arrivals could exacerbate social divisions and possibly foster a permanent underclass of Canadians. That certainly wouldn't be the Liberal way. Moreover, national unity politics also precluded cutting settlement services. After the failure of the Meech Lake Accord, Brian Mulroney had given Quebec a sweetheart deal on immigration, including an endowment for settlement that rose every year regardless of how many immigrants the province actually accepted. Quebec already received a disproportionate share of federal settlement money, an irritant to other provinces, particularly Ontario and British Columbia. Despite the obvious injustice, the Chrétien government entertained no thought of unilaterally revoking the arrangement in a referendum year. All this meant that if Marchi wanted to cut settlement services, he would have to take it all from the other provinces, further exacerbating the existing inequity. Cutting settlement services, as a result, simply wasn't an option.

With a guilty conscience, Marchi opted for the landing fee. He was working simultaneously on a White Paper on immigration and needed to settle quickly with program review. He told his officials he was ready to sell the user fee idea to his cabinet colleagues. They furnished him with international comparisons and analyses of countries, such as Australia, that had landing fees. Marchi had one caveat, though. The fee would have to be kept below $1,000; that was a psychological and political barrier he was not willing to cross.

Still, Liberals agonized. Copps complained that the government was abandoning its traditional tolerance for newcomers and behaving in a cavalier fashion towards a core constituency. "Liberals don't do this kind of thing," she insisted. The prime minister's representatives were also deeply troubled. Eddie Goldenberg and Chaviva Hošek sat in on the Program Review Committee sessions from beginning to end. Hošek also attended Social Development Committee meetings, where Marchi's planned White Paper was proceeding on a parallel track. Goldenberg and Hošek were the guardians of the party's values, the two people in the room for whom the big picture had to be about re-election, not finances. Both were Jews from Montreal, with a strong attachment to the immigration ethos. Hošek referred to the two of them as "squishy Liberals."

For her, like Marchi, the landing fee hit particularly close to home. She, too, had been born overseas, in her case in the chaos of postwar Czechoslovakia. Her family had come to Canada by way of Israel. Asked to explain her values, she would say: "I'm a Jew and I'm Czech. Those are very important things." She had also come of age in politics not in the Liberal Party like so many of her colleagues, but in the women's movement. Her politics were rooted in social advocacy. When she first heard of the landing fee idea at a Social Development Committee meeting, she spoke up, something even prime-ministerial advisers rarely do in cabinet sessions. "Sergio," others in the room recalled her beseeching him, "how can you do this? This is racist." Marchi responded that the alternative — curtailing settlement services — was even more odious.

Hošek and Goldenberg spent hours discussing every angle of the landing fee. In the end, her heart had to give in to what she called her Israeli aspect, which meant that if you said things were bad, she would retort, Compared to what? Massé observed all this with great interest. He respected Hošek and thought she, like many of the others in the room, had grown considerably during program review. "She was beginning to see that her game was trade-offs, not straight choices. And that in the game of trade-offs, you do not choose what is Liberal. You choose what is more Liberal than the other things."

Despite all the misgivings — and there were plenty — the landing fee proposal had one indispensable factor going for it, Marchi himself. In a cabinet system, especially a decentralized cabinet like Jean Chrétien's, it was very hard to reject the responsible minister's solution to a problem. It was incumbent upon opponents to at least offer an alternative. But without the benefit of officials steeped in the issues and numbers, other ministers operated at a disadvantage. Marchi had plenty of research to back him up. He saw this as the best way out. He was credible on the issue. He didn't like the solution. In fact, it was safe to say he hated the prospect of being stigmatized as its proponent. For him, defending the landing fee was an act of courage, not of convenience. But he was willing, and if it was good enough for Sergio Marchi, it had to be good enough for the rest of them.

Many Liberals in caucus as well as cabinet were wondering that fall just what was "good enough": were their standards slipping? Program review was only one of the issues that were bringing to light some self-doubt about whether they were still true Liberals.

Preparations were under way for Jean Chrétien to lead the first Team Canada trade mission to China, departing November 4. He would be accompanied by nine premiers, two territorial leaders, and more than 250 business people on an expedition that would eventually provide a public relations bonanza for the Liberals. But in caucus prior to the trip, there was more than a little unease at the Liberals' apparent rejection of their traditional positions.

Through the Trudeau and Turner years, the Liberals' foreign policy had focussed on human rights, arms control, the United Nations, the environment, and the conversion of defence plants to civilian production. Their China policy had included vigorous denunciations of the country's human rights record, complaints about China upgrading its stock of nuclear weapons, and protests about the "environmentally disastrous" impact of the massive Three Gorges dam project on the Yangtze River.

But in power again in the 1990s, the Liberals swiftly discovered economic and political advantages to rethinking their policy towards China. As the Chinese economy opened up to the world and became the new magnet of international business, Chrétien's pragmatic nature came to the fore. After becoming prime minister he promptly began wooing China's political leaders. At the APEC meeting in Seattle in November 1993, his special effort to cultivate President Jiang Zemin yielded the invitation to visit China. The notion of bringing the premiers along came out of a December 1993 first ministers' meeting in Ottawa. It was initially suggested by British Columbia Premier Mike Harcourt, who was a frequent visitor to the Asia-Pacific region, and familiar with the close relationships between business and political leaders in that part of the world. Chrétien quickly appropriated the concept.

Once the prime minister bought into the idea, other concerns were swept aside with remarkable alacrity. On March 19, Chrétien made his position clear with a series of blunt comments in a question-and-answer session at the Université de Moncton. There was no point, he said, in Canada lecturing China on human rights because Canada was simply too small a country, and China too large, to have any influence. "If I were to say to China, 'We are not dealing with you any more,'" he said, "they would say 'Fine.' They would not feel threatened by Canada strangling them." There was no point, he added, trying to act like "a big shot" in such a situation. On the other hand, Chrétien continued, Canada would continue to exert pressure in smaller countries where it might have more clout. As a country, Chrétien said, "you have to measure your strength. Sometimes you will have influence and sometimes you won't."

Those remarks caused a stir in political circles across the country and an internal uproar at the Foreign Affairs Department, which had been heatedly debating approaches to Chinese relations ever since Tiananmen Square. Even those sympathetic to closer relations preferred a more nuanced position. Some officials went to André Ouellet, who had echoed Chrétien's unsubtle tactics, with their concerns. The surest way, they said, for Canada to be treated as an inconsequential player was to describe itself as one.

The result was a carefully worded speech by Ouellet to the Canadian Institute for International Affairs in Ottawa on May 31, in which he sought to reclaim the middle ground between trade and human rights for the Liberals. Canada, Ouellet said, wanted to "promote dialogue rather than confrontation" with China. We believe, he said, that "China will achieve long-term stability only through greater respect for human rights and the rule of law." Canada would work with other nations to ensure that China respected its obligations under the United Nations Declaration on Human Rights, which it had signed in 1993.

But at the same time, other Foreign Affairs officials played the part of overzealous matchmaker, doing everything they could to push Canada and China closer together. If someone sneezes within the PMO, they sometimes said at the Foreign Affairs Department, everyone catches a cold at their offices at Fort Pearson. Now some officials embraced the notion of warming up to China with almost unseemly enthusiasm, outracing even their political masters in an attempt to get on side. The Canadian Forces frigate HMCS *Vancouver* was headed for the Asia-Pacific region, and Chinese military officials let it be known to Canada that a "goodwill" stop in several ports would be very welcome. Foreign Affairs was in favour, and said so in a memo written, appropriately enough, on Valentine's Day. The memo made its usual circuitous way across various desks, gathering the requisite signatures of approval, before landing in front of Raymond Chan, secretary of state for the Asia-Pacific region.

Chan, born in Hong Kong and a Vancouver MP, had more of a stake in Canada-China relations than most. In his previous life as a human rights activist, he had been thrown out of China in 1991 after meeting with dissidents. In his newest incarnation as a cabinet minister, he was a latecomer to Canadian politics but no novice at deciphering the intentions behind Chinese government actions. He was the last person to check the memo before it reached the desk of Ouellet for final approval. Chan knew that the Chinese government would see the gesture as a sign that Tiananmen Square had been stricken from Canadian memory. That was not the signal Canada should send, he thought. On the other hand, Chan felt certain the Chinese would not be offended if Canada told them that the frigate was unavailable. The Chinese put out feelers like this all the time, testing the temperature around them. In his first significant act as secretary of state and in the face of strong objections from department officials, Chan scribbled a note outlining his opposition to the move. Ouellet backed him, and the idea was scrapped.

The Team Canada trip itself was, by almost any measure, a great success. It generated more than $9 billion in signed agreements involving Canadian companies, and reaped a huge bounty of favourable press for Chrétien back home. He appeared relaxed and at ease on the international stage. A televised image of Chrétien breaking into a sprint on a stretch of the Great Wall evoked fond recollections of Trudeau's old élan. (Never mind that the entire affair was not so spontaneous as it seemed: a planning memo sent by the Canadian Embassy from Beijing several months earlier had specifically recommended that site because, among other things, "the climb is less physically demanding.")

But on the human rights front, not all was so smooth. One problem was the way the prime minister, in response to urging from Foreign Affairs advisers, tiptoed around the issue. Rather than utter the words "human rights," Chrétien was told by his China experts to use the phrase "good governance and the rule of law."

There were two difficulties with that, as the prime minister discovered to his chagrin. One was that Chrétien, when asked whether he had raised human rights as an issue, could not respond in the affirmative, because he had not used those words. He stumbled over his responses in the ensuing press conference as a result, and fumed about the matter later to aides. Another problem was that his advisers had been overly cautious: the Chinese side, as it turned out, would not have been upset if he had taken up the question. When Chrétien met with Jiang a year later at an APEC meeting in Osaka, Japan, he talked about Canada's desire to send a delegation to China to talk about "good governance and the rule of law." Jiang, when the remark was translated for him, looked baffled and asked his aide what Chrétien meant. At that point, China's foreign affairs minister intervened and told him: "He's talking about human rights." Jiang smiled, and told Chrétien that the two countries should work together on the issue. (The Canadians knew that because Raymond Chan was standing near Jiang and overheard the exchange, which was not repeated in English. When Chan later related it to the prime minister, Chrétien laughed, shook his head, and responded that he had wanted to say "human rights" from the outset, but was dissuaded by Foreign Affairs officials.)

The strong approval for Chrétien's Team Canada efforts — a tribute to a brilliantly executed communications effort — silenced most of the potential opposition within caucus. In the spirit of lowering expectations and then exceeding them, the government had signed more deals than advertised. And the Liberals had provided images that the television networks would find irresistible, from the planned (Chrétien's sprint up the Great Wall) to the opportunistic (his bicycle ride down a Shanghai street). John Tory, the veteran Conservative political organizer, figured the favourable coverage would extend the Liberal honeymoon an additional six months.

By now, even diehard Chrétien opponents could only marvel at his remarkable political touch. The most recent Angus Reid poll gave him a 71-per-cent approval rating, making him more popular than any Canadian political leader in the previous half-century. In the Finance Department, where they had their own particular brand of humour, the joke that fall was that while Mulroney's popularity had been lower than the prime rate, Chrétien's was higher than the ratio of debt to GDP. In an era of deep public cynicism about politicians in general, power enhanced rather than diminished Chrétien. He lapped it up. Other G-7 leaders took envious note.

Chrétien's popularity held no matter what he did. He had skilfully exploited Mulroney's penchant for pork-barrel and patronage, but, in office, he proved no saint himself. Before the election, Zussman and his group had pushed Chrétien to reform the system by which prime ministers personally filled some 3,000 government positions. At their February 1993 dinner at Stornoway, Judith Maxwell proposed the creation of an arm's-length agency, akin to the Public Service Commission of Canada, to manage these appointments. The group also wanted parliamentary scrutiny of high-level appointments. Zussman thought the idea a natural, given Chrétien's integrity agenda. It would mark a triumph of managerial competence over partisanship. But Chrétien thought there was no such thing as a neutral process. At some point, it became a matter of judgment. If others wanted to run for prime minister, they would take on that responsibility. He intended to exercise the prerogatives of the office. "It is better that I make the appointments and be accountable for them," others remembered him saying, "than someone else makes them and I be accountable."

By the fall of 1994, he had rewarded most of the key operatives from his 1984 leadership campaign, back when support for Chrétien had not been a smart career move. Before leaving for China, he put into motion a plan to name the only Trudeau cabinet minister to stand by him in 1984, his good friend Romeo LeBlanc, as Canada's twenty-fifth governor general. LeBlanc needed some time to get his affairs in order. A divorcé, he and his current companion, Diana Fowler, would have to arrange a speedy marriage. Meanwhile, Chrétien took off for China, accompanied by one of his young aides, LeBlanc's son, Dominic. His father had confided in him several days earlier. But Chrétien didn't know whether the younger LeBlanc had been informed. Dominic, in turn, wasn't sure whether he was supposed to know. At one point on the trip, Chrétien invited Dominic LeBlanc for a private swim at his hotel. They circled the subject warily, neither letting on.

Chrétien broke the news about LeBlanc's appointment to his cabinet on Tuesday, November 22, confirming a news leak from that morning. When would it be announced, several shocked ministers asked. Chrétien told them he was going to the Commons chamber directly from cabinet. Their hesitant reaction couldn't hold a candle to that of Reform leader Preston Manning. He touched off a furore in the Commons by condemning the appointment as "unwise and inappropriate." The Liberals were furious. House of Commons Speaker Gilbert Parent admonished Manning. Paul Zed, a rookie New Brunswick MP who had served as LeBlanc's ministerial assistant in the early 1980s, shouted across the aisle that Manning's father, a former senator, would be ashamed of him for his disrespect, then stormed out along with other Liberal MPs.

Chrétien shared the fury of his colleagues, portraying Manning's response as an unprecedented attack on the governor general rather than on the method of selection. In a fit of pique, Chrétien ignored his advisers and decided to follow up the next day with the appointments of John Bryden, his former New Brunswick campaign chairman, and long-time Liberal backbencher Jean-Robert Gauthier to the Senate. Responding to the ensuing uproar, he gave rare public voice to his poll numbers. "It is not very good for my humility, but if I were to discard all the people who have expressed confidence in this prime minister, then 75 per cent of the Canadian people would be disqualified." Aline gave him hell for sounding arrogant.

While Chrétien enjoyed his charmed existence, a succession of furrow-browed cabinet ministers continued to troop that fall in front of the Star Chamber to fight for the very lives of their departments. Industry Minister John Manley made his appearance in late October. To everyone's great surprise, this stalwart of the fiscal Liberals, one of cabinet's four Ms (Massé had joined the original three), resisted program review with all the means available to him.

Manley, who took the Red Book and its commitments to science and technology seriously, was overwhelmed by the size of the cut Martin sought. In their June meeting in his office, Martin had informed him that Industry would have to come up with a 60-per-cent spending reduction. Manley wasn't one for outbursts. Martin probably misread his mild reaction as concurrence. He cheerfully related how one of the other ministers seated in the same chair several days earlier had been catatonic.

"Just for the record," Manley replied, "although I may not show it, I *am* catatonic."

A forty-four-year-old tax lawyer, born and bred in Ottawa, Manley was a mild-mannered guy, a devout Christian, upstanding and even-tempered. His good nature masked an impressive intellect and strong ambition. He was a straight-shooter, a guy who, in the 1990 leadership campaign, held off his support until he could take time to evaluate the candidates. He was at home in Ottawa scraping wallpaper during the last of the policy sessions, half watching it on Newsworld. The discussion turned to the GST. Martin was anti-GST but pro some barely defined other. Copps was adamantly opposed. She went after Chrétien, trying to pin him down. He replied that taxes were complicated matters, and once they were in force they would be difficult to eliminate. Manley appreciated the maturity. He phoned Chrétien the next day with his endorsement.

After graduating from law school at the University of Ottawa, he had clerked for the chief justice of Canada, Bora Laskin. He was viewed as solid and stolid, a comer who was handed the Industry Department partly to satisfy Paul Martin that it would be in safe hands and partly because, as the past president of the Ottawa Board of Trade, he possessed the right credentials. Although popular with other ministers for his sober advice and thoughtful manner, he was the subject of a good deal of backbiting in both cabinet and caucus — by Martin included — for his failure to translate the Red Book's industrial policy thrust into a pro-active and coherent jobs strategy. He was respected, but regarded as too much the tax lawyer to sell a vision of a role for the government in the economy of the 1990s.

Because they liked him, other ministers blamed his department and particularly Harry Swain, the deputy, for Industry's perceived shortcomings. Swain, who had been employing his combative style around Ottawa for a number of years, had more than his fair share of enemies in the town. Among them seemed to be Martin. At their very first meeting early in the government's mandate, Manley and David Dodge had looked on in astonishment as Martin lit into Swain for the uninspired performance of his department.

Manley had a lot of time for Swain. But around town, the view was that the minister was poorly served. In some quarters, the tall, pencil-straight Manley, with his mop of hair and spectacles, was known as Beaker, after the lab-coated Muppet character of that name. The egg-headed Swain was nicknamed Bunson Honeydew, in honour of the character who, unawares, always seems to start a chain of events that end with Beaker being blown up. Swain, a veteran deputy minister, was seen as an obdurate figure more interested in besting the central powers in a complex game of chess than in furthering the interests of his minister. Without so intending, Swain undermined Manley, whom he respected greatly, with others in the system.

Program review frustrated Manley as much as it did Swain. He felt that some bureaucrat in the Department of Finance was trying to stuff his department into a pre-cut suit of clothing without due attention to the fit or the price. He had been mandated to come up with ways to spur growth and create long-term jobs, an assignment that flowed out of Martin's favourite chapters in the Red Book. Cutting into the sinew of science and technology would hamper those efforts. If the exercise really amounted to setting priorities and lopping off those programs at the bottom of the list in order to save those at the top, then did it make sense for all departments to shuffle to the guillotine? Like the Star Chamber of old, the process seemed designed not for the protection of the innocent but rather for the conviction of the guilty. Acting on mere suspicion, the Star Chamber was empowered to arrest a defendant and examine him in private. If he refused to answer, he was imprisoned. Program review didn't feel all that different.

Swain and Manley had misread the June meeting. They treated their target as an opening bargaining position. Manley was badly distracted at the time, trying to keep internal trade talks with the provinces from falling apart as they neared a looming deadline. Once freed of that, he and his officials reviewed their $1.1-billion empire, trying to make the numbers fit. Certain things were untouchable. An industrialized country needed a patent office. Someone had to manage a public resource like the radio spectrum. Constitutionally, they were required to look after weights and measures. So the savings would have to come in the department's core areas: the analysts who fed the government intelligence on the many sectors of the Canadian economy, the scientific agencies, and his department's biggest industrial support program, the $144-million Defence Industry Productivity Program (DIPP).

Ottawa's longest-standing and, by some accounts, most successful industrial support program, DIPP was created in the late 1950s in the wake of the Diefenbaker government's cancellation of the Avro Arrow jet fighter. It provided repayable grants to help aerospace companies defray some of the risks of new product development. Proponents, including

Manley, credited it with preserving the wartime legacy of an outsized Canadian aviation industry, helping companies such as Bombardier, Pratt & Whitney Canada, and Spar Aerospace to become global players.

The program review arithmetic made Manley ill. Industry's dogs were long gone. These were good programs, the very ones that Martin often extolled as examples of the proper role for industrial policy. DIPP was one of the few subsidy programs that actually met the tests for government intervention that Peter Nicholson had set out in the Purple Book. It countered the subsidies of competing nations, supported early-stage research and development, paid back royalties to the government, and promoted high-quality jobs in a strategic industry.

Moreover, as Manley and his officials tirelessly pointed out, DIPP beneficiaries were overwhelmingly concentrated in the Montreal area. Pratt & Whitney, the biggest DIPP recipient, was the largest industrial employer in the region. A referendum year above all wasn't the time to jeopardize those jobs, Industry argued. From its vantage point, Finance was engaged in seriously flawed short-term thinking, insisting on savings today that would actually harm the economy over the medium term.

Manley met privately with Martin and with Massé to argue the case for DIPP. He also spoke to the prime minister. Swain set up meetings with key deputies. To meet the targets, they argued, entailed undermining two of the main building blocks of the government agenda, jobs and national unity. They sent documents to all of the Quebec ministers and offered to set up briefings to explain the political ramifications flowing from an end to DIPP.

So when Manley went before the Program Review Committee in late October, he said it couldn't be done. As a good lawyer, he made a counter-offer, saying he could get rid of regional development responsibilities in northern Ontario and a support program for aboriginal entrepreneurs. But his target would have to be lowered. Swain argued that the proposed Industry cut represented just one-third of one per cent of government spending. The damage it would unleash wasn't worth it.

The committee members sadly concluded that Manley and, particularly, Swain were playing games with them. They felt embarrassed for a friend, but decided they had no choice but to reject his business plan. Finance suspected that, as an Ottawa minister, Manley simply didn't want to cut public service jobs. Industry was sent back to the drawing board, instructed to return when it had something serious to discuss.

He never went back. Ultimately, he sent the committee a report setting out a streamlining of his department and cuts to science programs. The offer went a long way towards meeting the target, but he said he could not get all the way there without sacrificing DIPP, whose essential nature he continued to argue. The committee sent him back a letter proclaiming DIPP's demise. "It was inconceivable to me that program review would end up with this conclusion," he said. "Perhaps I was naive."

Still deeply troubled, Manley tried one last desperate gambit. He sent a letter to the prime minister telling him that the committee was about to make a major political mistake. He didn't receive a reply until the day of the budget. He was in London, Martin's chosen representative to the British financial community. (Roy MacLaren was in Tokyo and Doug Young in New York City.) His department faxed him a reply from Chrétien containing the budget wording on DIPP. It had not been killed outright; it had been placed under review. But it had been shorn of all funding.

From Martin's perspective, the program review exercise was a smashing success, despite a continuing struggle to meet its targets. Not only did it deliver billions in savings, but it came with cabinet buy-in. He had felt isolated in the first budget, going round to ministers one on one, informing them of their fate like some fiscal Grim Reaper. It was no way to make friends, especially for a politician who still harboured leadership ambitions, and no way to educate a government. In program review, he got to define the universe, as he thought a finance minister should, but the others decided the best way to reach their destination. It was both more rational and better politics. He took some of the skeptical members of cabinet and brought them inside the tent, which was far preferable to the alternative. When the package went to full cabinet in January, it had the imprimatur of people like Brian Tobin and Sheila Copps and Herb Gray. They were a show-me committee, and he and Massé had shown them.

The granite resistance of the numbers to all forms of persuasion had changed people. For impressionable ministers like Tobin, McLellan, and Marchi, program review was like a graduate school in government, with the seminars led by Massé and the guest lectures provided by David Dodge and his Finance officials. Several of the committee members would later joke that they were probably swayed less by the power of the argument than by the Stockholm-on-the-Rideau syndrome that arose from being locked in a room up to three times a week, four hours a shot, with the government's leading fiscal fundamentalists. Either way, by winning over the committee, Martin had won over the government. If Herb Gray and Sheila Copps didn't kick up a fuss, how could David Dingwall or Diane Marleau?

It had been a voyage of discovery for the ministers. But the seas had been rough and the passage often left them feeling ill. Once, after a particularly taxing session, McLellan turned to Martin as they walked out the doorway and said, "Paul, what if what we're doing is all wrong?"

Copps, an emotion-driven politician, carried program review around in her gut. Normally, she slept soundly. Now she found herself lying awake in the middle of the night imagining the faces of all those public servants who were going to lose their jobs. It reminded her of the agony that befell her home town of Hamilton in the early 1980s, when the retrenchment of the steel industry destroyed lives. "It is a constant struggle to maintain your idealism," she told an interviewer on the eve of the 1995 budget.

Massé never, for a moment, lost his composure. He knew the government inside out and could puncture a false argument with a well-pointed question. But always he was polite, unruffled, the perfect technocrat. He kept the group on an even keel. Some of his internal critics, watching his performance, concluded that it was easier for him because he wasn't a real Liberal. "Marcel can work with anybody," one of them commented, damning him with the faintest of praise. "If you come from the bureaucracy, you are used to doing the bidding of your political masters, without any moral attachment. And Massé could do this. Nothing bothers him. Nothing flusters him. He's used to following instructions."

He and Martin made a brilliant team. The book on Massé at CIDA had been that he was a thinker, not a doer. Massé required the accompaniment of Martin's drive to lift program review from the theoretical to the real.

Each committee member crossed boundaries they never would have imagined in October 1993. They cut the CBC. They cut women's shelters. And they had sanctioned a user fee for those hundreds of thousands of immigrants who came ashore in Canada every year — people like their parents and grandparents — in search of a better life. They consoled themselves that their actions had been mitigated by their Liberalism. Although there was a landing fee, it would be accompanied by a loan program to help the poorest of immigrants. The Tories, they assured one another, perhaps falsely, would never have done that.

Even Herb Gray, the longest-serving member of the government, was shaped by the experience. He found it one of the most gruelling and intellectually challenging undertakings in a political career reaching back to the early 1960s. He was fascinated by the process, turning aside other demands to make sure that he was up to speed on the materials circulated before the meetings. He had been put on the committee as a sober, solid voice of the left. He had helped put in place many of the programs now being threatened. But he couldn't ignore the arithmetic. Jerry Yanover, the Liberal parliamentary expert who had worked closely with Gray over the years, recalled him castigating the Industry Department, one of his old portfolios. "The problem is that that department always has one solution to any problem, and that is to spend money," Gray, one of the last of the big spenders, confided. "That's no longer viable. There isn't any money."

But Gray, like Marchi and several others, hadn't buried his idealism. He had held fast to his principles for more than three decades in politics, even when banished to the back benches by Trudeau for much of the 1970s. He was politically committed to the 3 per cent and as such he couldn't ignore the irrevocability of the fiscal arithmetic. But he saw it as more a tactical retreat than an about-face. He would cut now to build later.

Gray found some solace in a passage from Joseph Schull's classic biography of Laurier, *The First Canadian*. The passage was from Laurier's famous speech to the Club Canadien in 1877, when he shook off the hesitation of his party leadership and the approbation of the Quebec clergy in a one-hour paean to Liberalism. The quote that Gray fixed upon included one of the most oft-cited in the Canadian Liberal pantheon, a touchstone of Liberal values for generation after generation of party activists. It read: "I am a liberal. I am one of those who think that always and everywhere in human things there are abuses to be reformed, new horizons to be opened up, and new forces to be developed." But as Gray read on, beyond the point at which most Liberals stopped, he found resonance with the difficult circumstances in which Liberalism now found itself. "The principle of liberalism," Laurier went on, "is inherent in the very essence of our nature, in that desire of happiness with which we are born into the world, which pursues us throughout life, and which is never completely gratified on this side of the grave. Our souls are immortal but our means are limited. We constantly gravitate towards an ideal which we never attain. We dream of good but we never realize the best."

It could have been the motto of the Program Review Committee — indeed, as the winter of 1994–95 set in, the motto for the entire Chrétien government.

15

MEXICAN STANDOFF

As Lloyd Axworthy's *annus horribilis* drew to a close, Ottawa's chattering classes glibly judged the human resources minister the Chrétien cabinet's most disappointing figure. It had been a long, hard fall from grace for the golden boy, the recollection of his Midas touch now confined to the deep recesses of the cortex.

As Ottawa settled into its winter routines — skating on the Rideau Canal, cross-country skiing in the Gatineaus, a poor imitation of professional hockey at the Civic Centre — the bone-tired and demoralized minister took a break for the holidays. For his fifty-fifth birthday on December 21, Axworthy's wife, Denise, sought to buoy him up with a party at their home. But there was no escaping his nightmare. A couple of the guests noticed a car parked across the street occupied by several unkempt men in their early twenties. They appeared to be watching the Axworthy house. The police, who had kept vigil after the December 17 demonstration, were long gone. The guests peeked out from behind the venetian blinds, uncertain whether they felt threatened or paranoid. After about ten minutes, the car finally pulled away.

Axworthy's mood would have cause to blacken further. In the upper reaches of Esplanade Laurier, patience had run out. It had been almost a year since the launch of his social security review, and it looked to the Finance officials as though all the movement had been backwards. Atlantic MPs were fomenting revolt against his plans for a two-tier unemployment insurance system. Privy Council officials working on the Quebec file were fretting about intrusion into provincial jurisdictions. Finance deputy David Dodge found the post-secondary education proposals appealing, but he couldn't help noticing that Axworthy's friends in the universities "were kicking the shit out of him."

The Finance officials agreed that Axworthy's insistence on fundamental reforms represented the right choice from a policy perspective. But
they needed to program in additional savings right away. Perhaps the
October 5 *Toronto Star* leak would prove prophetic. Far removed from
the spotlight, a small coterie of senior officials began beavering away in
November on a sweeping reform to federal social transfers, to be unveiled
in the February 1995 budget, that would effectively bury the social security review. In his first budget, Martin had put Axworthy on notice that if
he didn't produce the desired results by 1996–97, "alternative measures"
would be implemented. Axworthy's two years were drawing to a premature close. The alternative measures had been hatched. Just as the social
activists had feared, the Department of Finance was preparing to impose
its own unilateral fiscal fix on the country's social programs.

Martin had been deeply impressed by the ten-year deficit forecast that
Marcel Massé had ordered up in the spring. The unmistakable message
was that under any reasonable economic scenario the deficit would never
hit zero without a radical change of course. Indeed, the hard-earned progress
in getting it down to 3 per cent of GDP would most likely be washed away
by an upsurge in the next recession, as had happened to Wilson.

The social system had been constructed in the Keynesian model, complete with so-called automatic stabilizers, programs that would pump money
into the economy when it contracted. Now Martin wanted to make these
stabilizers less automatic, to control expenditures so they didn't go
through the roof in every recession. To achieve his 3-per-cent deficit target and put the country on a track towards what Finance officials
considered a sustainable budget would entail going beyond hacking and
slashing. Finance became obsessed with the need to totally restructure its
spending patterns, in effect to insulate government finances from the next
economic cold front. That required Martin, among other things, to revisit the question of social payments to the provinces, to consider a system
that would cut and restructure transfers at the same time. If that resulted in
dumping some of his problems on the provinces — well, they tended to
be in better shape than Ottawa in any case. If it also meant breaking commitments to Axworthy — as Nicholson had said, the first order of business
was stabilizing the patient.

This was the kind of challenge that Peter Nicholson lived for. He considered the entire transfer system a jerry-rigged system of lies, half-truths,
and jiggery-pokery. There was a pot called Established Program Financing

(Education)—the $2 billion that Axworthy wanted to turn into an endowment for student loans. But Ottawa imposed no conditions to require the provinces even to spend the money, as intended, on post-secondary education. The same was largely true for the pot called Established Program Financing (Health), the $7-billion cash transfer that gave Health Minister Diane Marleau the influence to make provinces conform to the Canada Health Act. In this case, Ottawa insisted that five principles of medicare be observed. While these obliged the provinces to refrain from extra-billing or user fees, they hardly amounted to specific standards. Ottawa had nothing to say about the definition of a medically necessary service: it was almost as variable a concept as Liberalism.

As Nicholson saw it, Ottawa would have a hard time cracking the whip even if it summoned up the will to do so, because of a decision made back in the Trudeau years. The EPF transfers had two components: cash grants, and the value of taxation rights that the federal government had ceded to the provinces in 1977. The revenue from these so-called tax points grew as the economy grew, but Ottawa no longer exercised any control over them. Under the existing formula, as the value of the tax points rose, the cash grants declined. The feds, who relied on the cash portion as a tool to enforce national standards, therefore found their influence waning.

The third major social transfer, the Canada Assistance Plan, was somewhat different. It was the last of the major federal-provincial cost-shared programs, a holdover from the Pearson era of federal expansionism. Under CAP, the federal government kicked in fifty cents for every fifty cents the provinces spent, with several strings attached. Finance hated the program because Ottawa could not control its exposure. If provinces raised their welfare rates or if the rolls swelled, the federal government was stuck with half the cost.

Finance had been trying to turn CAP into a block grant, a fund with pre-set limits like EPF, since the 1970s. In 1990, the Mulroney government moved to rein in its CAP bill by imposing a 5-per-cent unilateral ceiling on the growth of contributions to the three richest provinces, Ontario, British Columbia, and Alberta — a tactic that had the benefit, for Mulroney, of leaving Quebec untouched. In Ontario's case, the so-called cap on CAP ultimately led to the anomaly whereby Ottawa contributed only twenty-eight cents on the dollar for a welfare mom living in Ottawa versus fifty cents for one across the river in Hull. The arbitrary and discriminatory nature of the cap had poisoned federal-provincial relations.

Closeted in Dodge's twentieth-floor boardroom, the Finance officials designed a new system. In a late-night session with Martin, they recommended lumping health, education, and social assistance transfers into a single block fund, with its overall size determined solely by the federal government. The beauty of this creation was twofold: Ottawa would regain control over its expenditures, ultimately reducing cash transfers from $17 billion to $11 billion, and it would be able to keep them in check during a recession. In exchange, Ottawa would loosen the conditions it placed on provincial use of the money.

Such an approach would, of course, infuriate the provinces and undermine Axworthy's post-secondary proposals. But given the stubborn political problems with his social security review, the Finance officials convinced themselves they were effectively offering him an exit strategy for a losing policy initiative.

Before Finance fully apprised Human Resources of its intentions, it tested the block transfer idea before an audience more likely to be receptive, the national unity squad. Massé immediately saw the possibilities for a big public relations score in Quebec, which had long complained about Ottawa's interference in its social jurisdictions. Although the size of the transfers would be scaled back — there was no escaping that — the accompaniment of the offsetting promise to relax federal conditions would put some meat on Massé's assertions of federalism's flexibility.

In early December, a Human Resources official learned from a colleague at Finance about the magnitude of Martin's contemplated cuts to social transfers. Axworthy groused that he always seemed to be hearing about things through back channels. But he didn't fundamentally oppose the concept of combining the transfers, which approximated a scheme he had floated months earlier, called the Big Bang. In that plan, Ottawa would have withdrawn from joint programs, pumping the savings into expanded children's benefits. Only this time, the bang was a bit of a whimper: he no longer would get his hands on any new money to combat child poverty.

His most immediate concern was his desire not to eat the entire multi-billion-dollar cut himself. It was a far deeper cut than contemplated by the February 1994 budget. If it all fell on post-secondary education and social assistance, the two programs would be devastated, and any lingering hope of federal influence completely snuffed out. Axworthy again would be depicted as having lost at cabinet. He insisted that health transfers must be included in the cuts, even though the Liberals were the party of medicare, Canada's most popular social program. With health transfers included in the block grant, he would get some cover for the hit to his programs. "Like anyone, I didn't like the shit-kicking," he said, looking back on the period. "It was hard."

Health officials were in the dark until late December, and even then information was doled out sparingly. As soon as they heard rumours about a block transfer, they feared that they would get dragged in. Their minister, Diane Marleau, was a cabinet lightweight, without much hope of staving off the combined finagling of Martin, Massé, and Axworthy. The department itself was a shadow of its former glory. The officials lobbied fiercely to prevent health, the last of the great universal programs, from getting buried in the same crypt as post-secondary education and social assistance. But to no avail.

To the rationalists in Finance, Nicholson prominent among them, the separate fund called Established Program Financing (Health) was nothing but an illusion in any case. Money was money. The provinces simply deposited all their cheques from Ottawa in a single account and then spent them as they wished. But the Health officials found such logic wrongheaded. Whether EPF (Health) meant anything or not to Peter Nicholson or David Dodge, it certainly mattered to the health lobby groups, which, unlike most interest groups, still packed plenty of wallop. Take the separate transfer away, and they would howl that the Liberals had abandoned universal medicare, one of the party's strongest brand identities.

Martin felt nervous again by mid-December. The good news was that the economy had turned itself around, propelled by a 24-per-cent increase in exports over the previous year. Growth was moving along at its fastest clip since 1988. The economy had created an astounding 95,000 full-time jobs in November, equalling a record set in 1980. This buoyancy relieved pressure for stimulus in his budget. As the prime minister had said in September, the growth part of the cycle was the best time to bring down the deficit. So now was the time.

But soon after Martin had presented his revised budget forecasts in October, interest rates had taken off on him again. U.S. Federal Reserve Board chairman Alan Greenspan, continuing in his determination to snuff out incipient inflation, hiked rates by three-quarters of a point in November, forcing the Bank of Canada to follow suit. But unlike in the spring, this time Finance had anticipated the problem. From the moment Martin had appeared before the Commons Finance Committee in October, the department operated not from its so-called prudent scenario but from the worst-case scenario. The mandate granted by the prime minister and cabinet from June onward allowed Martin to plan his next budget with the assumption that rates would stay up, and if they ended up better than he planned, he would moderate his cuts. "My method of operating is to go to you and say I need $200, and if it turns out that I'm only going to need $175, I'll be able to give you back $25." Unfortunately, the targets kept moving and Martin never gave anything back. He did, however, grab more.

Securing the program review cuts proved tougher than expected. By early December, for all the blood on the floor and wounds to the soul, Massé was still short of his ultimate target. Some of the cases demanded political resolution beyond the committee's capacity. Agriculture Minister Ralph Goodale, for instance, still held out against a wholesale abandonment of the 1897 Crow Rate benefit, which he said would scorch the prairie soil for Liberals for at least a generation. André Ouellet, who seemed to possess total recall of ugly political moments, reminded the committee about the protests that had hit the Trudeau government when it tampered with the dairy subsidy in the 1970s, including the famous incident in which Agriculture Minister Eugene Whelan was drenched with milk on Parliament Hill. Quebec ministers, Ouellet explained, remained psychologically scarred by those protests. "Chrétien would have the same memories," he assured them. The prime minister would have to deliberate over many of these tough political issues himself.

By this time, it was clear that Martin was a far stronger character than Massé, and his agenda naturally predominated. Getting government right took a back seat to getting it smaller. There is not much evidence that Massé resisted in any case. At the end of the day, the only one of his six tests that really mattered was the final one, the affordability test. Everything got hit in program review — good, bad, and indifferent. A number of the cuts, like DIPP, would prove short-sighted and arguably counter-productive to the country's overall economic health.

Meanwhile, the budget strategy was threatened by the stubborn refusal of Liberal MPs to surrender much in the way of their parliamentary pensions. The decimation of the Tories remained fresh in Liberal minds, as did the knowledge that a number of defeated MPs still had not found work. The public almost universally considered the existing MP pension plan to be far too self-indulgent, an impression reinforced on a regular basis by the Reform Party and through a well-financed public relations campaign sponsored by the anti-government National Citizens' Coalition.

From Finance's point of view, the job of selling budget cuts would be all the more difficult without meaningful changes to the MPs' pensions. Politicians, rather than looking like indulged fat cats, had to be seen to be sacrificing, too. But on this particular issue, Martin could not rely on his usual powers of persuasion. As a multimillionaire industrialist, he didn't have to sweat life after politics, unlike many of his colleagues on the Liberal benches. Nobody really cared to listen to him preach about the symbols of restraint. Ultimately, after much agonizing, the Liberals agreed to reduce MPs' pensions, but not sufficiently to satisfy Martin. He refused to include the measures in his budget, thinking they would attract more fire than they would deflect.

On the morning of December 20, an unnoticed time bomb was placed beneath the cautiously crafted interest rate assumptions underlying the budget planning. Ottawa was overcast that day, with a light sprinkling of pre-Christmas snow. Along the Sparks Street Mall, Christmas music filled the air as shoppers worked down their lists of presents. Cabinet was scheduled to meet at 10 a.m., its last session before the holidays, and Marcel Massé would bring his colleagues up to date on the progress of program review.

Thirty-six hundred kilometres away, Mexico City was dry and warm. The congested capital had become something of a showcase for the apostles of the new global economy. From 1986 to 1990, Mexico had undergone a phenomenal economic transformation, shucking its highly protectionist garb and opening its arms to international business. But on that Wednesday, a massive and long overdue devaluation of the peso laid waste to the Mexican miracle, sparking panic among foreign investors. The government, defenceless against the overpoweringly negative market sentiment, had little choice the following day but to allow the peso to go into free fall.

In Ottawa, nobody yet recognized the significance of the peso crisis. Mexico would provide a lesson for nation-states in just how dependent they were upon the vagaries — even potential irrationalities — of the financial markets. "What it did was point out just how fickle offshore, short-term money is," Peter Nicholson explained. "It was a great object lesson in the psychology of the run. The Mexican experience was one of those practical object lessons that politicians understand a hell of a lot better than the theoretical arguments." But Martin, although he had been alerted to the situation by Gordon Thiessen, did not even raise the matter at cabinet.

It wasn't until early January that the so-called Tequila effect washed ashore in Canada. Shell-shocked international investors frantically transferred their hot money to countries that offered the protection of hard currencies with little risk. Canada, a midsized economy with a major-league national debt, failed to make the grade in this so-called flight of quality. The dollar came under attack, falling a cent and a half in the month after the peso devaluation. This, in turn, placed renewed pressure on interest rates, which rose 157 basis points (1.57 percentage points) over the same period. The spread between short-term Canadian and U.S. rates, which Martin watched so closely, more than doubled in this period, increasing to nearly two and a half percentage points.

Now Martin paid close attention. The peso slide assured that his budget would be forged in a crucible of crisis. All through January, the pressure tightened. With each successive turn of the screw — a critical editorial in the *Wall Street Journal*, an apocalyptic interview with an influential money trader, a debt warning by Moody's Investors Services — Martin was, ironically, bolstered in winning further concessions from his cabinet colleagues. Looking back months later, Dodge would cite the peso crisis as the second seminal event, after the June cabinet retreat, on the road to the 1995 budget.

Even before the peso crisis, Axworthy's people had been fending off new demands by Finance, which worried about falling short of the market's expectations. It wasn't just a matter of making the 3 per cent. That would be fine for public consumption, but professional economists would scrutinize the quality of the effort as well. The Finance Department had crafted a number of benchmarks that the budget would have to clear: items such as the volume of fiscal action; the ratio of spending cuts to tax increases; the structural changes to ensure that costs would not take off in future.

Finance was deeply concerned that the assumptions outlining the path to 3 per cent be seen to be sufficiently conservative. It would be a lot easier to make the 3-per-cent target by predicting strong revenue growth and low interest costs, but the economists might balk and the markets would react negatively. It came down to a judgment call: how safe did one have to be to satisfy the markets about the quality of the budget? To Martin, it was a no-brainer: err heavily on the side of caution. "My argument with individual ministers is, Do you really want to have gone through all of this pain and have this budget fail? I mean if you've gone through all this pain at least make this budget a success."

Between Christmas and New Year's, Nicholson arranged to meet with Axworthy's chief policy adviser, Giles Gherson, in Toronto, where they both were holidaying, and explain Finance's dilemma. Gherson was regarded as a good go-between because he was sympathetic to both Axworthy's and Martin's agendas. Nicholson explained Finance's concern that the budget planned would not be tough enough to satisfy the market. They were going to need more from Lloyd. Gherson did not dispute Nicholson's point, but argued that Axworthy had a mandate to re-engineer social programs, not destroy them.

As the toll from the Tequila effect mounted, Martin's budgetary rope stretched to the breaking point. He had exhausted the slack he had left for himself in adopting the worst-case scenario in October. Reviewing the figures with his officials in early January, it became clear that he would have to renege on many previous commitments. He had asked for $200 in expectation of needing $175. In fact, he needed $225.

Finance squeezed program review for additional juice, paying particular attention to Defence and Industry. As ministers puckered again, resentment began building towards Axworthy. His department's programs — with the small exception of the labour branch — had been excluded from the Star Chamber process. His lack of allies in cabinet now came back to haunt him. Why should job training merit a bye? other ministers steamed. Certainly, it didn't deliver much bang for its nearly $2-billion price tag. Moreover, it was the perfect program to hand over to the provinces, which claimed jurisdiction anyway. Massé's committee held a vigorous debate about whether Axworthy should be summoned to appear.

Martin dropped the bombshell about his latest, peso-induced shortfall at a cabinet meeting on January 11. He needed more money, another $1.6 billion, and so all bets were off. He spoke about Mexico and his worries that if Canada failed to meet market expectations it would be descended upon by financial sharks. Axworthy's programs, especially training, would have to be thrown in the pot.

Axworthy had once believed he possessed an ironclad guarantee of twenty-four months to put his reforms in place. He had paid up front in the first budget through the major cuts to unemployment insurance benefits and the promise to reduce transfers. His next step was to reflect on the results of his public consultations — the Human Resources Committee wasn't even scheduled to release the report into its cross-country hearings until mid-February — and then publish a White Paper setting out his reform plans in the spring. Clearly, further savings would be expected from him in 1996–97 and he was cooperating on the new block transfer, but nothing beyond a tiny $45-million contribution to program review was slated for the February 1995 budget.

"You're killing me," he told Martin. Martin responded that his arithmetic was unforgiving. If Axworthy helped him now, he would be there for him when social security review went forward in the fall. It won't go forward without money, Axworthy replied. With post-secondary education and welfare reform undermined by the block transfer, and training now on the table at program review, Axworthy had few levers left.

Finance would ultimately settle on a two-year cut in the block transfer of $2.5 billion and $4.5 billion. For decades, successive Liberal governments, using their spending power, had rolled the state forward from Ottawa into areas of provincial jurisdiction. Now they intended to yank it back. There would be a one-year grace period until the block transfer took effect, but once in place it would mark a radical and unilateral reworking of fiscal federalism, done on the run. Indeed, the matter hadn't even been subjected to a full and proper cabinet discussion. A number of important blanks would only be filled in later: the method of calculating the size of the block fund in future years, the formula for distributing it among provinces, and the conditions attached to it.

On Thursday, January 12, CBC-TV bureau chief Chris Waddell received a tip about Finance's plans. The following evening, chief political correspondent Jason Moscovitz told his audience that CBC had learned that Finance officials no longer were prepared to wait for Lloyd Axworthy to produce his blueprint for a new social regime for Canada. "Under the proposal, the provinces would get less money but more control over how that money is spent," Moscovitz said, correctly pointing out that the new block transfer served the interests both of the Finance Department and of the national unity strategists as a demonstration of flexible federalism.

Sharon Sholzberg-Gray was intrigued by the leak. Even though she was the wife of Liberal minister Herb Gray, she hadn't known the block transfer was in the works. (It was unlikely her husband knew either.) But in her capacity as a member of the Health Action Lobby, a coalition of health and consumer groups, it sounded remarkably familiar. Martin was under the impression that the block transfer was a new idea, invented for his needs. He couldn't know for sure, though. Officials were forbidden to disclose the advice they had given previous governments.

Sholzberg-Gray recalled that the Finance Department had floated a similar plan in the middle of the Gulf War, a block fund that was nick-named MOAT — for Mother of All Transfers. The department at that time was trying to address many of the same pressures: diminishing health transfers; runaway welfare costs; a fiscal need to squeeze the social envelope and a political need to retain federal influence. MOAT would have rolled all the social transfers — health, post-secondary education, social assistance, and equalization — into a huge amorphous blob of money that would be sent to the provinces, just like Martin's block fund (except that he had excluded equalization). Its bigger size would mean it would last longer, but the specific objectives of equalization, for instance, would be blunted. Ultimately, the Finance officials failed to sell MOAT to their political masters.

In the days after the leak, the Health Action Lobby held a meeting with Martin at the Department of Finance. He asked their opinion of the block fund concept. Sholzberg-Gray interjected to inform Martin, who knew nothing of it, about the earlier version and how it had failed to win Tory endorsement. "Maybe you had better find out why they rejected it," she suggested. Of course, he couldn't find out. Cabinet secrecy prohibited it.

On January 17, the Chrétien cabinet met for one of its special sessions on the top floor of the Lester B. Pearson Building. It was the last real opportunity for a gang-up on Martin before the budget. Some in Finance worried that the leak about the block transfer would galvanize the cabinet's left wing. A smaller group thought the absence of any public outcry in the ensuing days actually played into their hands. But the issue never really came to a head. As in June, serendipity dealt Martin the strong hand.

A number of ministers continued to suspect that Finance's hidden agenda went well beyond the 3-per-cent target agreed by cabinet. As they had in June with the first set of interest rate hikes, some argued that the Tequila effect represented merely a temporary spike and that Martin shouldn't overreact. (In a sense, they were right. Long-term interest rates returned to their pre-peso-crisis level three weeks before the budget was delivered, although short-term rates wouldn't fall back until June.) But in the panicky atmosphere, most ministers viewed the Mexican scare as a demonstration of the power of global markets to punish countries like Canada.

Martin now held enormous sway. In the wake of the peso crisis, his arguments became almost impossible to resist. The financial markets had made clear the Chrétien government was on probation. On January 11, the influential *Wall Street Journal*, the bible of the U.S. business community, had published an article describing the Canadian currency, like the peso, as a basket case. It cited as evidence the value of the Canadian dollar, sitting at an eight-and-a-half-year low against the U.S. dollar, as well as the country's chronic current account deficits, its high debt, the departure a year earlier of John Crow, and Quebec jitters.

The *Journal* followed the next day with a scathing editorial, entitled "Bankrupt Canada?" "Mexico isn't the only U.S. neighbor flirting with the financial abyss," the paper stated. "Turn around and check out Canada, which has now become an honorary member of the Third World in the unmanageability of its debt problem. If dramatic action isn't taken in next month's federal budget, it's not inconceivable that Canada could hit the debt wall and... have to call in the International Monetary Fund to stabilize its falling currency."

The editorial infuriated most Liberals. The idea of some neoconservative American scribbler passing judgment on Canada from his Manhattan office tower got far up their nose. The *Globe and Mail* felt differently. It reprinted the broadside verbatim, upping the pressure on the government to take decisive action. The tension continued to build right up to the January 17 cabinet retreat. That morning's *Globe and Mail* carried an interview, buried on the eleventh page of the business section, with Albert Friedberg, one of the country's most secretive and influential currency traders. Friedberg was quoted as saying that Canada would have to go through a "massive crisis" such as a 10-per-cent drop in the value of the dollar in a single day before its politicians mustered the resolve to fix its economic problems. He also predicted the International Monetary Fund would be compelled to intervene.

The markets, already in high anxiety over Mexico and the *Wall Street Journal* editorial, lost further altitude on Friedberg's comments, dropping a third of a cent in what one trader described as "a heartbeat." It was a Tuesday, the day the Bank of Canada set its weekly bank rate. Chartered banks, watching the signals from the central bank over the previous days, had already moved in the morning to raise mortgage rates by three-quarters of a percentage point.

As ministers gathered around the table to start the cabinet meeting, David Dodge took a phone call from Gordon Thiessen. The Bank of Canada governor informed the deputy minister of a hike in the weekly bank rate of a full percentage point, a huge one-day increase. That put rates at their highest level since November 1992, and nearly twice as high as when Martin had brought down his first budget eleven months earlier. Dodge passed a note to Martin, who opened the proceedings in dramatic style. He referred back to the previous cabinet meeting, and his decision to order more cuts because of the pressure on rates. "Let me tell you, to show you just how serious the situation is, I just got a note saying that there has been a 100-basis-point rise."

Once again, Martin had prepared carefully, reiterating his arguments about the disastrous cost of getting the budget wrong. The small measure of lingering resistance tended to be highly specific. Copps, Ouellet, and several others again expressed their dismay at Martin's continued desire to bring forward a massive reform of old-age pensions in the budget. Ouellet thought it would be political folly in Quebec, where seniors constitute a critical part of the federalist coalition. Copps argued that the content of the reform didn't matter. People would be so riled, they wouldn't be reading the fine print.

Diane Marleau kept up the battle to keep health out of the block fund. Axworthy didn't weigh in. Without his support, she didn't stand a chance of overturning Martin and Massé. In any case, the mood of financial crisis was so ingrained that it almost amounted to heresy to suggest that Martin might be going too far. "At the end of the day, no matter how well you prepare, there is no substitute for a 100-basis-point rise in interest rates," one of his top advisers commented. Paul Martin was unassailable.

Axworthy, incredibly, was still pinned down fighting the last war. The Canadian Federation of Students had called a national campus strike for January 25. Continuing his counter-attacks, the minister flew out to Calgary after the cabinet retreat for a colloquium meant to breathe new life into his education proposals.

Meanwhile, back in Ottawa, Noreau worried about Axworthy's obsession with the students. He stubbornly persisted in his plans for his income-contingent loans scheme, even with the knowledge of the new block

transfer, searching for a way to square the circle. All this was taking valuable time away from the real battle, with Finance. Axworthy was, it
became increasingly clear, engaging the wrong enemy.

Finance now had made clear the extent of the program review cuts it
expected from HRD: a whopping $1 billion over two years, more than a
third of the department's program budget. It would mean the loss of about
5,000 jobs and the gutting of training programs, the all-important human
investment part of the portfolio, the essence of the new Liberalism.

Axworthy's dilemma was all too familiar. Robert Reich, the American
labour secretary whom Axworthy had befriended at the Detroit jobs summit, had found himself in the same fix in Clinton's first budget. The
Democrats had also been elected on a jobs and growth agenda, with investments in human capital at its core. But each time the White House budget-
makers had gone through the numbers they came up short of their deficit
target. So, with each successive pass, more of the human investments
would be sacrificed. Clinton grew so frustrated at one point that he snapped
sarcastically at his staff: "We're Eisenhower Republicans here, and we are
fighting the Reagan Republicans. We stand for lower deficits and free trade
and the bond market. Isn't that great."

There was no denying it. Democrat or Republican, Liberal or Conservative, they were all beholden to the bond markets. Canada, a smaller
country with a deeper deficit crisis, was especially vulnerable to the sentiments of the proverbial twenty-five-year-old in red suspenders. Martin
had emerged from the January 17 retreat with a sweeping mandate to do
whatever it took to reach his budget targets. Axworthy, seeing no way
out, retreated into his shell. After the cabinet session, Dodge made some
efforts to arrange a talk. But Axworthy, brooding, did not return the calls.

Axworthy tended to personalize these matters. Dodge, with whom he
had a long history, was basically all right. He was better rounded than your
average deficit-obsessed Finance deputy. But Axworthy could hardly
abide some of the other Finance officials, who he felt resented greatly the
moderate, social side of Liberalism. They were radical crusaders, unable to
see beyond their own cause. As for Martin, Axworthy sometimes wondered what he truly believed in.

Communications at all levels were strained. Noreau and Dodge, who
never had an easy relationship, hardly spoke any more. Noreau found the
Finance demands outlandish. Essentially, he was being asked to present
a *de facto* program review plan in just six weeks, one that would radically

redefine his department's mission. At one point, he was summoned to the Privy Council Office and told Finance needed another $200 million. Coming out he ran into an acquaintance who said he wasn't looking well. "I just got beaten up," he sighed.

Noreau, the quintessential process bureaucrat, wondered on what authority these cuts were being ordered. Where was a cabinet discussion? Who had determined that Human Resources would tear itself apart? The orderly process of cabinet government seemed to be breaking down as Finance exploited the crisis atmosphere. Martin, it appeared, had seized control of the government of Canada.

Ever so gradually, the outline of a deal began to emerge. Gherson and Nicholson were the main negotiators. Finance's objective was simple: it wanted its savings. Axworthy wanted to retain the means to follow through on his employability agenda. The answer lay in tapping the $16-billion unemployment insurance fund. For Martin's budget, Axworthy would ante up $1.1 billion in spending cuts from his departmental budget — $600 million in the first year and $500 million in the second — so long as in the next round of unemployment insurance reform later in the year, he could dip into the UI fund to refinance training programs. Without the means to make human investments, he argued, the Liberals would be almost indistinguishable from Preston Manning's Reform alternative. "Unlike the Americans, where investments just dropped off the table, we simply put it on another table," Axworthy later said.

Martin, like the zoom lens on a camera, was now completely focussed on his budget. With the markets tracking his every move and compound interest clicking inexorably away, the fiscal future of Canada, indeed its sovereignty, was on the line. He didn't care that other ministers had problems, that some of the cuts would be counter-productive in the long run, even contrary to Red Book promises. He simply couldn't take the chance of coming up short. To some, he had become the kind of hacker and slasher he had so disdained. His adviser David Herle kidded that he now was minister of debt instead of minister of finance. It was something they would have to correct — later.

Martin was convinced the best way to conquer the deficit was through a blitzkrieg — a lightning-quick offensive with all guns blazing. That would set his stunned opponents — most of them extra-parliamentary groups ranging from public-sector labour unions to arts organizations but some within his own party — back on their heels. Each action would provide political cover for another action. It would be difficult to isolate a single measure politically, as had occurred with the partial deindexation of pensions in Wilson's first budget. Political momentum was on his side; the time to strike was now. The later it got into the mandate, the harder it would be. By the next budget, the Liberals would be in the back half of their term, thinking more and more about re-election.

Increasingly fearful of the market's judgment, he opened another front against Lloyd Axworthy. With HRD's departmental cuts now in hand, alongside the cuts to transfer payments, he went back at unemployment insurance. The two ministers had reached agreement in the fall about the overall size of Axworthy's next UI cut. It would take another 10 per cent out of benefits, roughly $1.6 billion starting in the 1996–97 fiscal year.

Now Martin started pushing Axworthy to let him unveil the UI benefit cuts right in the budget, four weeks away. That would allow the changes to go into force on July 1, 1995, six months or perhaps even a year earlier than would otherwise be the case. Finance figured that by moving up the date, it would be able to pocket the first $500 million of the annual $1.6 billion in savings right in the 1995–96 fiscal year. But it would also entail Axworthy pre-empting his elaborate reform plans in favour of a quick-and-dirty so-called reform of the type implemented a year earlier. Martin suggested Axworthy could separately introduce the human investments side of his reform in the fall, but Human Resources suspected that even if they got past Finance, they would be battling the national unity crowd by then.

His argument to Axworthy, as Martin later recounted in an interview, was the one he put to everyone. "What kind of social security review are you going to have if, as a result of not facing up to the deficit, I have to cut you three times as much in two years? I mean, you have a choice. We do it now, or in two years we are going to do a Mexico, we will have to do a Sweden, we will do an Ireland — that's what we will do."

Axworthy knew the argument well, even accepted its logic, but he was tired of the emphasis always being on Paul's needs. It was always, "You have to understand my position." Martin had a strong position, no doubt. But Axworthy also enjoyed a mandate from the prime minister. The government had been elected on a growth and jobs agenda. The importance of the social security review had been reiterated in June in a strategy document by cabinet as one of the five priorities for the first term. It had been reaffirmed in Chrétien's September 18 speech in Quebec City. Neither time did it rank below the deficit. This went back to the two-track strategy of the Red Book; they were companion objectives. Axworthy was tired, hurt, humiliated, and fed up with Martin's single-mindedness. Having been a good soldier, he did not wish to be a kamikaze pilot.

The attempted UI grab broke the dam of deep, almost despairing rage bottled up within Axworthy. The extraordinary events of the following days still remain shrouded in some mystery. Clearly, Lloyd Axworthy stood up to Paul Martin both publicly and privately, rocking the government in the process. But there is some dispute over exactly how much calculation went into his actions. In any case, the outcome was a private chat with the prime minister, in which the government's commitment to a social security review was reaffirmed. And Lloyd Axworthy never made that $500-million UI down-payment.

The crisis began innocently enough on Thursday, January 16, when Axworthy spoke at a seminar on social assistance that his department had sponsored as part of the social security review. Fittingly for how things had gone, a faulty fire alarm interrupted the proceedings twice. Trapped in the hotel corridor with reporters, Axworthy conceded for the first time that his social security review had become a shadow of its former self, a theme he touched upon as well in his prepared remarks. Drawing on that speech, the *Globe and Mail* published a front-page article on Tuesday, January 21, quoting Axworthy as saying that the government would have to secure the fiscal front before it could proceed with a comprehensive social security review. "We can only begin to lay foundations, stepping stones at this time." The article raised some eyebrows inside the government, but was generally judged within the bounds of acceptability.

One reader, though, was especially intrigued. Mark Kennedy, the *Ottawa Citizen*'s social policy writer, was scheduled to interview Axworthy later that day. He had put in a request the previous week, using the January 31 anniversary of the official launch of the social security review as a hook. That afternoon Kennedy put his tape recorder down on the round wooden table in the minister's office and sat back as Axworthy repeated the comments the *Globe* had carried, except this time in far sharper language. There was no need to prod him; Kennedy departed convinced that Axworthy had a message he wanted to get out.

On that same afternoon, Gherson went over to see Terrie O'Leary in her office at Esplanade Laurier. Gherson warned O'Leary that Axworthy

had reached the end of his rope. He felt betrayed by Martin's attack on
UI. Like Martin, Axworthy had a bottom line, Gherson said, leaving dangling what he might do about it. He never used the word "resign," but the
threat was implicit.

As they sat in the upholstered armchairs in her office, Martin, who was
fighting a bad cold, sauntered in through the passage that joined his office
with O'Leary's. Gherson filled him in. They decided to call Axworthy
immediately and arrange a meeting.

That evening, the two most powerful ministers in Jean Chrétien's cabinet retired to Martin's office for an hour-long heart-to-heart. Axworthy
calculated that he wasn't without some leverage. Martin needed him to
deliver UI reform. If it came out of the Department of Finance, it would
lack any semblance of credibility.

Axworthy reminded Martin of the emphasis his 1990 leadership campaign had placed on modernizing social policies. Martin, he recalled, had
advocated a new social contract in Canada, arguing that every dollar
invested in alleviating poverty today would save five dollars down the road.
Martin, who constantly invoked the social legacy of his father, was undermining Axworthy's attempt to renew social programs with his deficit fixation. As a result, "SSR is finished," Axworthy said. A proper UI reform, he
reminded Martin, was also a government priority. Finance had to back off
and give him room to do the reform his way.

Martin, in turn, spoke about the peso crisis and his fear that if his budget failed, the money traders would pounce and the government would be
forced into a second budget in April. Except Martin wouldn't be finance
minister by then. He insisted that he needed money from UI now, and
would play ball with Axworthy later. Still groping, he suggested they
could cut $3 billion immediately — a staggering sum — perhaps lower-
ing the benefit rate from 55 per cent to 50 per cent. Axworthy then could
use some of the savings to top up the working income supplement — a
benefit for poor families with children — in the fall, playing good cop to
Martin's bad cop. Axworthy countered that the social security review had
been designed to reallocate spending, not to make do with significantly
less.

Martin and Axworthy both felt it had been a good meeting, clearing
the air and re-establishing lines of communications. "It wasn't a big unhap-
piness meeting," was all Martin would say about it in the months afterwards.
But as was common in meetings between the two, they left with different

understandings of the outcome, and all the issues they had discussed resurfaced in the days to come.

Axworthy had made no mention of the Mark Kennedy interview, which was about to create a sensation. The next morning's *Ottawa Citizen* carried Kennedy's front-page story under the banner headline: "Axworthy shelves social policy overhaul." The article itself wasn't all that different from the *Globe* one. Again, Axworthy conceded the primacy of the deficit fight and said this would make it difficult to immediately finance his reforms. The aim would be to start designing the "architecture" of a new social policy and implement it once the fiscal situation improved. But the headline said it all.

Alec Jasen, Axworthy's press secretary, was alerted to the brewing storm when he was awakened shortly after 6 a.m. by a producer at Ottawa radio station CFRA. The morning program wanted to arrange an interview with Axworthy on the death of social security. Jasen couldn't figure out what had prompted such a call until he saw the *Citizen* headline.

For months, tensions had been running high over Axworthy's reforms. Now, with the added strain of the budget preparation, people snapped. Eddie Goldenberg told staff in the PMO that Axworthy had gone too far. Then, at a weekly meeting of key executive assistants, he scolded Patricia Neri, Axworthy's executive assistant, telling her the article was "totally unacceptable" and that a senior cabinet minister should know better. The prime minister wouldn't be pleased, he asserted. Peter Donolo, the PMO's communications chief, phoned Axworthy's office to discuss damage control and learned that the minister had left for Montreal.

Suspicions abounded that Axworthy must have an end game, although nobody could figure it out. The Liberal caucus was scheduled to hold a special pre-budget session beginning the following afternoon in Toronto. Perhaps he wanted to rally support to challenge Martin. Perhaps he had taken leave of his senses. Either way, the government could not afford to have the standard-bearer of left-of-centre Liberals looking victimized.

David Dodge, out for a pipe in the hours after the *Citizen* article hit the streets, bumped into David Walker and invited him to stroll with him. There were probably no two people in the capital who knew Axworthy better than Paul Martin's deputy minister and Martin's parliamentary secretary. Dodge had been at Princeton with Axworthy and had worked for him at Employment and Immigration in the early 1980s. Despite his current position and fiscally conservative outlook, he felt a great deal of goodwill towards him. Walker, a fellow academic, had known Axworthy since 1967 and had managed his election campaigns before running himself in 1988.

Dodge was animated, pointing out the seriousness of the article. It undermined the government's entire message — that the deficit battle was intended to save social policy, not stifle it; that Martin was a humane and reluctant budget cutter. He urged Walker to do what he could to make sure Axworthy was all right. Otherwise, the government could find itself in a pre-budget crisis.

The fierceness of the reaction to the Kennedy story caught Axworthy's people off guard. Axworthy was fully occupied attempting to stave off industrial action at the port of Montreal. The media pack had picked up the scent of the demise of the social security review and demanded a comment from him. The press was told that Axworthy would respond in Montreal. It was time to put the issue to bed.

When the 6 o'clock news came on, the image of an exhausted and monotonic Axworthy spoke volumes more than his words. His message came across as one of those listless fabrications of support extracted under duress. Back in Ottawa, both his own advisers and the prime minister's staff understood instantly that instead of dousing the flames, he had fanned them further. That night the CBC's *Prime Time News* led with an item declaring the social security review dead in the water. "I was just dead tired," Axworthy later admitted. "We made a bad judgment call. We should have done the scrum the next day."

A little after 7 p.m., the Prime Minister's Office phoned Jasen to ascertain the minister's whereabouts and was told to try him at home. Axworthy was invited to fly down to the caucus meeting the next morning on Chrétien's Challenger jet. No staff were to accompany him.

The following morning, February 2, he took a seat next to Chrétien. By all accounts, their discussion en route to Toronto was amicable and positive. Rather than scolding his minister, Chrétien reassured him that social security review remained a government priority and that he should not feel abandoned. Axworthy walked away with the assurance that the PM supported his right to manage UI reform. Now he could fend off Martin. The message, according to Eddie Goldenberg, was, "Lloyd, we need you, don't despair, it's not as bad as it sounds. It was very much a team message."

Inside the hotel conference room, Chrétien assured his caucus that Paul and Lloyd were working together and counselled the MPs to keep the faith. "Don't lose your cool. Paul will present an acceptable budget," he promised. He went out of his way to defend the block transfer, which had come in for a lot of comment by the MPs. Ottawa needed to regain control over federal money, he said. The provinces would, in return, be promised greater influence over social policies, but without constitutional changes. Ottawa could always reassert its role at a later date. "This is a strategic retreat," Chrétien informed them.

The crisis apparently over, government insiders were left to speculate about the motives behind Axworthy's public sulk. Some sources suggested it had largely been a gamble, with a lot of improvisation along the way. One Axworthy supporter called it high-stakes poker. The social security review was dying the death of a thousand cuts. Axworthy needed to save some portion of it. His comments represented both an attempt to rally sympathetic Liberal MPs in the run-up to the caucus and, more important, to gain the attention of a distracted prime minister.

Chrétien had never displayed much interest in the social security review and was preoccupied, in any case, by both the budget and his Team Canada trade mission that month to Latin America. He had been out of Ottawa almost continuously from the January 17 cabinet retreat until the day of the Mark Kennedy interview. At a critical moment, with his two most important ministers locked in combat, he hadn't been around to mediate. Axworthy had finally managed to sound the alarm loud enough to give him a jolt. "After four or five days, we had accomplished what we set out to do," commented an Axworthy ally. The $500-million UI down-payment was pushed back to the following year, giving Axworthy time to plan a comprehensive reform.

The January-February contretemps underscored one of the great weaknesses of Chrétien's style of governing. His revulsion at the central command structure of the Trudeau years had led, almost inevitably, to an overreaction in the other direction. In farming out greater authority to his ministers, he had left both himself and the support structures around him largely detached both from ministerial conflicts and, even more so, from overall government strategy.

It would be unfair to say of Chrétien, like Ronald Reagan, that he was a disengaged leader. He was, rather, highly selective in his engagements. Usually it was left to others — most often Goldenberg or Pelletier or Jocelyne Bourgon — to speak on his behalf. In Axworthy's office, they joked that Chrétien was the man behind the curtain, a reference to the unseen Wizard of Oz. "A lot of people speak for him and use his powers," one Liberal source said. He was, to be sure, very involved in budget planning and would play a major, largely unheralded role in the March fish war with Spain. But while he felt an attachment to the social safety net, the nitty-gritty of social policy wasn't his thing, especially the high-concept 1990s-style social policy that excited Axworthy. He rarely, almost never, used his bully pulpit to support the policies Axworthy propounded.

In the planning for the transition, he had chosen quite consciously to be his own chief executive officer and chief operating officer. But he behaved more like a chairman of the board. He desperately needed a strong second-in-command — the role filled by Don Mazankowski in the Mulroney government — with the authority and skill to broker differences between ministers. Instead, in Sheila Copps he had opted for a deputy prime minister with little in the way of authority and lacking any known affinity for conciliation.

Incredibly, Axworthy and Martin, the standard-bearers of the left and the right in cabinet, had been left to work things out themselves. It was reminiscent of Chrétien's instruction to David Zussman a decade earlier to work things out with Eddie Goldenberg. Without mediation, Martin, a powerful minister of finance with a head of steam and will of iron, ate the human resources minister for breakfast, reducing his social security review to the lonely outpost of unemployment insurance reform, and even there attempting to pre-empt him.

Axworthy's cabinet colleagues shook their heads in wonderment. Certainly, Martin was a powerful personality with a lot of momentum behind him. But Axworthy, they felt, tended to blink too soon. It was a curiosity of the Axworthy character that his closest associates had marvelled about right from the beginning of his career in federal politics. In some deep recess of his brain, one he may not even have been conscious of, Lloyd Axworthy didn't seem to mind losing and wasn't prepared to take the unpleasant steps necessary to win. By the time Pierre Trudeau resigned in 1984, Axworthy, after four years of contemplating the leadership of his party, had still not put an organization in place, despite the urgings of his senior advisers the previous summer. Again in 1990, he seemed to expect it all to fall into place without having to go around asking.

The first inkling of this mysterious ambivalence had manifested itself on May 22, 1979, the night Axworthy first squeaked into Parliament by 483 votes. It had been a hard-fought battle against an impressive Tory candidate, Sydney Spivak, a former provincial cabinet minister. But Axworthy had campaigned brilliantly, and David Walker, his campaign manager, felt secure that his friend and benefactor would prevail.

As the returns came in, the CBC decision desk declared Axworthy defeated. Walker checked the individual poll results. He told Axworthy the CBC must be mistaken and suggested the candidate just sit tight while he investigated. The next thing his campaign team knew, Axworthy, the Liberals' great white hope in western Canada, was on national television conceding defeat. As it turned out, the CBC had double-counted a couple of the stronger Tory polls. Axworthy had indeed come out on top. But his supporters were left with a queasy feeling from the episode: why had Axworthy gone out and conceded? Why was he so quick to accept defeat? He always seemed to them a bit conflicted: the admirer of the bare-knuckled poetry of the Kennedys versus the United Church, where having fought the good fight was as important as the outcome. Paul Martin harboured no such reservations.

16

WHO'S THE REAL PM?

In early February, a Finance official remarked to a colleague at the Human Resources Department that Paul Martin was still pushing where Michael Wilson would long ago have given up. With just three weeks left to budget day, Martin was battling on multiple fronts. He and Ralph Goodale had not yet settled the Crow: Goodale, fearing he would be the last Liberal elected on the prairies for a generation, was hanging tough for a major compensation package to assist farmers hurt by the end of grain transportation subsidies.

Martin and Goodale's personal relationship complicated matters. They went back to the 1968 leadership race when Goodale, then a teenage Trudeau youth delegate, had dropped by the Regina Inn to meet leadership candidate Paul Martin Sr. He struck up a conversation with the candidate's son, and a friendship blossomed. Goodale and Martin had been there for each other for over a quarter-century. The Saskatchewan politician provided the venue for one of Martin's earliest party speeches, at the 1981 provincial convention that chose Goodale as leader, and helped organize his 1990 leadership run. Martin, in turn, raised money for Goodale's party and went to bat for him when Chrétien formed his cabinet.

Goodale had a conversational knack for circling the earth without ever landing. Early in the term of the government, Chrétien was reading a newspaper on a flight out west and came across an article quoting Goodale commenting at length on a sensitive trade matter without uttering a word of substance. "Now that's how a minister should talk," he beamed to his aides sitting nearby.

Within Finance, the line on Goodale was that he would bargain until there was just one guy left in the room — and then he would wait until the hardy soul lapsed into unconsciousness. Goodale was a supremely cautious individual, a product of his personality and his experience. He had been elected to the House of Commons as a twenty-four-year-old in 1974, but saw his budding federal career go up in smoke at the next election with the Trudeau-fuelled Liberal immolation in western Canada. In the early 1980s he served as leader of the Saskatchewan Liberals, without a seat in the legislature for most of his term. After coming third in a tight three-way race in Regina in 1988, Goodale finally gave up on politics — or so he said. When he returned to the Commons in 1993 after almost twenty years, he was a politician not inclined to tempt fate.

Goodale's issue was compensation: how much, for how long, and in what form. He understood he could not save the Crow Rate. But after all the setbacks of his political career, he would resist anyone, even Paul Martin, who put his standing at risk. After months of haggling, he and Martin were still $900 million apart on Crow compensation and hadn't come to agreement on other cuts to farm stabilization programs, straining their friendship. But because of the relationship, Finance officials knew they could not apply the customary muscle.

Foreign Affairs Minister André Ouellet also gave Martin a hard time. He attempted an end run around program review. Ouellet, a canny politician first elected in a Centennial Year by-election, appealed directly (but unsuccessfully) to the prime minister about the proposed cuts to dairy subsidies and, for good measure, the relatively small hit intended for his department and the Canadian International Development Agency. Sheila Copps, another Program Review Committee member, also disputed her reduction, in Environment, and Martin had to keep a careful watch on several others. If he gave way to one minister, he felt his fragile cabinet consensus could shatter.

He also had to be cognizant of the unsettled dust from the Axworthy outbursts. Demoralized left-wing Liberals and their friends in the social policy community, reading Axworthy's press comments as a call to arms, had belatedly rallied to his side. On February 9, twenty representatives of Campaign 2000, a group battling child poverty, crowded into the minister's fourth-floor office on Parliament Hill for a long-scheduled session on the budget and social policy. Axworthy arrived from Question Period a few minutes late, striking those in the room as haggard and wary. His shoulders were bowed, his eyes projected suspicion. The obvious depth of his dejection took his visitors aback. He seemed thoroughly miserable at the prospect of subjecting himself to additional abuse. But the delegation had come in friendship. They discussed the block transfer, which he indicated was still in flux, and ways in which they could help him rebuild support for a social agenda in the face of what they considered a heavily hyped fiscal crisis. As the meeting progressed, Axworthy became more animated and comfortable. He put his feet up on the coffee table. For the moment at least, he had his constituency back.

In caucus, a ginger group of left-leaning Liberals, people like Winnipeg MP John Harvard, Toronto's Maria Minna, Montreal veteran Warren Allmand, and New Brunswick rookie Andy Scott, also regrouped. These social Liberals quietly gathered in private conclaves, preparing for one last push against Martin. By now, they saw no gain in attacking deficit reduction. They merely wanted cuts to social programs to be balanced by commensurate reductions in the tax benefits available to better-off Canadians through registered retirement savings plans. Social Liberals dominated the Commons Human Resources Committee, which brought down its report on the Axworthy reform plans on February 6. The Liberals on the committee went out of their way to fire a warning shot at Martin about the unfairness of cutting social programs while retaining RRSP deductions, even while attacking some of the more radical Axworthy proposals, such as a two-tier UI system.

But their passion could not compete with the hard logic generated by the financial panic and a well-orchestrated tax revolt. Martin had always believed that the weight of budgetary action had to fall most heavily on government spending, but he contemplated tax measures as well. Over Christmas, he gave an interview to Clyde Graham of Canadian Press, who badgered Martin into conceding that hitting his deficit targets was more important than leaving taxes alone. The story got picked up across the country, leading to irate calls from MPs back in their ridings. O'Leary screamed at him.

For months, she and Peter Donolo had warned Martin that the public was taxed out. It went well beyond tax rates. Measures to supposedly broaden the tax base or make it fairer — like the taxation of dental and health benefits — could be enough to ignite the tinder. In late December and early January, consumers had revolted against cable rate increases, forcing the cable companies into full retreat and capturing the attention of the budget planners in Esplanade Laurier. The *Toronto Sun* published the phone and fax numbers in Martin's office, encouraging readers to make their views known. They jammed the lines. One woman called on a Sunday when the office staff was off and demanded to speak to Martin. Her boldness evaporated when she learned that the minister himself had picked up the phone.

Even if Martin had been inclined to major tax measures, the Swedish experience in January would have pulled him back. The Swedish budget had relied heavily on tax measures rather than spending cuts, and the markets had responded by pushing the kronor down and interest rates up. "Sweden wasn't important for the fact that the rating agency moved against it," Martin explained later. "It was not important for the fact that their interest rates went through the roof. What Sweden was important for was that the markets would not give you credit for tax actions. A year earlier, the market didn't seem to care how you reduced the deficit. Sweden demonstrated the market had evolved."

Tensions at Finance were as taut as piano wire. The long hours, the ministerial horse-trading, and the continuing financial market turmoil took their toll. The place struggled against battle fatigue.

Officials were in a state of unrelenting anxiety that their efforts would fail to meet the expectations of the financial markets. Nobody could precisely locate the invisible line between confidence and lack thereof. A four-person team from the International Monetary Fund paid its annual visit to the department during the budget preparations. The IMF officials argued the 3-per-cent target was inadequate, urging the government towards "faster and front-loaded" fiscal action. The Finance officials privately welcomed another powerful voice calling for harder action.

To ensure the budget's success, Finance felt it needed to provide one more demonstration of its resolve, a big-ticket item of such symbolic value that nobody would doubt that the government was on a track from which it would not retreat. Martin, still pushing where other finance ministers would have backed off, had never given up on using the budget to redesign old-age pensions. If he was going to not just cut but restructure federal spending, how could he leave out a $20-billion spending item, one of the largest and fastest-growing of all government programs? Martin felt it was the last, and perhaps most important, piece of the puzzle.

The dramatic struggle of February 1995 over seniors' programs — a battle that pitted a prime minister against his minister of finance — was the untold story of the 1995 budget. After the budget was finally delivered, attention naturally focussed on the raft of measures implemented, from the scrapping of the Crow Rate to the full privatization of Petro-Canada to the revamping of federal-provincial social transfers. Martin would rightly enumerate these as evidence that his budget had been the most far-reaching since the end of World War II. But there was a big one that got away. At the highest reaches of the government, officials and advisers watched in fascination and horror as two very proud and very different men refused to bend.

In Martin's first budget, Finance officials had included a paragraph calling for preparation of a paper to "look at what an aging society will need in terms of services; and what changes are required to the public pension system to ensure it is affordable." Even this meek suggestion was furiously attacked and the paper went nowhere, although Finance continued its work on the plan. It bore the fingerprints of David Dodge, for whom pension reform was a long-standing and holy crusade. Dodge believed that with the greying of the baby-boomers, the system would collapse under its own weight. The annual cost, $20 billion in 1994, would rise 60 per cent over the next fifteen years. At that point, the baby-boomers would just be starting to queue up for their OAS cheques. The system, as Dodge liked to say, simply could not be sustained.

Finance liked to argue the seniors' issue in moral as well as financial terms. Seniors with good incomes siphoned off a huge chunk of money while younger families, struggling to keep their heads above water, made do with less and less government help. Just as in Paul Martin Sr.'s time, when the poverty of seniors represented an intergenerational scandal, so now a new intergenerational injustice appeared. The government was failing children and youth, the inheritors of the deficit. Around the Department of Finance, a favourite aphorism went something like this: In the old days, people left their kids the house. Then they left the house with a mortgage. Now they're just leaving the mortgage. Or, as U.S. President Herbert Hoover had quipped several generations earlier: "Blessed are the young for they shall inherit the national debt."

Finance thought it had a pretty good plan for addressing this inequity and, at the same time, contributing to deficit reduction. By now, sensitive to Martin's strong emotional attachment to his father's legacy, the department had learned to couch its proposals in terms of preserving social programs. Under its proposed scheme, benefits would be calculated on a sliding scale based on family income, not individual income. This would put the burden of cuts on better-off seniors and, most particularly, on middle-class couples collecting two pensions. But poorer seniors, those receiving the means-tested guaranteed income supplement as well as the basic pension, would pocket more. So there would be winners as well as losers. The saw-off point was set at a family income of $40,000: those below the line would be better off; those above, worse off. The universal pension scheme that Paul Martin Sr. had introduced in 1952 after years of campaigning would be no more. It would be replaced by an income-tested program that — while admittedly more sophisticated — bore a resemblance to the kind of system that Martin Sr. had sought to replace.

Nothing frightened politicians more, however, than the thought of tinkering with old-age pensions, no matter how impressive the justifications or progressive the plan. Unlike welfare recipients, seniors had the means, and the time, to mount a concerted political counter-attack: they wrote letters, they phoned radio shows, they demonstrated, and they came out to vote. The lessons had been driven home forevermore by the tiny giant-killer Solange Denis.

She had come to national prominence on June 19, 1985, a month after Michael Wilson had announced the partial deindexation of pensions in his first budget. She joined a small knot of seniors holding vigil in a cold drizzle outside the Centre Block. Shortly before noon, Brian Mulroney, trying to make a quick exit home for lunch, had the misfortune of running into the group. Ever the charmer, he engaged the seniors in relatively harmless banter for a few moments before being brought up short by the indignant Denis. "You lied to us," the white-haired woman reproached him in one of the most famous television clips in Canadian politics. "You made us vote for you, then, Goodbye Charlie Brown." She warned that the Tories would never win re-election if they tampered with pensions. Mulroney, trapped in a public relations disaster and knowing this was not the moment to fight his way out with a combative response, replied weakly: "I'm listening to you, Madame." She walloped him again. "Well, Madame is damned angry."

He listened well. Eight days later — after the prime minister had a private lunch with Wilson — the government reversed course. A grim-faced Wilson told the Commons that the government "recognized the anxieties" of senior citizens. Up in the public gallery, Denis, wearing a pink carnation and accompanied by her husband, took in the scene with satisfaction.

Now ten years later, Martin prepared to embark on the same journey as Michael Wilson. But he felt he had a more roadworthy vehicle. The department's reform package not only would save money and assure the affordability of pensions in future, but it also came tightly wrapped in Liberal values. The pain would come out of the hide of middle- and upper-income seniors. Unlike Wilson, Martin would see that the worse off would be better off.

Sheila Copps, hearing these rationalizations, figured Martin had been breathing the rarified air on the twenty-first floor of Esplanade Laurier too long. Her mother would be unnerved by any change, even the hint of change. She wouldn't give you the chance to explain that you were from the government and that this was actually good for seniors. Learning that Martin wanted to introduce the new system on Canada Day, she asked incredulously: "What planet is he coming from?"

Martin had a budget to worry about. Jean Chrétien had to worry as well about his cabinet. A prime minister must make sure that the fragile consensus at the heart of all governments remains intact. He must express the consensus and know when to pull an issue off the table because the elements of that consensus are not yet in place. Since he cannot afford to allow light to show between himself and his minister of finance, most of their business will be conducted in private. As well, in addition to being the leader of the country and of the government, the prime minister is also the party leader. As such, he must ensure that the conditions are in place for his government's re-election. He is the ultimate guardian not just of cabinet solidarity, but also of political prospects.

Chrétien tended towards the view of Copps and Ouellet on pensions. Changes to seniors' programs, as Madame Denis had demonstrated so well, were in the realm of whitewater politics. The rapids were fast and tricky. Large boulders would come at you out of nowhere. People were not prepared. Better, he figured, to portage. He told Martin the subject made him very nervous.

But Martin, totally obsessed with his budget needs and his fear of falling short of the invisible mark, couldn't take no for an answer. His fixation on compound interest was such that he thought of any delay in terms of the additional interest costs he would have to endure. He also worried that if he didn't strike while he enjoyed such enormous momentum, he could get swept aside by any number of factors: the Quebec referendum, a display of grey power, the approach of the next election.

Chrétien had been, as promised, a supportive prime minister. But on this one, he wouldn't defer. Twice in budget meetings in mid-February, Chrétien nixed pension reform. Martin either didn't notice or didn't care. In part, this may have been due to communications breakdowns. Martin tended to be blunt in his views; Chrétien purposely ambiguous. He was more likely to signal his disapproval obliquely than express it outright. "The PM doesn't like to say no," explained a Liberal insider. "He says 'I don't know about that' or 'I am uncomfortable with it.' That was his signal, and he had the expectation that Paul would come back next time with a changed position. But Paul didn't budge."

The finance minister emerged from his meetings with the prime minister increasingly exasperated, telling Goldenberg and other Chrétien advisers that he needed definitive answers, not only on pension reform but also on the budget's crucial economic assumptions. They thought these had been provided. It seemed to them that Martin's singular focus and hyper-competitiveness, attributes that had allowed him to push the budget process close to completion, had gotten out of hand.

Martin needed allies. He sought out Lloyd Axworthy, whose department had co-responsibility for pension reform and who liked the income-redistribution features in the Finance proposal. Axworthy had never fully given up the Liberal dream of a guaranteed annual income. Time and again, he would circle back to this touchstone. In pension reform, he found a building block towards that ultimate goal. The beleaguered human resources minister also understood instinctively that a package that would result in immediate savings of $800 million to $1 billion could relieve other demands on him. The alternative could be even deeper cuts to his departmental spending or more pressure on UI. Indeed, Martin told Chrétien at one of the budget meetings that without pension reform, he would have no choice but to go back after unemployment insurance. Chrétien told him to take it up with Axworthy, that he would agree to anything they could work out. But Axworthy refused to budge on UI, although he was willing to lend his name to the pensions package.

Late one afternoon in mid-February, Paul Martin climbed into a taxi and went to see another person who he felt would be critical to his chances of selling pension reform. It was a risky venture, totally out of character with the instincts of the Finance Department, but in keeping with the minister's. If he was going to keep pushing pension reform, he needed the personal assurance that his plan would fly politically as well as new arguments to throw at Chrétien.

Martin took the elevator to the fourth floor of a low-rise in the eastern part of Ottawa and made his way to Apartment 411. Seventy-three-year-old Solange Denis greeted him at the door.

The visit was a closely guarded secret, known to just a handful of his closest advisers. Who could account for Denis? Her fame, after all, had sprung from her willingness to shoot her mouth off. If she had blabbed about the visit, one of the deepest budget secrets would have been out in the open. Calls might have been made for Martin's resignation.

Martin came back buoyed. He told the inner circle — some of whom were apoplectic about the visit — that Denis had liked the plan. She collected the guaranteed income supplement herself, and would be among the winners. And she trusted Liberals; she was one herself. In an interview with the *Globe and Mail* several months earlier she had cheerfully confessed that at the time of her "Goodbye Charlie Brown" remark, she had been a committed Liberal doing volunteer work for veteran Ottawa-Vanier MP Jean-Robert Gauthier. It had been a Liberal government, she correctly recounted, that had given seniors their pensions in the first place.

Martin sought to overcome Chrétien's objections one by one. After being told that Daniel Johnson thought such a move would be harmful in the looming Quebec referendum, the finance minister rushed down to Montreal and provided the Quebec Liberal leader, a former colleague at Power Corporation, with a personal briefing on the merits of the proposal. He felt it went well and believed that Johnson's concerns had been assuaged. (PCO thought Martin heard what he wanted to hear.)

But Chrétien, like Martin, was adamant. A small group existed within the Privy Council Office to provide Chrétien with economic advice independent of the Department of Finance. Other PCO officials regarded the group, largely composed of ex-Finance officials, as overly sympathetic to the department's fiscal agenda. Indeed, within the Langevin Block, which housed the Privy Council Office, the unit went by the name Finance North. On this occasion, though, Finance's northern satellite broke from the mother ship. The PCO officials told the prime minister that while the pension plan had merit, the budget could fly without it.

On Friday, February 17, ten days before Martin would present his budget in the House of Commons, nearly all the decisions, including the final trade-offs on the block transfer, the Crow Rate, and unemployment insurance, had finally fallen into place — except pension reform and some continued jousting over the economic assumptions. Chrétien tended to be a bit more optimistic that the economy would turn in their favour. And if it didn't, they could always adjust course in the government's third year, the target date for 3 per cent. That afternoon, Martin and Dodge once again sat down with Chrétien and his top civil service adviser, the clerk of the Privy Council, Jocelyne Bourgon, to try to put the budget to bed.

Finance's state of high anxiety had not subsided. Late in the morning of the previous day, New York–based Moody's Investors Services had placed $428 billion in Canadian bonds under review. Canada stood in jeopardy of losing its prized triple-A credit rating. The dollar quickly fell another half-cent, dipping below seventy-one cents. The Bank of Canada responded by raising the cost of overnight funds, a percursor to another rate hike. "If the budget doesn't meet the markets' expectations, then Moody's is going to pull the trigger," said Jerry Ficchi, a Boston-based financial analyst. "If Martin doesn't produce, then it could get extremely ugly. There will be new lows on the dollar right off the bat, within the first five minutes." Martin reached back into the Red Book to remind the skittish markets that his 3-per-cent target was just an "interim" step towards the ultimate objective of a balanced budget.

Martin and Dodge once again extolled to Chrétien the superiority of the old-age pension policy the department had designed. Their system would be socially progressive and fiscally sustainable. Now was the time, they argued. It would be unfair to hit everyone else in the budget — farmers, welfare recipients, students, artists, public servants, immigrants — and leave upper-middle-class seniors alone. The crisis atmosphere and the calls on so many others to sacrifice would provide political cover for an overdue and inevitable reform. Even Solange Denis accepted the logic.

Chrétien had reasons for seeing it differently. In many ways they spoke to the profound personality differences between him and his finance minister. Martin was a doer and risk-taker, an entrepreneurial politician who would undertake ten tasks in the hope that nine of them would succeed. On the other hand, Chrétien's inclination, in the words of a senior government official, was to do no things and get none wrong.

Chrétien fit the great British political scientist Michael Oakeshott's description of a true small-c conservative: preferring "the familiar to the unknown, ... the tried to the untried, fact to mystery, the actual to the possible, the limited to the unbounded, the near to the distant, the sufficient to the superabundant, the convenient to the perfect, present laughter to utopian bliss." The characteristics of a political conservative, Oakeshott had written in his 1956 essay "On Being Conservative," "centre upon a propensity to use and to enjoy what is available rather than to wish for or to look for something else; to delight in what is present rather than what was or what may be." Martin, the innovator, spotted opportunity in pension reform; Chrétien, the conservative, fretted over needless upset.

He told his finance minister that he had a good budget, but the seniors' initiative could be one step too far, the political tripwire that detonated the entire effort. Then there was Quebec. The referendum would probably be held in June. It was a time to avoid unnecessary adventures. For Martin, the issue always came down to the question, Why take a chance of the budget failing? For Chrétien, the final question was, Why take any chances with Quebec?

Again the meeting broke up with Chrétien saying no and Martin stubbornly refusing to acknowledge the verdict. The issue had grown well beyond the merits of pension reform. Martin's insubordination was unprecedented. Intentionally or not, he had challenged the ultimate authority of the prime minister. The officials had seen many things in their years padding around the corridors of power, but they had never seen a stalemate of this sort between the two most important figures in a government. Martin had been told no three times by the prime minister, and still he persisted.

"It got to the point where Chrétien had no choice but to draw a line in the sand and say, 'I'm the prime minister and you're the finance minister. I am saying no,'" commented one observer close to the standoff. "If he didn't cut it off, he wasn't going to be PM any more, effectively. Paul was going to be *de facto* PM."

Martin retired to a boardroom next to the clerk's offices with Eddie Goldenberg. Like others, Goldenberg had watched in horror as the situation spun dangerously out of control. The time had come to bridge their differences, to make them understand each other's points of view. Although his primary loyalty was to Chrétien, Goldenberg's connection with Martin was long and deep. Their fathers, both progressive Liberals, had attended all three of the great Liberal policy conferences of the twentieth century: Port Hope in 1933, Kingston in 1960, and Aylmer in 1991.

Martin returned to the department in the early evening, disconsolate. His officials awaited a definitive answer, either way. The reform plan sat

on a shelf ready to go. But its inclusion or exclusion would require adjustments to the charts and tables, the budget booklets, the speech itself. The
clock was ticking down. Word spread that Martin still lacked an affirmative answer to his demands. Anticipating his foul mood, the bureaucrats
scattered back to safety on the floors below.

Martin closeted himself with his top political advisers: O'Leary, David
Herle, Peter Nicholson, Elly Alboim. They had lived with the stress of this
budget for months. The distinction between night and day, weekday and
weekend had blurred. They were worn out, nerves jangled, physical health
deteriorating. The exhaustion clouded their judgments, incapacitating their
ability to take a broader perspective. O'Leary was running a fever, suffering from an undiagnosed case of strep throat. At times she felt so weak
that she could neither stand nor sit. Staffers would find her prostrate on
the floor of her office, her face beaded with perspiration, her voice reduced
to a croak. Now, after all the effort, they faced failure. Martyrdom held
greater appeal for some.

His advisers, political and bureaucratic, shared Martin's analysis that
the absence of action on pensions could sink the entire budget effort. Without one more bridge, not only would they fail to traverse the raging river,
they would probably be consumed by it. They would appear weak to the
boys in red suspenders, who, like it or not, held the fate of the country in
their hands. Martin's people continued to fret as well over the prudence of
the economic assumptions and the size of the contingency fund.

In the privacy of Martin's office on that Friday night ten days before
the budget speech, the minister of finance and his kitchen cabinet discussed
his options, including whether he would submit his resignation. He was
adamant that he would not deliver a budget that didn't make his grade.
Martin considered this issue absolutely fundamental. He was the minister
of finance. He would wear the ignominy of a budget failure for all time. He
had the option as well of just stalling, of not announcing a budget date,
the absence of which was already beginning to raise eyebrows, until the
pressure built in his favour.

Martin never uttered the word "resignation" to Chrétien. But senior
officials in the Privy Council Office understood the gravity of the deadlock between the prime minister and the minister of finance. They, too,
held discussions, informal but sober ones about the various contingencies.
If the minister of finance quit on the eve of a critical budget, it would
plunge the country into an immediate financial crisis. Speculators would

pile on in a feeding frenzy, putting the dollar under tremendous pressure. The Bank of Canada would be forced to jack up interest rates as it struggled to stabilize the situation. The government's fiscal credibility would be absolutely in ruins.

It would be necessary to bring down the budget immediately, they concluded. They would have hours, not days, to try to restore order. The prime minister would have to be prepared to either quickly appoint an acting finance minister or else deliver the budget himself. Few officials actually believed such a scenario would come to pass. They couldn't really imagine Martin putting the country into such a spot. But they were in the business of thinking the unthinkable.

The government was teetering on the edge of an unprecedented crisis. Eddie Goldenberg existed for such moments. His extreme caution and awkward manner made him a much maligned figure in Ottawa. Goldenberg often found himself perplexed by instances in which people saw him as an impediment when he actually considered himself to be supportive. They simply failed to understand, he would explain, that his role required him to ask the hard questions. If he didn't, nobody would. When a given policy initiative got past him, he wanted to make sure that all the potential pratfalls had been identified. Any other stance would be irresponsible.

Goldenberg, the son of one of the country's great labour conciliators, understood that the time for debate was long past. Back in the opposition days, he had been among a group of advisers who had argued strenuously that the Liberals should slay the free trade dragon once and for all by coming out foursquare in favour of NAFTA. Chrétien had nixed the approach. The others, licking their wounds, wondered what they should do. Goldenberg reminded them the leader properly had the final say. Advisers were paid to provide their best counsel. Then they implemented the decisions of their political masters, no matter what the decision, always with due attention to minimizing the risks.

In the preparation of the Red Book, time and time again Goldenberg displayed a genius for brokering compromises, usually through the use of language intended to obfuscate rather than illuminate. The impasse between Chrétien and Martin now cried out for his talent for identifying solutions where none seemed evident.

Goldenberg worked over the weekend on a formulation that would allow both of these stubborn, deeply entrenched men to save face. Employing the sort of shuttle diplomacy made famous by former U.S. secretary of state Henry Kissinger, he cobbled together a compromise in which each could find strong echoes of his own position. He made Martin see that Chrétien, too, had legitimate concerns, that the ground had not been politically prepared for such a radical action and that Quebec posed a special problem. But that didn't mean that Martin could not have his way in signalling his seriousness to the markets.

On Tuesday the 21st, with six days to go, Chrétien and Martin met alone. They both accepted the terms of the peace pact. Martin would not get his old-age pension reform in 1995. But he could have it the following year. And he could flag it in the budget itself, outlining the basic principles — undiminished protection for those receiving the guaranteed income supplement; the phasing out of benefits as income rises; and the provision of benefits based on family income — that underlay the Finance plan. For Chrétien, nothing would happen before the referendum. And there would be time to prepare public opinion for future changes and further debate the particulars. Only after that meeting did Martin announce that the budget would be delivered the following Monday.

The budget, for the second year in a row, said that the human resources minister and the minister of finance "will release a paper later this year on the change required in the public pension system to ensure its affordability." This time, it put a timeframe on implementation, promising that changes would be legislated to take effect in 1997.

Martin hated to lose, even to half lose. In the aftermath of the pension battle, his officials worried whether he would be in top form to sell the budget. But his ability to shake things off stood him in good stead. Within twenty-four hours, he regained his focus.

He and the department remained on tenterhooks right until budget day. They never got over their fear that the budget would flop because of the absence of a serious pension initiative, that it would fall one measure short, and then choke on that single failure. They made up some of the lost savings by forcing some of the program review cuts forward by a year or two and through a neat accounting trick involving the creation of the two-dollar coin. But the absence of the structural change, with all its symbolic value, wore on their shot nerves.

At the same time, the episode sealed the bond between Martin and his officials. Nicholson had noticed a thaw setting in earlier in the fall, in the build-up to the release of the Purple and Grey Books. "You still had this odd cold snap. But the global warming trend was there," he said. Some of the more easily bruised figures would never forgive Martin the aggravations of the early months. But they also knew — and appreciated — that he would go to the wall for their common agenda, the one he seemed to have dismissed back at the chaplain's office in the Hôtel-Dieu Hospital fifteen months earlier. Now, on the eve of their second budget together, Martin and his department were at peace — or as peaceful as it ever got under his frenetic leadership.

17

CANADA REMADE

On the Saturday before budget day, Paul Martin, clad in denim shirt, blue jeans, and a well-worn pair of loafers, rambled around his office reading through his speech yet again. He placed the small green lectern borrowed from the House of Commons on the table in his office, leaning over it as he would on Monday. Martin had once again retained Larry Hagen to craft his thoughts into phrases that resonated. His policy guru, Peter Nicholson, a phrase-maker of some repute himself, also lent a hand.

Martin knew it would be the most important speech of his life, but he also understood that the public had a limited attention span, even for such a sweeping document. He would have to get across the complexity of his budget, he figured, in one hour — no more time than a viewer would devote to a television drama. He had requested information on other budget speeches: in an earlier era, they had sometimes gone on for twice as long. But Michael Wilson was always thoughtful enough to inflict the bad news in under sixty minutes.

On first read, it had come in at about an hour and twenty minutes. "I took an axe to it," he said. He cut and pasted for hours and hours, taking out a bit here and a bit there, reordering the paragraphs and adding back the bare basics. He would edit something in the French text and then switch and edit something else in English. It drove his aides wild. They had to check each one against the other to ensure that the minister of finance was delivering the same budget message in both of Canada's official languages.

His throat getting hoarse, Martin's run-through that Saturday morning clicked in at an hour and twenty-two. A visitor asked how he felt. "Browned off," Martin replied. How long a speech do you think the public will tolerate, he demanded to know. Then his sense of humour broke through the cloud cover for a moment. "I guess I am my father's son," he commented. "It took him an hour just to do the introductions."

Later he would compare it to the story of the loaves and fishes. "We kept taking out chunks of fifteen to twenty minutes and the goddamn thing kept growing by fifteen or twenty minutes. We still can't figure it out." But nobody around the Department of Finance was laughing that weekend, especially when Martin's wife, Sheila, phoned Terrie O'Leary on Sunday morning — with a little over twenty-four hours to go — and said that the speech was still too long and he was driving her crazy. He was coming in.

Nearly all the senior officials were at their posts that weekend. They had put the budget to bed, but plenty of preparation remained in selling it. They pored over the so-called Q-and-A books, trying to anticipate every question that might be asked of the minister or his advisers. The thought of being stopped cold by some innocent question nobody had ever considered mortified everyone.

Word spread about Martin's impending arrival. About ten of the advisers, including speechwriter Hagen, piled into his boardroom on the twenty-first floor to help him with the last-minute cuts. They reviewed every line, voting whether it should stay or go, with Peter Daniel, the department's communications chief, issuing regular warnings that if they didn't get the text to the printers post haste, there wouldn't be a budget speech.

With the text finally dispatched in the afternoon, Martin was out of sorts. He wandered back and forth between the ministerial suite and the deputy's floor right below. He dropped by Nicholson's office several times, plopping himself down on the couch, getting up, going back upstairs, impatient to get the show started. "Paul doesn't like a situation where the play isn't still going on. He doesn't like to sit around waiting," Nicholson noted.

Like Martin, Canadians from coast to coast waited anxiously to get the monkey off their back. The pre-budget period had been brilliantly stage-managed. Two decades earlier, in a clever paraphrase of Keynes, John Turner had said in a budget speech: "Economics is too important to leave to the economists. The choices to be made are essentially political decisions." Martin may have failed to convince the team at Finance of his economic brilliance, but by February 1995, they fully appreciated his political skills. His performance since the October appearances before the Finance Committee had been flawless. In the summer, before the selling had swung into high gear, fewer than one in five Canadians had named the deficit when asked which issue should receive the greatest attention from Canada's leaders. By February, just in time for his budgetary assault, it had climbed to one in two in an Angus Reid poll, vaulting over unemployment to take over the top spot for the first time.

Martin's outside communications consultants, Elly Alboim and David Herle, had been given top security clearance and practically lived in his department. Along with Peter Daniel, they had set the stage for Martin's performance. Daniel's return to Finance in the summer of 1994 had put the final piece in place for Martin's elevation of communications to a central role in the departmental power structure. Daniel enjoyed great credibility with the minister. He didn't hesitate to speak his mind and, to Martin's thinking, had things worth saying.

In the old days, communications had been viewed internally as a necessary evil, peripheral to the main functions of the department. After a policy had worked its way through the system, the communications people would be duly informed and assigned to push it out the door. Now the communications function began at the front end of the policy process. If it couldn't be communicated, if it didn't fit a communications plan, it never got near the door.

By the time the budget was ready for delivery, almost every measure had been test-marketed. Jean Chrétien would call it a Holiday Inn budget: no surprises. Whenever Finance secured final agreement on a given initiative, Martin would gently float it at a consultation session or refer to it in response to a question in the House of Commons, taking the sting out of the tail. The only exception would be the happy discovery that there would be no personal tax increases.

On Monday morning, Martin, determined not to stumble, went through the speech yet another time. He leafed through his briefing books. At lunchtime Dodge, O'Leary, and Nicholson went over to the media lock-up at the Ottawa Congress Centre. The media and professional economic commentators were always given access to the budget documents several hours before its public presentation so that the reporters could query officials about technical details and begin preparing their stories. Security was tight at the lock-up, so called because once in the room nobody was allowed to leave until the finance minister rose in the Commons. Phone lines were disconnected until that moment. Cellular phones were not permitted.

The trio from Finance, along with Peter Donolo, the prime minister's communications director, wandered around the room. The budget resembled the opening night of a Broadway play. In this case, the producers felt pretty good about their offering, but what mattered was the audience's reaction. And the audience would take its cues from the professional reviewers, the journalists and economic experts in the room for the preview. "We thought we had a pretty good budget, not an A-plus budget, but certainly not a C budget," Nicholson said. "But I — and I think I was typical — was nervous that the markets would, for whatever reason, start to turn thumbs down on it and that there would be a snowballing effect."

Nicholson canvassed the opinions of about ten people, economics writers like Bruce Little and Andrew Coyne from the *Globe and Mail* and Greg Ip from the *Financial Post* and several of the bank economists present. He felt immediately encouraged, particularly by their positive reaction to the conservatism of Martin's economic assumptions. "There wasn't really a single negative word coming out of any of them," Nicholson recounted. "That's like when you see the first twenty-five polls reporting in a riding. Unless it's a dead heat, you get a pretty fair idea of where it's heading. So I was really quite confident that we had passed the market muster."

The foursome met in a prearranged spot after about forty-five minutes to compare notes. Dodge and O'Leary phoned the early returns in to Martin. The decision desk was calling the budget a winner. "As soon as they phoned and said the talking heads like the assumptions, then I knew that from a market point of view, we were okay," Martin recounted.

At 3:30, Martin dropped by cabinet, where his colleagues learned for the first time the breadth of the budget and discovered that pension reform had not gone ahead. As the cabinet sat around reading the budget, Donolo slipped in to let them in on the good news from the lock-up. The press had bought in. A few gripes here and there, some of the expected grumbling about the destruction of the old Canada, that sort of thing. Donolo had his talking points with him, the pithy page of rejoinders he and his staff regularly prepared to fend off hostile queries. They all rehearsed their lines. It was essential that everyone sang from the same hymn-book.

Just before heading into the Commons chamber, Martin and his wife, Sheila, stopped by Chrétien's third-floor office for a photo session with the prime minister and Aline Chrétien. Chrétien observed that Martin had forgotten the flower customarily worn by the minister while delivering his speech. Peter Donolo suggested the omission would symbolize the government's commitment to restraint. But Chrétien insisted, "We must honour tradition." So after a brief search, someone located a vase of flowers in a nearby office and snipped off two red carnations, and Chrétien and Martin, suitably outfitted, descended the west staircase together.

Martin rose at 4:30, a very different finance minister from the one who had stood in the same spot a year earlier. He proceeded to outline a document breathtaking in its ambition. "Mr. Speaker, there are times in the progress of a people when fundamental challenges must be faced, fundamental choices made — a new course charted. For Canadians this is one of those times.

"Our resolve, our values, our very way of life as Canadians are being tested. The choice is clear. We can take the path — too well trodden — of minimal change, of least resistance, of leadership lost. Or we can set out on a new road of fundamental reform, of renewal — of hope restored."

More than an economic statement, he presented a blueprint for a new Canada, or perhaps a return to an older Canada, the one that had existed when C.D. Howe and Paul Martin Sr. had sat around the King and St. Laurent cabinet tables. The budget, as one strategist commented, marked the Liberal Party's return to the "pragmatic centre."

Spending would be reduced by more than $25 billion over three years; tax increases would amount to $3.7 billion. After all the cuts kicked in, program spending as a proportion of the overall economy would revert to 1950–51 levels. Every department of government would be smaller, save Indian and Northern Affairs, some by as much as 50 per cent. The Trudeau legacy of regional development would be seriously whittled down. Business subsidies would be slashed by 60 per cent. The CBC, even after winning a bit of a reprieve, thanks to friends in the Prime Minister's Office, took enough of a jolt that its president, Anthony Manera, fell on his sword the next day, saying he would not preside over its dismantling. The remaining shares in Petro-Canada, a Liberal creation, were to be sold. The annual $560-million Crow Rate subsidy, dating back to the previous century, was eliminated. (Goodale, in the end, secured a $1.6-billion compensation package.) Dairy subsidies were rolled back 30 per cent despite the bitter memories of the 1970s. An immigrant family of four would have to pay $3,150 to get into Canada.

The block transfer had been contentious to the last minute. The Prime Minister's Office worried that the magnitude of the cuts — $7 billion over two years — would destabilize provincial finances and rebound on the federal government, especially in pre-referendum Quebec. The language over national standards also had gone down to the wire. But Martin and Massé had prevailed, both on the size of the cuts and in signalling Ottawa's willingness to allow the provinces more autonomy.

The party that had embraced the public service extended its pay freeze into a fifth year and announced the elimination of 45,000 jobs, a 14-percent reduction in the federal workforce. There would be a generous offer of early retirements and buy-outs. But contractual job guarantees would simply be legislated away. After months of hoisting his cabinet colleagues on a variety of petards, Massé, the Ottawa-area minister who had promised to protect public servants, had been politically prevented from defending his own backyard. "This is by far the largest set of actions in any Canadian budget since demobilization after the Second World War," Martin crowed.

As Arthur Kroeger, the retired mandarin, had said when trying to persuade Martin to take the job, the minister of finance, with the support of the prime minister, enjoyed the means to reform the entire government. Martin had gone one step further, changing the relationship between individual Canadians and the state. In a post-budget analysis Kroeger, deeply impressed, commented that Martin's budget presented the closing bookend on "50 years of activist, interventionist and, above all, self-confident government." The opening bookend had been Mackenzie King's White Paper on Employment and Income in 1945, which had ushered in both the Keynesian era of macroeconomic management and the postwar social agenda. Kroeger did not disguise his astonishment that the Liberals, who had shown no such inclinations when taking office in November 1993 or even through their first budget the following February, had arrived at this particular juncture in history.

"It marks the end of Canada as we know it," Ontario Premier Bob Rae declared upon digesting the budget. Labour leader Nancy Riche pronounced the score Moody's 1, Canadians 0.

The suspicions of left-wing Liberals that Martin had designed his prudent economic assumptions with a mind to going beyond 3 per cent proved out. In the background documents to the budget, Finance acknowledged that using the less conservative assumptions of private economic forecasters, the deficit would actually fall to $19 billion in 1996–97, 2.3 per cent of GDP. In his speech, Martin boasted that the downward track established "in this budget will continue in the years thereafter."

Naturally, Martin wrapped up his budget speech with a quote from the old man looking over his shoulder, his father. Larry Hagen, with the help of William Young, the historian who had toiled on the elder Martin's memoirs, had managed to dredge up a relatively favourable quotation from a politician who hadn't liked finance ministers. "Government must not live in the past... Every day there are new needs to be met. If inflation is to be fought, unemployment countered and something done, and soon, to get Canadian prosperity back into its stride, the government must begin to plan ahead — not timidly, not tentatively — but boldly, imaginatively and courageously."

Martin looked around the Commons. "Those words were spoken by my father in 1957 — for his time. That is what I believe we have done today, for ours." Then Paul Martin departed the chamber to face a country in transition.

For the rest of the day and evening, Martin made the rounds of television studios, demonstrating his mastery of the material and his focus on his message. "Is this the beginning of the end of government as we know it?" asked Pamela Wallin on *Prime Time News*. "Are we really going to be talking in the future about what you're not doing as opposed to what you're doing?"

"Not at all," Martin replied, the stock opening answer of the media-coached. "It's the beginning of the beginning for modern government going into a very different era."

Throughout his discussion with Wallin, Martin appeared to be losing a battle to suppress a grin. It had been a terrific day. Once again, he had performed superbly. Of course, he hadn't left much to chance, including his media interviews. Unknown to Wallin, and all his other interlocutors, Martin was wired with an advantage.

That morning, two of his outside communications advisers had departed for Montreal and Toronto. A pair of citizens' panels, one French and one English, had been assembled to view the budget speech and some of Martin's subsequent television interviews. Each member of the group had been equipped with a hand-held gadget called a Perception Analyzer. These allowed them to twirl a dial as they watched to indicate the points they found favourable or unfavourable. Their collective response showed up on a chart, like an ECG.

The technology was relatively new. Elly Alboim had become

acquainted with it during the 1993 election campaign when the CBC had used it to gauge the reactions of a group of viewers to the leaders of the main parties. The segment had made for fascinating television. In his new role, he suggested it to Martin. Several weeks after the minister's October presentation to the Commons Finance Committee, they tested reactions to the various passages. The beauty of the technology was that it provided a precise and instantaneous response as each word was being spoken. You could tell exactly what worked and what didn't.

On budget day, they pushed the envelope by trying out the procedure in real time. As Martin appeared live on television, the English and French groups reacted generally favourably. But when he spoke near the end of his speech about the faults of separation, the graphs headed straight down in Montreal. As he wrapped up, his advisers asked the participants about this reaction. The panellists responded that a budget was an economic statement and that he should not have injected political rhetoric.

Martin's media interviews had all been arranged to take place in the Parliament Buildings. As the results from the focus groups trickled into his office on the fifth floor, O'Leary would run downstairs and brief him between appearances. He then made the necessary adjustments. It was like inside trading on the information highway. In his appearances on the French networks, he refrained from discussing his budget's contribution to national unity.

The next morning, Martin participated in a conference call with 400 clients of the big U.S. brokerage house Salomon Bros. Challenged about the staying power of the government as it got deeper into the electoral cycle, he revealed some of the political thinking behind the budget. Pointing out that the Reform Party constituted his main political opposition in most of Canada, he said his challenge lay not in fending off accusations of being too hard but in proving he was not too soft. "We won this election primarily on our votes in Ontario and western Canada. In virtually every one of those ridings, the Reform Party — this is the far-right party — came second. So when I go into my caucus, what they're looking at is who is their opposition in the next election. And that opposition isn't saying cut less; they're saying cut more. So in terms of the electoral cycle, let me tell you there is going to be no let-up on that. The political imperative in this country, in fact, says there can be no let-up on deficit cutting."

Martin had long been convinced, largely by O'Leary, that while the economic objective was to slay the deficit, bring down interest rates, and promote growth, the political payoff would come through restoration of the Liberal reputation for economic competence. The managerial party had lost that lustre over the previous generation. When Martin was travelling with Chaviva Hošek in preparing the Red Book, he had been struck by how many people, particularly in western Canada, dredged up the subject of Allan MacEachen's 1981 budget as proof that the Liberals knew nothing about running an economy. After the 1995 budget, Martin and O'Leary believed that would change.

Canadians seemed to agree. The Angus Reid Group was out in the field the night after the budget, polling 1,023 Canadians. Sixty-nine per cent thought the government was on the right track, a majority in all regions. That was up from the 55 per cent who had given the thumbs-up to the previous year's budget. Indeed, four in ten Canadians thought the government had moved too slowly on deficit reduction; just one in ten thought it was proceeding too quickly. Reform voters were more favourably disposed towards the budget than any other group.

Canadians understood that the budget would be tough on them personally and on their communities. Nearly six in ten thought it would exacerbate unemployment and would erode the quality of social programs. Even among those brooders, though, two-thirds gave the budget their broad endorsement. And, most important for Jean Chrétien, more people now said they would be likely to vote Liberal. The budget had lifted the party to 63-per-cent popular support, its highest standing yet and a five-point gain in two weeks.

Martin had pulled it off. He was riding higher than any finance minister for generations. Around Ottawa, people spoke of him as the economic prime minister. Even Massé seemed surprised by what his cabinet twin had accomplished. He confessed to a newspaper interviewer that until a few months earlier, he would have given the exercise at best a one-in-five chance of succeeding. Those close to the deliberations of the previous year revelled in the ironic outcome of the 3-per-cent goal. It had been meant to position the party in the moderate but responsible middle of the deficit debate. They had no doubts that the radical budget they had just delivered owed its existence more to an election promise than to the fiscal circumstances of the country. Without the Red Book or the spur of interest rate hikes, few could imagine Martin having ever got it past Chrétien.

Martin would later compare the execution of the 1995 budget to his early days in business. His first job at Power Corporation, he recalled, had involved being parachuted into problem companies to help work out their troubled finances. There Martin first encountered bankers. When the young executive would bring them a plan of action, they would invariably deride it as inadequate. They wanted Power to inject more equity into the business, a demand it habitually refused. "I learned quickly that if you over-promise to the bank and then you can't deliver, the bank loses patience. But if you go in with a plan the bank finds insufficient, you'll have a huge fight, but nine times out of ten they will go along. And if you deliver on your targets in the three- to six-month timeframe, then it will be that much easier the next time out."

When Martin arrived at Finance, he felt that the markets were holding a gun to his head. First, they challenged him over John Crow and then over the 3 per cent. These markets reminded him of the bankers of his younger days. He needed to build confidence in order to regain control. By under-promising and over-delivering, he succeeded. In the aftermath of his second budget, few commentators spoke any more about the inadequacy of the 3-per-cent target.

One year and voluminous amounts of water under the bridge later, Martin returned to the *Globe and Mail* for another post-budget editorial-board meeting. The paper had spent the better part of the previous twelve months savaging him and his party in its editorials and columns. This time, the meeting proved a relaxed, pleasant affair. After the session, Martin and David Olive, the editor of the *Report on Business Magazine*, prepared to go grab a beer. Globe editor-in-chief William Thorsell hurried down the escalator after them. He had a gift for Martin, which he had forgotten to present. In the lobby of the paper's offices, he gave the minister of finance a giant cardboard blow-up of a photograph of him that had appeared on the cover of the February issue of Olive's magazine. All was forgiven.

18

LIBERAL GUILT

In the aftermath of Paul Martin's radical budget, members of Canada's natural governing party searched their souls for the meaning of Liberalism in the 1990s. In small knots around Parliament Hill, social Liberals vacillated between admissions that the finance minister's actions had probably been unavoidable and queasiness about the new Canada being created. After they had gone around briefing the various party caucuses on budget day, the Finance officials had joked that only the Liberals reacted negatively. The jest rang at least partly true, right up into the cabinet.

Ministers like Sheila Copps, Sergio Marchi, David Collenette, Ron Irwin, and David Dingwall, who drew their political inspiration from the social justice rhetoric of the Trudeau years, held heartfelt discussions in corridors and offices about their ineffectiveness as a group as compared with the business Liberals. They had gone into public life to build pyramids. Instead, they found themselves dismantling the edifices of previous Liberal generations. They had been elected to create jobs. Now they had laid off 45,000 public servants. The government to which they belonged had sent strong signals that Ottawa would allow the provinces greater latitude over social policy. Whether in the environment or unemployment insurance or the CBC or human rights, these Liberals could not easily reconcile their values with the record.

Jean Chrétien, the boss himself, added to their misgivings in his first post-budget interview. Asked by CBC Radio host Peter Gzowski on *Morningside* about the changes the Liberals had wrought, Chrétien took a provocatively decentralist line. "For years the provinces said, 'Let us run these programs.' I said, 'Fine, run them.'... This is changing, yeah. It's changing to respond to the requirements of the provinces that they say, 'We need more flexibility.'" As for medicare, Chrétien, one of its great public defenders, shocked fellow Liberals with his minimalist inter-pretation of their most cherished accomplishment. "Nobody loses his home because somebody has a problem with his teeth or his eyes, nor-mally," he remarked before suggesting a reduced role for Ottawa.

The bitter irony was not lost on the social Liberals. By and large, many had supported his leadership because of his association with Trudeau Liberalism. Now he seemed to have abandoned the cause. The Red Book had spoken of a two-track economic policy, "matching a drive for jobs and growth with a comprehensive approach to controlling debt and deficits." What, they asked one another, had happened to the first track? They com-mitted themselves to righting the balance in the back half of the mandate, to returning the government to the jobs track, to the Liberal track.

Not everyone shared the sense of betrayal, however. For a larger group of Liberals, this had been the budget from heaven. Martin enjoyed a wide following in caucus, particularly among the Class of '93. Elected for the first time two years earlier, many from western Canada and suburban or rural Ontario ridings, these MPs tended to be more fiscally conservative than holdovers from the 1980s. Unlike the veteran Liberals, isolated in the time capsule of Parliament Hill, members of the new intake could draw upon their own recent experiences in the private sector or municipal gov-ernment or in almost any other institution in understanding the way ahead for Ottawa. They had lived the reality of doing more with less. They under-stood that global competition had rendered the old rules obsolete. They did not feel particularly threatened by the rise of a new individualism, one highly suspicious of the supposed good deeds of a centralizing Big Brother state. The evident ease with which the budget had gone over with Canadians put the wind in their sails.

Martin had managed matters brilliantly, but a bit of luck always helps. Prairie grain farmers, counting the blessings of unusually high grain prices, resigned themselves quietly to the loss of the Crow Rate subsidy. Public servants failed to muster any sympathy from a general public similarly bat-tered. Even the provinces, deprived of billions in transfer payments but given a one-year grace period, seemed in a stupor.

But mostly Martin had a single person to thank for the acquiescent mood, as he readily confessed at a party on a Saturday night in late March. Members of Parliament were stuck in Ottawa that weekend for an emer-gency sitting to pass back-to-work legislation in a railway strike. The finance minister, asked why so little opposition had materialized in the wake of his budget, offered up a simple two-word answer: Brian Tobin.

On Thursday, March 9, after a four-hour chase through the fog-shrouded north Atlantic, Canadian authorities had fired four bursts of .50-calibre machine-gun fire over the bow of a Spanish fishing vessel called the *Estai*, which had been operating in international waters off the Grand Banks of Newfoundland. Over the next five weeks, as Canada unblinkingly and uncharacteristically stared down the Spaniards and the European Union, Tobin proved himself a superb communicator and brilliant tactician. He turned an obscure, slimy bottom-feeder called the turbot into a symbol of national pride. Internationally, he succeeded in framing the issue in environmental terms. He stood for the conservation of an endangered species against the greedy Spanish fleet. European attempts to portray the dispute as an egregious example of extraterritorial application of domestic law didn't stand a chance.

In New York, at a United Nations conference in the middle of the crisis, Tobin astounded the UN reporters with his rhetorical flights and his telegenic media field trip to view the *Estai*'s illegal nets, which he had ordered shipped down from St. John's and hung on a barge. He so outshone his European opponent in presenting his case that a British journalist working for a Portuguese paper stood up and applauded at the end of a Tobin press conference. You don't necessarily have to agree with him to recognize a great performance, the reporter explained.

Conspiracy theorists, watching the fisheries minister in action, couldn't help but suspect the timing of the turbot war had to be more than a coincidence. Whatever the motivation, a war, even a fish war, did its part in distracting people from the full implications of Martin's handiwork.

Among the troubled social Liberals in cabinet, Sergio Marchi mourned the most deeply. He had been stigmatized, as he had feared, as the father of the modern head tax. The immigration groups, his former friends, were relentless in their criticisms of the $975 landing fee. "I don't see any vestige of Liberalism in this. This could just as easily have come from the Reform Party," said David Matas, president of the Canadian Council for Refugees, plunging the knife into the minister. His associate at the council, Nancy Worsfold, then twisted the blade. "I'd like to know whether Sergio Marchi's father could have paid that much money when he came to Canada." It was the kind of question Marchi had asked himself, indeed the

kind of question nearly all Program Review Committee members had
considered in those tormented months leading up to the budget.

Marchi slipped into a deep post-budget funk. "Is this what being a
Liberal is about?" he would ask repeatedly. His officials got their hands
on a private Insight Canada poll that showed the right-of-landing fee to
be hugely popular, with a 74-per-cent approval rating. Marchi didn't want
to hear about it. He figured that people supported the measure for all the
wrong reasons. Concerned about his depressed state and fearful he might
somehow try to undo their handiwork, his officials would phone downtown
to Finance and the Privy Council Office, prevailing upon their counterparts to get Martin or Jean Pelletier or Chrétien to slap Marchi's back and
remind him of the importance of his initiative to the entire government.

Months would pass before Marchi could rekindle the fire in his belly.
In the autumn, in a dream come true, former New York governor Mario
Cuomo, his political hero, agreed to address a fundraising dinner in
Marchi's riding. His speech was a highly sentimental and personal recount-
ing of the Cuomo family tale, the quintessential story of the immigrant
family striving against the indignities of prejudice and persevering to see
a son become governor of New York. It was Cuomo's story, but it could
just as well have been Marchi's.

Cuomo bemoaned the decline of the ethics of tolerance and compassion in modern politics. Probably the same thing was happening in Canada,
he suggested. "But I'm not going to speak for you, that's Marchi's job —
to make sure these lessons are remembered here in Canada."

The budget was followed two weeks later by the Budget Implementation
Act, Bill C-76. As befits a budget bill, the legislation had been drafted in
secret. It passed through cabinet without a ripple on Tuesday morning,
March 14.

The following day Sheila Copps took a closer look at the legislation
that would turn the budget into law. It almost left her speechless — no
mean feat. Perusing the section on the new block transfer, called the
Canada Social Transfer, she concluded that the principles of the Canada
Health Act, to be embedded in the new bill, had been significantly watered
down in the drafting process. Her natural suspicion of Finance — heightened, like that of other social Liberals in the budget's wake — now
achieved record altitude. Without any debate, without even a rudimentary
discussion around the cabinet table, the Department of Finance, as far as

she could tell, intended to defang federal stewardship over medicare.

She worked the phones, alerting Health Minister Diane Marleau, who had fought long and hard to keep health out of the block transfer in the first place. Marleau often took her lead from Copps and now she, too, became agitated. Health Department officials, however, couldn't credit a conspiracy theory. The budget documents and the budget speech both promoted the Liberals' unswerving commitment to the five principles. Chrétien and Martin had spoken about them at every stop. Even the Finance bureaucrats, never a popular bunch in the eyes of the Health officials, didn't have it in them to be so sneaky.

Copps took her concerns to the prime minister, advising him the government would be "crucified" if the bill was introduced without changes. He gave her the go-ahead, as chair of the cabinet's Social Development Committee, to clear the matter up. She swung into action, suggesting to Martin and Gray that they delay the bill's introduction.

Copps had her detractors in cabinet. But Jean Chrétien could not be numbered among them. He didn't know her well when he left the House of Commons in 1986 or even when she ran against him in 1990. But he came to appreciate her when he returned as leader. Chrétien admired the way she could get under Brian Mulroney's skin. He believed that most of Mulroney's mistakes were forced mistakes, when he lost his control over some provocation or another. And Shrill Sheila, as Mulroney called her, seemed to have an intuitive sense of how to fluster him.

In Copps, Chrétien saw something of himself. He respected her well-honed instincts, consulting her frequently on political issues. "Sheila is a great politician," he said shortly after she resigned over the GST imbroglio in May 1996. He had already decided to return her as deputy PM.

Chrétien felt genuine sympathy for anyone, like Copps, so readily dismissed as a lightweight. He had battled against the same accusations throughout his political career. In the treatment of Copps, he could see the same arrogance of the elites so long directed at him by the francophone notables. For his money, he would take political smarts over sophistication every time. She, in turn, served him loyally. She might bad-mouth others, but her record resounded with a paradoxical mixture of extreme self-interest and absolute fealty to the leader, whether David Peterson or John Turner or Jean Chrétien.

Her relations with others verged on open hostility, however. She was embroiled in constant battles: fighting her officials; fighting her provincial counterparts; fighting her fellow cabinet ministers. You were with her or against her — black or white. As she had in opposition, she worked best when she could identify an enemy, and then blast away. Unlike most politicians, she was not overly perturbed by a lack of universal adulation.

"I always say it's crap if I think so," she acknowledged in a 1995 interview, contrasting herself with some other ministers. "Others butter you up with a lot of buttery words and then trash you anyways. I don't. That's my Achilles' heel, but also my plus." If she had ever taken the Briggs-Myers personality test recommended by psychologists, Copps would have been revealed as an extroverted, intuitive, feeling, judgmental person — with little nuance in any of the categories. Her inclination on issues almost always relied on intuition — usually solid — rather than reflection. As a consequence, she tended not to do her homework, eschewing knowledge in favour of what she called common sense.

Copps didn't get along particularly well with Paul Martin or with the hot rookie in Justice, Allan Rock. The conventional wisdom in Ottawa was that she was determined to undermine any potential leadership rivals, although clearly with Martin's people, who spared no opportunity to trash her, it cut both ways. She even sparred with Brian Tobin, a fellow Rat Pack graduate and one of her best friends in cabinet. Tobin, as part of program review, decided to get the Fisheries Department out of the regulation of freshwater lakes, dumping it on the provinces. He wanted to replace the Fisheries Act with an Oceans Act. But the Environment Department depended on the Fisheries Act for its legal authority to regulate the ecology of the Great Lakes. This conflicting interest strained their friendship. At one committee meeting, Copps startled others in the room by screaming at Tobin.

To some extent, Copps's various battles, with Roy MacLaren at International Trade or with Natural Resources Minister Anne McLellan, reflected the natural tensions of an environment minister operating in a government so heavily committed to a jobs and growth agenda. In the Red Book, one of the eight chapters had been devoted exclusively to sustainable development — Paul Martin had been environment critic at the time and had thrown his energies at that subject with the same intensity he would later focus on the deficit. But devotion to environment issues had not survived the transition to government. Only very late in her time in the portfolio, after she read an article by Harvard University business guru Michael Porter called "Green and Competitive," would Copps attempt to reconcile her activities with the government's pro-business orientation.

As a Trudeau-style Liberal, Copps also found herself in conflict with the government's desire to pursue "national reconciliation" through greater cooperation with the provinces. While outsiders tended to view the natural schism of the Chrétien government on left-right lines, in fact the more profound debate took place between advocates of a strong central government like Copps, and those like Massé, who thought that devolving power would situate government services closer to the people. Massé had targeted environmental protection early on as a natural area for such cooperation. He liked to offer up as an example of wastefulness the fact that both levels of government sent inspectors to measure effluent from pulp mills. Copps didn't defend duplication, but nor did she necessarily accept the provinces as the logical repository for such responsibilities.

In June 1995, environment ministers from across the country met in Haynes Junction, Yukon, to sign a major federal-provincial agreement on environmental management. But Copps balked at the last minute and refused to approve the pact. The provincial ministers were livid. Soon the bad blood spilled into public, particularly in a series of nasty exchanges with Alberta Environment Minister Ty Lund, whom Copps accused of having made racist statements in a private meeting. All this did little to aid the cause of the Chrétien government's desire for national reconciliation.

At least these incidents had a point. Copps thought the bureaucrats were interested more in going along to get along than in advancing the cause of environmental protection. But her gratuitous ill treatment of Anne McLellan, a frequent adversary, and Revenue Minister David Anderson at a Social Development Committee meeting on child support late in 1995 could not be so easily understood. The pair normally sat on cabinet's Economic Development Committee, but both had a strong interest in the child support issue and chose, as ministers sometimes do, to attend the meeting. Upon seeing them enter, Copps, in a stage whisper, asked the Privy Council official serving the committee, "What are those right-wing ministers doing here?" The embarrassed official, at the behest of the chairwoman, requested the departure of the two interlopers.

After Copps alerted Martin to the flaw in the budget bill, the finance minister asked David Dodge to investigate. Dodge concluded that Copps had indeed caught something that could embarrass the government. Martin phoned her at home that evening and said he understood that she didn't accept calls from deputy ministers, but that Dodge was with him and wanted to clear up the matter. The deputy got on the phone and apologized.

He insisted Finance had no hidden agenda, chalking up the matter to a snafu.

On Thursday, Marleau and her advisers gathered in her office to work on the offending section. Copps kept in constant touch by phone. With the text in their hands and Finance on the defensive, they decided to push to add the word "health" to the Canada Social Transfer. The Health Department hadn't wanted any part of the new block transfer, but if others chose to lump it together with post-secondary education and social assistance, the department insisted the health component be advertised in the title.

The block transfer was rechristened in Marleau's office the Canada Social and Health Transfer. Officials faxed the changes to Gray. Then Sharon Schollar, Marleau's executive assistant, suddenly realized that the new name wouldn't do. The acronym CSHT would be pronounced C-SHIT. They flipped around the words "social" and "health," turning the transfer into the CHST.

Key questions surrounding the CHST had been left unanswered as it was forged in the crucible of budgetary confusion and secrecy. Would the cash portion continue to shrink after 1997–98, or would Ottawa impose a cash floor in order to maintain a measure of influence over social programs? If there was to be a cash floor, when and at what level? How would the available cash be allocated among provinces, on a population formula or with consideration of the relative strengths of provincial economies? This was a matter of extreme importance to Ontario and British Columbia, who complained the existing system treated them unfairly. What conditions would Ottawa attach to the transfers and how would it enforce them? Nobody wanted to stir up a hornet's nest in the budget run-up; as often happens in politics, ambiguity had ruled the day.

The cash floor quickly percolated to the top of the social Liberals' concerns. They thought that if Ottawa guaranteed that it would always maintain the transfer at a reasonable level, the provinces would stop treating the federal government as a lame duck. The Chrétien government had drawn its line in the social policy sand at medicare; it said it would stop any province from introducing two-tier health care. But as its contribution to health care dwindled, provinces increasingly resented the dictates of Big Brother. Alberta had openly challenged Diane Marleau by allowing private, for-profit clinics to charge facility fees to users while collecting public funds. Now, with the massive cuts to transfers contained in the budget, social Liberals despaired that they would be without clout — if not right away, certainly in a few years — to enforce provisions of the Canada Health Act.

Keith Banting, a Queen's University academic with impeccable social policy credentials, caused many Liberals to sit up and take notice in his post-budget testimony before the Commons Finance Committee. He said Canadians would never stand for the open and explicit repeal of the Canada Health Act. But the quiet erosion of the cash transfer led to the same end — by stealth. In May, the Liberal majority on the committee, hardly a left-winger among them, sent a powerful message to their own government, recommending that Finance "commit that there will be a cash component to the CHST in the future, and that it will be sufficient to enforce compliance." Paul Martin took notice.

Marcel Massé had been attracted to the block transfer because he thought (incorrectly, as it turned out) it could be sold in Quebec as a decentralizing measure: the federal government would cut some of the strings on social programs, disproving the charge that Ottawa always rejected Quebec's aspirations. The budget preserved only the five principles of medicare and the condition that provinces not discriminate against new residents applying for welfare. It eschewed use of the word "standards" (which implied enforcement), mandating Axworthy instead to develop, "through mutual consent, a shared set of principles and objectives." Those two seemingly innocuous but vague words, "mutual consent," would provide the battleground over the following weeks between Liberal centralists and devolutionists.

Axworthy, who would be wrongly pegged as a defender of the status quo, actually didn't mind the block transfer. He had long advocated greater clarity between federal and provincial spheres of influence in his social security review and now claimed at least partial paternity of the CHST, which he saw as an offspring of his failed Big Bang. In the words of one of his officials, he viewed the block transfer as "a neat, albeit brutal, federal-provincial clarifier." Indeed, he told social policy groups throughout the spring that national standards had really been a figment of their imagination and that the new system would actually allow him to impose greater accountability.

Axworthy believed he had an approach superior to the methods of the past, something he called a social audit. He had borrowed the idea in part from an annual report on foreign trade practices produced by the office of the U.S. trade representative, which exhaustively catalogued trade violations in hopes of shining a public spotlight on the perpetrators. In exchange for Ottawa's money, Axworthy wanted the provinces to provide an accounting of their social programs, measuring them against a variety of performance benchmarks. The information alone could be powerful in exposing instances of provinces failing to make the grade or spending foolishly. But Axworthy also wanted to be able to impose fiscal penalties if provinces fell short.

Which is where he and Massé parted company. Clearly, it would be impossible to persuade a separatist government in Quebec — indeed any Quebec government — to sign on. Axworthy hoped he could work with a majority of the other provinces. Or merely on a one-to-one basis with those willing to negotiate. But Massé would not countenance any approach that could result in the isolation of Quebec.

It all came down to the meaning of "mutual consent" — the words that had been inscribed in the budget after hours and hours of argument. Martin and Massé took mutual consent to mean that no conditions would be introduced without the approval of each and every province. But nobody had formally conferred such a definition on the term. In the French version, because of sloppy drafting, the phrase looked even more suspicious.

With the referendum approaching, the Quebec press suddenly found a national unity story in the budget bill. Although the social Liberals loathed the bill for its devolutionist bent, the Bloc Québécois had argued in the weeks after the budget that it actually represented a centralizing thrust. One of the subsections stated that national standards could be maintained "in the operation of other social programs," and a different section defined social programs to include post-secondary education. Combined with the ambiguity over mutual consent — and the accidental substitution of the vaguer term in French — a case could be made that Ottawa had equipped itself with the means to intrude into post-secondary education.

On March 31, Chantal Hébert, the influential *La Presse* reporter, made just such a case after consulting two lawyer acquaintances. That set alarm bells ringing among Quebec ministers. The CHST, a supposed referendum asset, threatened to degenerate into a serious liability. Massé contacted Martin to discuss remedial measures. Over the next few weeks, *Le Devoir* also picked up on the theme. When Parliament returned from its Easter break, the Bloc Québécois went back on the attack. In high dudgeon, the Bloc accused the Liberals of trying to sneak through Parliament "a centralizing assault, the likes of which we have not seen since the shameful patriation of 1982" — precisely the historical parallel Massé so anxiously wanted to avoid. In early April, the Privy Council Office, asked to sort out the confusion, stated that cabinet had never determined whether mutual consent meant unanimous consent. Axworthy still had some wiggle room.

By late April, with a referendum perhaps less than two months away, Chrétien's exasperated Quebec ministers searched for ways to shut down the Bloc. The ministers discussed amending the legislation to more explicitly restrict Axworthy's manoeuvring room. To Axworthy, the block transfer had been motivated by fiscal needs, not as a means of refashioning federal-provincial relations. The budget specifically placed him — the minister of human resources — in charge of the dossier. He deeply resented Quebec ministers working his beat.

On May 1, the Bloc raised the pressure a notch by giving notice in the House of Commons that it would introduce a motion the following day denouncing the federal government for restricting the provinces "to the role of mere consultant by imposing on them new national standards for all social programs... which will enable the federal government to interfere even more in such areas as health, post-secondary education and social assistance, all of which come under exclusive provincial jurisdiction." The Liberals learned about the Bloc motion at suppertime. The machinery of government snapped into action: it was decided that Axworthy and David Walker, Martin's parliamentary secretary, would speak to the matter. Officials stayed late into the night preparing their remarks.

By this time, Finance had already drafted proposed amendments to ward off the Bloc's objections. It had settled on a definition of mutual consent that stated that only provinces agreeing to new shared principles and objectives would be bound by them. Unanimity would not be required and nothing would be imposed. The agitations of the Quebec ministers had resulted in the Privy Council Office briefing Chrétien on the matter in the last few days of April. PCO expected him to approve the amendments, at which time it intended to convene a meeting to hammer out the final details with Lloyd Axworthy, Sheila Copps, Herb Gray, Diane Marleau, Marcel Massé, and Lucienne Robillard, the new labour minister brought into the government to lead the referendum fight. But now the Bloc motion intervened.

The morning of the Bloc motion, Tuesday, May 2, was a cabinet day, so the Quebec ministers gathered at 8 a.m. for their weekly pre-cabinet tête-à-tête, the so-called Tuesday-morning group. Although they enjoyed no official status as a cabinet committee, the Tuesday-morning group had grown increasingly influential over the previous months, a fact that bred deep resentment among ministers from other parts of the country. When the Quebec ministers, who were always joined by Jean Pelletier, learned the game plan for handling the Bloc motion, they panicked. They could hardly believe the task of responding would fall to two Manitoba MPs, neither with a strong grasp of French or of Quebec politics. Moreover, they couldn't be sure that Axworthy would not use the opportunity to expand rather than contract his reach. Agreeing that the issue needed to be put to rest once and for all, they cut off early and marched next door to see Chrétien before cabinet.

Axworthy was summoned from upstairs and found himself jammed into Chrétien's office with the most senior Quebeckers in the government. Axworthy had no objection to being bumped for a Quebec minister; Martin and Massé would replace him and Walker. But there was more to it than that. Although parliamentary procedure precluded the government from introducing any amendments at that point, the Quebec ministers intended to read the drafts into the record right then and there. Three out of four were basically cosmetic, but even Finance had acknowledged in a private memo that the fourth, which ruled out any future national standards, would probably cause Axworthy problems.

As cabinet gathered for its 10 a.m. start, Martin, who almost never spoke in government debates, headed downstairs to the Liberal lobby. By all accounts, he was in a foul mood. He liked to practise his speeches, to roll the thoughts around in his head until he had shaped them into a form with which he felt comfortable. By the time Martin arrived, Lucien Bouchard was already on his feet, pinning back the ears of the centralizing Liberals.

Giles Gherson, Axworthy's policy adviser, was down in the lobby carrying a copy of the remarks originally intended for his boss. In his previous incarnation as a journalist, Gherson had come to know Martin fairly well and had heard stories about his explosive temper. But he had never witnessed an eruption. He approached the finance minister, who was without any prepared remarks, and offered him Axworthy's speech. Martin physically brushed Gherson aside: "I don't need your goddamn speech," he growled. Then his assistant, Ruth Thorkelson, rushed in with a copy of the remarks Finance had prepared for David Walker. Martin took one look and exploded in a torrent of abuse, stopping everyone in their tracks. The speech was largely in English. How could he respond to a Bloc motion in English? Officials back in the department were ordered to translate the remarks, and fast. The place was a madhouse. As they completed a page, they sent it directly to a fax machine in the Liberal lobby, where it was run to Martin, who was sitting in the House listening to Bouchard. He made minor adjustments. The final pages didn't arrive until after he rose to speak at 10:35.

Martin characterized the Bloc motion as an empty shell bearing no relation to the reality of the situation. Under the new system, there would be fewer, not more, conditions. But in order to clarify matters, both he and Massé would introduce amendments. "The minister of human resources development will invite all provincial governments to work together, through mutual consent," Martin stated. "This means that absolutely no conditions will be imposed to the provinces. Mutual consent means mutual consent. Both parties will have to be in agreement."

Later in the debate, after Question Period, Massé, taking his turn, painted Axworthy further into the corner. Except in health care, no standards would be demanded of the provinces, he reiterated, other than that they not impose a residency requirement on welfare applicants. He made sure there would be no attempt to push federal influence forward into post-secondary education. And he assured the House that further discussion would be based on "principles and objectives," not on the potentially more intrusive "standards."

Right until the end, Axworthy tried to get Massé to ease up. Standing under the south archway of the Liberal lobby, the pair went back and forth in quiet but intense discussion. Axworthy seeking breathing space and Massé refusing to cede it. By the end of the day, any hopes of using the CHST to push the central government forward had been resoundingly rebuffed.

By late spring, despite their continued high standing in the polls, fractures could be detected throughout Liberal ranks. Justice Minister Allan Rock was battling religious and rural Liberal backbenchers over both gay rights and gun control. Three government MPs voted against his gun bill on second reading, and more threatened to break ranks when it came back to the House. Chrétien stripped the trio of their committee work, sending a strong message that whatever arguments occurred in the family were to stay in the family. He demanded loyalty to the party that had got them elected.

On April 26, Chrétien devoted his wrap-up caucus speech to the discipline issue, warning that those voting against the party would pay a price. "I need to look like a leader. I cannot afford to look like I can be pushed around," he said, linking their unruliness both to his own popularity and to the prospects for federalism in Quebec. He told his MPs that he had voted for abortion even though he personally opposed it. That was the mark of a mature political party, he insisted. If they succumbed to single interests, they would end up with the credibility problems of the U.S. Democrats.

The budget, despite its political success, continued to roil the Liberals. A prominent MP, strolling on the Sparks Street Mall, provided a succinct reading of the caucus mood in early June. "Varying levels of discomfiture, I would say." That same week, a rookie MP from northern New Brunswick named Pierrette Ringuette-Maltais shamed many of her colleagues with a stirring speech in caucus about the meaning of Liberalism. She told fellow MPs that her mother had never learned to read. But here was her daughter, a member of Parliament, thanks to the equal opportunity policies of former Liberal premier Louis Robichaud. Did Liberals still believe in such values? she wondered. Veteran Montreal MP Warren Allmand, a former cabinet colleague of Chrétien's, stated publicly that he still believed in Liberal values. That was why he intended to vote against the budget.

Paul Martin was sensitive to the unease in Liberal ranks; he probably felt some of it himself. He bristled at suggestions that he had turned his back on classic Liberalism. The dissent, especially that part of it directed at him, disturbed him greatly.

Martin decided to tackle the issue head-on with a major speech in Ottawa, where it would attract media coverage. He put his top advisers to work on the address, including Peter Nicholson and speechwriter Larry Hagen. Typically, Martin practised and practised, even trying out an early version of the speech before a live audience, but without any national media, at a May 23 fundraiser in York North, in the Toronto area.

At about the same time, Maude Barlow, a former Liberal who headed the left-wing Council of Canadians, delivered a blistering attack on the Martin budget to the annual meeting of a non-profit housing association. The speech, entitled "Straight Through the Heart: The Liberals Abandon the Just Society," put forth the arguments she would make in her book of the same name. Half an hour after Barlow returned to her office, she got a message from Terrie O'Leary. Soon she heard from Richard Mahoney, a close friend who also happened to be part of Martin's inner circle. She agreed to sit down for dinner with the finance minister later in the summer.

On June 22, Martin staked out his territory for fellow Liberals and the media before the Ottawa-Carleton Board of Trade. He set his speech in the context of his own family, saying off the top that his son had recently been reading Paul Martin Sr.'s memoirs and had asked how the Liberalism his father had set out in the recent budget differed from his grandfather's Liberalism. "[To] those who feel we have turned our backs on our past — let me make two points," Martin told the audience. "First, economic failure has never been a tenet of Liberalism; second, Liberalism is a belief in a better future: it is not a set of programs fixed in time." In his father's time, the task of Liberalism was to define itself in a period of abundance; today, his obligation was to define it in a period of austerity. But deficit reduction, while essential, did not begin to embrace the Liberal vision, he stated. It only made that vision possible. "Our goal in beating the deficit is not simply to make the bond market feel better. Our goal is to be in a position to tell the bond market to get lost."

Next on his agenda came Maude Barlow. Despite her absolute opposition to everything Martin had authored in government, Barlow actually felt great affection for him. They had co-chaired a series of policy conferences in the mid-1980s and she, like so many other women, had been impressed by his charm. Once upon a time, he had been a founding member of her nationalist organization — in a different phase in his life — and he had delivered the keynote address at its annual meeting in 1989. "He's impossible not to like," she declared.

Liking him as she did, she often found herself rationalizing his behaviour. She thought of Martin as the pilot of the *Enola Gay*, the warplane that dropped the atomic bomb on Hiroshima. In abstract terms, she reasoned, he knew he had unleashed a powerful weapon that would wreak havoc below. But he could never truly imagine the extent of the devastation. She persuaded herself that he had no real appreciation of the battered women's shelters and children's museums and handicapped workshops that would be destroyed by his actions. Bomber Martin was just too high up.

They finally broke bread in July. Martin asked Barlow to think of the country as a shelter for homeless men that found itself in hock. It could choose to continue as normal until the whole place closed down, or it could shut a wing immediately in order to ensure its future. But Barlow came at it from an entirely different perspective. Where had the debt of this homeless shelter come from? she demanded. Why couldn't it find a different way to relieve it? Why didn't people care any more about donating to it? What had happened to the political culture? They debated back and forth, the cut and thrust that Martin so loved.

"It was a fascinating evening," she said afterwards. "He's a very nice man who doesn't live on the ground." He had failed to win a convert in Barlow. But that he had cared enough to bother spoke volumes about Paul Martin.

19

THE LEGEND OF
MARY SIMMS

While others on the party's left stewed in their springtime torpor, the Chrétien government's best-known social Liberal felt renewed. Lloyd Axworthy found no joy, of course, in surveying the wrecked dreams of welfare and post-secondary education reforms. But in overhauling unemployment insurance, he had at least one institution left to bash with his handbag. Over the months to follow, he would again demonstrate his absolute abhorrence of the status quo, confirming he was more the reformer than the left-winger.

This final chapter in Axworthy's term as human resources minister had begun the morning after the February budget. While his grieving department tallied the casualties from Martin's blitzkrieg — its program spending cut by 35 per cent, 5,000 employees to lose their jobs — Axworthy had already moved on. "Yesterday's budget was unquestionably a seminal occasion, a once-in-a-generation event," he told a luncheon audience of information technology specialists at Ottawa's Westin Hotel. "The times they are a-changing."

He recounted for the audience one of the early scenes from the film *The Madness of King George*. The firebrand politician and opposition leader of the day, Charles James Fox, is strolling through the halls of Westminster alongside the dour prime minister, William Pitt. "Do you admire anything, Mr. Pitt?" Fox asks. "A balance sheet," replies the stolid Pitt. "I like a good balance sheet."

In addition to his departmental cuts, the budget had set out a new balance sheet for UI, ordering up the further cut in benefits of 10 per cent — about $1.6 billion — to be in place for Canada Day 1996. According to Axworthy, half those savings — $800 million — would come back to him for new employment programs. He would bundle that princely sum with other leftover money to create something he called the Human Resources Investment Fund. HRIF (the acronym conjured up images of someone clearing their throat) would concentrate all its fire on just two goals: employment programs for jobless Canadians and the battle against child poverty. (In short order, the second objective would again fall victim to jurisdictional concerns; children were seen as a provincial responsibility.)

In laying out his thinking, Axworthy took a couple of gratuitous swipes at his shell-shocked department, giving full cry to his decades-long loathing of the Ottawa bureaucracy. His speech derided Human Resources' panoply of services as an "alphabet soup of bureaucratic command-and-control programs." He likened these offerings to barnacles and catacombs. "Well, all that's going out the window," he vowed.

The officials, licking their wounds across the river in Hull, could hardly believe the news reports. They had shared his passion for the social security review, working their tails off in response to his whims. Now not only had the budget crushed the effort, but thousands of them would end up on the dole themselves. And their minister — the alphabet-soup king himself — was publicly dumping on them. Jean-Jacques Noreau, Axworthy's deputy, fired off a note to the minister blasting him for his "totally unacceptable" remarks.

On the surface, Axworthy looked to have been as badly burned as anyone by the cuts to his departmental programs. But his success in fending off Martin's advances on UI provided a saving grace unavailable to any other minister. Industry Minister John Manley had no new pot of money to refinance his Defence Industry Productivity Program. Ralph Goodale could not replenish his farm support programs. But Axworthy could dip into the $16-billion UI fund to make himself whole again. "I may have lost the dough in the budget," he remarked later, "but I kept myself in business for another day."

Axworthy didn't merely want to tinker with UI in the grand tradition of two decades of timid ministers. He intended to give birth to a reform of the breadth and scope of the one that Labour Minister Bryce Mackasey had bulldozed through in 1971. Mackasey's generous nature and the era of plenty had transformed UI from an insurance policy into an entitlement for those who, by dint of circumstance, did not work year-round. Year after year, the same individuals would file their claims, often paying premiums for as little as eight weeks and collecting benefits the rest of the year — Loto 8-44, as the system came to be known on the east coast.

But in the new era of less is more, the 1970s Liberal concept of universality gave way to a new credo: "mutual responsibility." Governments no longer accepted sole responsibility for society's ills; individuals would have to bear the brunt, too. Axworthy set out to alter the system so that it rewarded those who squeezed out an extra week or even hour of work and penalized regular users. In so doing, he offered both a carrot and a stick. The carrot could be found in the move to an hourly instead of weekly formula to qualify for UI, which provided incentives to work additional hours and, for the first time, covered part-time workers. The stick had two sides: a so-called intensity clause, which would ratchet down benefits for repeat users of the system; and a new method for calculating benefits that would average down benefits for those who couldn't put together at least twenty weeks of work. Seasonal workers, whom Axworthy had been accused of stigmatizing in his social security review, would suffer the most. In these changes, he would find the $1.6 billion in cuts.

Axworthy's reform would also come with a good-news element. He intended to shift the emphasis of UI from providing the unemployed with financial support towards providing them with the means to support themselves. This would entail investing in human capital: the so-called active measures approach so fleetingly mentioned in the Red Book and endorsed internationally by the Organization for Economic Co-operation and Development. The active measures — such things as wage subsidies to employers, training programs, and aid to help the unemployed start their own businesses — represented the Liberal part of the reform, the part that truly excited Axworthy. He would be on the leading edge of policy. It would take money, of course. But the budget, Axworthy proclaimed, gave him $800 million to work with.

Or did it? The budget papers didn't say so explicitly. They spoke of "savings" of 10 per cent from UI reform. But 10 per cent of what: the $16 billion the program paid out in 1995–96, or the $12-billion payout projected for the year the UI legislation would take effect? And whose pocket would the savings go into? In the weeks after the February budget, it became clear that Martin wanted the entire sum for deficit reduction. The officials in Finance viewed Axworthy's repeated statements about *his* $800 million as an ill-concealed attempt at wish fulfilment. As far as they were concerned, if Axworthy wanted $800 million, he could cut more deeply into UI benefits, a prospect that didn't cause much lost sleep at Esplanade Laurier.

The opposing interpretations over the numbers so frustrated other ministers that they walked out of a cabinet committee meeting on UI in late May demanding that Martin and Axworthy come to an understanding before deliberations proceeded. The pair remained behind with Eddie Goldenberg, Chaviva Hošek, and Suzanne Hurtubise, a Privy Council official. Ultimately, after much haggling, Finance agreed to accept just $1.2 billion for the deficit fight, the lower of the two possible 10-per-cent figures. But that meant Axworthy had to reduce benefits by $2 billion, not $1.6 billion, in order to generate his $800 million for human investments.

With Paul Martin now mollified, Axworthy found himself engaged with a new foe — less powerful perhaps, but every bit as resolute and probably even more resourceful.

By the late spring of 1995, when he turned his attention fully to Axworthy's UI plans, Brian Tobin had already catapulted himself into celebrity status with his handling of the fish war with Spain. Brash, passionate, and blessed with the lyricism of a native Newfoundlander, Tobin quickly established himself as Axworthy's main antagonist on UI. Day after day, week after week, from May to December, these two veterans of the left of the party bobbed and weaved, Axworthy with his eye on the big picture of changing the economic behaviour of Atlantic Canada, Tobin focussed on the deleterious effects on the little guy.

Tobin pushed Axworthy to the wall, and kept pushing. Often he relied upon surrogates. In caucus, a volunteer army of Atlantic MPs was at his beck and call. He worked closely as well with the Atlantic premiers, particularly New Brunswick's Frank McKenna. Axworthy had been in government a long time and had witnessed plenty of cabinet battles. But he had never seen anyone as relentless as Tobin. "It was highly unusual," he said.

Tobin had been raised on a U.S. Air Force base in Newfoundland, and had schooled himself in the American approach to conflict. He spoke openly of his admiration for the American tendency to be, as he said, in your face. "They express their self-interest clearly and unabashedly," he stated. "Americans will generally take a situation as far as they can take it."

That pretty well summed up the fisheries minister himself. The temples had greyed and he had surprised his colleagues with his sense of fiscal maturity, but his pleasure at the gamesmanship of politics remained intact and, fiscal responsibility notwithstanding, he never compromised his advocacy of the interests of his hard-luck province. He drew his line around what he regarded as certain core values — among which unemployment insurance was prominent. A cynic might have suggested — and there were several around the cabinet table — that his core values had to do with what hurt or helped Newfoundland and, by extension, its favourite son in Ottawa. But to Tobin, just because something was good politics didn't mean it wasn't also the right thing.

Nothing builds credibility among politicians like political success, and Brian Tobin had chalked up more political success than even Paul Martin. The fish war had turned him into the hottest political property in Ottawa, generating a standing ovation from journalists and MPs at the annual press gallery dinner in May. On closer examination, however, his performance, although brilliant in parts, was spotty in others. Tobin excelled at the grand gesture and could seduce a microphone at a thousand paces. His willingness and ability to make his case publicly put tremendous pressure on his cabinet and bureaucratic adversaries. In the run-up to the fish war he brought boundless energy to the task of grinding down the resistant officials in Foreign Affairs, and he understood implicitly the buttons to push in convincing Jean Chrétien of the righteousness of Canada's course.

But it was difficult to ascertain Tobin's end game. At every step along the way, his instincts told him to escalate the war. When the Europeans missed deadlines or flouted his dictates, he agitated to ratchet up the pressure with more boat seizures. Chrétien stopped him.

In fact, the fish war represented Jean Chrétien's finest moment, as much as or more so than Brian Tobin's. The two had a good deal in common. Both were guided by their instincts, and both viewed the world through the most political of prisms. Like Chrétien, Tobin had come to the House of Commons at a very young age, in his case twenty-five, and quickly distinguished himself. Chrétien relied upon Tobin for political and communications advice on matters ranging far from his fisheries portfolio. Chrétien didn't begrudge Tobin his ambition; he respected his political smarts and paid close attention to his views.

Tobin had a story he loved to tell whenever introducing Jean Chrétien: in the worst of storms, he'd say, the captain of the ship would turn the wheel over to the most experienced seaman to bring the crew home to safe harbour. Now Chrétien, the old hand with the seasoning to know when to fish and when to cut bait, demonstrated the value of the seasoning Tobin lacked.

Throughout the fish war, Chrétien proved himself secure enough as a political leader to allow Tobin the spotlight. But he didn't hesitate to reel in his cocksure minister when he sensed him overstepping the bounds. Even while Tobin waged the war, Chrétien charged Gordon Smith, the deputy minister of foreign affairs who had previously been stationed in Brussels, with making the peace. "The guy who controlled the game was the prime minister," one of his cabinet ministers remarked after the fish war ended. "Brian wanted to seize a second and a third and perhaps a fourth boat, but the prime minister said, 'We've done enough.'"

Chrétien employed one of his favourite analogies, the one about Jacques Plante, the 1950s goaltender with the Montreal Canadiens, in rendering his judgment. He told Tobin that he was well positioned, the goal was blocked. He should force his opponent to make the next move. Chrétien was no more a strategist than Tobin, but he understood instinctively that Canada's interests did not lie in a protracted and bitter row with an ally like the European Union. Success would not be measured by the number of impounded ships. Canada, less than one-tenth the size of the EU, would get hurt. "My gut feeling is we've gone as far as we can. I don't want to start a war," Chrétien told a group of Liberal MPs in the midst of the crisis. Later, he explained the need to prevent a trade war "because that can cost jobs."

Ultimately Gordon Smith, Chrétien's diplomatic envoy, brought home an honourable if imperfect peace pact. But if Tobin had not pushed the envelope on an issue that had defied the ministrations of the foreign service professionals for the better part of a decade, there never would have been negotiations, let alone a deal. Tobin, to borrow the words of baseball slugger Reggie Jackson, was the straw who stirred the drink.

Still flush with success two months after the *Estai*, he prepared to turn his energies against Lloyd Axworthy's UI plans. Tobin, like most Atlantic Canadian politicians, lacked Axworthy's faith in training and other such programs. He had seen the government of Canada produce too many hairdressers in remote Newfoundland outports. Axworthy seemed to think that if you trained people, jobs would come. The Atlantic politicians preferred the jobs up front. Until then, they would fight to maintain benefit levels.

After Martin and Axworthy settled on the money in late May, the proposed UI bill went to a special joint cabinet committee of social and economic development ministers, with veteran André Ouellet in the chair. In contrast to his sullen performance in the social security review débâcle, Axworthy worked the room fairly well, quickly responding to the points raised in committee. He had a powerful package in hand, one aimed at breaking with the entitlement mentality. By now, the referendum in Quebec had been postponed from June to the fall. Axworthy wanted to get out in front of it. As he sailed through the committee, it looked like he might make it. After several weeks of hearings, Ouellet gave the UI package approval to go to full cabinet.

Tobin, taking note of Axworthy's success in the committee, chose not to attend the final meetings. It was a clever tactic. Normally, members of the committee, having had plenty of opportunity to express themselves already, did not speak to an issue at full cabinet. By staying away, Tobin could declare himself outside the committee consensus, permitting him to rejoin the battle at full cabinet.

At the end of June, Tobin made his move. Chrétien had scheduled one of his thrice-yearly cabinet retreats for June 26 and 27. Axworthy's UI plans would be on the agenda and Chrétien himself would be in the room. Tobin had gone to the extraordinary lengths of retaining his own UI expert to run numbers for him, a former Finance official named Heather Robertson. She worked through Axworthy's cabinet documents and created case studies for Tobin. They had the inspiration to put names to these creations. An imaginary woman named Mary Simms was about to become Tobin's most effective weapon.

Liberal cabinet retreats are held on the ninth floor of the Lester B. Pearson Building, home of the Foreign Affairs Department. The room, with its view across the river into Quebec, had been designed for large diplomatic receptions. On days of a cabinet session, officials would draw curtains around a portion of the room and set up a rectangular box of tables.

When the agenda turned to UI, Axworthy, seated as usual two chairs to the left of the prime minister, launched into a detailed explanation of his reform plans. It sounded well thought out, tough, but Liberal. Then Tobin pounced, saying he had some data that suggested the impacts could be far more severe than Axworthy was saying. Seated at the far end from Axworthy, on the short end of the rectangle, he proceeded to spin a sad tale about the invented Mary Simms.

Simms worked in a fish plant in his riding on the northwest coast of Newfoundland, managing to scratch together twelve weeks of work a year, just enough to qualify for UI. Axworthy's proposal to base her benefits on a twenty-week work period, even though she had actually worked only twelve, would reduce her UI payments precipitously. Moreover, his intensity clause, under which repeat users would be penalized, would put her on a downward spiral towards absolute poverty. Axworthy had said that nobody would receive less than $100 a week under his proposal. But Tobin showed how, over time, her benefits would be ground down to $82 a week. Nobody could live on that, he insisted. She would be worse off on UI than on welfare.

Alarmed, ministers wanted to know how anyone could survive on $82. Axworthy, thrown on the defensive, challenged Tobin's assumptions. Tobin had presented a worst-case scenario that failed to take into account the more lenient treatment of low-income recipients. But Axworthy hadn't been prepared for such a blindsiding. The mood in the room turned against him.

The plight of Mary Simms immediately caught the prime minister's attention. She seemed real. She probably voted Liberal. Her dire predicament had come about through no fault of her own. She wanted to work; there simply wasn't enough opportunity in her remote community. As the member of Parliament for New Brunswick's Beauséjour riding from 1991 to 1993, Chrétien had first-hand experience with seasonal workers, many of them Acadians. He felt a natural empathy with them, with their love of Canada and their economic circumstances.

It fell to Chrétien, in the time-honoured practice of cabinet government, to call the consensus — in other words, to give voice to the will of the cabinet, which did not vote formally. The fate of Axworthy's reform plan rested on the prime minister's reading of the room. The other ministers could tell he had been impressed by Mary Simms. Clearly, he found resonance in her fate, as Tobin had intended. But Mitchell Sharp had taught him that a prime minister must never rule outright against the responsible minister, which could be construed as a sign of non-confidence and possibly lead to a resignation. Instead, he should simply send a matter back for further study. Which is precisely the course Chrétien took. Axworthy's proposal was good, he pronounced, but it needed some more work. They would look at it again in August. With that, Tobin had succeeded in taking the wind out of Axworthy's sails. The human resources minister had been told his offering wasn't good enough, but hadn't been told what it would take to bring it up to scratch. Tobin now had the wind at his back.

In the aftermath of the meeting, the protagonists held an acrimonious meeting in Axworthy's Parliament Hill office. The Newfoundlander trotted out his favourite victim again. He reiterated that the economic circumstances in her community made it impossible for her to find more than twelve weeks of work. Giles Gherson wondered how much work she had found a few years earlier, when it took only ten weeks to qualify for UI. He bet that back then she couldn't get more than the minimum either. Tobin took great umbrage at this attack on the integrity of his imaginary constituent. He gathered up his papers and stomped out of the office.

Over the summer, Axworthy sought to shore up his political support. Gherson and other staffers made the rounds of the Atlantic lobster circuit, hoping to drum up goodwill by explaining their plans to MPs on their own turf. Over the course of UI reform, Axworthy would attend nine Atlantic caucus meetings in spite of the slings and arrows directed his way. He worked hard to come to an accommodation with Tobin, who always maintained that he supported the thrust of the reforms, just not the particulars. Axworthy offered up a panoply of measures meant to offset the impact: a $300-million transitional job creation fund, an extended phase-in period for the measures that would penalize repeat users, and community development projects that would allow individual MPs a say in the allocation of temporary jobs. Axworthy promised as well that his $800 million in active measures would be tilted heavily towards Atlantic Canada.

As part of these remedial measures, his department proposed a special supplement that would put additional cash in the hands of low-income UI recipients with children. Axworthy had never lost his emotional attachment to the notion of a guaranteed annual income, despite its high cost. He excitedly told a number of friends over the summer that his low-income supplement for UI would join with the existing GST tax credit, the child tax benefit, and the guaranteed income supplement for seniors to form major building blocks of the cherished dream of a generation of social Liberals. Over time, the remaining blanks could be filled in.

Axworthy returned to cabinet in late August. In the low-income supplement, he had found his retort to Tobin's poor, woebegone Mary Simms. In order to make his point loud and clear, Axworthy now appropriated the creation of his rival. He kindly furnished Ms. Simms with two children so that she could qualify for the low-income supplement. He happily elaborated on the benefits she thus would enjoy.

But just as Axworthy thought he had overcome the Atlantic dissent, he found himself again bumping up against the political calendar in Quebec. As the summer drew to a close, Ottawa was seized by referendum fever. Thanks to the Tobin ambush in June, he had failed to get far enough out in front of the referendum. It was clear that, one way or another, UI would become a referendum issue. Axworthy argued that it would be better to unveil his plans immediately than to allow speculation to continue and subject them to the darkest possible interpretation. He thought he had a good story to tell with the investments he would make to put Canadians back to work. Why leave Ottawa vulnerable to accusations of having a hidden agenda? But the size of the cuts and the potential jurisdictional squabbles over training made Quebec ministers nervous. They wanted the announcement delayed, and they carried the day.

The government's attentions, for the next couple of months at least, would be turned entirely to Quebec. On September 11, Quebec Premier Jacques Parizeau disclosed that the fate of Canada would be determined on October 30. Lloyd Axworthy would have to wait.

20

STRANGER IN
HIS OWN LAND

If Jean Chrétien had any unshakeable belief after a lifetime in politics, it was that Quebeckers would never vote for separation. As the debate over the formulation of the referendum question formally started in the province's National Assembly in September 1995, the only bets being laid in federalist circles involved how much the No side would win by.

At the outset, few of the key players on the No side imagined they would get less than 55 per cent. A tidy, symbolically important figure would be anything above 58 per cent; with that, they would have a majority of the francophone vote alongside the massive No they would get from anglophones and allophones. Chrétien refused to get into the numbers game. But Eddie Goldenberg thought they would hit 60 per cent at least — the same result as the 1980 referendum — and perhaps even climb as high as 62 per cent. Paul Martin, fresh from an August test run of speeches in rural areas, thought it could be anywhere from 62 to 65 per cent. There was no passion out there for politics, he said, and without that, the Yes side was "dead in the water."

By contrast, the Yes side began the campaign in apparent disarray. In early September, Pierre Drouilly, a prominent sociologist and poll analyst and professed sovereigntist, released a study that concluded, based on past voting trends in elections and the previous referendum, that the Yes side was doomed no matter what it did in the campaign. The sovereigntists were trying to portray themselves as a nonpartisan coalition with roots far beyond the PQ, but those efforts were hurt by the obvious fact that the two main figures, Jacques Parizeau and Lucien Bouchard, didn't think much of each other. Federalists, in fact, considered Parizeau's leadership of the Yes side to be an asset for the No. With his arrogance and upper-class mannerisms, someone joked, he was the sort of person who sends his shirts out to get stuffed rather than starched. Parizeau and Bouchard sniped at each other regularly in private, and their comments and body language towards each other made it obvious that they were allies only by obligation.

On the No side, the formal role of leader fell to Daniel Johnson. The federal Liberals were fairly comfortable with Johnson. He was a prickly customer whom one former colleague described as being "as warm as a tombstone." But he had proven himself an effective campaigner, staving off a Liberal rout in the 1994 provincial election, and he was a staunch federalist. Two weeks after the provincial Liberals lost the election in September 1994, Johnson's people started meeting on a weekly basis with federal officials and advisers to coordinate referendum strategy.

Everyone agreed on the basic thrust. They would hammer away early on economic issues, focussing on the uncertainties and potential losses Quebeckers faced if they voted Yes. That phase of the campaign would culminate in the expected televised debate October 15 between Johnson and Jacques Parizeau, the official leaders of the No and Yes sides. After that, they would switch to emphasizing the positive virtues of Canada. Chrétien would make three speeches in Quebec, along with a fourth public appearance in Montreal hosting a dinner for visiting Chinese Premier Li Peng. In his speeches, Chrétien would appear thoughtful and prime-ministerial, a dramatic switch from the fist-waving figure of 1980 who taunted separatists in deliberately chosen Frenglish by saying that they wanted a new country so they could all be ambassadors, driving in Cadillacs with "un flag sur le hood."

From the start, the Yes side positioned itself as "the camp of change." Change was the mantra of the 1990s. With unemployment levels stuck at around 10 per cent, governments everywhere reducing services, young people leaving university wondering if they would ever have real jobs, and older people wondering if they would still have their present jobs five years from now, defending the status quo was a dangerous strategy in dangerous times.

In the 1980 referendum campaign, the Yes side jumped out to an early lead when the Parti Québécois showed up far better prepared than the opposition Liberals for the debate on the issue in the National Assembly. This time, federalists thought, the battleground would shift to the House of Commons. Some Liberals wanted Parliament adjourned until after the referendum. They weren't sure if it was a good idea for Chrétien to go head-to-head with Lucien Bouchard, the country's most eloquent orator.

Chrétien was spoiling for a scrap with Bouchard. He was tired of Bouchard constantly portraying him as an enemy of the Quebec people, and with his long experience in the House, he was sure Bouchard could not trip him up. At a September 18 caucus meeting, with exactly six weeks to go until the vote, Chrétien was in a feisty mood. As for Bouchard, he said, the fact he would be opposite him in the House was "a good opportunity. I have no lessons to learn in democracy from him." Then he added as an afterthought: "You know I would like to kill these guys, but I have to remain civilized." Civilized, yes, and calm as well. Chrétien's advisers constantly fretted about his combativeness in the House, which they thought played well enough in the chamber but badly on the small box in people's living rooms. They sometimes showed him videotapes of his Question Period performances to illustrate the point.

That day, and the following one as well, Aline Chrétien showed up in the House for Question Period. Friends knew it was something that she always did when she was concerned that her husband was feeling nervous. Very early on, Chrétien made clear to his caucus that when it came to strategy for Quebec, their role was to listen and obey, not to suggest or question. Whenever MPs pressed to make a contribution, he rolled out the example of how Manitoba MP Jon Gerrard and his wife had spent two weeks touring Quebec, meeting people and learning about life in the province. But there was a time to speak up and a time to shut up, and now was the latter. Cabinet ministers speaking in Quebec, or about it, would submit their texts in advance to the Prime Minister's Office or the Privy Council Office for approval.

In Montreal, where day-to-day preparations for the campaign took place, everyone was generally satisfied as September neared its close. The most senior representatives of the federal and provincial Liberals met daily at the provincial party headquarters on Saint-Denis Street. On the federal side, Goldenberg shuttled between Montreal and Ottawa, sometimes several times a week. John Rae took leave from his job at Power Corporation to work full-time on the campaign. Others who regularly attended meetings from the federal Liberal side included Montreal lawyer Eric Maldoff and former Trudeau-era cabinet minister Serge Joyal. Jean Pelletier usually remained in Ottawa as the daily phone link between them and the prime minister. The Tories were also present, usually in the person of Senator Pierre-Claude Nolin, a wily veteran organizer.

Relations with the provincial Liberals were surprisingly good, given the testy history between the two parties. The provincials were usually represented by Pierre Anctil, Johnson's chief of staff, and John Parisella, Robert Bourassa's former chief of staff. The feds liked Parisella — now working for a Montreal ad agency but still a trusted adviser to Johnson — whom they considered the one rock-solid federalist at a high level in the provincial party (other than Johnson himself). They were still suspicious of Anctil for his nationalist leanings, but had learned to respect him for his obvious political savvy and professionalism.

At lower levels, niggling incidents exemplified the different approaches between the referendum allies. Provincial organizers insisted that at every No rally, there had to be three Quebec flags for every two Canadian ones. When the two sides discussed proposals for their joint televised ad campaign, the provincials vetoed presentations that mentioned Canada by name. Similarly, the provincials flexed their muscles over a video showing person-on-the-street interviews that was to be shown at the official No side launch at Montreal's Metropolis nightclub. The video would show Quebeckers explaining different reasons why they planned to vote No. First the provincials insisted that all those interviewed should be drawn from the membership list of their party. Then they vetoed any interviews where the subjects evoked their pride in Canada.

According to Quebec electoral law, the formal referendum campaign was limited to four weeks, meaning that October 2 marked the official kick-off. But by late September, both sides had been campaigning hard for more than two weeks, since the September 11 start of debate in the National Assembly. The Yes side still appeared dispirited and divided, the animosity between Bouchard and Parizeau barely concealed. Scandal erupted over a series of provincial studies intended to prove the merits of sovereignty. There were questions about improprieties in the awarding of contracts for the studies, and their findings didn't always make the case for sovereignty over federalism. All the poll news was good for the No side. A large poll commissioned by the CBC and several Quebec newspapers, conducted in mid-September and released October 2, showed a lead of 55 to 45 per cent for the No. The No side had its own poll, run by Grégoire Gollin and his company Créatec: a sampling conducted between October 2 and 5 gave the No side a lead of 48 per cent to 41 per cent, with the remainder undecided.

Paul Martin made his first major campaign appearance in Montreal in early October. He gave a well-reviewed speech in which he warned that an independent Quebec would face difficulties in signing the North American Free Trade Agreement and in gaining membership in the World Trade Organization under the existing terms that it enjoyed as part of Canada. As well, the pro-federalist business community spoke up.

In retrospect, No organizers admitted, the early speeches should have been leavened with more upbeat news. Even as the overwhelming majority of people thought the Yes side was doomed, a few people detected trouble ahead for the No. Two of them were Parizeau and his chief of staff, Jean Royer. Parizeau had made Quebec independence his life's work. Since 1980, he had devoted many hours to thinking about how and why things had gone wrong in the first referendum. He concluded that the 1980 campaign had begun with high emotion — with René Lévesque and PQ MNAs making sometimes tearful exhortations on the need for a nation — and had ended in a scuffle over statistics. That, he said, could never be allowed to happen again.

On the No side, the provincial Liberal headquarters became the official centre of activity. It was spread over four stories of a nondescript building on an otherwise fashionable stretch of Saint-Denis. Its design highlights were a freight elevator almost the size of many of the offices, and a paint scheme of the sort of chalky colours that owe their inspiration to hockey-arena locker rooms. A receptionist was on duty twenty-four hours a day. In the early weeks of the campaign, the first arrivals came in any time after 5 a.m., and there were always a few stragglers turning out the lights around midnight. Rae, a habitual early riser, usually rolled in about 6 o'clock, looking as serene and crisply turned out as if he had just come back from a full grooming session. When Goldenberg was in town, he slouched in, rumpled and bleary-eyed, about an hour later, a notoriously bad early-morning person, as he readily confessed.

Later on some people spent twenty-four-hour shifts in the building, and no matter what the hour, someone was always on the third floor. That was the real nerve centre, laid out over four perpetually untidy rooms dominated by handwritten wall charts, fax numbers taped to the wall, and an impressive collection of empty Dunkin' Donuts boxes. Tensions were exacerbated by the physical structure of the place. The rooms were open-concept, in a nod to democracy and all-inclusiveness that everyone publicly praised and senior organizers privately despised. There was nowhere to go to hatch a secret plan or have a good argument. It was hard to find a place just to think.

The nerve centre was known as "the War Room" — always in English — as a conscious tribute to the documentary movie of the same name about the Democratic campaign to win the White House in 1992. Many of the key No organizers watched the movie several times, and the dishevelled, stripped-down look of the Montreal offices signalled a deliberate attempt to re-create the feel of that campaign.

The No side had already rolled out all its big artillery by the end of September, hoping to build such a big early lead that the other side would simply collapse. At a September 24 rally of businesspeople in Montreal, the CEO of Standard Life Assurance Company, Claude Garcia, had said it would not be enough to simply beat the sovereigntists. Rather, he said, to end the interminable debate sapping Quebeckers' energy, the margin of victory should be enough to "crush" the sovereignty movement. Initially the remark passed without notice. The ultranationalist daily *Le Devoir*, in its report on the event the next day, did not even mention Garcia. But when Parizeau's chief of staff, Royer, heard about the remark, he was particularly struck. It seemed to exemplify a growing sense of arrogance among No supporters. It became a feature of Yes ads that suggested the No side was contemptuous of all who opposed it.

On October 2, the two sides paused long enough in their full-time campaigning to formally launch their full-time, now official, campaigns. The No side staged an impressive show at the Metropolis nightclub in downtown Montreal, where 2,500 people listened as Daniel Johnson promised that "the winds of change" were blowing across Canada and would lead to big changes in the federal system. Parizeau appeared on provincewide prime-time television to launch the Yes campaign, and then set off on a psychedelically decorated bus to tour Quebec's hinterland.

Chrétien made his first campaign appearance in Quebec on Friday, October 6, at a rally in Shawinigan. There were three weeks and three days remaining till the vote, and the unofficial campaign — counting back to the start of debate on September 11 — was half over. There was no doubt at this point that the federalists were winning the battle, and the war. Chrétien's conciliatory speech, delivered in a low-key manner, looked good on the late-night newscasts, where it led most lineups. When Rae drove back to Montreal that night, he was convinced the campaign was "in the bag."

Two days later, Yes organizers summoned reporters to a news conference at which they announced that in the event of a Yes vote, Bouchard, rather than Parizeau, would serve as "chief negotiator" with the rest of Canada over the terms of separation. On the No side, the initial response was surprise, but no alarm. They had always thought that Bouchard might, at some point, replace Parizeau. Some No side planners doubted that Bouchard, slowed by a prosthetic leg, could lead a gruelling campaign for long. The arguments for both sides remained the same, said Marcel Massé, in his rational but politically obtuse way, and so did the players. After the initial furore, the Bouchard effect would subside. Goldenberg, Rae, Pelletier, and others felt that. "Who could have thought," Pelletier asked rhetorically after the campaign was over, "that they would overthrow their leader in the middle of the campaign, and that everyone would just accept it?"

But with Bouchard's new prominence in the campaign, everything changed. Robert Bourassa often quoted one of his political idols, Harold Wilson, who said that in politics, a week is a long time, and a year is an eternity. Now, the three weeks remaining in the campaign suddenly became a very, very long time.

Bouchard turned the debate to the emotionally satisfying terrain of "partnership." You can have it all, a sovereign Quebec with a stake in Canada, he told his audiences. The argument was an extension of the old notion of Canada as a pact between two founding nations, French and English. The way to get the bargaining power to achieve that was to vote Yes. A Yes vote, Bouchard told an audience in Joliette, was like giving a strike mandate to a union leader who has to negotiate a new contract with management. The more the rest of Canada squawked, the more he portrayed the vote as Us against Them. The existing Yes ads, which sometimes seemed more federalist than those of the No side, were in sync with the new message. While the No side downplayed mention of Canada's national symbols, one of the most widely used print ads for the Yes featured the Canadian loonie — which, the Yes side promised, Quebeckers could keep when Quebec became a sovereign state linked with its Canadian partner.

Almost overnight, the Yes campaign achieved what Parizeau knew was necessary, shifting the terrain from reason back to passion. He had made a remarkably selfless gesture in stepping aside for Bouchard, and it put the No side in a quandary. Bouchard was formidable: a truck driver's son who quoted Molière, and a political man for all reasons and seasons. The feds knew it would be a mistake to attack him personally. They also thought it would be a mistake to change tactics, because it would look as though they were running scared. True, the average size of crowds at Yes rallies tripled, and the Yes headquarters reported calls from hundreds of people daily wanting to volunteer. But it would pass. Rae, Goldenberg, Parisella, Anctil, and company watched closely, but calmly. They had all ridden out similar storms in other campaigns, or so they thought.

The initial polling results gave support to that confidence. The first in-house Créatec poll, taken the previous week, had shown the No with a lead of 48 to 41 per cent among committed voters. The next poll was taken between October 10 and 12, when the excitement over Bouchard's appointment was in full bloom. It showed a No lead of 49.1 per cent to 42.8 per cent for the Yes — only a tiny change within the statistical margin of error.

But the reverence for Bouchard grew instead of dissipating. It was, one No organizer remarked, as though people had decided to ignore his previous return to public life from near-death and were now staging his welcome-home event. They wanted to touch his coat and even feel his prosthetic leg. Bouchard, caught up in his own incendiary rhetoric, sometimes made mistakes other politicians hang for in the media, but it didn't matter. At one rally, he talked about Quebec's falling birth rate, remarking that Quebec society "is one of the white races that has the least children." He refused to discuss the controversial provincial government-commissioned reports on the costs of sovereignty, dismissing them as part of a previous campaign. They ceased to be an issue. At another rally, he said that a Yes would have "something magical about it. The whole situation is changed with the wave of a wand."

Bouchard, it seemed, could say anything he wanted, and people believed him. Frank Graves, a partner in Ekos Research of Ottawa, ran regular polls using the same 1,000 Quebeckers to sample their reaction to events. Bouchard later said he regretted his remark about the "white races." But when he said it, support for the Yes among Graves's poll group went up. Rae sat in on focus groups organized by Créatec. Even when focus group members watched clips of Bouchard making controversial statements, they insisted he either didn't say those things, or was cited out of context.

Many of the economic arguments from 1980 were turned on their head. In that referendum, many people said they voted No because they thought a sovereign Quebec couldn't afford services like old-age pensions and medicare. Now, in an era of cuts in government programs, people didn't believe the federal government could sustain such programs either. Polls showed a majority of Quebeckers believed that they paid more into the federation through taxes than they received, even though this was demonstrably not the case. Some respondents in focus groups said that they planned to vote Yes because they would save on taxes by paying at only one level instead of two. It was all terribly frustrating for the No side strategists, silently watching the groups from behind one-way mirrors. After the campaign was over, John Rae joked that he could empathize with the title character on the *Murphy Brown* sitcom, who in one episode is so enraged by the inanities and inaccuracies offered up by a focus group that she stomps into their room and begins berating them.

The real slippage in the federalists' own polls started a week after Bouchard's *de facto* take-over of the Yes campaign. A Créatec internal poll taken between October 15 and 17 showed the No side barely leading, with 47 per cent of committed voter support to 45 for the Yes. Chrétien was unfazed. Asked about poll results, he responded that at a similar stage of the 1980 campaign, "the results were much more close than this time and it finished 60 per cent to 40."

Still, some feds worried. By October 15, with only fifteen days left till the vote, they had expected their percentage of the vote to be growing, not shrinking. This was the day the televised debate was supposed to take place — the point at which the No campaigners had planned to wind up their economic arguments. But it had fallen through.

The No team realized that they needed to drum up more positive emotion. In daily meetings, organizers tossed out all sorts of ideas for events that, they hoped, would create the sense of pride that was lacking. The notion that got the farthest out of the gate was to stage a gathering featuring former prime ministers. When the idea was presented to Chrétien, he was unimpressed. "Do we really need these guys?" he asked an aide. But he made the necessary calls to Trudeau, John Turner, Joe Clark, Brian Mulroney, and Kim Campbell to see if they would cooperate. Chrétien half hoped that one or all of his predecessors would say they could not make it, so the idea could be shelved.

All the former leaders accepted Chrétien's invitation. But in the week before the planned October 24 event, the organizers' enthusiasm waned as the polls headed due south. Mila Mulroney, attending a rally of women for the No side in Montreal, jumped the gun and cheerfully told reporters that her husband expected to participate in a rally "next week." At the Saint-Denis Street headquarters, one provincial Liberal recalled, Chrétien's organizers "went ballistic" when they heard her comment. The event was cancelled the next day. Instead, they decided on what eventually became the October 24 mass rally in Verdun.

Overall, they stuck to their game plan, even though the Yes organizers had altered theirs. There wasn't much time for change even if everyone would agree, and agreement was not certain. Besides, they just couldn't believe what was happening with Bouchard out there. It was, one senior No organizer said later, as if the entire province had decided to allow itself to be hypnotized.

On October 18, Chrétien spoke to the Quebec City Chamber of Commerce. His speech, written by Eddie Goldenberg and Chrétien's press secretary, Patrick Parisot, aimed to dispel the notion that the rest of Canada would agree to a partnership, and to puncture the magical aura around Bouchard. It was a difficult balancing act, a prime minister venturing into a home province suspicious of him, speaking on behalf of the rest of the country and against Quebec's favourite son. But Chrétien managed it well. He spoke confidently, his self-assurance a welcome relief from the pinched, fidgety manner he often projected when constrained by a prepared text and TelePrompTer. He took aim several times at Bouchard's magic wand reference, exclaiming that in "the real world, there are no magic wands and people have to pay their bills." He suggested that a shift in powers between the federal government and the provinces was needed and likely because "the state of public finances is such." In a nod to voters who thought he was against the notion that Quebec was different from the nine other provinces, he described it as a place that "by its language, its culture, and its institutions forms a distinct society."

That was a step across the Rubicon towards recognizing Quebec as the land of the Formally Distinct Society. At the end, he briefly departed from his text and talked about the heavy burden of being prime minister, and the historic legacy that came with the office. Watching him, Rae said later, he was struck forcefully by the notion of "what a huge sense of responsibility comes with the job, and how aware the prime minister was of that."

But the speech, while well received, was overtaken by events. The day before, Paul Martin had given his second speech of the campaign, this time to businesspeople in Quebec City. He again referred to the immediate economic dangers a sovereign Quebec would face. Without membership in NAFTA, Martin said, Quebec would lose its open borders with the rest of Canada and the increasingly open border to the south. The result, said Martin, would be "the economic isolation of Quebec." And "what would this jeopardize? Ninety per cent of [Quebec] exports; close to one million Quebec jobs."

It was too much. Whether accurate or not, it was an apocalyptic notion, especially after all the inflammatory rhetoric of recent weeks. One million jobs! Parizeau pounced. His air of self-assurance for once perfectly complemented his remarks. He told reporters scornfully that Quebec only had 3.2 million people working — so if the feds inflated job loss estimates any more, they would have to import unemployed people from other provinces. The newscasts that night and the headlines the following morning were full of comment about Martin's remarks, none of it favourable. When the first report came in to the TV room at No headquarters, it took "about one and a half seconds," Anctil later said, for the No side to realize they had a major new headache. Many on the provincial side were astonished by the speech. Although it had been vetted in advance in Ottawa, no one had shown it to the provincial Liberals. "We had absolutely no idea this was coming," said Grégoire Gollin of Créatec. "It was a very severe blow."

With one remark, the credibility of one of the No side's most trusted figures was cast into doubt. Martin and other federalists argued that the media was using selective judgment. Quebec Deputy Premier Bernard Landry, after all, had recently suggested that Ontario had 433,000 jobs at stake if it didn't agree to a partnership with Quebec, and no one had jumped on him. Months later, Martin still refused to say he had erred, and insisted that numerous statistics and studies supported his figure. Besides, he pointed out, he had talked about the number of jobs at risk, rather than actually saying all those jobs would be lost. No matter. The finance minister headed from Quebec City directly to the nationalist bastion of Saguenay–Lac Saint-Jean, where he was trashed on talk shows, cursed in coffee shops, and torn to pieces in taverns. Bernard St. Laurent, a veteran political reporter with CBC Radio, did a series of more than twenty random street interviews in Montreal over the following three days. The depth of anger over the remarks, he said, was "unbelievable. People are saying this is the final straw, they're not going to listen to this scare crap any more."

In that week beginning October 16, all households in Quebec received a pamphlet containing the principal arguments and promises of the Yes and No sides from the province's chief electoral officer. The debate between the federal and provincial Liberals over the wording of the text had begun during the summer and continued until the day before it went off to the printer. It revived, on a larger scale, the debate over whether an offer of new powers to Quebec should be made during the campaign, or at all. The provincials wanted some sort of commitment, but the feds weren't buying, and the document was deliberately ambiguous about the timing and specifics of any future changes. No one at senior levels around Ottawa liked the idea of specific promises; not Chrétien, nor Pelletier, nor Rae, nor Goldenberg. On the provincial side, Anctil and Parisella were increasingly frustrated at their inability to get a straight answer from the federals. At least the provincials committed themselves, Anctil told one acquaintance. "When I am in favour of something, I tell them I will recommend it to Johnson. But they never commit to anything: they just keep saying, 'Trust us, you will like what we decide on,' and then they won't say what they decided on."

The tensions showed on Thursday morning, October 19. There were now twelve days remaining to the vote, and the first really bad poll results had just arrived. The Yes side, according to various polls, was gaining ground swiftly, or leading. Everyone agreed it was time for Chrétien to play a more prominent role. The previous day, the key participants had arranged to meet to make some crucial decisions. Goldenberg made the two-hour drive from Ottawa that Wednesday night, wishing, not for the first time, that he could get "frequent-driver points" for the commute.

The October 19 meeting took place in a boardroom in Daniel Johnson's offices in Place Ville-Marie in the heart of Montreal's downtown. The participants included Anctil, Parisella, Goldenberg, Rae, Montreal lawyer Michel Vennat, Lucienne Robillard, and businessman and former civil servant Michel Bélanger. There was further disturbing news: Gollin reported that his polls showed an even split between those who thought there was an economic risk in seceding from Canada, and those who thought there was an equal risk if Quebec remained part of debt-ridden Canada. Goldenberg was shocked. He had never contemplated losing the advantage of the economic arguments. They began planning for the mass rally on the 24th. They also decided that Chrétien should appear on television on the 26th. Although Radio-Canada was the usual vehicle of choice for prime ministers, they opted to accept a previous invitation to appear on *Mongrain*, a popular talk show on TVA, the private television network. Its audience was huge, and its viewers more blue-collar than Radio-Canada's; they were more likely to be undecided voters.

Now, as they had ever since the federal Liberals had come to power, the provincials urged them to commit themselves to some kind of transfer of powers to Quebec. Again, the question of control over labour market training came up. As usual, there were no specific answers. Suddenly, the usually genial Parisella exploded. "God damn it," he shouted, slamming his fist on the table, "you've got to give us something!" The outburst from Parisella, considered by the feds their one true ally on the provincial side, stunned everyone into silence. Goldenberg and Rae promised to take the matter to the prime minister for consideration, and left shortly afterwards. Parisella was mildly embarrassed. Anctil put his left arm around him, and shook his hand with his right. "You know, John," he said with a smile. "For the first time in my memory, you sounded more nationalist than me."

On Saturday morning, with Chrétien in New York City for ceremonies marking the fiftieth anniversary of the United Nations, the No side held a strategy meeting at the Saint-Denis headquarters. The Saturday-morning meetings were attended by more people than the weekday sessions. On this day, the group included the highly respected poll analyst Maurice Pinard, Pierre-Claude Nolin, Grégoire Gollin, Goldenberg, Eric Maldoff, Anctil, Parisella, John Rae, and Chrétien's press secretary, Patrick Parisot. By now, the feds were thinking more seriously of offering increased powers to Quebec, although that wasn't widely known. Gollin told the No strategists they had to switch to a more positive message, that their present theme was too much of a downer for voters. "I said that we had surrendered the emotional terrain," Gollin later recalled — which was exactly what Parizeau had hoped for. They decided that Chrétien should go ahead with plans now under discussion for a televised address to the nation. Johnson showed up later, and was briefed on the planned contents of Chrétien's speech to the rally next Tuesday. They agreed that it would contain some concessions to Quebec, although the final details weren't clear. While everyone debated the topic, Johnson went out campaigning.

About four hours later, Johnson returned to No headquarters, which was uncharacteristically quiet. With Chrétien away and no major events scheduled, many people, exhausted, had taken the rest of the day off. Johnson's perpetually mournful basset-hound appearance was heightened by a furrowed brow and palpable air of dismay. "I think I screwed up," he said.

He had just inadvertently made big news on a slow day. In answer to a reporter's question at a No event, Johnson said that he would welcome a statement by Chrétien before the referendum that would open the door to a constitutional amendment recognizing Quebec as a distinct society. If Chrétien disagreed with Johnson now, he would embarrass his provincial counterpart and create the image of discord at the very highest level of the No camp at the worst possible time. That was, in fact, precisely what happened. Asked about the remark while in New York, Chrétien said he did not intend to discuss constitutional amendments. "We're not talking about the Constitution," he said. "We're talking about the separation of Quebec from Canada."

Later, Chrétien's people suggested that he was not briefed properly about the content of Johnson's remarks, and didn't intend to sound so unequivocal. But the response was certainly interpreted that way. "Chrétien dit non à Johnson" was the headline the following day in the Sunday edition of Montreal's *La Presse*.

Serious damage control was in order. After back-and-forth calls between Montreal and New York over a sixteen-hour period, Johnson read out a joint statement on Sunday afternoon. He and Chrétien had meant the same thing all along, Johnson insisted. "We state unequivocally that Quebec is a distinct society. We remind you that we have both supported the inclusion of this principle in the Canadian Constitution every time Quebec has demanded it." But, as reporters immediately reminded him, that wasn't entirely true, given Chrétien's past to-ing and fro-ing on Meech Lake.

Later some federal Liberals bitterly suggested that Johnson's remarks had been calculated, that he wanted to force the feds into concessions that they had already moved towards in the official No side pamphlet, and to be seen within his own party as the person who had single-handedly initiated change. If true, it was quite Machiavellian. And Johnson was a tough man to figure, cold-eyed and contrarian. But federal Liberals who had seen him at headquarters that day rejected the notion. Johnson was so obviously distraught when he returned to the offices, Goldenberg told a friend. Either Johnson was sincere in his regrets or he was the world's greatest actor. And his often-wooden speaking style and lack of personal warmth suggested the latter wasn't the case.

Goldenberg and Patrick Parisot had spent the rest of their Saturday huddled together over Parisot's laptop, working on the text for Chrétien's upcoming speech at the Tuesday rally. They kept at it for close to nine hours, Goldenberg offering up concepts, and Parisot, with his ear for Chrétien's speech patterns, putting it into language the boss would feel comfortable with. At about 8, they yawned at each other, and Parisot suggested that Goldenberg go back to the hotel while he finished up. After a dinner at a nearby delicatessen, Goldenberg returned to his hotel at 10 p.m. to find his phone light flashing and desperate messages directing him to call Parisot "most urgently." When he reached Parisot, the press secretary sounded frantic. Had someone died, wondered Goldenberg? Almost as bad, responded Parisot, the text had vanished from the computer's memory. All their work appeared lost. Goldenberg, usually the cause of such intensity rather than the recipient of it, smiled, relieved that the news was no worse. "Between us, we probably remember 90 per cent of the speech word for word," he told Parisot. "Get some sleep, we need it." Early the next morning, Parisot woke him up with the bulletin that his wife had located the missing text on the laptop's hard disk drive.

For many people, Monday the 23rd was the worst day of the campaign, a relentless march towards chaos punctuated by small explosions and fire-fights. Exactly one week remained till the vote. Everything was in free fall; published weekend polls put the Yes in the lead, and they had been taken before the latest Johnson-Chrétien débâcle. Bouchard and Parizeau were now cautioning their followers against overconfidence, while panic and division on the No side were rampant. The bad news continued all day. Newfoundland Premier Clyde Wells, the *bête noire* of Quebec nationalists, told reporters he was not prepared to grant Quebec any special constitutional status even as Pierre Paradis, Johnson's parliamentary leader, publicly pleaded for Chrétien to do precisely that. French President Jacques Chirac, Cheshire cat smile and all, appeared on CNN's *Larry King Live*. In response to a query from a Montreal caller and King's follow-up question, he suggested France would swiftly extend diplomatic recognition to Quebec in the event of a Yes vote.

Brian Tobin's day began with his usual morning gathering of senior departmental and political staff in his office boardroom. His schedule was so mind-numbingly normal that it suddenly seemed surreal to him. He was to fly to St. John's to speak to the Board of Trade, do some work on fish licence fees, then go on to Nova Scotia for a Liberal fundraiser. "At a certain point," he recalled later, "I was looking at this thing, and looking at the day's activities, and said, This is absolutely crazy. I'm sitting here planning the week as if nothing was going on. And I said to my staff, Cancel the day, cancel the week." Then he retired to his office and began working the phones. He called contacts in Newfoundland and British Columbia to see if they thought it would be possible to organize a giant unity rally in Montreal on Friday. Everybody wanted in.

Tobin wasn't alone in thinking of a giant rally. Phil O'Brien, a prominent Montreal businessman, had been talking with friends in the Montreal business community for a week about staging a giant march of Montreal federalists. And Pierre-Claude Nolin had had a similar notion. A senator who played a key role in Mulroney's two electoral sweeps of Quebec, he was the Tories' senior point person on the No organizing committee. The previous Friday, he had been at lunch with an otherwise nonpolitical federalist francophone friend who was bemoaning the apparent lack of interest of other Canadians in the campaign. The friend, Nolin recalled later, made "a cry from the heart," asking if the rest of Canada even cared about the result. Nolin, chewing on his sandwich, was shocked. The No side had worked hard to keep the rest of Canada away from the debate. Perhaps that had been a grievous error. He resolved to raise the issue the next day. He didn't have to: at the Saturday meeting at No headquarters, Rae brought up the notion of a giant rally and said: "Will you all agree?"

The idea percolated in various quarters through the weekend. Based on the tentative agreement of the Saturday meeting, Nolin went on Monday to Montreal city hall and requested a permit for a rally for the following Friday, October 27. At this point the Montreal organizers were thinking of a rally mostly for Quebeckers. They would have five days to put it all together, with no window for delay. The permit, in Nolin's name, anticipated a crowd that would total between 10,000 and 15,000 people.

Back in Ottawa, most ministers planned to go from the House on Monday to a No rally in Marcel Massé's Hull riding, at which Daniel Johnson would speak. But Tobin buttonholed some ministers in the lobby and chamber and told them to forget the rally, they had more important things to discuss. He arranged for them to meet for dinner at Café Henry Burger in Hull. The group included Anne McLellan, Sergio Marchi, David Anderson, Lloyd Axworthy, and Ralph Goodale.

They knew the campaign was floundering. They had seen the furore over the weekend over Chrétien's response to Johnson. Tobin pulled few punches. He was livid about the way Chrétien had been fenced in by the Quebec Liberals and his own advisers. He felt the PM wasn't getting the straight goods, and that the No side would lose unless the prime minister took direct charge immediately.

Tobin, six months past the fish war, had a healthy respect for the love Canadians felt for their country. He had received more than 10,000 letters during the dispute, including poems and paintings. He had touched a nerve and felt that nerve needed to be touched again, or Canadians would discover they had sleepwalked over the edge of the constitutional abyss. The more politically attuned ministers, like Tobin and Sheila Copps, had been frustrated for weeks about the lack of emotion in the campaign. Now they bought into the idea of a massive rally. They would push the next day to put aside the talk of balance sheets and let Chrétien be Chrétien. While the other ministers caught the end of the Hull rally, Tobin returned to his office to brief more MPs.

Early Tuesday morning, Goldenberg was in Jean Pelletier's office in the Langevin Block discussing Chrétien's televised address to the nation with Pelletier and Parisot when John Rae called from Montreal. He had the latest poll numbers from Gollin, and they were very bad. The No side now trailed the Yes side by seven points, with six days left. The three men sat in Pelletier's office for the next five minutes, alternating between stunned silence and questions about when, or whether, to tell Chrétien the news. Before a key speech, Goldenberg thought, was not a particularly good time. When you've got bad numbers, he later explained, you tell the prime minister after, rather than before, a big event because there is nothing that can be done about it anyway.

But then the telephone rang in Pelletier's office. It was Chrétien, wanting to talk to Goldenberg. They chatted for several minutes before Chrétien asked Goldenberg if he had the latest poll numbers. There was no choice, so Goldenberg told Chrétien the bad news without hesitation. Chrétien, after several seconds of silence, was sanguine. We have our work cut out for us, he said.

Cabinet met at 10 a.m. Chrétien discussed his planned speech in Verdun that night in general terms, telling the ministers he would offer Quebeckers hope for change. Chrétien did not throw that open for further talk. He said he would decide. He planned to be more active in the final week of the campaign, he said, laying out the events to follow. He acknowledged that the No side was behind, but he did not say precisely how grave the situation was. Chrétien departed cabinet early.

Then Tobin put his idea for a massive rally on the table, and said he needed to know right away. A lot of work would be needed to transform the Montreal group's Quebec rally into a pan-Canadian event. Alfonso

Gagliano, an innately cautious politician in the Chrétien mould, was hesitant. He expressed concerns about whether the No side could deliver the necessary organization on such short notice. Several ministers worried about the possibility of violence. In a telling comment, Lucienne Robillard said the conversations were pointless, that others had decided that it would be a go. For some fellow ministers, her remarks echoed with a bitter refrain of how far she had fallen from grace in the campaign. When she first came into cabinet in early 1995, she was treated as a star, even as a saviour in Quebec. She was to be for Chrétien in 1995 what he had been for Trudeau in 1980: the daily federal presence at rallies. But she was soon eclipsed by Jean Charest. Now Robillard appeared increasingly ignored by the press.

Watching the others hesitate, Tobin, at the far end of the oval table, put down his pencil with a dramatic flourish. Dripping with sarcasm, he reminded them that the country was in play, and they were losing. Did they want him to go ahead or not? No one challenged him.

Tuesday night was rainy in Montreal. The federalists demonstrated the strength of their organization, as well as the sense of urgency on their side. The Verdun rally had come together in less than four days, after a final decision at the Saturday-morning meeting in Montreal. The organizers had originally thought of using the Montreal Forum: there was a contingency plan to do so, and they waited until Sunday night before deciding on Verdun, a suburb southwest of Montreal. It was better to have an overflow crowd in a smaller place than a larger crowd that can't quite fill a bigger hall. Verdun, seating 7,000, was safer, if less dramatic, than the 18,000-seat Forum. It was also much cheaper to rent.

Half an hour before the rally began, the roads to the arena were jammed with incoming traffic for close to two kilometres in every direction. Even Chrétien could not get through. Three blocks from the arena, he and Aline got out of the car and walked hand in hand, with Rae alongside, and security guards hurrying behind. People opened their car windows and offered best wishes, while children waved. Young men in tank tops stood on their balconies silently, many of them Yes supporters. There was one heckler along the way, a man who kept shouting "Oui, oui."

Closer to the arena, the group bumped into Jean Charest and his wife, Michelle Dionne, who had also abandoned their car. They entered the arena together, damp from the rain, and went to a holding room deep in the bowels of the aging arena to meet Daniel Johnson. Chrétien was pumped full of adrenaline. He had seen the scores of buses outside, the huge television screens, and thousands of people standing patiently in the rain. Finally, the federalist camp was energized.

Still, his speech was not the stemwinder that many in the audience were hoping for. He was up first, before Jean Charest and Daniel Johnson, because the organizers wanted the TV news people to have plenty of time to digest, cut, and edit his message before the late-evening news. The message was that Chrétien now supported recognition of Quebec as a distinct society without reservation, within the Constitution or outside it. A No vote, he said, "does not mean giving up any position whatsoever with regard to Canada's constitution." All paths were open for change, and "any changes in constitutional jurisdiction for Quebec will be made only with the consent of Quebeckers."

There they were, two of the main elements of the failed Meech Lake Accord: recognition of Quebec as a distinct society, and a form of constitutional veto. Chrétien did not promise to entrench either in the Constitution, and was no more specific about either promise. His remarks drew jeers from Quebec nationalists, and concern from the rest of the country. But it allowed No supporters to go among the 20 per cent of undecided Quebeckers who would decide the future of Canada, and argue that the prime minister had said that the status quo was not good enough. In his three campaign speeches, in Shawinigan, Quebec City, and now Verdun, Chrétien each time pushed the notion of a distinct society a little further, not unlike a swimmer who tentatively lowers himself into potentially cold and perilous waters by inches at a time.

Chrétien's Verdun speech also promised to meet a third Quebec demand, for control over labour market training. It was something that Daniel Johnson had wanted for more than a year. Now, at the eleventh hour, Chrétien relented. The promise further hindered Lloyd Axworthy as he neared completion of his ambitious plans to reform unemployment insurance.

Chrétien was followed by Charest. He delivered what most people agreed was the best speech by a No spokesperson in the campaign. He described the realities of partisan politics, and the divisions between parties. Then he told how he, his wife, and Jean and Aline Chrétien had met on the street and come to the arena together. He turned to the prime minister, seated behind him, and said: "When it comes to Canada, Prime Minister, you and I walk on the same side of the street every time."

That evening, polls later suggested, was the start of an extraordinary, event-filled two-day period in which the No side arrested its slide and turned the campaign back around. But no one knew that then. The following day, Wednesday, October 25, was, Jean Pelletier later said, the worst of all for him because "we were not permitted to make any mistakes. Not a one."

The day began with an extraordinary meeting of the Liberal caucus. With five days to go until the vote, Chrétien stood ready to deliver an emergency television address to the nation that evening about the perils that would follow a Yes. Several MPs in the room privately noted that the date, October 25, marked the second anniversary of their election victory. It should have been a morning of festivities. Instead, they felt as if they were trapped in a palliative care unit. Chrétien tried to explain to caucus what had gone wrong. Bouchard's ability to get away with "the big lie" of risk-free separation was, he said, the most unusual situation he had encountered in more than thirty years in politics. Chrétien vented his pent-up frustration towards the Quebec media, blaming it for giving the secessionists momentum by happily reporting a "big pile of shit." He spoke about a friend who had called him the night before, so nervous about the campaign that he hadn't slept for three nights.

But it wasn't over yet, he insisted. The tide had started to turn the evening before in Verdun. Now he would reach out to the 35 per cent of Yes supporters who, according to polls, didn't really want to break up Canada. Chrétien recalled his visit the previous weekend to New York City for the fiftieth-anniversary celebrations of the United Nations. It was inconceivable to the outside world that Quebec would separate, he said. Presidents and prime ministers from some sixty countries had approached him to express their puzzlement that anyone would rip asunder such a successful country. A group of Islamic leaders had told him they were praying for Canada.

But it would take more than prayer right now to provide solace to Chrétien, a temporarily exhausted and spiritually wounded warrior. He turned, bowed his head, and cried. Jane Stewart, a third-generation Liberal politician and the caucus chair, had known Chrétien since the times he had visited her family farm in southern Ontario. She stood and embraced him. Throughout the Parliament Hill caucus room, Liberals surrendered to their emotions. Brian Tobin, David Dingwall, David Collenette, Sergio Marchi, Christine Stewart — tears streamed down their cheeks.

Chrétien turned to leave, but Jane Stewart urged him to continue. Regaining his composure, he stiffened and glared around briefly, clearly hoping everyone would forget or at least ignore his momentary loss of control. He reminded the stunned Liberals that there were five days left in the campaign. Remember the federal election; remember the lie then that he was going down to defeat in his own riding of Saint-Maurice. He choked up again briefly as he recalled how in August 1993 Parizeau had referred to him in his home town as a cretin, but he fought back the emotion. (Parizeau had never apologized for the remark.) "Remember we live in the best country in the world," he said, finding solace in a familiar mantra. "The people of Quebec will not fall into the trap of the magician."

Then Jean Chrétien went out to do what he did best: fight for Canada. He strode past the reporters waiting outside, his lean frame tilted forward. As always, he was moving fast.

Jean Pelletier was not in caucus when the prime minister broke down but received a phone call describing the incident. Pelletier was concerned, he said, for both "the state of the caucus, and the state of Mr. Chrétien." The caucus, he quickly ascertained from several members, was not a problem. When he called across the street to Chrétien's office on Parliament Hill, his fears vanished. "I knew," recalled Pelletier, "that he was in full control." And he added drily, "It is permitted that even statesmen get to show their feelings on occasion." Similarly, when Goldenberg went to see Chrétien in mid-afternoon to show him a proposed text for his television address, he found Chrétien serious, but upbeat. Goldenberg had not been in caucus but was not surprised when he heard that it was there that Chrétien had been at his most emotional. Caucus, Goldenberg felt, was Chrétien's second home: all of his emotions welled up in him when he was there.

When Chrétien showed up that afternoon at his Parliament Hill office to tape his television broadcasts, he was calm, but looked drawn and showed all of his sixty-one years. He and Pelletier liked to joke, Pelletier said, that "it is fun to have the experience of a sixty-year-old, but it would be nice to have the energy of a forty-year-old." But this was no time for jokes. The prime minister was grumpy when he sat down in his office to tape the broadcast. The furniture was rearranged to accommodate the television lights, and the usual pictures of Aline and his grandchildren were moved to a table behind him, so that they showed up in the background of the broadcast. Family and the consequences of breakup were themes of the speech. The woman doing makeup fussed over Chrétien, telling him he would need something to cover the circles under his eyes and look younger, but he was impatient. "I don't care if I look old," he snapped.

In his English and French comments, Chrétien spoke slowly and carefully, but the strain of the campaign was evident in his haggard expression. No one should delude themselves into thinking this was about constitutional change, dislike of government or politicians, or any of the traditional, lesser grievances, he said. The issue at stake "is our country. To break up Canada or build Canada. To remain Canadian or no longer be Canadian. To stay or to leave."

Bouchard came next. Everyone worried that with the force of his rhetoric, he might blow the prime minister right off the television screen. Under the terms of the Emergency Broadcast Act, Chrétien was not required to give Bouchard equal airtime, but there was never a question of excluding him. The No camp understood how bad that would look. They refused to allow Bouchard to see Chrétien's speech in advance. The Yes side, in turn, refused to say whether Bouchard would tape his own remarks in advance or go live, and respond extemporaneously to the prime minister. Chrétien advisers breathed a collective sigh of relief later that afternoon when Bouchard's office called Radio-Canada to say he would tape.

Advisers in the Privy Council Office briefly considered a plan that revolved around the Montreal Canadiens game to be televised that night on Quebec's private Quatre Saisons network, beginning at 7:30. Chrétien was speaking at 7 p.m., Bouchard at 7:15. Some advisers thought that they should stall Chrétien's start just enough so that Bouchard's rebuttal would run past 7:30 and cut into the televised start of the game. That might sway some annoyed, undecided voters whose real priorities were other than a referendum. In the end, they thought better of it.

The next day, the consensus in francophone Quebec and some English-language media was that Bouchard had won the duel of the cameras. He spoke briskly, eloquently, and confidently. He was soothing about the future after a Yes vote, and told Quebeckers they should be calm. But the only review that counted was Quebec public opinion. As the polls later showed, the dramatic turnaround for the federalists came during precisely the period of the Verdun rally and Chrétien's televised speech. Between October 22 and 24, the federalists' internal polling of 1,000 respondents had shown the No down by five points; their next poll of 700 respondents, taken October 25 and 26, put it ahead by 3.7 points. That speech, said Gollin, "was the real turning point for the No, because of the promises of change. It gave uncertain voters a reason to come back to the No."

Other factors came into play. On Wednesday, Bill Clinton gave a press conference in Washington, and Canadian reporters were tipped in advance that he might address the Quebec issue. Asked about the consequences if Canada broke up, Clinton launched into a glowing endorsement of Canada's role on the world stage that left no doubt where he stood. The remark came less than a week after his secretary of state, Warren Christopher, had warned that a sovereign Quebec should not assume it would automatically be accepted into NAFTA under the existing terms of the agreement. Those comments — and Clinton's in particular — reflected the assiduous efforts of Ambassador Jim Blanchard to bring the White House into the debate. The Americans had always intended to get involved if they could be sure that an intervention from Washington would help the federalist side rather than hurt. In the summer of 1995, the State Department ordered up a poll measuring attitudes in Quebec and the rest of Canada towards the United States. In Quebec, Bill Clinton had an astonishing 74-per-cent approval rating — far higher than any other leader, including Bouchard. And 62 per cent of Quebec respondents thought the opinion of the United States towards a sovereign Quebec was important, compared with only 55 per cent in the rest of the country. Those findings helped Blanchard in pressing Clinton to get involved.

As well, the rest of Canada was now entering the debate at official and grassroots levels. Most of the provincial legislatures passed resolutions supporting, with varying degrees of commitment, recognition of Quebec as a distinct society. In Toronto, 4,000 people turned out for a hastily organized pro-Canada lunchtime rally. In dozens of elementary school classrooms across Canada, teachers drafted students to write letters, in French, to their counterparts in Quebec, asking them to stay in Canada.

On the planning of the Montreal rally, things were moving very fast. Tobin, in an appearance on Wednesday on CTV's *Canada AM*, mentioned that Canadian Airlines was offering discount fares to anyone wanting to attend the rally. Air Canada joined in, and the two airlines discounted fares by up to 90 per cent to anyone in Canada wanting to fly to Montreal on Friday, as long as they returned within twenty-four hours. The bus companies followed suit, and hundreds of companies offered workers the day off to attend the rally. One such employer was the federal government, which gave employees in Ottawa the day off in order to attend.

The politicians had their hands all over the organization of the event, but for once, they knew when to get out of the way. This was to be a gathering of the common people, with minimal participation by politicians. Many premiers and members of the federal cabinet would attend, but only Quebec politicians would speak.

Everyone saw this as an occasion for Canadians outside Quebec to let off steam, to release the fears and emotions that had built up as the news from Quebec got progressively worse. The provincials, led by Anctil, were nervous for precisely that reason. They had visions of drunken nineteen-year-olds from out west staggering into the bistros of Saint-Denis Street, speaking English and waving Canadian flags at 2 in the morning. Even if that didn't happen, they were vaguely horrified at the notion of what one provincial organizer sardonically called "Operation English Canada Saves the Day." They wanted the message to be that Quebec federalists were willing to stand up and be counted. That was typical of the difference between the provincial and federal Liberals. The provincials thought it was a Quebec debate, and were leery of involvement from anyone else. The federals thought the Quebec Liberals were too parochial, and scared of risk.

For better and for worse, there was no stopping the notion of a pan-Canadian rally of the sort that Tobin had envisioned. On Thursday night and early Friday, every airport at every major Canadian city was jammed with people lining up for special charter flights: some spent ten hours in the air commuting both ways, and as little as four hours in Montreal. Every bus in Ottawa and Toronto was rented by organizers. Estimates were that between 15,000 and 20,000 people came from outside the province.

No one ever agreed on how many people attended the rally. Federalist organizers claimed 150,000. Lucien Bouchard, who mocked the rally as an exercise in hypocrisy, estimated 35,000. RDI, the all-news network of Radio-Canada, earned the eternal enmity of federalists when its reporters agreed with that estimate. Months later, the CBC hired an expert at crowd estimates who, working with photographs and video, put the count at about 75,000.

The speakers included Chrétien, Johnson, Charest, Quebec Liberal backbencher Liza Frulla, who was considered the most charismatic speaker in their caucus, and several "ordinary Quebeckers." All spoke enthusiastically, but few in the audience understood much of what anyone said, because the sound system was inadequate for such a huge open square on a chilly day when the wind was whipping in everyone's faces.

Several minutes before the rally was to start, Sheila Copps announced to organizers that she also intended to speak. Everyone had agreed that only Quebeckers would make speeches, but no one wanted to refuse the deputy prime minister. Marie-Hélène Fox, a well-connected Liberal organizer to whom Copps made the demand, got on her cell phone to ask for instructions. A series of urgent calls went up the organizing chain in minutes, involving PMO officials, Nolin, Anctil, and other provincial Liberals. No, was the unanimous answer. After an embarrassed Fox relayed the decision to her, Copps, furious and incredulous, stomped off the stage escorted by a PMO official while some Liberals standing nearby snickered.

Everyone on both sides of the referendum debate behaved themselves. Yes supporters heeded pleas from their side to stay away so as not to provoke any incidents. On the No side, most people went home feeling better about themselves, believing that they had tried to do something to save the country. As a phenomenon, it was without equal in the country's history. But the actual effect on the referendum result was negative, experts on both sides later agreed. Quebec's francophone media took a hostile tone. The *Journal de Montréal*, the province's biggest newspaper, described it as an "invasion" by English Canada. The No side's tracking polls showed support had peaked the day before the rally, when they led by 3.7 per cent, and fell to a margin of 2.5 per cent by Saturday.

Grégoire Gollin, for one, thought the idea ill conceived and ill received when he went to the final No strategy meeting the following morning. In fact, he advised everyone to downplay the importance of the rally as much as possible. Quebeckers, he said, "perceived this as Ottawa and corporate Canada sticking their noses in. It was a bad idea from the start."

The rally, for all intents and purposes, was the final significant event of the campaign. By the weekend, people at No headquarters generally agreed they would win, but no one felt comfortable about guessing the margin. Estimates varied wildly, in part because of the seesaw nature of the polls in the last week. Some people were back to guessing a 60-per-cent No vote, others were in the low 50s.

At the Yes headquarters, they were just as confident of a sovereigntist victory, though they projected a tighter margin. Parizeau was so convinced of victory that he taped two broadcasts that were to be aired only in the event of a win. In one, with TVA's anchor Stéphane Bureau, he jovially recounted how he would have resigned in the event of a No vote. In another, he taped a victory speech. The latter was shown to the news directors of Quebec television stations, who were brought together in great secrecy at the state-run Radio-Québec television headquarters to watch it. (In a foreshadowing of the Yes side's final frustration after coming so close, there was a long delay in running the tape because they initially could not find a videocassette recorder that worked properly.)

The Yes side planned carefully for the aftermath of victory. Bernard St. Laurent, the CBC reporter who had good connections at high levels on the Yes side, later reported that plans had been so complete that for the first four days after the vote, Parizeau's agenda was broken into ten-minute segments. It included calls to key heads of government, such as Chirac and Clinton, and to people on the money markets in New York, Toronto, London, and Tokyo. His chief of staff, Jean Royer, offered to bet John Parisella $25,000 on the outcome. Parisella refused.

Chrétien spent Sunday night at 24 Sussex with Aline, receiving several guests. The prime minister was, one visitor said later, like a caged cat. He knew things were close, his gut instincts had deserted him in this campaign, and it remained possible he could lose the country. He called David Zussman, who had been told some poll results by Frank Graves from Ekos Research. Chrétien pressed for more information. "Why don't you call Frank?" Zussman suggested. Chrétien wasn't sure he knew Graves personally. Sure you do, Zussman told him; they had golfed together last summer at the Royal Ottawa.

At 10 o'clock, the phone rang at Graves's home and a familiar voice identified himself as Jean Chrétien. At first, Graves thought it was a friend, pulling a fast one. But he had a caller identification panel on his telephone, and it showed the call coming from the Privy Council Office (which had routed it from 24 Sussex). So, Chrétien asked, how would the vote go? Graves said that he was "cautiously optimistic." They chatted for several more minutes, and then Chrétien thanked him and hung up.

The next day, as everyone waited for the polls to close, seemed endless. Chrétien voted in Shawinigan at 10:15 a.m., then flew back to Ottawa. He made a series of telephone calls in the afternoon. One was to his long-time colleague Saskatchewan Premier Roy Romanow, who was in Montreal to do television commentary that night. The result would be very, very close, said Chrétien, although he added that he expected the No would win. Regardless of the result, he would go on television that night to reassure people that Canada would continue, everything would still function.

The 2:15 p.m. Question Period in the House of Commons was uncharacteristically quiet. All the Bloc Québécois seats were empty, without even a piece of paper on their green felt tabletops. There were many empty seats among the twenty allotted to Quebec Liberals. The session began with an impromptu singing of "O Canada," led by New Brunswick Liberal MP Pierrette Ringuette-Maltais. The gallery was packed with kids from across Canada attending a Terry Fox seminar in Ottawa. A woman in an Atlanta Braves baseball cap sat sleeping in the official guests section; a slightly more attentive but clearly confused visitor was Dr. Antje Vollmer, vice president of the German Bundestag.

Voter turnout was massive. At about 7 p.m., with an hour to go till the voting ended, No workers began gathering at the Metropolis club in Montreal, the same place they had used to launch the campaign. Then, everyone had been upbeat. Now, no one knew what to think.

Of Chrétien's inner circle, Rae was at the Metropolis with his wife, while Chrétien and Aline were joined at Sussex Drive by Goldenberg, Zussman, Pelletier, Peter Donolo, Patrick Parisot, Chaviva Hošek, and all-purpose adviser Jean Carle. Martin voted in Montreal, then drove to Ottawa to watch the results with staff and friends. Visibly edgy, Chrétien paced from room to room as the results trickled in, while aides channel-surfed. The early news was bad. The tiny Magdalen Islands were first to report in, because they operated on Maritimes time, ahead of the rest of Quebec. They had voted No in 1980, but this time, they went Yes. Through the first hour and a half, the Yes held its lead. Montreal, where federalists were counting on a massive No vote, was one of the last regions to have its ballots counted. There was no one clear moment when it became apparent that the No side would squeak through: no eureka, as Chrétien liked to say.

At 24 Sussex, Chrétien kept pacing. He retired to the basement for a while with Zussman, who always calmed him. The mood remained sombre until the vote broke through to 50 per cent at 9:35 p.m. Then it hovered at that level, barely moving. Chrétien spoke to Johnson once, about an hour later, when the outcome was more secure. "We were sure of the western part of the province," Pelletier said later. "When the first votes came in, it was all in the east. We knew rapidly that we couldn't reach 60 [per cent]."

In Montreal, Rae couldn't stop pacing either. About half an hour after the first results came in, he went up to Pietro Perrino, the provincial Liberals' director general, and asked if he had a fix on the likely result. We'll be okay, Perrino said. After that, Rae didn't want to bother Perrino any more, and he didn't particularly want to be bothered himself. He wandered around, found a deserted corner, and sat down, listening to the cheers and jeers following the results echoing from the string of television sets scattered through the club.

When it finally became clear that the No had squeaked through, it was time for various No side speakers to comment publicly on the result. In the excitement, no one had decided the order in which speakers would appear. Brigitte Fortier, a federal Liberal activist with good contacts with the provincial party, drew up a schedule on the back of a napkin. Johnson spoke, then Charest. Again, Charest was electrifying, but few heard him. Less than two minutes into his remarks, the cameras cut away as Chrétien began his speech from Ottawa. Charest, a good team player throughout the campaign, was furious at what he perceived as a deliberate snub. Federal Liberals blamed a communications mixup.

On Chrétien's way into the Parliament Buildings, he passed a small knot of bystanders who cheered him. Summoning up a smile, he said: "We won." When it came time to speak to the nation, Chrétien stuck to his hastily prepared text. He had practised it twice before, reading it from a TelePrompTer, and in the face of such a divisive result, it was no time to improvise. Addressing the nation, and Quebeckers in particular, he called for calm, asked everyone to accept the democratic result, and repeated that the commitments made in the last week of the campaign would be honoured. "The people have spoken, and it is time to accept the verdict," he said.

Then he walked to his waiting car to return to 24 Sussex and a shorter night of sleep than he was accustomed to. As always, the prime minister moved fast. To some of his colleagues, the big question in coming days would be how to slow him down.

21

APRÈS LE DÉLUGE

On the morning after the referendum, Jean Chrétien was up and at his desk in his study at 24 Sussex Drive shortly after 7 a.m., as usual. Ahead of him lay a quick caucus meeting at 8 a.m., followed by an all-day cabinet session. Chrétien was determined to move swiftly on his commitments to Quebec. He had promised in the final week of the campaign to grant Quebec formal recognition as a distinct society and a veto over constitutional change on matters affecting the province, and he intended to keep his word. He was no longer troubled by previous objections he might have had to Quebec's constitutional demands, nor did he see any irony in the fact that he was the person meeting them. As Jean Pelletier said later, "Chrétien is a practical man, not an ideologue. If a formula no longer answers the need of the day, he looks for something else."

Even before the referendum campaign began, the Liberals had been planning a post-referendum charm offensive. They wanted to appear more cooperative in areas where the federal government and the provinces shared control, such as health care and the environment. On September 27, Chrétien wrote a note to Sheila Copps, in her role as environment minister, pointedly suggesting that she end jurisdictional disputes she was entangled in with several provinces. "Dear colleague," the letter began, "I am writing to seek your assistance in the management of several potentially difficult issues during the period of national reconciliation which will follow the referendum." Proposed actions would be studied on several fronts, the letter continued, including "health care, social policy and environment in order to demonstrate both federal commitment and leadership in forging a stronger federation."

After the referendum, the feds were prepared to go to ridiculous extremes to avoid antagonizing the provinces. At one point in November, the TVOntario public network asked the prime minister to do a testimonial for a feature the network was planning about outstanding teachers. The PMO refused, explaining solemnly to the network's Ottawa bureau chief that it was inappropriate for Chrétien to do so because education was a provincial responsibility.

As Chrétien sat down with his cabinet that Tuesday morning, Canadians from coast to coast were looking to him for leadership. But for now, his main concern was upholding his promises — and salvaging what remained of his credibility in Quebec. He was fixated on the hastily conceived commitments made at Verdun a week earlier.

His ministers, feeling the need to purge their pent-up fears, conducted an emotional post-mortem. They were shaken by how close they had come to losing the country, and there were conflicting feelings of relief, frustration, exhilaration, and exhaustion. Sheila Copps broke into tears at one point. They had made it only halfway around the table when Peter Donolo slipped in, just before lunch. The overall tone of the morning media coverage was not kind to the prime minister. The *Globe and Mail* had called him a diminished figure. Donolo wanted the ministers to point out that the federalists had been trailing until the prime minister entered the fray. He had pulled it back from the brink. But Lucienne Robillard strongly objected. They could not do that, she protested: it would look as though they were blaming Daniel Johnson. In fact, some of them did.

Everyone — from reporters to cabinet ministers — looked forward to Question Period that afternoon. How would Lucien Bouchard behave after coming so close? At 2:15 p.m., House of Commons Speaker Gilbert Parent called for oral questions. Bouchard, to his left, rose and opened with a query about unemployment insurance. Across the aisle, Brian Tobin listened with particular interest. Much of the media commentary afterwards described Bouchard as having retreated into business as usual. But Tobin read it differently. In UI, he figured, the separatist Bouchard had discovered a breach in the federal line, one he could probe until he broke through.

Tobin had toured the Gaspé in the dying days of the campaign with Patrick Gagnon, the only Liberal MP in eastern Quebec. At stop after stop, they ran into friendly people, self-declared Liberals all, who planned to vote Yes because they wanted Lucien Bouchard to be strong enough to save UI. The Gaspé was much like parts of the Maritimes, full of seasonal workers and with a traditionally high unemployment rate. Tobin didn't buy into the conventional wisdom that Quebeckers had come within a whisker of rejecting Canada because of federal refusals to reopen the Constitution. He thought their flirtation with separatism had a strong bread-and-butter element to it, with a sense that Ottawa was about to sell them out on unemployment insurance, that the federal government had detached itself from their lives.

Heading into October, Quebec Liberals were still disturbed about Axworthy's plans for labour market training. He was intending to decentralize, but on his own terms. That would entail blowing up the department's top-heavy command-and-control programs, and farming out authority to individual Canada Employment Centres. The Quebec ministers thought Axworthy should go farther in distancing the federal government from the provision of training, and that he should interpret training to include most employment programs. They didn't want to sidestep the provinces. Rather, their idea of getting out of labour market training was to hand the money to the provinces, leaving them in charge of the distribution. As Bouchard spoke, it was plain that Axworthy was again caught in the Quebec maelstrom.

The post-referendum fallout was just beginning. The western premiers were gathered in Yorkton, Saskatchewan, that Tuesday for a meeting scheduled weeks previously. The premiers closeted themselves in the local Holiday Inn. At 10 p.m., they sent out for pizza. They did not have their officials in the room with them, and the atmosphere was informal, the conversation forthright. They talked for a while about the personal pressures that bind politicians in power. Alberta's Ralph Klein complained about how his wife, Colleen, was being subjected to a kicking in the media about alleged insider trading in a Calgary-based company, Multi-Corp. Inc. Roy Romanow dispensed advice to British Columbia's social services minister, Joy MacPhail — who was filling in on the first night for Premier Mike Harcourt — on how to handle the so-called Bingogate controversy. When they finally turned to Quebec, Klein proved to be the most aggressive on the topic. He felt the country had been hijacked by Quebec. Now it was time to turn to the grievances of others. The premiers decided that the provinces should take the lead.

Romanow contacted Newfoundland's Clyde Wells, who held the rotating position of chair of the annual first ministers' conference. On behalf of the western premiers, Romanow suggested that Wells investigate the possibility of holding a special meeting of all the premiers. On Wednesday, the western premiers issued a communiqué that called for what they considered truly national decision-making in the days ahead, but it was widely interpreted as a power grab at the expense of a weakened Ottawa. Wells reported back that there was not sufficient consensus among the provincial leaders for a meeting. Some of the premiers he had talked to felt that they would look divided.

Chrétien, still bursting with nervous energy, wanted to strike quickly and decisively. He was already fed up with the second-guessing under way across the country about the referendum campaign. In caucus on Wednesday, he stuck his hands in his pockets and launched into a long recitation of what he saw as the key moments of the campaign, and their effects. He was impatient with those who suggested the final result was so close as to amount to a tie. "In a hockey game and a tight one," he said, "nobody says it was a tie. We won, God damn it." And for all those who faulted his dozens of advisers, "I had none, God damn it: when you are prime minister, you are alone."

Jacques Parizeau had announced on Tuesday his decision to resign as premier of Quebec. While others speculated over Bouchard's intentions, Chrétien had no such doubts: in caucus, he spoke of his rival's ascension to the premiership as a fait accompli. Now, he said, was the time to corner Bouchard and leave him with some unpalatable choices.

But already it was clear that the prime minister's enthusiasm for quick action was not widely shared. The pleas to Quebec and the passions that had ignited the massive pro-Canada rally in Montreal the previous Friday had already dissipated. Reg Alcock, speaking for western MPs, said that offers to Quebec would not be well received in his region. Ontario caucus chair Sue Barnes said that jobs were the big concern in Ontario, more so than the questions of distinct society and a veto for Quebec.

Later that day, Chrétien flew to Toronto to give a speech at a $500-a-head Liberal fundraising dinner. In his first lengthy public comments on the referendum since the night of the vote, he took an unusually forceful line. Canadians, he said, had been "extremely generous" in sitting quietly by while Quebec held its referendums on the province's constitutional future, but enough was enough. We Canadians, he said, "have done it twice and we cannot carry it on forever." Although he did not go farther in his remarks, it was the first public sign of the growing belief among himself and key advisers that somehow, some way, the feds should take steps to ensure that the sovereigntists were not always dictating the terms of the debate.

Chrétien stayed overnight for a secret meeting the following morning with Ontario Premier Mike Harris. The prime minister desperately wanted to line up six provinces willing to support a constitutional amendment on distinct society. Under the Constitution, such an amendment required seven provinces representing at least 50 per cent of the country's population. Chrétien felt that if he could get six outside Quebec, then he could put Lucien Bouchard — or whoever succeeded Parizeau — on the spot. The Quebec premier would then look like the rejectionist, the one who stood in the way of change.

Chrétien felt he could count on the three Maritime provinces, while assuming that Wells would never agree. He also figured on the support of two of the prairie provinces, Manitoba and Saskatchewan. Romanow was uneasy about the notion. "I told him," he said later, "that this is a tough sell out here." But he also made it clear that Saskatchewan would not block change if Chrétien could line up the requisite number of other provinces. On the other hand, Alberta and British Columbia could not be expected to support anything that smacked of special status for Quebec.

That left Ontario. Chrétien and his advisers were encouraged by the fact that Harris had supported both the Meech Lake Accord and the Charlottetown Accord. And the Ontario legislature had passed a resolution in the late stages of the referendum campaign asserting recognition of Quebec's "distinct character within our country."

Harris arrived for the meeting at the Westin Harbour Castle Hotel, overlooking Lake Ontario, at about 7:30 a.m. on Thursday, and proceeded to a sprawling suite on the top floor with a panoramic view. A large Canadian flag stood near the window. The Ontario premier was ill with flu, and running a fever. He hadn't wanted to meet that day, but federal officials had pushed hard.

Harris had an idea of what to expect. Ontario government officials had spoken with their federal counterparts the previous day. Chrétien wanted to move quickly to give Quebec an effective veto, guaranteed by the federal government, over any constitutional change that would affect it. As well, Chrétien wanted to recognize Quebec's distinct status in the Constitution using language based on the so-called Canada clause in the failed Charlottetown Accord. That provision would not override the Charter of

Rights, satisfying what had always been Chrétien's chief objection to any such move.

The two leaders sat in armchairs facing each other. Eddie Goldenberg was with the prime minister, and Guy Giorno, a young Tory lawyer and policy adviser, accompanied Harris. Goldenberg asked Giorno not to take notes. Harris had expected Chrétien to show him a draft of the motion and the proposed amendment, but the prime minister stuck to generalities. He described his two-pronged plan. He said he would have enough provinces lined up to force Quebec into a corner if Ontario signed on. The legislation would make Bouchard look intransigent if he refused to go along.

Harris felt Chrétien was acting precipitously and told him so. He pressed Chrétien to explain why he needed to move so quickly. Each time, the response came back to Chrétien's promises a week earlier in Verdun, and the need to deliver on them. Harris argued that the country was not ready, and neither was Ontario. "Jean, I tell you as a friend," he said, "it's a mistake."

Harris wondered about the federal government briefers. He had made plain on several occasions that he would not agree to constitutional changes without a referendum. It was more than a matter of the legislature; he had to carry voters, too, and that seemed difficult. As well, it would distract him from the economic agenda upon which he had been elected five months previously.

Chrétien didn't give up. As the meeting wound down, he asked Harris: "Can I have your support?"

"No," Harris answered.

Without Ontario, Chrétien would be forced to fall back on a secondary plan to pass a federal resolution recognizing Quebec as a distinct society, outside of the Constitution. Disappointed, he flew back to Ottawa for a cabinet meeting that brought more bad news. The initial doubts expressed on Tuesday within cabinet and caucus over the need for swift action on Quebec had congealed into outright hostility in some quarters. On Wednesday and Thursday, political aides took soundings of the public mood — perusing newspaper columns and editorials, monitoring radio and television, and telephoning contacts. The message was unmistakable: anything smacking of special status for Quebec was definitely not on. The fire of the pre-referendum unity rally the previous Friday in Montreal, when people seemed ready to promise almost anything to keep Quebec in

Canada, was now reduced to ashes, the embers cooling quickly. Hard-line talk-show hosts like Rafe Mair in British Columbia and Dave Rutherford in Alberta were already on the warpath against concessions to Quebec. Chrétien's aides believed that similar sentiments in rural Ontario provided the real explanation of Mike Harris's unbending stance in the morning meeting with the prime minister. As now seemed perpetually the case, federalists in Quebec dismissed the suggestions to appease them as too weak, while the rest of the country considered them too strong.

In this second post-referendum cabinet meeting on Thursday afternoon, many of his ministers urged Chrétien to slow down, consider his options, and allow the country to catch its breath. He could keep his promises later, they argued, as part of a more comprehensive package. Even Allan Rock, the minister whose department would be responsible for putting the veto and distinct society promises into practice, expressed strong reservations about the prime minister's hellbent determination to proceed. As justice minister, he worried about the difficulty of translating Chrétien's ambiguous musings on distinct society and the veto into law. Caucus and some of the left-liberal ministers were deeply troubled by the loose talk of decentralization. They felt that the absence of a discernible federal presence was part of the problem, not the solution. Very few ministers, with Sheila Copps one of the exceptions, backed immediate action.

It was a tough meeting for the prime minister, one that participants described as unusually brutal and frank. Chrétien took it from all sides, but as prime minister, he chose to trust his instincts. As had Harris, his ministers concluded that his desire to press ahead had to do more with a need to save his own credibility than with a permanent solution. When Chrétien pounded the gavel to end discussion, he made clear that he intended to proceed.

It fell to Rock to put flesh on Chrétien's bare-bones promises. Senior Justice Department officials and his ministerial staff worked feverishly to make sense of it all. To them, the issues looked far more complex than the prime minister seemed to think. Who, for example, would have final say in Quebec on a veto over constitutional change? Would it be the people, in the form of a referendum, or the National Assembly? Chrétien did not make that clear in his Verdun speech. Privately, his preference was that it be given to "the people." But provincial Liberals were adamant that it should go to the National Assembly, so there was the risk of splitting the already weakened federalist side.

Chrétien was preparing for a gruelling trip half a world away that would begin with a Commonwealth meeting in New Zealand. From there, he was supposed to visit Australia briefly and then go to Osaka, Japan, for a meeting of the Asia-Pacific Economic Council. But he set his planned November 7 departure back a day to allow him to be in the Commons to speak to whatever measure was put forward.

On Thursday night, Chrétien had Jean Charest over to dinner at 24 Sussex. Charest, too, urged the prime minister to slow down. Like other Canadians, he argued, the people of Quebec were exhausted by the referendum process and in no hurry to revisit constitutional issues. It would be better to deliver more later rather than some watered-down notions of distinct society and the veto right now. Chrétien listened but didn't agree. At the same time, he made several oblique suggestions to Charest about his own future that could have been interpreted as encouragement to go after the leadership of the Quebec Liberal Party in place of Daniel Johnson. Charest, who was already cross at the Liberals for bumping him from national television on referendum night, was further annoyed by that. He thought the Liberals, after treating him with care and respect before and during the campaign, were now casually dismissing both him and Johnson.

On Friday, November 3, House Leader Herb Gray's office frantically prepared to give the forty-eight hours' notice required to introduce the veto bill, which had leapfrogged ahead of the distinct society motion. After the meeting with Harris, Chrétien knew he could not get agreement on a constitutional amendment on distinct society, and so he put the matter temporarily on ice. But formidable problems remained on the issue of a veto. The drafts coming over from the Justice Department didn't hold together. Using the Verdun speech as their guide, the drafters kept bogging down on the deliberate vagueness of Chrétien's promises. He hated precision, and was almost incapable of it. Years ago, he had responded to a reporter's question about the Constitution by saying, "Why ask me, I'm not a lawyer." But he *was* a lawyer, and in the aftermath of the referendum, that was more clear than ever.

On Friday morning, Allan Rock had several conversations with Chrétien, trying to dissuade him from pressing ahead. Rock, a rookie MP and minister, told the prime minister that, of course, he was on the team and would do whatever he was told — but he had very definite questions and concerns. He had worked closely with his department officials during the week trying to prepare a cohesive draft. He did not want to produce a document that would be so mushy as to be irrelevant, and he feared that was the danger they faced. Rock spent what he later described to friends as a "terribly uncomfortable morning" in his office, agonizing over unsatisfactory drafts and dreading his impending press conference. The prime minister still clung fast to his determination to act immediately.

Shortly before noon, Rock was relieved to get a call from a Chrétien adviser telling him to stand down, that they would not proceed that day. Rock walked across the street to the Langevin Block to see Jean Pelletier, and told him that in his view, the government should halt its efforts entirely, and form a cabinet committee to study different options for action. Pelletier pulled a piece of paper from his pocket and said: "Here." It was a list of ministers, including Rock, who would form just such a national unity committee. Rock felt lighter than air. He returned to his office and took his staff to the Parliamentary Restaurant for what he later described as an "utterly blissful" if brief lunch.

By Saturday, Chrétien had a terrible cold. He stayed in bed in the morning, then got up to make a brief appearance at a Liberal national executive meeting, then went back home to bed. That afternoon, word reached Ottawa that Israeli leader Yitzhak Rabin had been assassinated. It was decided that Chrétien would leave on Sunday for Israel in order to attend the funeral. From there, he would fly on to New Zealand, and pick up the rest of the planned trip. At the PMO offices in the Langevin Block, the lights burned until the early hours of Sunday morning as aides tried to arrange hotel accommodation. The Israelis wouldn't put up Chrétien. His aides studied a large map of the region trying to find a safe, convenient place for him to stay. Eventually, Canada's honorary consul in Cyprus came through with a block of rooms in Nicosia.

Just as it seemed that nothing was going as planned, things got markedly worse. That night, Aline Chrétien pumped her husband full of cold remedies and sent him off to bed. Shortly before 3 o'clock in the morning, she heard a commotion in the hallway. Thinking it was the staff getting their bags ready for the next morning, she went out into the hall to shush them so they wouldn't disturb her ailing husband. But there were no staff members around. Instead, she confronted a strange man brandishing a knife and putting a glove on one hand. He had roamed the grounds of 24 Sussex, RCMP investigators later ascertained, for more than twenty minutes before entering the house by breaking a side-door window. Aline retreated into the bedroom, locked both doors, woke Chrétien, and called the RCMP. The prime minister, groggy from the effects of medication, initially told her she was dreaming. But then, as he became fully conscious, he picked up a fifteen-inch stone Inuit carving to use as a weapon. After a seven-minute wait that seemed much longer, an RCMP detachment arrived and arrested the intruder.

Chrétien phoned and woke up Eddie Goldenberg. "We have a problem," he said in the cold, flat voice that he reserves for when he is furious. No one knew who the intruder was, or what had motivated him. The already edgy PMO staff, home just a few hours from the Langevin Block, phoned and roused one another with the shocking news.

The experience deeply rattled Chrétien for many months. On the flight overseas, visibly upset, he speculated to reporters that the incendiary language used by sovereigntists in the referendum campaign might have sparked the incident. The RCMP's incompetence made the prime minister angry, but over time, he directed his fury as much at the manner in which the incident was treated as a joke in some quarters. The images of the confused intruder, equipped with a small knife, frightened away by the prime minister's wife, and the Chrétiens preparing to do battle with an Inuit carving all became fodder for editorial cartoonists, satirists and radio morning-show hosts. But as far as Chrétien was concerned, it was an assassination attempt, plain and simple. The weapon was more like a hunting knife than a penknife, and Chrétien maintained that the intruder had clearly intended to plunge it into the sleeping prime minister.

When Chrétien returned from his trip two weeks later, he returned to the matter of his unfulfilled promises, even before the unity committee could begin drawing conclusions. By now, it was clear that the only way to achieve action on recognition of Quebec as a distinct society was via a federal resolution. Constitutional change would have to wait. As for the veto, he was still thinking only in terms of Quebec, as he had promised in Verdun. But the restless Liberal caucus soon made it clear that that was not acceptable. How, backbenchers and ministers asked, could we give Quebec a veto without giving similar status to Ontario, which was larger? And once that happened, what about the rest of the country?

Despite those objections, the prime minister gave no public or private sign through most of November that he was considering vetoes for any part of the country outside Quebec. Even at that, his proposal amounted to "lending" Quebec Ottawa's veto in instances where Quebec's interests could be affected. An actual constitutional amendment to provide Quebec a veto, which would require unanimous provincial consent, was an obvious non-starter. The unity committee, which was meeting two to three times a week, proceeded on that basis until November 27, when Eddie Goldenberg walked in with a new document, rendering all its previous work obsolete. The prime minister had reversed course and would announce a veto formula based on the aborted Victoria constitutional agreement of a quarter-century earlier, a long-standing favourite of his. Each of four regions — Quebec, Ontario, the west, and Atlantic Canada — would be given equal weight. And it would be publicly announced that very day, along with federal recognition of Quebec as a distinct society and a proposal for Ottawa to shift control of labour market training to the provinces.

The problem was that under the formula, British Columbia, the third-largest and fastest-growing province, with a society and culture markedly different from the three prairie provinces, was nonetheless lumped in with its neighbours. Along with Alberta and Ontario, it was one of only three "have" provinces paying more into federal coffers than it took out. Chrétien apparently didn't appreciate the great psychological and economic changes that had occurred in B.C. since 1971, when the four-regions concept had first been broached.

Political disaster loomed, as some ministers immediately understood. Tobin, privy to the new plan as a member of the unity committee, argued forcefully that B.C. should also get a veto, that the prime minister could gain badly needed points in that province by getting out ahead of the curve and recognizing the province's growing importance and clout. It, too, formed a distinct society. But Chrétien, caught in his time warp, stuck to the old formula. He did, however, accept Tobin's suggestion that he inform caucus before making the regional veto plan public that afternoon.

Tobin, with his genius for communications, came up with the idea of gathering the Liberal MPs in their private lobby behind the curtain of the House of Commons following Question Period. Chrétien stood on a table and told them his plan in a sort of pep rally. Tobin felt the gesture lent an air of urgency and unity to the day. Pumped up, Chrétien then went across the street to the National Press Theatre. The prime minister said the moves would achieve "change without revolution, progress without rupture." That wasn't the way that many other people in the country saw it. Predictably, Lucien Bouchard denounced the measures as insufficient for Quebec and ridiculed the prime minister for envisioning Quebec as "one of many chicks nicely arranged around the mother hen."

Almost immediately, there was trouble on nearly every front. The promise about training brought its own distinct set of difficulties. In his November 27 statement Chrétien had agreed, belatedly, to Quebec's demands for full control over labour market training. But whatever did that mean? He said the federal government would withdraw from programs that included training, apprenticeship, cooperative education, and programs based in the workplace. "We are prepared to help workers that need training to return to work or obtain a better job, but we will do so only with the consent and cooperation of the provinces," Chrétien told reporters.

Axworthy had grown impatient with traditional training in any case. But he wanted to hold on to other employment measures, ones that some in Quebec regarded as belonging in the training envelope. Some Quebec ministers still weren't satisfied, but the prevailing view in the PMO was that Axworthy could not be dealt another defeat. As always, the situation was fluid.

Nor was Brian Tobin finished with Axworthy. As Axworthy neared the finish line in late November, Tobin played his final card. He had been consulting closely throughout with New Brunswick Premier Frank McKenna, whose province was heavily dependent on seasonal work.

Tobin let McKenna know that he was engaged in an intensive cabinet battle with Axworthy and that any help from him would be appreciated. Tobin told McKenna that the UI bill was in its final stages, and despite his best efforts, it would devastate the region economically and threaten Liberal political hegemony. He wanted the New Brunswick premier to use his position to write a letter to the otherwise preoccupied Chrétien, who needed a reminder about the potential political consequences of Axworthy's reform. McKenna and Tobin dictated lines back and forth to each other on the phone, both getting angrier as they went along. In extraordinarily strong language, the letter beseeched Chrétien to reconsider Axworthy's "devastating" plans. "Prime Minister, I beg of you to take the time to examine the ramifications of this legislation," McKenna wrote. He and Tobin made sure to link their concerns to Chrétien's larger national unity worries, warning that the UI bill "will create a political backlash from the Ontario border east, the likes of which has never been seen before in this country."

Axworthy felt betrayed by the letter. For one thing, he correctly sensed Tobin's hand in its drafting. Second, McKenna had always portrayed himself as the great social reformer, a politician who, on his own turf, cut welfare rates to the bone to finance active social measures. One of Axworthy's first public acts as minister had been to arrange a fact-finding trip to New Brunswick to study McKenna's innovations.

On Wednesday, November 29, the Atlantic premiers descended on Ottawa to inform Chrétien personally of their concerns. All along, the prime minister had wanted to avoid getting caught in the middle of the Axworthy-Tobin battle. But after receiving the McKenna letter, he felt he had no choice: he had to intervene. Tobin scored some further concessions, including changes in the number of weeks used to calculate UI benefit levels. But the basic architecture of Axworthy's reforms remained intact.

Meanwhile, the Quebec ministers got together to discuss a last-minute appeal of their own to the prime minister. They still didn't think that Axworthy's plan — which they regarded as only a limited withdrawal from labour market training — would wash in Quebec. They began drafting their own letter to Chrétien. Axworthy got wind of their intentions and took aside Martin, who had been supportive over the previous months. If the letter went out, he said, the government would have one angry human resources minister in its midst. There had been enough interference, he declared, hinting at the possibility of resignation. Besides, if he didn't get the UI bill introduced in the next few days, Martin's coming budget, which depended on the reforms being in place, would be undermined. He succeeded in breaking apart a Quebec consensus. In the meantime, Chrétien flew off to Africa for the annual meeting of the Francophonie. The letter never went out.

On Friday, December 1, Axworthy's Employment Insurance Bill finally limped into the House of Commons. It had been a long, hard slog for the minister. He had first set out to reform unemployment insurance under Pierre Trudeau in the early 1980s. Now, in the dying days of 1995, he explained that the key to his reforms lay in changing people's attitudes: he wanted Canadians to focus less on benefits as an entitlement and more on developing opportunities to earn income. "I go back twelve years, wanting to make sure that we have a system that is much more conducive and open and encouraging to work than the one we have now," he said. Despite all the opposition, and the late changes he had made, he felt tremendous satisfaction.

Meanwhile, the west was up in arms. For close to a week after the November 27 announcement, the Liberals sat unblinking in Ottawa while the negative responses rolled in from Alberta and B.C. about the government's distinct society intentions for Quebec and especially its veto plans for four regions of Canada. Political aides monitoring responses had no trouble gauging the mood: offices of British Columbia MPs were bombarded with protesting phone calls, provincial politicians were harshly critical, and callers to open-line radio shows denounced Ottawa. Some of the letters were "very vituperative, almost pathological," said MP Ted McWhinney, a former professor of constitutional law.

Chrétien and his advisers couldn't, or wouldn't, comprehend the firestorm the proposal had sparked, particularly in B.C. Two years after Chrétien had named his cabinet, the weakness of the B.C. contingent came home to roost. The six MPs from the province often spent as much time fighting one another as they did working together to pursue B.C. interests. Backbencher Herb Dhaliwal and Secretary of State Raymond Chan had once clashed for the nomination in the same riding, and still didn't get along with each other; Hedy Fry and Ted McWhinney were considered by colleagues to be shameless egotists forever considering themselves poised on the edge of cabinet; Anna Terrana hadn't created any kind of profile; and Anderson, the one MP from the province in the full cabinet — a reluctant choice at that — had immediately made a bad impression once he got there with his involvement in several minor controversies. None of them could be said to have Chrétien's ear. There were no British Columbians in the Privy Council Office, and no senior advisers from the province in the Ottawa back rooms. Inside the PMO, the senior western Canadian was a twenty-something Albertan named Raj Chahal, a relatively junior official in the PMO's pecking order, with responsibility for the entire west and the added assignment of "advancing" foreign trips.

The upset held at a steady roar that showed no signs of abating. Liberals in the province felt panicked by the intensity of the reaction. Some thought the political fallout comparable to the outrage that had greeted the National Energy Program in Alberta in 1980. Nonetheless, Chrétien did not budge, insisting the package would go ahead as planned. "To you the members from B.C., close the file and deal with your normal work," he admonished them at a caucus meeting. "Do you think that Rafe Mair will become a Liberal if we change?" British Columbia had 47 per cent of the population of the west, he said, so it had an effective veto anyhow. What was the problem? He reminded the shaky MPs of the party's high standing in the province. But they noted that the latest poll had been taken before what they now considered a catastrophe.

On Monday, December 4, Anderson met with the unity committee and pleaded for relief. He warned that the negative response in B.C. was overwhelming. He was almost desperate in his insistence on some action. Other B.C. MPs transmitted similar messages. Ted McWhinney wrote Chrétien a letter, explaining that population growth and immigration had changed the province so profoundly in the previous twenty years that it could no longer be lumped in with other western provinces, the same argument Tobin had made a week — it seemed an eternity — earlier.

At first, Anderson had tried to play it both ways, arguing against the exclusion of British Columbia from the club of big hitters but accepting the prime minister's argument that by virtue of its size, it would effectively control the western veto in any case. Now he argued passionately that something had to be done. That brought opposition from Alberta minister Anne McLellan. She and Anderson and his wife, Sandra McCallum, were very close friends, so much so that McLellan was godmother to one of their children. But on this issue, the two ministers from the westernmost provinces parted company. She warned that a veto for B.C. would cause anguish in Alberta, which would feel left out. Rock and Tobin still supported B.C., but Marcel Massé and some others worried that a fifth region would further water down the effect in Quebec. Some ministers initially sympathetic to the B.C. case thought the government would look as if it was improvising if it gave in at such a late date.

On Wednesday, Chrétien, who had returned from Africa, met with caucus. He told them that if he gave a veto to B.C. based on its population levels, he would have to do the same for Metropolitan Toronto, and so on. Not for the first time, he lamented that B.C. was almost as difficult as Quebec. He didn't seem prepared to entertain any possibility that he had misjudged the situation.

Anderson asked for, and finally received, a one-to-one meeting with the prime minister and persuaded him to hear out the province's small contingent of Liberal MPs. Before suppertime, the PMO contacted the group, giving its members ten minutes' notice of a meeting with the prime minister. It was held down the hall from Chrétien's third-floor office in the

Centre Block. They met for twenty minutes, peppering Chrétien with prognostications of the dire consequences that would befall them. At the end of the session, Chrétien thanked them for coming but gave no indication whether he had changed his mind.

He had, although he left it to Allan Rock to make the announcement at a news conference the following afternoon. Rock, flanked by his B.C. colleagues, made official the government's capitulation. "In a word," he said, "the government has listened." The measure, the government pronounced, also meant that Alberta would effectively gain a veto as well, because it had more than 50 per cent of the population of the three prairie provinces. In British Columbia, Andrew Petter, the provincial minister responsible for constitutional affairs, said his government was still unhappy with the legislation, which would allow Quebec and Ontario to maintain the constitutional status quo: it didn't want anyone to have vetoes.

In Quebec, nobody thanked the prime minister. The Bloc Québécois pointed to the change as further proof of the worthlessness of Quebec's veto; the proof was that it had taken just a week or so for B.C. to achieve what Quebec had demanded for years. Falling short of a constitutional amendment, Chrétien also piloted a motion through Parliament on December 11 committing the federal government to recognize a limited form of distinct society status for Quebec. The Bloc Québécois and Reform voted against.

The contretemps with British Columbia underscored Chrétien's stubborn streak. Once he decided on a course of action, little short of divine intervention — or a near full-blown caucus insurrection — could dissuade him. That was evident in early November, when he had insisted on pressing ahead with his plans for Quebec despite the objections of almost everyone else in the government. Events at the end of November and the beginning of December also exposed how removed he was from political currents in Canada's third-largest province. Since becoming prime minister, he had spent more time out of Canada than in visiting the more far-flung regions of the country — even those as important as B.C. Without personal contact, a politician such as Chrétien, who relied so heavily on his instincts, was forced to engage in political combat stripped of his best weapon.

22

STARTING OVER

As the holiday season approached, Canadians found themselves in a deep collective funk. They had even lost their will to shop. The year-end pulse-taking by the nation's pollsters, a more recent but no less pervasive tradition than St. Nick himself, threw up a portrait of a nation in utter despair. "In 20 years of analyzing poll results, this year's set of findings is the blackest I have ever examined," veteran pollster Allan Gregg wrote about his 1995 sample for *Maclean's* and the CBC. The results were sufficiently apocalyptic for the magazine to title the issue "Can Canada Survive?"

Gregg discovered that one in three Canadians — and one in two Quebeckers — believed that by the end of the decade Canada, as they knew it, would cease to exist. Their malaise drew on a rich aquifer of anguish, most of it relating to the country's profound sense of economic insecurity. Almost 90 per cent expected unemployment insurance and welfare to be less generous or eliminated entirely within five years. A similar number thought that young Canadians would find it even harder to secure meaningful work. About 80 per cent expected to see the end of the Canada Pension Plan. More than 60 per cent felt universal health care would expire. One of the *Maclean's* writers turned to Leonard Cohen to capture the mood as Canada approached the millennium: "I have seen the future, brother: it is murder." Despite all the pain that Canadians expected to endure in bringing the deficit under control, only 2 per cent believed it would be eliminated altogether. Far more thought it would be higher rather than lower.

The economic pessimism came as no surprise to retailers. The sharp upturn in consumer confidence in Chrétien's first year in office had evaporated. In the last quarter of 1994, consumer confidence had plunged precipitously, falling to its lowest non-recessionary level since figures were first compiled in the 1960s, according to the Conference Board of Canada. Small wonder. In 1994, the economy had produced some 400,000 jobs. In 1995, the figure fell below 100,000, not nearly enough to keep up with new demand from school-leavers and immigrants. The public sector, in declaring war on deficits, had actually destroyed tens of thousands of jobs. While the Liberals still floated high in the polls, confidence in their economic management had begun to erode, a disturbing trend for any government but particularly for one that had staked so much on jobs and growth. Asked by the Angus Reid Group how well the Liberals had done in keeping their election promises on jobs, 68 per cent judged the government poorly.

A couple of years earlier, shortly after declaring his Liberal candidacy, Marcel Massé had told a journalist acquaintance that the only way governments would ever get their deficits under control would be to siphon off all the benefits of the next economic recovery for themselves. That, in essence, had occurred. Polls showed that up to 80 per cent of Canadians believed the 1990–91 recession had never ended, a figure that paradoxically grew as the tepid recovery lengthened.

On top of all this, Canadians had been forced by the near-miss of the referendum to confront their constitutional ghosts once again. Positions from one end of the country to another appeared, at least on the surface, beyond reconciliation. On the morning after Jean Chrétien's election as prime minister, the *Globe and Mail*, analyzing the balkanization that had taken place with the Bloc in Quebec and Reform in the west, had written: "It will take the skill of a magician and the nerve of a high-wire artist to govern the country after Canadians gave vent to their regional frustrations yesterday." The *Maclean's* poll of December 1995 underlined the point. Canadians outside Quebec held fast to the conviction that the country constituted a partnership of ten equal provinces, entitling Quebec to absolutely no special privileges. In most of the country, the traditional view of Canada as a pact between two founding people — French and English — had withered and practically died.

As his dispirited members of Parliament prepared to head home in mid-December, Jean Chrétien delivered a pep talk. He asserted that three-quarters of the Red Book promises had already been kept, and that he had succeeded in meeting the Verdun commitments. For all the blackness of mood, the Liberals still stood at the mid-50s in the public opinion polls.

The methods of the government in Ottawa, well on its way to its 3-per-cent deficit target, appeared moderate and competent compared with the slash-and-burn policies being employed in Ontario.

"Spend good time with your family," Chrétien urged the MPs on December 13, the second-to-last sitting day before the holidays. "Be optimistic," he said, invoking the sunny ways. "A Liberal is someone who always speaks positively."

It was Lucien Bouchard's final day in Parliament before heading off to become premier of Quebec, and that afternoon he and Jean Chrétien met face to face for the first time ever. Bouchard had requested the meeting, sending a note across the floor of the Commons. Both leaders had been in gracious moods that day. Chrétien interrupted Question Period to salute Bouchard, saying that "in politics there is a certain amount of confrontation, but there are also moments that we appreciate." Bouchard, in turn, defended Chrétien against the intemperate remarks of Reform leader Preston Manning.

The PMO had set aside ten minutes for the meeting. It was extraordinary in the cloistered chamber of Canadian politics, and even more so in the Quebec anteroom, that two figures of such prominence, both graduates of Laval Law School, only five years apart, had no personal history. In the early 1960s, long before they would become the titans of their age, Trudeau and Lévesque had debated each other twice a month in the privacy of Gérard Pelletier's home. Perhaps the lack of connection between their successors said something about how isolated Chrétien was from Quebec, or how isolated Bouchard was from Canada as a whole.

Bouchard took the elevator to Chrétien's office. They met alone, breaking the ice by talking about their respective brothers, both medical researchers in Montreal, and their good relationship. The prime minister then lit into Bouchard for the highly charged personal invective he had employed against Chrétien in the referendum. Bouchard would later confess he had been taken aback. He hadn't realized how wounding his words could be. He vowed to be more circumspect in future, to keep his attacks on a more substantial plane. Finally, the two settled on a subject of common interest: the dire straits of the Quebec economy, on which they pledged cooperation. In the end, they spent forty-five minutes together.

Jean Chrétien remained a moderate in politics, the conductor seeking to make soothing music out of the clanging political notes being sounded across the land. He had always been at his best as a deal-maker, locating the common ground on which a compromise could be constructed. He had demonstrated this talent as the energy minister negotiating a heavy-oil upgrader for Lloydminister and, most famously, in delivering Trudeau a constitutional deal in late 1981. Trudeau hadn't liked the final shape, but Chrétien had convinced him it was the only deal possible.

Chrétien clearly had his own bottom line: he wouldn't countenance discussion, for instance, of a confederated Canada, one in which Ottawa, like Brussels in the European Union, would be relegated to the status of a creature of the provinces. But he was willing to stray far and wide in taking whatever action he felt would hold Canada together. To a pragmatist, the completed transaction mattered more than the principles underlying it. "For me, I look at what works and what does not work," he said in an interview in mid-1996.

Now Chrétien instructed the cabinet unity committee to concentrate on non-constitutional measures that responded to the traditional demands of Quebeckers. But he had also decided that he would never be held hostage to another Quebec referendum with no control over the timing, question, or interpretation of the result. His views had hardened considerably from the early fall, when he had attacked Reform for its tough questions about Canada's negotiating terms in the event of a Yes vote.

Now he favoured an in-your-face strategy that would fence in the separatists before they could once again put the play in motion. In caucus, Doug Young, tough-minded and fluently bilingual, put the case for an aggressive strategy in terms of a hockey game. "What we find frustrating," he told Chrétien, "is playing on their ice, with their rules and their referee. We need to have our own rules." The prime minister signalled his full agreement for what would become known as Plan B, marking a sharp reversal from his earlier "What, me worry?" position.

The referendum gnawed at Chrétien — and not just the prospect of going through it again. He seethed at the damage to his own reputation. "We won, God damn it," he told one group of Liberals. "We won. Under a crooked question." (To Chrétien, the question amounted to "Do you want to stay in Canada and pay half the taxes?") In almost all remarks, public and private, he would seek to deflect any possible blame: the No strategy had been letter-perfect until Bouchard took over from Parizeau in mid-campaign; he had so outperformed Bouchard in the House of Commons at the start of the campaign that the Bloc leader had fled to find a more favourable field of combat; nobody could have predicted Parizeau stepping aside; the Quebec media had been shamefully biased; the federalists had won every week of the referendum except two; he had personally saved the day in the final week. Chrétien, the victim of the big lie for many years, had his own particular spin on his limited role in the referendum. He had been blocked from participating in the campaign by the No committee, he would state, which, under Quebec law, was controlled by the provincial opposition leader, Daniel Johnson. Only in the last week, trailing by seven points, had he been permitted to play a more active role. In less than a week, he wiped out that seven-point deficit and took the No side over the top.

All this conveniently left out the fact that he had always planned to intervene in the campaign just three or four times, as Trudeau had in 1980, and that among the reasons for his limited role were his confidence of victory and his understanding that he could be a liability. Certainly he had not been excluded from the referendum strategy. John Rae, his closest associate for nearly thirty years, had participated in every meeting.

Increasingly, Chrétien fretted about an overabundance of democracy in Canada. He would come back from his trips overseas and report on the puzzlement of foreign leaders over Canada's willingness to allow such votes to take place. The president of Mexico had responded to his own national crisis by stating unequivocally that the country was indivisible. The Belgian prime minister said he would never tolerate such a process.

As Christmas approached, Jean Chrétien concluded he would have to take dramatic action to put his government back on track. For two years, he had forsworn changes to his cabinet. He had stubbornly resisted suggestions of dumping weak or embattled ministers, taking pride in the longevity of his ministry as compared with Brian Mulroney's. The original cabinet, sworn in at Rideau Hall on November 4, 1993, remained intact but for the addition of Lucienne Robillard, for whom the government had manufactured a by-election to strengthen itself for the referendum. For Chrétien, Quebec representation remained his biggest headache. Robillard had failed to make much of an impression in the public arena. Paul Martin had proven Chrétien's faith in him as finance minister well placed. But his million-person remark in the referendum had badly hurt the government at a critical moment. Michel Dupuy's credibility stood in negative integers. Marcel Massé gave all indications of being a quick learner, but on political matters, his learning curve was ascending from zero. André Ouellet's worn image in his native province after twenty-eight years in Parliament could best be discerned in the fact that the government chose to have him overseas in the final days of the campaign. "Modern politics is always calling for changes," Chrétien explained in an interview in May 1996. "And I felt that after two years and almost a half, things had to be changed."

He secured the change he most wanted with ten days left in the year. On Thursday, December 21, Bruce Hartley, Chrétien's executive assistant, went to the Ottawa bus station a little after 9 in the morning and picked up a young political science professor from Montreal toting a canvas knapsack. They drove to the prime minister's cottage at Harrington Lake. There, Jean Chrétien offered Stéphane Dion an opportunity to serve his country.

Dion stood apart in Quebec society as an accomplished francophone academic who happened to be a strong federalist. In fact, like most young intellectuals of his generation, Dion had flirted with separatism. "When I was a teenager, I was for the Parti Québécois," he admitted in a 1996 interview. But in the 1980 referendum, he discovered he lacked passion for the cause. While others threw themselves into the battle for nationhood, Dion was off studying for his Ph.D. in Paris. In that cosmopolitan setting, he began to develop a distaste for nationalism. On referendum night, he joined others for a live telecast of the results at Maison Québec. He watched as his friends broke down and cried, particularly at René Lévesque's moving concession speech. "Myself, I felt nothing. I was like an observer. I listened to Trudeau. I listened to Lévesque. I was only in the mood to analyze these results."

His increasingly favourable view of Quebec in Canada was made all the more interesting by virtue of his bloodline. Dion's father, Léon, had been one of the most prominent intellectuals of the Quiet Revolution, a highly influential federalist but a strong advocate of loosening the bonds of Confederation in order to better reflect the central fact that it consisted of two nations with different languages, cultures, and histories. In the Meech impasse, Léon Dion had counselled Premier Robert Bourassa to hold a knife to the throat of Canada, a tactic with which his son did not agree.

During the referendum campaign, both Chrétien and his wife, had watched Dion's debates and commentaries on television. "I said this guy is not a timid guy," Chrétien recalled. "You know, he was defending

Canada very well, and there was not this ambiguity that we see in so many people in Quebec. It did not exist in him. He knew exactly what he wanted."

As Chrétien idled away hours in airplanes in early November, flying to Israel for Yitzhak Rabin's funeral and then on to Asia for the Commonwealth summit and the Asia-Pacific Economic Council meeting, he had plenty of time to contemplate the mess he had left behind in Canada. His thoughts kept returning to Dion. Here was a young, credible francophone who believed, as Chrétien always had, that Canadian federalism was not inimical to Quebec's interests. Chrétien had met Dion only once, just for a handshake in a television studio after an appearance on the popular public affairs program *Le Point*. But he had a strong gut instinct that the forty-year-old professor could inject life into his moribund Quebec bench. After he returned home, Chrétien picked up the phone in his residence on Friday, November 24, and asked his office switchboard to track down Dion.

The operator left messages on his voice mail at the Université de Montréal and at his home. Coincidentally, Dion was in Ottawa for a conference that weekend on the future of Canada. He returned the call and told Chrétien he was staying at a friend's house within sight of 24 Sussex. Chrétien invited him to lunch. "He came with his pack on his back," Chrétien recalled. He kept the visit a complete secret. Not even Jean Pelletier knew. "Dion was very much my idea," Chrétien crowed.

The prime minister asked Dion his views on why the referendum had been so close and what he thought should be done now. "It was easy for me," Dion recalled, "because I had my conference notes."

Over lunch, Chrétien got to the real point of the invitation. "I said, 'Would you like to join my party? And would you like to help me?' " He made it clear he wanted Dion at his cabinet table, without specifying a portfolio.

Dion replied that he was a professor and could serve better in that capacity. Had Chrétien thought about Pierre Pettigrew, another noted Quebec federalist? Chrétien had, but he insisted that he wanted to talk about Dion, not Pettigrew. Chrétien told him to think it over. There wasn't a big rush. He asked Dion to call him before Christmas.

Dion returned to Montreal and took only three people into his confidence: his wife, Jeannine Krieber, also an academic, and his parents. Krieber, a little bit more adventurous than her husband, liked the notion of a new challenge. His mother, Denise, replayed the stories of pathetic politicians who had sat around their dinner table over the years, forever complaining about their powerlessness in the face of a stubborn leader and mourning their family breakdowns. She didn't want that kind of life for her son.

As for Léon Dion, one of the most influential Quebeckers of his generation, he reacted like any father. Stéphane already had a good career in academe and was developing an international reputation. He would be off to Europe in a few days for a round of lectures on the Quebec situation. Why risk it all on an adventure?

Dion had pretty well decided to turn the offer down. But Europe, as it had a decade and a half earlier, made a deep impression upon him. In Madrid, Barcelona, and Brussels, he learned how profoundly concerned others were with the fate of Canada. If Canada could not survive, how could they hope to hold their countries together in the face of secession movements? "When I left I was inclined to say no, and when I came back I was inclined to say yes."

Now, as they sat out at Harrington Lake contemplating the close of an overly eventful year, Dion said he would come to Ottawa, but only if he was put in charge of the national unity file as minister of intergovernmental affairs. It would be quite an assignment for a rookie politician. A generation earlier, when another Université de Montréal academic, Pierre Trudeau, had made the pilgrimage to Ottawa to save Canada, he served a sixteenth-month apprenticeship as parliamentary secretary to the prime minister before becoming justice minister. The demand didn't faze Chrétien. Intergovernmental was precisely the job he had in mind for Dion. "I knew that I was to use him there before I called him the first time," Chrétien said. But he stalled. He needed to figure out how all the pieces of the puzzle would fit, how he would handle Robillard and Marcel Massé without ruffling feathers. "I said, 'I don't know. I will plan my cabinet. Let me think on it.'"

At noon, Hartley returned Dion to the bus station. The professor grabbed a sandwich to eat on the bus to Montreal. Over the holidays, his father gently reminded Dion that Chrétien was a supremely cautious politician. He didn't have it in him to hand such a sensitive position to a rookie. "Then I will not go," Dion shrugged.

Meanwhile, Chrétien had given his staff the go-ahead before Christmas to prepare a new Speech from the Throne. If he was to renew his team, the government should also renew its plan, he figured. Two themes, above all, stood out: national unity and jobs. Both had been the subject of intense cabinet scrutiny by special committees since November. The jobs committee was the culmination of months of agitation by the social Liberals. By the fall, they held a strong hand because of the economy's anemic job performance. From November 1994 to July 1995, the economy had created just 5,000 jobs. Pressure was building on Martin to spend big on a second infrastructure program. David Dingwall, the public works minister, openly conceded that the first infrastructure program had been an enormously costly exercise in job creation. But he would add with a wink that it had done the trick politically. Chrétien, as a prime minister must, watched Martin's back, ensuring that the big spenders wouldn't control the jobs committee. He named Agriculture Minister Ralph Goodale to chair it, his most obvious qualifications being an earnest competence, a westerner's parsimony, and a quarter-century-long friendship with Paul Martin. Discussions quickly ran up against the reality that governments in the 1990s — particularly broke governments — exercised little control over job creation.

Of the two committees, the unity one clearly generated more interest. Marcel Massé, once again in the chair, had gained valuable experience with show-me committees in program review. But this time out, he lacked the irrefutable logic of deficit arithmetic. Everyone was entitled to an opinion about the best course of the country, and nearly everyone exercised that prerogative. Ron Irwin, the bluff Indian affairs minister, was the most impassioned and immovable centralist on the committee. Massé needed to sway the cabinet's Ontario wing if he was to have any hope of achieving a consensus, but where some of the other Ontario ministers seemed willing to compromise, Irwin dug in his heels. He could not easily countenance the thought of Ottawa devolving its social responsibilities to the provinces. But even without Irwin, getting agreement on a plan of action would have been tough.

The committee met with Montreal sociologist Maurice Pinard, the dean of Quebec pollsters. He showed them historical data that shed light on the emotional motherlode into which Lucien Bouchard had tapped during the referendum campaign. Pinard traced opinion surveys back to the 1960s. The simple finding: Quebeckers had shucked the objective manifestations of their economic colonialism far more thoroughly than the psychological ones. The memory of every historical humiliation remained alive in their psyches.

After Pinard, Frank Graves of Ekos Research Associates met the committee. His presentation, while sobering as to the strength of the separatist threat, provided support for the kind of response the Ontario ministers thought appropriate. Graves provided compilations of polls taken over the previous two years that convincingly demonstrated that the average Quebecker wanted the federal government to maintain or increase its role in their lives, including in labour market training, a finding that flew in the face of conventional thinking. The devolutionist argument, he maintained, led to a diminution of pro-Canada feelings in Quebec.

Graves's presentation included one other important aspect. The federalists had, in fact, won the economic arguments in the referendum, he asserted. Unfortunately, Lucien Bouchard had moved the debate onto a different terrain. Graves suggested that Ottawa stop thinking of the Quebec challenge in terms of economics and politics. Federal vulnerability, he maintained, existed in the realm of symbols and culture. "What Bouchard did was shift the logic of the debate out of the territory of economists to the territory of culture, to meaning, symbols, humiliation, historical destiny — and he did it with a tremendous amount of charismatic authority. Then, on top of that, he satisfied those soft nationalists, who retained an attachment to Canada and worried that the project amounted to a risky economic adventure, that he could get a better deal."

The analysis made an impression on Massé. He remembered that he and his schoolmates had called one another *les Canadiens* and referred to the English as *les Anglais*. Now young people in the province called themselves Québécois. The language had been appropriated, as had so many symbols. But he wasn't prepared to stop pushing on labour market training. Quebeckers had called for change. His own riding organizers had told him they would have trouble coming out to fight next time if it entailed another defence of the status quo.

While the unity committee groped towards a consensus, Chrétien prepared for his third Team Canada trade mission, a January trip to south Asia. Jacques Parizeau naturally demurred again, but so did two others this time: Roy Romanow and Ralph Klein. It seemed a symbol of the country's fragile unity.

Once again, Team Canada signed a ton of deals. But the press had grown bored with the same old story. Instead, human rights surfaced as a major theme in the dispatches back to Canada. For two years, Chrétien had paid scant attention to the subject, needlessly offending all kinds of

Liberals with a bloody-minded approach that refused to acknowledge even a moral imperative in waging the good fight, particularly in China. Suddenly, confronted in India by a media-savvy thirteen-year-old from Thornhill, Ontario, named Craig Kielburger, he realized he had been too unambiguous in his approach. The kid, stumping the continent in a crusade against the exploitation of child labour, embarrassed Chrétien into a private meeting at his next stop, in Pakistan, and made plain to him that the government needed to recast its image in more Liberal terms. From that day forward, human rights, at least rhetorically, returned to the agenda.

Chrétien continued to think through the cabinet shuffle on the trip. He had already told Dion before departing that Intergovernmental Affairs would be his. And that Pierre Pettigrew would also join the cabinet. On his last stop, at Kuala Lumpur, Chrétien put a list together on the back of a square coaster while drinking a beer in his top-floor suite at the Regent Hotel. He ran out of space and asked for a second coaster. He had decided on a major generational change, particularly in Quebec. He had canvassed his ministers as to who would be running in the next election, with a mind to replacing the outgoing ministers in a second shuffle in the summer or fall. Now he decided to combine the two events. That would mean the early departure of André Ouellet and Roy MacLaren. Michel Dupuy would be dropped, and Sheila Finestone would be removed from the second tier of ministers. Brian Tobin had departed earlier in the month for Newfoundland to take over from Clyde Wells as premier.

Back home on January 20, Chrétien immersed himself in the work of his unity committee. Massé had found his elusive consensus, but at the price of content. The report stayed largely in the realm of generalities. In place of actions, he offered up a list of long-winded values, each one attached to a policy area. There was, for instance, compassion and sharing, which entailed a continued role for the federal government in maintaining a national social policy. Another value was pragmatism in the pursuit of a higher standard of living, which linked into the idea of a stronger role for Ottawa in national economic policy. Accommodation, tolerance, and mutual respect related to Canadian identity, and freedom and democracy had to do with speaking with a single voice in the world. The report set out areas of activity that Ottawa could easily vacate (some had been effectively deserted as a result of program review), a few areas where the federal presence should be stronger, means to buttress Canadian identity such as Flag Day, and recommendations for a unity information office to counter "the separatist myth."

Nobody on the committee was fully satisfied with the outcome. Several conceded its banality. Separate from the report, Massé sent a letter to Chrétien setting out personal recommendations on which he could not obtain a consensus. The most important of these was that Ottawa must renounce its spending power, the means by which it had wielded its influence over social policy in the postwar years. (The Ontario ministers feared this would preclude future federal initiatives in the social field, such as a national daycare program.)

On January 25, the same day he formally received the unity committee report — Eddie Goldenberg had helped with the drafting, thus ensuring there would be no surprises — Chrétien unveiled his new cabinet. In the weeks before, he had reminded Goldenberg that he had been appointed to cabinet in his thirties by Lester Pearson in the year the prime minister turned seventy. (Trudeau had also entered cabinet on that day.) Pearson had purposely recruited a new generation of Quebeckers. "I have to do the same thing," Chrétien said. (It was left unstated that Pearson had been a unilingual anglophone from Ontario seeking credible spokespeople in Quebec, whereas the current prime minister hailed from Quebec himself.)

For more than thirty years in politics, Chrétien had distinguished himself by his unwillingness to court risks. Now, to the surprise of Léon Dion and others, he moved with uncharacteristic boldness in what looked as much like a change of government as a cabinet shuffle. Stéphane Dion's appointment as intergovernmental affairs minister grabbed the headlines. Chrétien had placed a political novice — a theoretician — in arguably the most sensitive (or perhaps the second most sensitive, after Finance) post in his ministry. Pierre Pettigrew, a former provincial Liberal aide also in his early forties, joined the full cabinet at the same time. Neither had ever held elected public office. Neither was a member of Parliament. Both had been parachuted directly into cabinet, putting a lot of Liberal noses out of joint. Chrétien called by-elections for March to get seats for the two. Pettigrew, given the new title of minister of international cooperation, had far more political experience. Some Liberals wondered why he hadn't been given the bigger assignment.

"Today we turn the page to a new chapter," Chrétien said in presenting his revised team.

In the early months of his government, Chrétien had spoken often of the harsh consequences he would rain down on ministers who failed to make the grade. In fact, he had proven extremely indulgent of under-achievement, taking greater pride in the longevity of his first ministry than in its performance. In part, this flowed from his well-developed sense of loyalty in politics. He also remained conscious of the dangers of yielding to the braying media pack when a minister, like Dupuy or Dingwall, stumbled. Chrétien believed that Brian Mulroney had been too quick to dump Defence Minister Robert Coates in 1985 for no greater offence than that he had visited a strip bar in Lahr, West Germany. By succumbing so easily in his first ministerial scandal, Chrétien thought Mulroney had only succeeded in encouraging the media in subsequent cases.

In the first year of government, Chrétien had clearly shown his determination to hang tough. Revenue Minister David Anderson had stepped in cow-pat after cow-pat, seriously eroding the government's credibility in British Columbia. Instead of bouncing him — not that any strong replacements recommended themselves — Chrétien had asked Randy Pettipas, the PMO's senior political aide for western Canada, to head up Anderson's office.

Pettipas hesitated. "I feel you're sending me to a sinking ship," he said.

"I wouldn't send you to a ship I didn't think you could salvage," Chrétien replied.

In the shuffle, Chrétien again salvaged rather than replaced his weaker ministers. Of the underperformers, only Dupuy was dropped, probably more because of his status as an older Quebecker than because of his competence. Diane Marleau was shuffled to Public Works, where her difficulty in expressing herself would be of less import; David Dingwall went to Health, where he couldn't lay his hands on any discretionary money to indulge his penchant for pork-barrel politics; Sheila Copps would go to Heritage, playing to the strengths of her emotional appeals for Canadian identity, in both official languages.

Chrétien now gave Lloyd Axworthy, who had been deemed too anti-business to go to Foreign Affairs two years earlier, the job he had coveted for so long. With the crusading Craig Kielburger as a foil, Axworthy arrived at the Pearson Building bubbling over with ideas about putting human rights back into the policy mix. He wanted submissions prepared quickly for the prime minister and cabinet. He intended to be a reformist minister, he informed his new bureaucrats as he sent them off in a dozen directions. He remained the antithesis of Jean Chrétien.

In Human Resources, Chrétien replaced Axworthy with Doug Young, his no-nonsense transportation minister. Young was from northern New Brunswick, the part of the province highly dependent on seasonal work. The area had been rocked by demonstrations against the Axworthy UI bill in December and January. Liberal ministers had discussed the likelihood of such an outcry many times in preparing for the release of the Axworthy package on December 1, but they were shaken nonetheless watching on television as Young was burned in effigy and junior minister Fernand Robichaud was shouted down by an angry crowd.

Young's appointment came with a clear message: as one of cabinet's fiscal conservatives but a minister naturally sensitive to the regional concerns, he was to calm the politics without undermining the economics of UI reform. He was also to go further than Axworthy in getting Ottawa out of training, an issue that continued to fester. He had wanted a business portfolio like International Trade or Industry and was deeply distressed by the appointment to a department he considered in utter disrepair. But Chrétien had been impressed by Young's toughness in Transport. He wanted someone who could blast through the bureaucratic obstacles at HRD and who could communicate in French. He told Young he knew it would be a difficult assignment that could take a personal political toll, but he needed results.

Martin, of course, was untouchable. But in order to make room for Dion, Chrétien moved Marcel Massé from Intergovernmental Affairs to the presidency of Treasury Board, the government's accounting arm, located several floors below the Finance Department in Esplanade Laurier. From Treasury Board, Massé would carry forward the program review, keeping intact his successful alliance with Martin. Spotted in the cloakroom at Rideau Hall for the swearing-in, Martin joked, "I'm just here to make sure nobody spends any money." Then he saw his partner hanging up his coat. Martin put his hand on Massé's shoulder and repeated: "Marcel and I are here to make sure nobody spends any money."

On Massé's performance at Intergovernmental Affairs, the record had been mixed. After initial resistance because of his lack of credibility around the cabinet table, he had won the government over to his technocratic prescriptions for renewing the federation. But this strategy — perhaps because of its late adoption, perhaps because of its lack of poetry — had failed to win Quebec. Chrétien still thought highly of Massé and mollified him with an appointment as political minister from Quebec, which, while keeping him active on the national unity file, also underlined the dearth of political experience on the Quebec bench.

The referendum result drove the shuffle, and nobody pretended otherwise. British Columbia had also been shown in the previous months to be badly in need of stronger voices around the cabinet table. But no effort had been made to bring in fresh blood. The only change came with the elevation of Hedy Fry, who had been denied a cabinet post two years earlier, to a junior post in charge of the status of women.

Taken as a whole, the shuffle could be interpreted as a deliberate attempt to shift the balance of power towards the devolutionist side of cabinet. Chrétien had added two fresh faces from Quebec, endowed with the credibility of new messiahs. He had moved stubborn, centralizing ministers out of two of the areas in which he wanted to provide examples of a more flexible federalism: Axworthy from Human Resources, which still had to negotiate the "principles and objectives" of the new Canada Health and Social Transfer (Foreign Affairs had no federal-provincial dimension); and Sheila Copps from Environment, where she had resisted overtures to the provinces.

As the professor in politics, Stéphane Dion launched his career with a highly unusual two-page essay outlining his course curriculum. Entitled "Regaining Confidence in Canada" and handed to reporters at Rideau Hall, it furnished both the raison d'être for his move into politics and an explication of the goals he would pursue. "I am proud to be a Quebecker and a Canadian, and I will do everything I can do to help show how these two loyalties can complement each other so well," he wrote. Fresh from his trip to Europe, he argued that Canada owed it to the rest of the world to survive.

He stated clearly and with great eloquence the case for the recognition of Quebec's distinctiveness in the Constitution. He also put forward arguments for decentralization, saying a strong Canada must not be confused with a strong federal government alone. "We as Canadians have nothing to fear from decentralization. We know it well enough to make it our ally. A strong federal government must not be confused with a centralizing government. Restricting itself to its own role will only make it more effective."

The essay disturbed a number of his new colleagues, who thought he had plenty to learn about the teamwork of cabinet government. But Chrétien didn't mind. Dion had told his new boss he had to explain himself. Chrétien had read the essay and figured he could live with it. He thought it the state-ment of a professor. "You know, he was teaching politics. To be in poli-tics is a big step." Challenged on risking so much on a rookie, Chrétien replied: "Oh yeah, but I'm around. You know, I work well with him."

Chrétien introduced his new ministers at a special caucus meeting in Vancouver — chosen to try to make amends for the veto imbroglio — on January 30. "I had to make changes because I had to do something about Quebec," he confided. "You should know that the changes in cabinet have changed the mood in Quebec."

Meanwhile, a group of Toronto-area MPs, including renegade John Nunziata, used that caucus meeting to put the government on notice that they had run out of patience with the lack of progress on the GST. They demanded changes in the next budget. Deputy Prime Minister Sheila Copps informed reporters that the dreaded tax would soon be history. Later she clarified her remarks, saying it would be "elaborated" on in the coming budget.

Chrétien had other matters on his mind. The national unity report had spoken about the need to strengthen Canadian identity, which, to Chrétien, meant the beloved flag. He had been around to vote for a Canadian flag in the 1960s and had marked its thirtieth anniversary the previous year with a ceremony and a patriotic advertising campaign. His advisers told him that the flag resonated as a national symbol, even in Quebec.

The prime minister seemed to want the whole country draped in the Maple Leaf. He ordered up a Flag Day for February 15, 1996. At the Vancouver caucus, he instructed his new transport minister, David Anderson, to hoist more flags at Montreal's Dorval Airport and even told his new revenue minister, Jane Stewart, to print more flags on the millions of forms her department distributed. Sheila Copps, with typical gusto, estab-lished a phone-in line to distribute one million flags by Canada Day, not bothering to wait to find a source for the flags or the money to pay for them.

Flag Day turned into a fiasco. A group of UI protesters heckled Chrétien. Frustrated, he cut his remarks short. As he strode back to his car amid a small sea of schoolchildren, one of the protesters, a professional demonstrator named Bill Clennett, got in his way. Chrétien grabbed Clennett by the throat and shoved him aside. The manhandling quickly became its own symbol. For many commentators, the picture of a violent Chrétien in dark sunglasses dredged up the old caricature of the street brawler, which played so poorly in Quebec. *Le Devoir* accused him of "brutalizing" the demonstrator. Others chalked the incident up as one more sign of the post-referendum morass into which he had sunk. "Get a grip, Jean," the Vancouver *Province* advised.

In cabinet, Dion quickly made his impact felt. He and Pettigrew had consciously decided they could not afford to hold back while learning the ropes. They served as a sounding board as the government translated the work of the unity committee into a Speech from the Throne. "Okay, Stéphane," fellow ministers would ask, "you are on *Le Point* tonight and Jean-François Lepine is saying to you, 'Is there substantial change in this document?' What's your honest answer?"

Dion thought it wasn't enough, not in labour market training nor in other areas. Like Massé, he argued that Ottawa had to promise to restrict use of its spending power in fields of provincial jurisdiction. In his blunt way, which was often mistaken for arrogance, he told Chrétien in front of the cabinet that if Ottawa could not see its way clear to meet such a basic Quebec demand, then he, Dion, had to wonder why he had bothered joining the government. Few ministers spoke to Chrétien so forcefully. Indeed, when Lucienne Robillard had made similar arguments, they seemed to accomplish little other than agitating the prime minister. But he appeared unperturbed by Dion.

After thirty-three years in politics, Chrétien found Dion refreshing. "To have this very intelligent guy not knowing anything of how to get elected and looking at politics from the top, it was very fascinating to me," he said. Chrétien knew Dion had a lot to learn, that the transition from teaching politics to living it would be huge. But he looked forward to nurturing the young guy with the knapsack.

Governor General Romeo LeBlanc read the Speech from the Throne on February 26, laying out for the first time the federal government's post-referendum plans and its renewed emphasis on jobs. The press trashed it for its leaden prose and warmed-over bromides. Clearly, the jobs section lacked vigour. But on national unity, the Throne Speech broke new ground for a government previously wedded to the status quo. "On October 30, the people of Quebec voted in a referendum to stay in Canada. At the same time, the referendum result gave a clear message that Quebeckers want change in the federation. This desire for change is broadly shared across Canada. The government will act on a responsible agenda for change for all of Canada."

To constitutional aficionados, the agenda looked remarkably like the Charlottetown Accord. Ottawa said it would not use its spending power to create new shared-cost programs in provincial realms without the consent of the majority of provinces, as Massé and Dion had wanted. (Ontario ministers embedded several qualifiers in the statement.) Any province could drop out of a new program, such as daycare, and be compensated, providing they established a comparable initiative. The government signalled its withdrawal — again — from labour market training, forestry, mining, and tourism, straight out of Charlottetown. Ottawa also announced its willingness to reach co-management arrangements in social housing and environmental protection.

A strengthened economic union would be the quid pro quo for this devolution. The Speech from the Throne flagged Ottawa's intention to press for a national securities commission to replace provincial regulation in an era of global capital markets. Ottawa also wanted to set up a single national tax collection agency and a unified food inspection service. All this would be pursued at a federal-provincial ministers conference in the months ahead, the first in two years. The government gave no date, but officials began preparing for a June confab.

As political commentators studied the Throne Speech, Paul Martin neared completion of his third budget. Despite the success of his slashing budget of the previous year, he still lacked the fervour of a true fiscal fundamentalist. In a private pre-budget consultation with the Business Council on National Issues, Thomas d'Aquino, the council's persuasive chairman, lobbied Martin to establish a zero deficit target immediately and put himself in a position to begin paying down the debt. Martin thought the suggestion ludicrous. Unlike d'Aquino, he had to concern himself with the public's pessimism about jobs. He couldn't wait until the debt-to-GDP ratio fell to 40 per cent before addressing the clamour. Moreover, like many Liberals, he was watching with close interest the social unrest unfolding in Mike Harris's Ontario. The Liberals wanted to present a contrast as humane budget-cutters. "I won't go to war to pay down the debt," he snapped at d'Aquino.

Still, Martin remained the government's chief advocate of deficit reduction, and his advisers knew that his third budget would be scrutinized for the pace of deficit reduction it set out. For the first time since the election, the Liberals would have to disclose a new target beyond 3 per cent. Chrétien and Martin had already agreed the next benchmark would be

2 per cent. Once again, it didn't appear to be too onerous an objective. Indeed, the downward momentum built into the previous budget would probably take them close without many added measures.

By now, Paul Martin had been finance minister for two and a half years. He and his department had developed a mutually beneficial modus vivendi. Respect, if not affection, flowed both ways. His outbursts occurred less frequently and were better understood. In August, Martin took his senior officials and outside advisers out for supper to thank them for their contribution. He presented each with a handsome memento: a picture frame containing a signed cover of the budget and a personalized thank-you letter. To Dodge, he wrote: "There is no doubt that no minister in government is better served by his Deputy, and for that I am grateful." The deputy, who many had thought would depart after the first budget, had decided to stay put through a third.

The minister remained a conflicted personality. Over Christmas, he had read a book called *The End of Work* by the American economic commentator Jeremy Rifkin. He had returned from the holidays singing its praises. The Finance officials shook their heads. Rifkin belonged to a long line of writers who argued that productivity gains killed jobs. The advances of technology, he wrote in *The End of Work*, led to mass unemployment. Dodge, a labour economist by training, rolled his eyes.

The Rifkin thesis flew in the face of Martin's Purple Book of fifteen months earlier, with its message that productivity growth inevitably led to more, not fewer, jobs, although often after a rough transformation. But Martin thought Rifkin struck an important chord with his critique about the maldistribution of productivity gains. All around him he could see the public's distress that the promise of the global economy — that a rising tide would lift all ships — had not materialized. In Canada, the economic anxiety of the public at large juxtaposed uncomfortably with high bank profits and escalating corporate compensation packages. Outside Canada, the chattering classes spoke darkly about a backlash against globalization. Cape Breton coal miners and New Brunswick seasonal workers, fearing for their way of life, embodied such sentiments. Martin thought Rifkin merited more serious consideration. He couldn't find a soul in his circle who agreed.

While increasingly sympathetic to the jobs issues, Martin continued to resist the worst of the pressures from cabinet's left wing. He had received a timely boost when job creation figures, awful for the better part of the year, suddenly turned upward in the last few months of 1995. Chrétien teased him, telling MPs: "We will be spending money on youth even if the minister of finance doesn't want to." Then, with a giggle, he plunged the dagger. "He's not like his dad was."

Martin had no intention of trying to bring down another radical budget in 1996. This would be a transitional budget, taking the Liberals from the total deficit focus of 1995 towards what he hoped would be a stronger jobs focus in his pre-election 1997 budget. The main measures in 1996 would tie up the loose ends from the previous budget, most visibly on pensions and the CHST.

In the summer of 1995, the government had hired Ekos Research Associates to test public attitudes to old-age pension reform. The sample questionnaire came back with a typographical error in it. Instead of reading: "Is it okay to restrict benefits to those seniors most in need?" the question asked: "Is it okay to restrict benefits to *hose* seniors most in need?" Upon spotting the mistake, Ekos president Frank Graves commented, "There are no typos, only interpretations."

In the end, seniors wouldn't be hosed, thanks in large part to an unholy alliance between Lucien Bouchard and Jean Chrétien. Martin had been right in fearing that if he didn't bully his reform through the previous year, the ground might shift under him. When he could not include the reform in the 1995 budget, Finance began planning for a mid-year strike, to take place right after a winning referendum. But by August, with the referendum delayed and the prime minister still dug in against pension reform, even the die-hards in Finance had to accept that their time had not arrived. Chrétien had always been troubled both by the idea of changing the rules of the game for people so advanced in their retirement planning and by the special vulnerability this could create in Quebec. In late summer, as he prepared for the referendum, he talked with Martin about the need to reassure existing seniors that they would not be affected.

As the campaign started, Bloc leader Lucien Bouchard used his perch in the House of Commons to whip up fears, not unreasonably, that the Liberals had a hidden agenda to attack pensions once they secured a No vote. Chrétien phoned contacts around the province and realized the effectiveness of the separatist claims. He accused Bouchard of scaremongering and put out the message without equivocation that "existing seniors" would be unaffected by any changes. Once Chrétien gave his word publicly, Martin had no choice but to fall into line.

Quebec also figured into the discussions over the Canada Health and Social Transfer. The new block fund was scheduled to come into effect on April 1, 1996, and Ottawa still had not come to grips with major decisions, such as the particulars of the cash floor under the transfer. Martin had committed himself to such a floor, but had studiously avoided saying when it would be established or at what level. Finance wanted to let the transfer drift down to $9 billion before it hit the floor. Social ministers like Axworthy, David Dingwall, and Diane Marleau naturally argued for a higher sum, in the region of $12.5 billion, an amount they thought would permit Ottawa to retain a strong measure of influence over provincial health and welfare systems in future talks on principles and objectives.

In this, they found an unusual ally in the person of Marcel Massé. The unity committee had found great resonance in medicare as a tie that binds Canadians, Quebeckers included. A higher cash floor would send a strong signal, they reasoned, that Ottawa did not intend to abandon its responsibilities. Massé thought it had to be over $10 billion. For Chrétien it was an easy call. The cash floor would be set at $11 billion.

Paul Martin also had to make his peace with John Manley in their year-and-a-half-long battle over the Defence Industry Productivity Program. From the summer on, as Quebec-based aircraft manufacturers threatened to relocate work to the United States, it became obvious to most ministers that the government had made a mistake in suspending DIPP in the previous budget. Martin and his people put the blame squarely on the shoulders of Industry, insisting they had always liked the program but could not interfere with how the department allocated its own money. Manley, who had worked feverishly to save the program, deeply resented the implication that he had killed DIPP. By the autumn, it had become clear the program would be revived in one form or another. From then on, the debate raged, like so much else in the Ottawa of the 1990s, over who would foot the bill. Finance still expected Industry to cover the costs by shuffling other spending. Manley repeated his arguments of the previous year that he had nothing left to reallocate. In the end, with the jobs pressures building on Martin, he agreed to meet Manley halfway.

Martin brought down his third budget on March 6, 1996. It spoke to a two-track Liberal policy. For the first fifteen minutes or so of his speech, he addressed the markets about the government's unswerving commitment to continued deficit reduction. But he insisted that the pace had to

be a measured and humane one. In any case, few squawked any more at
the minister of finance's failure to commit himself to a zero deficit. As
with his experiences with bankers three decades earlier as a Power
Corporation troubleshooter, Martin had accumulated sufficient credibility
by repeatedly meeting his targets to earn the benefit of the doubt. Next
Martin spoke to the provinces, telling them he would place the floor under
cash transfers. Then he spoke to the economic anxieties of Canadians,
announcing that the government would invest in the future, reallocating
$315 million over the next three years to additional spending on youth
unemployment. He set aside another $250 million for Manley's Son of
DIPP.

Martin's pension reform package was a work of beauty, but it had been
a mess putting it together. Until a couple of weeks before, Finance had
been working on a scheme that would have protected existing seniors, but
only until the year 2005, when new arrangements would kick in. Those
under sixty-five would have seen their pensions change right away. With
two weeks to go, Martin's communications advisers convinced him he
was flirting with political disaster. Commentators would poke holes in
the argument that existing seniors had been protected. With the clock running down, Martin revised his plan. The final package contained all the
elements Martin had championed a year earlier, but now it delayed their
implementation until 2001. Today's seniors would be, as Chrétien had
promised, unaffected for as long as they lived. So now would anyone over
sixty. That took the sting out of the tail for most seniors' groups, although
it also provided less in the way of future savings.

In the days after the budget, Martin's office notified the media that he
would visit a seniors' apartment building in the east end of Ottawa on
Sunday afternoon. The reporters descended upon the real star attraction,
the still spunky, seventy-three-year-old Solange Denis, the woman who had
destroyed Michael Wilson's first budget and whom Martin had secretly visited a year earlier and kept in touch with since. Despite the blandishments
of reporters, she refused to be budged from her ironclad support for the
Liberal government's plan to reform old-age pensions. People in her age
bracket, she happily noted, would not be affected.

As Martin walked in for the event, he caught sight of his favourite
senior seated on the aisle. One of the residents was playing the piano at the
front of the room. The consummate performer took his tiny, grey-haired
friend by the arm and led her in a brief waltz.

23

THE GET SHEILA TAX

In the wake of the 1996 budget, Paul Martin privately made an admission that Jean Chrétien might have liked to hear. The prime minister had been right after all, Martin confided to friends, in blocking the pension reform a year earlier — a veto over which Martin had almost gone to the wall. Martin now had a fairer package, and one that had gone down smooth as a nip of brandy. Martin saw benefits in having someone around to temper his overweening drive "to do things tomorrow, to get on with it." Chrétien's political instincts, Martin acknowledged, tended to be better than his own. That's what made the two of them such a formidable combination.

The pension episode served as the final lesson that convinced Martin that the implementation of a policy was as important in the 1990s as the policy itself. That's why he put so much stock in his communications advisers. In fact, Martin happily articulated the five easy lessons from his trio of budgets: tell people what you're doing before you do it; give people time to adjust between the announcement of a measure and its implementation; if adjustment help is required, provide it; bend over backwards for fairness between different groups so nobody feels unjustly targeted; don't announce something before you have worked out the details.

Don't announce something before you have worked out the details. If only the Liberals had thought of that earlier, they might have averted the April débâcle over the goods and services tax, a Tory disaster that the Chrétien government managed to convert into its own. The 1996 budget was supposed to have been the one to put the GST issue to rest, once and for all. Chrétien had said so in an interview with the *Ottawa Citizen* several months earlier. He had also promised his caucus that the party's campaign promise on the GST would be fulfilled by early 1996. But tax reform had proven a hugely complicated issue, and so the budget passed with just the slightest of nods in its direction. In his speech, Martin couldn't even bring himself to utter the initials GST, fearing they would become a flashpoint that would overwhelm everything else. "We are working very hard to replace the federal sales tax" was the best he could do.

Liberal expediency on the GST had been bred in the bone. In the 1990 leadership race, the three main contestants had stood divided on the consumption tax, then in the process of being legislated by the Mulroney government. Sheila Copps opposed it with the considerable indignation she could muster, as did her Rat Pack mate John Nunziata, a minor leadership candidate. Paul Martin shared their conviction, calling for its abolition, but acknowledged that the revenue would have to be replaced. As a candidate who had positioned himself as the policy Liberal (in contrast with the idea-less Jean Chrétien), it fell to him to offer up a host of ill-considered alternatives. Chrétien, the most experienced and cagiest of the trio, warned that taxation was a political minefield and that once a tax was implanted, it was best to stay clear. When asked what he would do, the frontrunner invariably told reporters that if they wanted to see his budget, they would have to wait until he was elected.

Chrétien knew of what he spoke. He had seen a Liberal government come under heavy fire at the start of the 1970s over tax reform and had watched the sinking of Allan MacEachen's 1981 budget over tax measures. Chrétien himself had been badly burned in 1978 by a sales tax initiative he had introduced in the first of his two budgets as finance minister.

But after he won the leadership of his party, the furore over the GST kept escalating. The Liberal-controlled Senate resorted to every device at its disposal to block passage of the GST into law that fall. Mulroney, desperate to break the filibuster, invoked an obscure passage of the Constitution to expand the Senate by eight, thus gaining a majority for his party in the upper chamber. Passions ran extraordinarily high on Parliament Hill, including in the Liberal caucus room.

Chrétien's political standing had ebbed significantly in the preceding months as he had bobbled issues on several fronts. Now his unwillingness to take an unequivocal stance on the GST made the Liberals look weak on the hottest political issue since free trade. In October 1990, national polls showed the NDP, resolutely opposed to the GST, surging past the Liberals into a strong first-place showing, adding to the misgivings of many Liberals. (The poll was probably skewed by the election that month of an NDP government in Ontario.)

In late October, Chrétien took a shellacking at an exceptionally rowdy meeting of caucus. MPs shouted out of turn and pointed accusatory fingers. Even allies, like Brian Tobin, berated him for his lukewarm backing of the senators. Chrétien held his ground, saying that he would announce at a fundraising brunch on the coming weekend the establishment of a special commission of tax experts to draft "fair taxation" policies for the next election. By the time Sunday rolled around, though, Chrétien and his advisers had decided that the announcement would not be enough. He told a cheering crowd of about 700 Liberals that "the Mulroney GST will disappear" under a Liberal government. "I am opposed to the GST. I have always been opposed to it. And I will be opposed to it always."

Jean Chrétien would forever rue going against his gut. On several occasions in the next couple of years, he tried to backtrack slightly. But the adverse reaction convinced him he was trapped. All this made it even more galling in early 1993 when a stream of Liberals, including Paul Martin, approached him and suggested he reverse the GST promise. Now that they felt close to victory, they could see the folly of their abolitionist position. But Chrétien decreed that it was too late. He had tied his credibility to the issue. "I feel stuck," he confided to a visitor as the 1993 election approached.

Chrétien did his best to water down the GST commitment in the Red Book while still refusing to abandon it. On page 22, the Liberals promised to give the Finance Committee of the House of Commons a one-year mandate "to report on all options for alternatives to the current GST. A Liberal government will replace the GST with a system that generates equivalent revenues, is fairer to consumers and to small business, minimizes disruption to small business, and promotes federal-provincial fiscal cooperation and harmonization." There was no mention of abolishing, scrapping, or killing the tax, only of replacing it.

On the cusp of power, he meticulously toned down the GST rhetoric in the campaign. He invariably answered questions about the tax by adding that the $18 billion in revenue would have to be made up in another way. He eschewed grand promises, slipping only once in the heat of an interview to say he would scrap it. But Sheila Copps, his deputy leader, lacked Chrétien's self-discipline. She had a quick mind and an even faster tongue. On October 18, 1993, with the election already in the bag, she represented the Liberals at a CBC-TV town hall meeting, uttering words that would come back to haunt her and the party. "I've already said personally and very directly that if the GST is not abolished, I'll resign. I don't know how clear you can get. I think you've got to be accountable for the things that you're going to do and you have to deliver on it."

After the election, the Liberals followed through on having the all-party Finance Committee examine the options. In the meantime, Martin pressured his department for alternatives. The bureaucrats, of course, thought the GST superior to all other possibilities, which is why they had recommended it in the first place. Nothing had changed. They humoured Martin with at least twenty different formulations, all so obviously inferior that he would be ridiculed for bringing any in. The officials were delighted when the Finance Committee came back and reported that the best alternative would be simply to harmonize the GST with provincial sales tax regimes. But as much as Martin tried, he could not persuade the provinces, particularly the western ones, to come on side. The new Conservative government in Ontario flirted with the idea for a few months before realizing that for consumers, harmonization represented a tax hike. Martin would later refer to this marathon dance as the "torture of the damned."

By the time Liberal MPs arrived in Vancouver for their caucus meeting in January 1996, patience had worn thin over the oft-promised GST reforms. Jittery MPs in the suburban beltway around Toronto felt vulnerable. The Harris Tories had swept the suburbs and now appeared to be following through swiftly on their commitments. These MPs, sitting in ridings not naturally Liberal and highly tax-sensitive, made a lot of noise about the GST. Trapped by the press, Sheila Copps restated her promise to resign. Martin by now had pretty well concluded that changing the GST — once again disrupting business — would be worse than not changing it. Indeed, business groups were telling him to let sleeping dogs lie. But Chrétien had a promise to keep, and a caucus restless at his failure to do so.

The caucus tantrum did little to help Finance in a new round of negotiations with the Atlantic provinces, which seemed willing to harmonize, for a price. Every time a Liberal MP delivered an ultimatum to Martin, it weakened his negotiating hand. The Atlantic premiers could sense his desperation to secure at least a partial victory.

Meanwhile, his communications advisers conducted focus groups aimed at identifying a strategy for selling partial harmonization of the GST as a fulfilment of Liberal commitments. The panels suggested that Canadians had patiently sat by for two years waiting to punish the Liberals for dissembling on the GST. They would not be denied their day of reckoning. Martin's outside communications strategists at the Earnscliffe Strategy Group recommended a course they thought perfectly in keeping with the new demands on politicians for integrity in the 1990s. The Liberals would apologize for failing to do what they had said. Never mind the Red Book, Canadians remembered the rhetoric: they hadn't heard the word "harmonization" a lot from 1990 to 1993. The Liberals had said they would scrap the GST. The public would not tolerate any verbal contortions now; that would deepen their cynicism. Apologize, let Canadians vent their cathartic anger, and then get on with life. "The whole point of the strategy," a Martin adviser would later remark, "was to have a bad day."

Peter Donolo, the prime minister's communications chief, bought into the strategy, as did Eddie Goldenberg. The two of them practically moved into the Finance offices in April, as the department put the final touches on the package. Donolo and Terrie O'Leary made the rounds of various ministers to sound them out. On April 16, accompanied by David Dodge, they met with Sheila Copps and her staff in her office on the fifth floor of the Centre Block. She didn't like the apology any better than the idea of settling for harmonization. At cabinet she had attacked such an approach as inadequate, and now she forcefully stated her view. "That's a stupid idea," she insisted about the apology. The government had to emphasize the positive aspects of its actions and not dwell on the negative, she maintained. On Friday, April 19, Copps learned that Martin would go ahead with the apology strategy.

The prime minister represented the bigger impediment at this point. Chrétien didn't think he had anything to apologize for. To his suddenly legalistic thinking, Martin's deal to harmonize the GST with the Atlantic provinces, which the Liberals hoped would be followed by deals with other provinces once the logjam had been broken, fulfilled the Red Book commitments. The GST would be replaced with a system generating equivalent revenues; it would be accompanied by changes to make it simpler to administer; it would, in his estimation, be fairer to consumers and small business (the tax, for the first time, would be embedded in the sticker price of items, as in Europe); and it would promote federal-provincial cooperation (through a common collection agency) and harmonization. So why say you're sorry?

Meanwhile, John Nunziata had raised the stakes. Even before seeing the GST package, he had decided to hold the government's feet to the fire by voting against Martin's budget bill for failing to deliver on the promise.

Nunziata was absolutely unimpressed by talk of harmonization, scolding the media for falling into his government's trap of equating that with fulfilment of the campaign promise. On April 22, Chrétien booted him out of caucus, instantly turning him into a GST martyr, a man who had stood up for principle in sharp contrast to the prime minister, who punished him, and the deputy prime minister, his former Rat Pack partner, who had made a similar promise and was now fudging it.

For the second time, Jean Chrétien went against his gut on the GST. Faced with a full-court press by Donolo, Goldenberg, and Martin, he relented on the apology. The words were toned down to make it less fulsome. Martin's prepared remarks would read: "We were mistaken to have believed that, once it was anchored into place, a completely different alternative would be within reach, responsibly."

The next day Paul Martin unveiled his widely rumoured GST deal with the Atlantic provinces. Taking questions from reporters after reading his statement, Martin went further with his apology. "We made a mistake. We made an honest mistake," he said. Just to make sure that nobody missed the significance of his unusual act of contrition, Donolo circulated among the reporters, playing up the Martin apology. Seeing that the first bulletin from Canadian Press didn't mention it, he phoned reporter Rob Carrick to remind him of its newsworthiness.

When Chrétien saw the newspapers the following morning, he hit the roof. The headlines made it sound as if the Liberals had apologized for breaking a promise. That did not reflect the wording to which he had agreed. He ordered a transcript of the Martin press conference. Chrétien's normally icy anger was red hot this time. The morning was still young when he imparted his latest thoughts on the apology strategy to Donolo. Others caught an earful as the day went on. Chrétien was not prepared to play along with any strategy designed to purposely have a bad day. In Question Period that afternoon, he took a decidedly different tack than Martin, defiantly reading over and over again from page 22 of the Red Book as proof that the Liberal promise had been kept.

Liberal MPs, watching the spectacle from the back benches, thought back to a barbed quip Chrétien had uttered a month earlier in caucus. The GST would have a different name, he had stated. "It will be called the PMMT — the Paul Martin Memorial Tax."

Copps didn't know it yet, but she was in deep trouble. As the GST announcement began to spin out of control, she was otherwise occupied escorting the visiting Prince Charles around northern Manitoba. Meanwhile, Canadians were watching repeated replays of her 1993 televised pledge to resign. Copps had scheduled a press conference back in Ottawa for Thursday on the unrelated matter of a new Copyright Act. She had cobbled together a fragile caucus consensus on the bill and wanted to strike before it fell apart. Before the press conference, she talked on the phone with Peter Donolo, who was relatively unperturbed about her problem. He figured that Canadians would hold the blunt Copps to a less demanding standard. John Nunziata represented the bigger concern that morning. He would precede her with his first press conference since his expulsion. Donolo wanted to make sure she didn't inflame that situation with an unnecessary denunciation.

Naturally, the reporters cared far more about the GST than the Copyright Act. Copps offered an explanation but not an apology. "I think that making a fast-lip comment in the course of an election campaign should not put me in a position of having to resign," she told the assembled reporters. In fact, if every shoot-from-the-lip comment required her to resign, she would be in a revolving door, she added. Then she went further. She revealed that several days earlier, she had passed a jocular note to the prime minister in the middle of a Commons debate saying, "I resign." Chrétien, she laughed, had passed it around the benches to other MPs for their amusement before returning it to her, unaccepted.

Copps had made a grievous error in judgment in shooting her mouth off about the joke. All those hours locked in Ottawa meeting rooms had apparently dulled her vaunted political instincts. Somehow, she seemed to think that Chrétien, as prime minister, served as her ultimate arbiter, rather than the public. Not only had she not been contrite, she seemed downright cheeky about it all. The following day, she accompanied Prince Charles to Hamilton. There were scattered boos for her at the war museum.

On Monday, Copps filled in for Chrétien in Question Period. Again, she exacerbated the situation with another off-the-cuff remark that her resignation would needlessly cost taxpayers $100,000 for a by-election. (In fact, she underestimated the cost by $400,000.) That night, she experienced her apparent epiphany at the bank machine on the corner of Queen and Bank Streets in downtown Ottawa. Turning from the machine, she could not bring herself to make eye contact with the customer behind her, a crisis of major proportions for a person so naturally gregarious.

Tuesday began with cabinet and then a regular weekly lunch with her deputy minister. Copps looked thoroughly distracted. Before Question

Period, she asked her executive assistant and close friend Danielle May-Cuconato to come into her office. They spoke for a while and May-Cuconato emerged to arrange calls to several key figures from Copps's 1990 leadership campaign, inviting them to an emergency meeting at 3 p.m. Question Period was brutal as Reform sought her head. Copps sat there as Chrétien and Martin rose repeatedly to her defence. Early in the onslaught, she leaned over to Chrétien, whispering in his right ear that he should not preclude her resignation in any of his answers.

After QP, she returned to her office. She placed a call to her old Rat Pack buddy Brian Tobin. He told her as a friend that the issue was one of integrity and that she probably had no choice but to resign if she hoped to restore her reputation. Indian Affairs Minister Ron Irwin dropped by to tell her to tough it out, that the government needed her in cabinet. At 4 p.m., the leadership group and her staff sat down with Copps. Clifford Lincoln, her former parliamentary secretary and a man who had demonstrated his own sense of integrity in resigning from the Bourassa cabinet over language rights in the late 1980s, joined them. Copps announced that she wanted to resign. What did they think?

Joe Thornley, an Ottawa communications consultant and member of the Liberal Party executive, led off. He talked about integrity and the importance to Copps of her reputation as a straight-shooter. She had no choice but to resign. "It's the only way you will be able to save your integrity and honour." May-Cuconato agreed. So did Clifford Lincoln. By this time her office had learned that CTV had sent a crew to Hamilton to probe anti-Copps sentiment in her stronghold. Thornley advised that they move quickly to put together a resignation announcement and thereby preclude the network from further undermining her position in her home town. He and her press secretary, Duncan Dee, went off to draft a statement. Meanwhile, Copps got on the phone to her husband, labour consultant Austin Thorne, who was in St. John's on business.

A few minutes later, she came into the outer office and said that Thorne wanted to speak with the group over the speakerphone. He challenged whether the punishment fit the crime. "If you look at the magnitude of the offence — bluntly put, it's chicken shit," he said. Her advisers reviewed their line of reasoning with Thorne. At the end, his voice came back over the speakerphone. "Sheila, these people are right," he sighed. "You have to resign."

By now, it was close to 4:30. Copps wanted to make her announcement at 6 p.m. May-Cuconato called downstairs and told Bruce Hartley, the prime minister's executive assistant, that Copps needed to see Chrétien urgently. The two met at about 5 p.m. Chrétien had to keep it short because of a commitment immediately afterwards. But he made clear to her that he saw no reason for her resignation. The media's harassment campaign notwithstanding, to his thinking the Liberals had kept their promise and therefore so had she. Cabinet government implied collective responsibility. Chrétien took inordinate pride in having gone so long without losing a minister. It spoke to his government's integrity. He didn't want to break the string, particularly not with his deputy prime minister. And not over the GST. He seemed blind to the harm to Copps's integrity.

At 5:30, she headed back down for a second meeting, this time with advisers in the room. Again Chrétien stalled, asking her to sleep on her decision. He said he wanted to arrange a quickie overnight poll in her Hamilton East riding. Copps then went home and kept a promise to her daughter to exchange one of her hamsters for a guinea pig.

She called the prime minister at home at about 9:45 p.m. to say she had decided to make the announcement in the morning and that she wanted to do it in Hamilton. Again he asked her to sleep on it and said they would talk in the morning. Chrétien then phoned Eddie Goldenberg, informing him of Copps's intentions, and asked him to find out the bare minimum period for a by-election. That night, Copps later said, she slept better than she had in several days.

At 6:45 a.m. Wednesday, her phone rang. Chrétien asked if she had made up her mind for certain. Yes, she replied, she would resign later in the morning. Chrétien was by nature a scrapper. His instinct, whenever under attack, was to fight his way out of the corner. He acceded to her will with reluctance. "I said tough it out," he acknowledged in an interview.

In the ensuing days, Copps grew resentful towards Martin. She felt that his spin doctors had sought to differentiate between her problem and the party's problem. She also had heard from sources that Martin supporters had claimed she had been pushed out by Chrétien. "All I will say," she told *Maclean's*, "is that there's been a campaign by some people with their own agenda to undercut whatever I do." Martin tried to make amends by showing up to speak at her nomination meeting, but the wound was deep.

Chrétien's anger over the handling of the GST matter had not subsided. He felt that the government should have brazened it out, that the apology had shown weakness and attracted more trouble. "We are facing a major problem," he told caucus on the morning of the Copps resignation, in an obvious swipe at Martin. "The replacing of the GST has not been very good." Martin's apology, he stated, had "put Sheila on the spot." In an interview a week later, he claimed that the problem had been not the apology itself so much as the media interpretation of it. Martin had meant to say the mistake was to believe the changes could be done all in one shot, that every province would sign on to harmonization at the same time, he contended. "Everybody wants me to apologize. Well, apologize for what? There is nothing to be shameful about."

But there was no disguising that he was steamed at Martin. Martin's people, in turn, complained that the prime minister could not fairly judge their strategy because he had undermined it on its first day. Canadians had been deprived of their desire to take their licks at the Liberals for the GST. Instead of working it out of their system, they now felt doubly angry at Liberal duplicity.

Ultimately, the biggest victim was not Sheila Copps. It was, as Chrétien soon realized, the Red Book, the symbol that these Liberals would be different, they would be accountable. The Red Book had served Chrétien and his government well. The plan had been to roll it out at the beginning of the next election as proof of promises kept. Now that would be problematic. The events of late April and early May had turned the Red Book into a symbol of promises broken. Suddenly, reporters began asking again about the unfulfilled daycare commitment or the Liberals' quick switch on NAFTA.

The GST débâcle underlined the sharp differences between Jean Chrétien and Paul Martin. Martin felt that the style of politics in the 1990s demanded that public figures come clean with their voters when they fell short. This would enhance their credibility, he believed, not detract from it. Chrétien, on the other hand, recoiled from signs of weakness, preferring not to spill his own blood in the shark-infested waters of national politics. They had differed before — and would probably differ again. Martin, a born activist, viewed politics as a medium through which society reformed itself so as to be better prepared for the challenges of the future. His was a governing mind. Chrétien, a natural conservative, viewed politics more as a means of preserving existing goods. Mountains should be climbed only when it was absolutely impossible to get around them. He cared more for the consensus than the content. His was the political mind.

Their differing approaches over the Liberal infrastructure program, the most important and expensive of all their Red Book promises, had been instructive. Martin viewed the program as an opportunity to invest in the cutting edge of the economy. He always talked about infrastructure in terms of fibre-optic networks and export highways connecting Canadian manufacturers with the United States. Chrétien had earned the present of a gold shovel from a construction union for his mantra about using the money to build roads and dig sewers. The disposition of the money seemed secondary to him; the key lay in improving the mood in the country. It could be argued that Martin would have invested the money more wisely for Canada's long-term benefit. But it could equally be argued that without Chrétien's ability to connect the infrastructure program to the common guy, the Liberals might never have had the chance. Their divergent orientations condemned them to perpetual tension. At the same time, each brought something particular to the table — the basis of a profitable partnership.

To some close observers, the GST incident pointed to differences stretching well beyond mere tactics. They simply felt that Jean Chrétien had reached a station in life where he was incapable of admitting error. The prime ministership invests even a regular guy like Jean Chrétien with quasi-imperial powers. On a Saturday night in early 1996, for instance, Chrétien sat at home watching a Grand Prix racing event from Australia. In the last laps, it looked as if Canadian driver Jacques Villeneuve would win. Chrétien picked up the phone and ordered the PMO switchboard to patch him through to Villeneuve. Pagers went off all over Ottawa as the desperate switchboard sought advice from Chrétien staffers. Someone suggested seeing if Information had a public relations number for the race. It worked. Moments later, Villeneuve (who finished second) sat in his pit, speaking with the prime minister half a world away.

Such power made it difficult for anyone to maintain perspective, a position not helped by Chrétien's continued high poll ratings. It was hard to believe in one's fallibility when everyone constantly assured you of your infallibility. "He almost pretends those campaign clips don't exist," an astonished Martin adviser remarked of Chrétien's unwillingness to accept that the Liberals had strayed well beyond the Red Book in their 1993 promises. "You guys, you don't want to read page 22. That's my problem on integrity," Chrétien himself said in an interview the week after the Copps resignation.

A pattern had emerged. He had steadfastly refused to accept any responsibility for the near-loss of the referendum, rejecting any criticism by asserting that until he had entered the fray, it had been lost. He tended to describe the events as if he had not been a party to them. Chrétien had reached a juncture in life at which he may have been beyond saying he was sorry.

Nearly seven years earlier, when he had begun preparing his second run for his party's leadership, he had gathered together a group of Trudeau-era ministers and MPs to solicit their support. They came with all kinds of advice, suggesting he listen to this person or that person on policy and tactics. Chrétien cut them off. "For thirty years, I've been listening," he said. "I'm tired of always listening. Now it's time for others to listen to me."

Spring arrived late in Canada in 1996. Calgary experienced a snowstorm in early May. Ottawa had flurries on the Sunday before the Victoria Day long weekend. Liberals accepted that the honeymoon had finally ended, if not the previous November when they limped out of the referendum campaign, then certainly in the pummelling they had endured over the GST.

For the first time since early 1994, the Gallup poll put them below 50 per cent. But they were still benefitting enormously from the lack of ready alternatives. The Bloc Québécois looked listless under Michel Gauthier, who had succeeded Lucien Bouchard, and the Reform Party was locked in internecine warfare over gay rights in the week after the GST mess, much to Chrétien's delight. Meanwhile, a sifting of the ashes of the Conservatives and New Democrats failed to produce any signs of a phoenix rising.

But the heights the Liberals commanded were slippery. The jobs and growth agenda on which they had been elected continued to produce too few jobs and too little growth. In April 1996, the Bank of Canada — riding the crest of six years of lower-than-American inflation, strong exports, and the new orthodoxy of deficit reduction — delivered Paul Martin his long-sought payoff from the deficit fight, as interest rates slipped below those of the Americans. But Martin was forced to wait for the increase in jobs that the government had hoped would flow from low interest rates. Public opinion polls gave the Liberals low marks on jobs, but somehow, perhaps because of the masterful sales job on the deficit, Canadians did not mete out the customary punishment. Job anxiety and political unpopularity, once yoked together, had become decoupled.

Still, a veteran political warrior like Jean Chrétien knew he wasn't home free. In its short tenure, his government had withstood two direct threats to the integrity of the nation. Both posed an even graver menace to his government than the inadequate jobs performance. Neither had been fully quelled.

In the first crisis, Paul Martin, Chrétien's choice for Finance, had risen to the challenge of staving off the bondholders and credit rating agencies. In confronting the fiscal crisis so energetically, Martin had allowed the government to retain control of its economic sovereignty. In the process, he had redefined the postwar consensus. Government, at least the federal government, would no longer be there for all Canadians — the social welfare state was now the mutual responsibility state. Canadian farmers had never been so exposed to the marketplace, at least not in the postwar era. The same was true for the unemployed, for users of the transport system, for Cape Breton coal miners and British Columbia lighthouse keepers. In the next recession, the indigent would be wards of the provinces: the federal government, by implementing the block transfer, had severed its direct link. In every area of civic life, the relationship between Ottawa and its citizens was profoundly reordered.

Martin had gained tremendous credence for heading off fiscal disaster. By mid-1996, it became clear that the European economies — Germany's included — would have a tough time making the 3-per-cent deficit target appropriated by the Liberals from the Maastricht treaty. Canada looked poised to chalk up the best deficit record among G-7 nations. But the victory remained tentative. Despite Martin's success in scaling back the government of Canada by more than 20 per cent — back to the size his father had found so inadequate in the early 1950s — the deficit would still ring in at about $20 billion in 1996–97. The national debt was continuing on its upward trajectory. And the Liberals had not yet lived through a recession. It would be many years before the momentum of compound interest would be sufficiently slowed for Ottawa to boldly exercise its sovereignty, for Martin to become more a builder than a dismantler.

The second threat cut to the core of Jean Chrétien's mission in life, and remained even less certain of a satisfactory result. If deficit reduction was a matter, as Martin asserted, of irreducible arithmetic, the preservation of national unity would have to be pursued in the less precise realm of art.

Canadians had built a wonderful country on a rickety foundation. They had strung themselves tenuously across thousands of miles of rough terrain, stubbornly defying for a century and a quarter the logic of surrender to the superpower next door. But in the 1990s, the global economy made

it increasingly difficult to defend the traditional cultural or economic ram-
parts: the east-west economy fabricated by Sir John A. Macdonald had
given way to a vibrant series of north-south economies. In this new world
without frontiers, Ontario cared more deeply about the competitive pressures from Michigan and Ohio than about the needs of Nova Scotia and
Prince Edward Island. British Columbia's fate depended more heavily on
the U.S. Northwest and the Orient than on the provinces on the other side
of the Rockies. When people spoke about the pressures for bilingualism
in Vancouver, the relevant second language was Cantonese.

These new economic and social realities exacerbated the tensions at
the heart of Canadian existence: the chronically challenging accommodation between French and English. The October 1993 election, in throwing up two protest parties, had brought the country's regional divisions and
jealousies into uncomfortably sharp relief. The vision of two founding
nations handed down through the generations now competed with a
western Canadian view of the country as ten equal provinces. Typically,
Chrétien had sought a halfway house: his formula of four, then five,
regions for a *de facto* constitutional veto. But nobody, not even those
provinces promised their own veto, seemed grateful for Ottawa's gift. Nor
had the country proven itself receptive to the recognition of Quebec's distinct character. Indeed, the new veto formula all but guaranteed that distinct
society would never make it into the Constitution. The threshold of seven
provinces had proven elusive; five regions would be insurmountable.

Nonetheless, Chrétien ordered the printing of a pamphlet trumpeting
his fulfilment of all the Verdun promises and had it distributed to every
household in Quebec. Technically speaking, he had kept his word — that
was what mattered to him. His approval ratings sank to new lows in his
home province.

Canada indeed looked like two nations: the nation that trusted Chrétien
more than any other living politician; and the nation, huddled along the
St. Lawrence River, that held him in utter contempt. In February, when he
had choked a protester on Flag Day, Canadians outside Quebec applauded
his assertiveness. But inside Quebec he was chided as Mad Dog Chrétien.
A poll showed that 63 per cent of Ontario residents found his behaviour
acceptable while 72 per cent of Quebeckers found it inappropriate.

As he prepared for a June first ministers' conference, satisfying provincial ambitions became the sine qua non of Chrétien's government. He
hoped to win agreement to implement the devolutionist agenda laid out in

February in his second Speech from the Throne. In the run-up to the meeting, his government offered the provinces $2 billion to take over labour market training, including the active measures Axworthy had once promoted as the Liberal portion of his UI reform. His ministers accepted the judgment of Stéphane Dion and Marcel Massé that they must lance this particular boil in Quebec.

Chrétien, ever flexible about solutions, was prepared to preside over a very different Canada from the one he had embraced upon arriving in Ottawa in 1963. "That was a time when society needed changes and we had the money to do it," he explained. The intention had always been "when the program will be mature, we will withdraw. And very often we forgot to withdraw." It was pure pragmatism. He would again deny the frigid waters below the ice the opportunity to gobble up Jean Chretién. He now took the separatist threat seriously. In demonstrating that Canada could change, he would perpetuate the Canadian fact, the ultimate duty of all Canadian prime ministers.

But ever the incrementalist, he rarely received credit for the halting progress made. In finally ceding control over job training, he looked more like a desperate quarterback throwing a Hail Mary pass than a confident leader presiding over a reordering of the federation. The same could be said for the distinct society commitment. Not only did it appear unattainable. Increasingly, it looked an irrelevant palliative. Chrétien wasn't the sort to mount the bully pulpit to thump for his cause in any case. In the rest of Canada, where he stood tall, he guarded his political capital like the king in the counting-house. Although he made sure to insert a line in favour of distinct society whenever he travelled to Vancouver, it was usually just that — a single line. He always appeared a step behind the play, offering up too little, too late, without much verve — perhaps the inevitable consequence of being a transactional prime minister, one who preferred to manage problems rather than anticipate them.

When Chrétien felt frustrated, he would turn to the same biography of Sir Wilfrid Laurier that Herb Gray had pulled off his shelves to provide comfort during program review. Chrétien identified strongly with Laurier; he never forgot his own father's pride at having once shaken hands with the great Liberal in Trois-Rivières. "When I feel I have problems, I pick up in my library the biography of Laurier by Joseph Schull and I read a chapter and I feel very good. I feel I don't have much wrong because he had not only the French and English, he had Catholics and Protestants," he explained.

Chrétien had attended classical college in Joliette, not far from Laurier's home town. His college played hockey and football against Laurier's alma mater in L'Assomption. As a student, he had visited the home where Laurier was born. Later, he would challenge his nationalist professor for disparaging Laurier as an anglophone because of his schooling at McGill University. "In those days you did not argue with the professor," Chrétien recalled, seated in an armchair in his office below an oil portrait of the country's seventh prime minister, an exact duplicate of the one that hung in his cabinet room. "He threw me out of the class."

In the aftermath of the referendum, he might well have reviewed the chapter on Laurier's travails over the Manitoba Schools Question, in which Schull had written: "The possible and the attainable were his sphere of action, and the more the tumult rose the more that sphere contracted." The words echoed through the century.

Laurier had ushered Canada into the twentieth century, just as Chrétien now wanted to take it into the twenty-first. Both these parliamentary warhorses — Laurier sat for forty-five years in the House of Commons — had been great pragmatists, seeking to hold the middle ground in eras in which the views of the nation had polarized and hardened. Both came, over time, to a similar view of Canada. Laurier had been Canada's original free trader. Chrétien, who had signed NAFTA and led the Team Canada trade missions, took great pride in being lauded by private business as the trade prime minister. Laurier had embraced provincial rights. Chrétien, more through circumstance than through conviction, now also emphasized the autonomy of the provinces. They shared a suspicion of the state, but also a willingness to harness its power.

Mostly, though, they shared a lineage as national unity Liberals, politicians who came out of rural Quebec to dedicate their careers to the reconciliation of the two partners of Confederation. Laurier had governed Canada for fifteen years, earning the sobriquet from his biographer of "the first Canadian" for his tireless efforts to bridge the country's natural divisions. But ultimately, the ice gave way beneath him.

Jean Chrétien, confident of appearance but fearful of soul, had begun his prime ministership with references to Laurier's expansive portrayal of the French fact in Canada. But he was enough of a student of the old master to remember as well the opening words in Trois-Rivières of Laurier's disastrous 1911 election campaign. "I am branded in Quebec as a traitor to the French and in Ontario as a traitor to the English. In Quebec, I am branded as a jingo and in Ontario as a separatist. In Quebec I am attacked as an Imperialist and in Ontario as an anti-Imperialist. I am neither. I am a Canadian. Canada has been the inspiration of my life. I have had before me as a pillar of fire by night and a pillar of cloud by day a policy of true Canadianism, of moderation, of conciliation." The middle collapsed and the voters rejected Laurier. But Canada had survived him.

Surveying his first two and a half years in office, Jean Chrétien knew that history would judge him on his ability to reconcile the regions in an era when deficits and the global economy had weakened the ties that bound the country and when regional chauvinism flourished. He, too, sought a calm oasis in the ever-contracting middle ground. In the tradition of Canada's greatest prime ministers, he embraced ambiguity on the overarching questions of the day. But every day in the House of Commons, the Bloc and Reform insisted on the kind of clarity that he felt would divide rather than illuminate Canadians.

Never philosophical, Chrétien cringed when asked in a mid-1996 interview to contemplate his destiny as Canada's twentieth prime minister, the disciple of Laurier. "I don't like this question because I don't care much about my place in history," he demurred. "It's not my style. My style is to be a good prime minister, to know that I have tackled the problems one by one, and that the overall result was pretty good." As the country teetered, he remained the defensive specialist in politics. His vision was to survive until tomorrow.

AFTERWORD

On June 20 and 21, 1996, as summer settled upon the country, Jean Chrétien, the premiers of the ten provinces, and the leaders of the two territorial governments finally sat down as a group to discuss the future of Canada. It was their first meeting since the referendum, indeed the first in two years. Even Lucien Bouchard came, but with the strict proviso that he would talk only about the economy. Any mention of the Constitution would compel him to walk out. Alberta's Ralph Klein delivered the same warning, as did British Columbia's Glen Clark. Even Chrétien, who had held out the promise of constitutional change at the Verdun rally six nights before the referendum vote, retreated to his earlier pronouncements that Canadians wanted their leaders to deal with the economy; he hadn't been elected to discuss the Constitution. He wanted success out of the first ministers' conference — the size of the success didn't matter. He would not, according to his senior aides, head down dead-end streets.

When they had promised such a gathering back in the February Throne Speech, Chrétien and his advisers had harboured bigger hopes. Stéphane Dion had travelled the country in the late winter and spring like some constitutional Don Quixote. The ministers and officials he met had the impression of a well-intentioned but hopelessly naive neophyte tilting at windmills. He made the mistake in Alberta of imploring his interlocutors to consider Quebec's needs. In British Columbia, he pitched distinct society to a provincial government that had forsworn the Constitution and, in the midst of a crisis over salmon stocks, seemed to care only about getting a piece of federal fisheries management.

By the time the meeting began, Chrétien, in classic style, had succeeded in reducing expectations. This would be a series of small steps on a long road to improving Canada. The ultimate goal, Eddie Goldenberg and other advisers confided, was to prove to Quebeckers that Ottawa was the agent of change and not the defender, as the separatists always claimed, of the dreaded status quo. The meeting would not be definitive. Dion, with bigger ambitions, looked lonely as his political benefactor distanced himself.

Chrétien and Bouchard, aware that Quebeckers wanted them to work together on the deteriorating economy, behaved themselves. Bouchard even expressed a willingness to participate in another Team Canada trade mission to Asia in early 1997. But Glen Clark, the new British Columbia premier, threw a tantrum over his failure to make progress on his fishery concerns. The agenda of a single province couldn't be allowed to dominate the agenda of the country, he spat out about Quebec in one of his more temperate statements. British Columbia had telegraphed its pique in advance of the meeting, but once again Chrétien seemed unable to comprehend the alienation brewing at the other end of the country. He sat dumbfounded, along with most of the other premiers, as Clark informed them over dinner at 24 Sussex Drive that he just might forsake the Team Canada mission himself. New Brunswick Premier Frank McKenna, who never allowed emotion to get in the way of hard calculation, reminded Clark with some puzzlement that nobody benefitted more from Asian trade relations than British Columbia. Perhaps the other premiers should just go somewhere else.

All in all, though, the meeting did not go badly, at least when measured against the low threshold set for it. Sergio Marchi, now in Environment, had moved forward on the harmonization of standards with the provinces that Sheila Copps had resisted. The provinces applauded. Doug Young appeared hell-bent on repeating the feat he had accomplished at Transport of getting Ottawa out of the nation's business; this time, at Human Resources, social services were his target. The provinces, filling the vacuum left behind by the collapse of Lloyd Axworthy's social security review, now took the lead in social policy reform. These were not the centralizing Liberals of the past. Even in areas they thought would be more efficiently run on a national basis — such as securities industry regulation — they spoke in terms of partnership, not leadership.

In the days after the first ministers' conference, journalists and senior bureaucrats puzzled over what had actually transpired. Chrétien's small-steps approach had failed to ignite any passion. Quebec's media elite ridiculed the effort. In the Privy Council Office, plans were already afoot for a third wave of initiatives. The national unity strategists had worked through the hastily conceived Verdun promises and had received little discernible credit for them. The government had sought to pacify Quebec, and other assertive provinces, with its devolutionist strategies. Now the cabinet turned to measures to strengthen the attachment of Canadians, especially Quebeckers, to their country. In this, Chrétien would rely more heavily on the newly re-elected Sheila Copps to manage the promised unity information office and speak out in her passionate manner for Canada. Without obvious answers, the Liberals seemed to be resorting to trial and error. They were making it up as they went along.

The circus continued, but more and more the spotlight fell on the ringmaster. Six summers after the failure of the Meech Lake Accord, Jean Chrétien remained a deeply mistrusted figure in Quebec. As chief salesman, he seemed incapable of overcoming a decade and a half of stigmatization. Liberals increasingly asked themselves if he had become too much of a symbol himself in Quebec to make the case for Canada. The weekend after the first ministers' conference marked Quebec's Fête Nationale. Chrétien had once complained bitterly that the separatists, in turning him into a pariah, "have stolen my feast." A year earlier, he had quietly observed the holiday in Shawinigan. This time around, he didn't even bother with the pretence of spending the weekend in his native province. As his fellow Quebeckers celebrated, Chrétien remained in Ottawa, throwing his own party for family members.

Canada Day fell on the following weekend. Chrétien put in an appearance on Parliament Hill at noon, wading into the enthusiastic crowds, feeding off its energy in the way that politicians so adore. More than 100,000 people filled the lawns below the Parliament Buildings. Chrétien addressed them from in front of the Peace Tower, the same location where he had launched his campaign to become their prime minister three summers before. This time the Peace Tower clock remained silent, its hands frozen in time. The tower, indeed the entire building, stood swaddled in scaffolding and green netting.

The prime minister chose to use the facelift as a metaphor for his attempts to refurbish the Canadian federation. "You know, Canada is a little bit like the Parliament Buildings behind us," he said. "They were built carefully, skilfully, lovingly by those who came before us. So was Canada. But even the best building in the world needs hard work to keep it great.

It needs refurbishing. It needs renovating. It needs constant restoration. For these great Parliament Buildings to stay great, we have to keep working on them. And it is the same with Canada — we have to keep working on it — every day, every year, because we want Canada to remain great."

Chrétien probably didn't know it, but etched into the window on the west side of the Peace Tower above him was a telling quote from Proverbs in the Bible: "Where there is no vision, the people perish." Canadians, in love with their country but frustrated by it, had looked to their prime minister for a vision, one that would build on their achievements and hold on to Quebec. But they had elected as their leader a man not prone to great visions, indeed one inherently suspicious of them. He possessed an impressive storehouse of folk wisdom, to be sure. And he understood the psychology of the masses better than most. But if he was to save Canada, it would be a careful and gradual salvation. Eight months after the referendum, he had fallen back on the cockeyed optimism that all would turn out well, on Laurier's sunny ways.

"Together, step by step, we have built a country that is the envy of the world, a country in which we all feel great pride. And working together, we will move into the twenty-first century with confidence and hope, knowing that we continue to live in the best country in the world," he told the crowd. "Vive le Canada. Bonne fête, Canada."

INDEX